★★★ PRAISE FOR ★★★
FOR TIMES SUCH AS

"Welcome to the voice of a new generation pushing the boundaries of Jewish thought and practice with clarity, urgency, and passion. Refusing the division between radical politics and deep religious commitment, Katz and Rosenberg lay out the spiritual offerings of each month of the Jewish year and provide a guide for creating political rituals that are grounded in and flow from each season. I cannot think of another book that provides such a helpful overview of the holidays while also centering left perspectives and practices."

—Judith Plaskow, author of *Standing Again at Sinai: Judaism from a Feminist Perspective*

"I wept when I read this book, recognizing its call in my bones. When my great-grandmother's grandmother, a rabbi's wife, walked out of her shul in Ukraine, she was walking toward the sacred, revolutionary, old/new Judaism this book proclaims. I am polishing my bedside table to receive it."

—Aurora Levins Morales, author of *Rimonim: Ritual Poetry of Jewish Liberation*

"A wise and courageous book—an extraordinary testament to the vibrant creativity of the Jewish Left and essential reading for all of us who yearn to ground our spiritual and political lives in the practice of justice, care, love, and liberation."

—Julia Watts Belser, author of *Loving Our Own Bones: Disability Wisdom and the Spiritual Subversiveness of Knowing Ourselves Whole*

"This book is as practical as it is political, as piercing as it is poetic. It makes accessible ancient sources as well as a huge array of modern ones, seamlessly weaving the most traditional and the most radical ideas and practices, making them not only copasetic but inseparable. Beautifying Jewish ritual (in the authors' own queer interpretation of *hiddur hamitzvah*), this book is both a welcoming entry point for any individual as well as an engaging and challenging resource for community leaders. *For Times Such as These* is a historical document reflecting the nature of our times, accounting for the development of Jewish ritual across history, and making room for its future promise. 'By showing kavod, honor, to our elders, wrestling with the stories we've inherited, we can be transformed,' write the authors, who have given us the opportunity to join them in this beautiful queer chain of tradition."

—Zohar Weiman-Kelman, author of *Queer Expectations: A Genealogy of Jewish Women's Poetry*

"*For Times Such as These* is a love letter to both Judaism and Jews. With humility and rigor, Rabbis Katz and Rosenberg guide us through the Jewish year's stories and practices, while simultaneously amplifying the political passions, spiritual yearnings, and ethical demands of Jewish, anti-Zionist, queer abolitionists who in the twenty-first century are refusing to cede Judaism to the Right. This book is sure to become a standard reference in home libraries for a deep dive as you turn the page of your Radical Jewish Calendar or prepare for the next holiday, in the rabbi's office, as a textbook for Intro to Judaism classes, as a way for non-Jewish comrades to access Jewish cultural life, and as a historical record of this moment in the long arc of Jewish time. It is an inevitable and essential contribution to our lineage that began with rebellious Esther and will continue until liberation is won for us all."

—Rabbi Alissa Wise

"*For Times Such as These* is a beautiful, practical, abundant gift to Jewish radicals. It sets out a spacious, generative, grounded approach to thinking about Jewish ritual, Jewish resistance, and Jewish time. This book offers support for a wide range of ways to observe Jewish time and practice Jewish being right now, in these times of ecological crisis and rising fascism, where we badly need to plug into countercultural, earth-based wisdom about resistance and survival. It complements, updates, and expands the existing literature on the Jewish year, proliferating inroads toward radical, connective, restorative, inclusive Jewish practice. This book will become the dog-eared reference text, full of folded pages, dried flowers, and tear stains, that accompanies us through the tumult that is underway and that is on the way."

—Dean Spade, author of *Mutual Aid: Building Solidarity During This Crisis (and the Next)*

"Katz and Rosenberg invite us to explore the ritual rhythms of the Jewish year. This welcoming guide brings together a diasporic political lens with accessible rabbinic teachings to help cultivate new forms of radical community."

—Anna Elena Torres, author of *Horizons Blossom, Borders Vanish: Anarchism and Yiddish Literature*

"This is a unique and impressive work that provides valuable information and commentary. It's a must-read for anyone who wishes to live their life in Jewish time connected to social justice work."

—Rabbi Rebecca Alpert, professor emerita of religion, Temple University

FOR TIMES SUCH AS THESE

FOR
TIMES
SUCH AS
THESE

A Radical's Guide
to the Jewish Year

RABBI ARIANA KATZ & RABBI JESSICA ROSENBERG

WITH ILLUSTRATIONS BY SOL WEISS &
INCANTATIONS BY DORI MIDNIGHT

Wayne State University Press

Detroit

Illustrations © Sol Weiss. Incantations © Dori Midnight.

ISBN 9780814350515 (paperback)
ISBN 9780814350522 (e-book)

Library of Congress Control Number: 2023938717

Cover illustration and design and interior design by Lindsey Cleworth.

Wayne State University Press rests on Waawiyaataanong, also referred to as Detroit, the ancestral and contemporary homeland of the Three Fires Confederacy. These sovereign lands were granted by the Ojibwe, Odawa, Potawatomi, and Wyandot Nations, in 1807, through the Treaty of Detroit. Wayne State University Press affirms Indigenous sovereignty and honors all tribes with a connection to Detroit. With our Native neighbors, the press works to advance educational equity and promote a better future for the earth and all people.

Wayne State University Press
Leonard N. Simons Building
4809 Woodward Avenue
Detroit, Michigan 48201–1309
Visit us online at wsupress.wayne.edu.

כִּי אִם־הַחֲרֵשׁ תַּחֲרִישִׁי בָּעֵת הַזֹּאת רֶוַח וְהַצָּלָה יַעֲמוֹד לַיְּהוּדִים מִמָּקוֹם אַחֵר וְאַתְּ וּבֵית־אָבִיךְ תֹּאבֵדוּ וּמִי יוֹדֵעַ אִם־לְעֵת כָּזֹאת הִגַּעַתְּ לַמַּלְכוּת׃

On the contrary, if you keep silent in this crisis, relief and deliverance will come to the Jews from another quarter, while you and your father's house will perish. And who knows, perhaps you have attained to royal position for times such as these. (Esther 4:14)

Bless this book with wine drops and lipstick stains.

CONTENTS

PART 1

SETTING THE TABLE

INTRODUCTION

When Are We?

As in every generation, we are writing in the midst of great change. In every generation, our ancestors[1] have wondered how they could possibly bear this teetering on the edge, the unknown future. We, too, balance on the promises and threats of upheaval.

Our earth is shaking, splitting, and roiling with the damage caused by human greed. Even as we try desperately to repair our relationships to the Earth so that life can be sustained, we know there is damage that cannot be undone. Fascism is again, or still, on the rise in the United States and worldwide, working to violently silence the movements that seek justice, liberation, and life. Colonization of Indigenous land, white supremacy, and systemic racism's crush on Black people and People of Color in the United States, built into the bedrock of the nation-state, are trying to tighten their hold. The capitalist mode of production that values accumulation of wealth and power for the very, very few, at the expense of life for all, dominates our days. We write in a time of global pandemic, revealing again and again the interconnectedness of our struggles.

There are also, as always, possibilities for transformation. In our time writing this book, we've seen a wave of campaigns that bring abolitionist principles into public discourse and expand people's imaginations of what is possible. We've seen encampment support and mutual aid become normalized in our neighborhoods, cities, and synagogues. We see movements rising and growing. We've seen the edges of global consciousness shifting under the stress of a horrific plague. We see people and communities dreaming and building new economies that center and sustain life and well-being. And we see people turning with curiosity toward our own bodies, turning toward each other, toward tradition and ritual, toward earth and sky and spirit. We see people practicing fierce fighting and fierce caring. We see movements motivated by love and moving toward liberation. We see transformation and the possibilities of transformation.

As in every generation, we have wondered how we can bear the teetering between possible worlds. As in every generation, we turn to the tools our ancestors left us to make meaning, make it through, and, we hope, tip the balance toward the good.

Why This Book?

Melanie Kaye/Kantrowitz z"l[2] died in July 2018. A writer and organizer, Kaye/Kantrowitz's work explores Jewish life, identities, communities, and histories in nuanced and critical ways, while deeply engaging with building power and changing the world.[3] As readers, we could feel her organizing in her writing. As organizers, she gave us permission to write. When she died, we pulled her books off the shelves and stacked them all around us: "She left us so many gifts," we said in awe. "We have to give gifts. We have to write more, and share more." We started writing this book, what we called a "leftist Jewish yearcycle book." This book is an offering, a gift to the ancestors, movements, communities, and family that feed us and nurture us, agitate us and love us.

We decided on a yearcycle book for a few reasons: because we were already part of making a calendar together, and this seemed like a natural, if intensely more involved, outgrowth of that. The eighth edition of the Radical Jewish Calendar is currently in production. The calendar follows the Hebrew months, and features art from radical Jewish artists and Jewish and leftist holidays and histories, both broadly defined. We also decided to write a yearcycle book because there is so much contained within the rhythm of the Jewish calendar, deeper and more nuanced than what so many of us have had access to. The Jewish holidays contain the core stories of Jewish people; holiday rituals create space to traverse the expanse of human emotions; the Jewish yearcycle connects us with the earth and seasons; and Jewish holidays incite community and connection, they turn us toward each other. In short, we believe the Jewish yearcycle is medicine for our times.

This book brings together our two core life commitments, blessedly entangled in our hearts and days: revolutionary politics and Jewish tradition. Over the course of this book, we will try to both show and tell the political commitments and the Judaism to which we are committed. To begin, we will say that we want a world organized around caring for life. That is the core of our politics and our Jewishness. Because we care about nurturing, loving, and sustaining life, we oppose all of the interlocking systems that destroy people and planet:

We oppose racism and white supremacy in its many expressions, all systems that oppress and degrade based on racialized hierarchies, and the particular ways anti-Blackness has shaped the structures of the societies in which we live. We understand antisemitism, Islamophobia, and anti-Arab racism as deeply interconnected with a white supremacist, Christian nationalist worldview, and understand that our lives depend on uprooting these interlocking ideologies. We oppose misogyny, patriarchy, transphobia, and all forms of gendered violence. We fight the ways ableism creates a normative, healthy mind and body and then designs the world around that, shamefully discarding all who do not fit the mold. We oppose colonization: the historical and ongoing land theft and genocide of Indigenous people everywhere. As we'll unpack further in this book, as U.S.–based Jews, we have specific obligations to articulate anti-colonial analysis of the United States, and to oppose the colonialism perpetrated in our name through the establishment of the modern state of Israel. In that vein, we are anti-Zionist because the State of Israel was created by modern political Zionism, a European-originated colonial project to create a Jewish supremacist state in historic Palestine.[4]

We oppose fascism, ethno-nationalism, and militarism in all places, and bring this analysis to our understandings of worldwide struggles for liberation. We see that all of these ideologies that degrade life are fed by, woven together in, and nurtured by capitalism, an economic system that requires the objectification of people and the earth, alienation of people from our humanity and creative flourishing, and wealth hoarding by the very few at the deadly expense of the vast majority of life.

It is very easy, in 5783/2023, to name what we are against. What are we for? What does organizing around care for life look like in practice?

We dare to claim revolutionary politics because, indeed, we want to turn the world upside down in order to make it right side up. We know that the earth is abundant and there is enough to go around. Right now, most of the earth's abundant resources are hoarded in the hands of the few, and systems of governance that control so much of our day to day lives control the flow from that hoarded resource. We seek to turn that upside down, redistribute land, wealth, and power, so that all of us have the resources we need and the power to collectively make decisions that impact our lives. We dream and work for a world in which all have what we need to survive and thrive, and are able to contribute meaningfully to the well-being of the whole. In this book when we say leftist, we refer to a wide collection of political traditions of life-centering ways of organizing society: direct democracy and anarchism, as opposed to imperialism and state control; socialism and communism and creative forms of economic democracy, instead of capitalism. We believe the diversity of political analyses is a strength, reflected and represented through Jewish history, and we encourage continued specific articulation of political frameworks that shape our thought and action. To transform society in these ways requires and would force a transformation of all of the system of hierarchy and oppression we outlined, into relationships of care, respect, and love. This world we are working for is not magically without hurt or struggle; instead we have ways of holding ourselves accountable to harm and supporting each other to reflect and transform. We strive for every step toward liberation to embody liberation: to organize in ways that prefigure, create today, the world organized around care that we seek. Our political commitment to love means we practice cultivating pleasure, deepening joy, celebrating all there is to celebrate, noticing and increasing beauty. We do this because our humanity depends on it and deserves it, with the side benefit of it flying in the face of everything capitalism and white supremacy try to take from us. When we say left, we mean the broad and varied movements of people working for more or less that vision, in a myriad of ways.

When we say Jewish, we mean 3,000 or so years of cultures, traditions, histories, texts, rituals, foods, songs, prayers, and stories. We say Jewish tradition to encompass all of it: halacha (הֲלָכָה), law, minhag (מִנְהָג), custom, and everything that's been passed down. When we say Jewishness and Jewish tradition we mean the rituals taught as normative Jewish practice, across diverse Jewish cultures, like making a seder on Passover and telling the story of the Exodus. We also mean practices created outside the rabbinic patriarchy, like our grandmothers' recipes at those seders, and practices that evolve to respond to our political realities, like putting an olive on the seder plate to embody our commitments to justice in Palestine. All of it is Jewish tradition.

We are writing this book positing that these politics and this Jewishness don't just happen to coexist in our lives; they are co-constitutive, they construct one another. Through lifelong exploration of how our politics and our Jewishness form each other, we can both deepen and grow into more nourishing practices and lives.

We wrote this book, exploring the Jewish yearcycle, as an offering for those who are bringing, and who want to bring, Jewish tradition into these tumultuous times, and who are creating, and who want to create, Jewish lives and new-old forms of Judaism and Jewishness. We say new-old to try to capture the process that we will explore of studying, valuing, and practicing our millennia-old inherited traditions while transforming them for the times we are in and our lives. Everything in this book is very old, older than our memories. Everything in this book is brand new, every day. As we hope will be abundantly clear, we love Jews, in all of our human frailty. We love Judaisms, Jewish traditions and cultures and practice. This book is an offering to strengthen Judaisms that can help us imagine and live into the transformed world by centering commitments to justice and liberation. This book is for all of us who want to embody our political commitments in our ritual lives and want our ritual lives to serve the work of deep transformation.

In this introduction we will untangle our motivations for this book. In the first section, Frameworks, we will explore the worldviews and values that underlie the rest of the book, and the implications for the Judaism we are building. From there, we will journey through every month, diving into traditional origins and contemporary expressions of the holidays. In the final section we provide brief summaries of the parashiyot (פָּרָשִׁיּות), the section of the Torah that is traditionally read every week, as it is an integral part of the yearcycle. In our time writing this book we've seen the exponential expansion of leftist Judaisms; this book is one in what we know will be a crowded shelf of offerings for these times.

For Times Such as These

We titled this book "For Times Such as These," inspired by the interplay of Jewish and leftist relationships to knowing what time it is, and to obligation. The name comes from Megillat Esther 4:14, when Mordechai is organizing his niece, Esther, to leverage her position and privilege to protect her people.

כִּי אִם־הַחֲרֵשׁ תַּחֲרִישִׁי בָּעֵת הַזֹּאת רֶוַח וְהַצָּלָה יַעֲמוֹד לַיְּהוּדִים מִמָּקוֹם אַחֵר וְאַתְּ וּבֵית־אָבִיךְ תֹּאבֵדוּ וּמִי יוֹדֵעַ אִם־לְעֵת כָּזֹאת הִגַּעַתְּ לַמַּלְכוּת:

On the contrary, if you keep silent in this crisis, relief and deliverance will come to the Jews from another quarter, while you and your father's house will perish. And who knows, perhaps you have attained to royal position for times such as these.

Immediately following this, Esther jumps into action. We call in the discernment and bravery of this femme hero who strategically evaluates her role and her context and takes bold action in time of crisis. Esther leverages the power she has to show up for her people, knowing her people have her back. This pasuk (פָּסוּק), verse, invites us to think about who we are, and what we can do in whatever moment we're in. It invites us to see our power when faced with overwhelming circumstances. It calls us to rally and show up, calling on our people and our rituals, for times such as these.

In leftist movement spaces, we regularly ask each other, in the words of revolutionary organizers and philosophers Grace Lee and James Boggs, "What time is it on the clock of the world?"[5] Being reflective about what time it is in the span of history helps us know where we are in revolutionary struggles, and helps us to organize accordingly.

Jewish frameworks of time can help us orient to the world with more alignment between our values, visions, and actions. Attuning to the cycles of our organizing allows us to see patterns, too: boom in energy and mobilization, the need for reflection and pause, steady pressure over time, long-term relationship building and community care. Both of these time-keeping strategies offer us tools for being in time that help us live more sustainable, nourishing lives: Judaism offers us scaffolding for our days, weeks, seasons, and years, and a collective story within which to orient. Leftist movements for justice offer us methods of understanding the world, and our places in it, relative to dynamic cycles of change. Through Jewish ritual cycle, through leftist organizing cycles, we both relax into rhythms of time that are much bigger than us and orient ourselves to taking action in time, individually and as part of intergenerational collectives. In our lives, we are not rigid about either Jewish or leftist times, but understand that we will go through natural cycles of ebb and flow in relation to ritual, prayer, and organizing. Living in Jewish time helps us crane our necks, to see forward and backward through millenia, to times before and after capitalism, white supremacy, and Zionism, countering all the limits of imagination that those systems instill.

The Jewish concept of knowing what time it is traditionally comes with a theological understanding of chiyyuv (חִיּוּב), obligation to mitzvot (מִצְווֹת), to Jewish commandedness: there is a correct time for each prayer. Most, though not all, of our leftist Jewish communities have rejected a Judaism of obligation and commandedness. In its place are modern, religiously liberal notions of free choice to practice what, when, and how we like, and to leave the rest. As discussed, we are committed to reimagining and reconstructing Jewish tradition. And, as leftists, we reencounter the Jewish relationship to commandedness with different perspectives on obligation than the traditional versus liberal, halachic versus non-halachic binary of contemporary Jewish life. From Black liberation movements and leaders we learned the words of Assata Shakur that "It is our duty to fight for our freedom; it is our duty to win." In this book we seek to invoke and invite new Jewish leftist relationships to duty and tradition. We hope you will join us in creating a Judaism of obligation: not to abstractions or rote, performative, ritual but to each other, our people, our communities, the earth, and all life on it. These times, we believe, call on us to embody and stretch into profound commitments.

*
* *

What Is Jewish Time?

The Jewish calendar blends lunar and solar timekeeping: Months begin on the new moon, while the year is calculated on how long it takes the sun to return to the same point in the sky. Because the solar year is longer than twelve lunar months, an additional month is added every two to three years, totaling seven times every nineteen years.[6] This serves to keep the festivals fixed in their seasons: Sukkot, a harvest festival, around the autumn equinox, Pesach in the spring, and Shavuot at the harvest of the firstfruits. Each month begins at Rosh Chodesh, literally the head of the month, on the new moon. Rosh Chodesh is celebrated by davening (to daven, דאַוון: Yiddish, to pray) Hallel, the service of Psalms sung in praise for new months and holidays. Rosh Chodesh traditionally was a day of rest for women, and the tradition of Rosh Chodesh circles has been continued by feminists.[7] The oldest of the celebrations on the Hebrew calendar always fall in the middle of the month, under the bright light of the full moon. This means that the Hebrew calendar and the Gregorian calendar, a solar calendar not tied to the moon, overlap but don't match up: Hebrew months and Gregorian months have common overlaps (i.e., Tishrei always begins in very late August, September, or early October). In the Hebrew calendar, there are four different new years, marking different seasonal changes.[8] In this book we begin with Tishrei, the month at which the count of the Jewish year changes. The Hebrew calendar year counts from the story of creation according to the Torah's telling of time in Beresheet.[9]

The Hebrew week is also counted around the story of creation, leading up to Shabbat, the seventh day. From Beresheet 1:5, "וַיְהִי־עֶרֶב וַיְהִי־בֹקֶר יוֹם אֶחָד" "there was evening, and there was morning, a first day," the new day on the Hebrew calendar begins at sunset, erev (עֶרֶב), the evening. In this book we will discuss every Jewish holiday, except for one that occurs every week! Shabbat begins at sundown on Friday night, the beginning of Saturday.

Beresheet 2:2–3 says:

וַיְכַל אֱלֹהִים בַּיּוֹם הַשְּׁבִיעִי מְלַאכְתּוֹ אֲשֶׁר עָשָׂה וַיִּשְׁבֹּת בַּיּוֹם הַשְּׁבִיעִי מִכָּל־
מְלַאכְתּוֹ אֲשֶׁר עָשָׂה:

וַיְבָ֤רֶךְ אֱלֹהִים֙ אֶת־י֣וֹם הַשְּׁבִיעִ֔י וַיְקַדֵּ֖שׁ אֹת֑וֹ כִּ֣י ב֤וֹ שָׁבַת֙ מִכָּל־מְלַאכְתּ֔וֹ אֲשֶׁר־
בָּרָ֥א אֱלֹהִ֖ים לַעֲשֽׂוֹת׃

On the seventh day God finished the work that had been
undertaken: [God] ceased on the seventh day from doing any
of the work. And God blessed the seventh day and declared it
holy—having ceased on it from all the work of creation that God
had done.

For twenty-five hours we observe Shabbat by behaving like God did—
ceasing from the work of creation. Creative labor is prohibited,[10] and the
day is spent focusing on that which brings delight and pleasure (good food,
time in community in prayer and study, sex, naps, song, Frisbee, and so
on). Shabbat is an opportunity to envision a time of liberation, outside
of capitalism and the alienation from our labor, a time of abundance and
enoughness for everyone. Shabbat is m'eyn olam haba, מֵעֵין עוֹלָם הַבָּא, a taste
of the world to come.

Jewish life and time keeping simply does not make sense without Shabbat. Each of the days of the week point toward Shabbat; we count down
the days until we get to relax, gather, and reflect. Shabbat is the animating
force behind our weeks and our observance. The flavor of the seasons of the
year, the holidays in each month, and the messages in Torah may change.
Shabbat is the constant that returns each Friday at sundown. Regardless of
what each week brings, we are called to step out of the crush and unending
flow demanding we sell our labor and maximize our productivity, to be a
part of time out of time.

Jewish tradition offers us structures for not only the year, season,
month and week but, in fact, every hour of the Jewish day. We hope this
book creates a container in which many kinds of deepening into Jewish
time can take place.

Who We Are

Though we wouldn't meet until becoming classmates at the Reconstructionist Rabbinical College in 2013, we grew up a block from each other in Jenkintown, Pennsylvania, a suburb of Philadelphia, on Leni-Lenape land. We surely passed one another on the way to the bagel shop.

Jessica was raised in a Reconstructionist congregation that began as a lay-led havurah,[II] cofounded by her parents, that met in the Reconstructionist Rabbinical College beit midrash for the first decade of her life. Jessica is a descendent of three generations of Jewish communal organizers: Jessica's great-grandparents, who arrived in Philadelphia from Poland and Ukraine, were founding members of the West Philadelphia Jewish Center; her grandparents were original members of Beth Hillel in Wynnewood, PA. From her parents, Shelley and Ken z"l, and from overhearing board meetings in the living room, she learned that Jewish communities should be life-giving and values-aligned, and that it is up to us to build them. She had the longest Bat Mitzvah of anyone she knew, and then quit Hebrew school, telling the rabbi that she couldn't abide by the theology of the High Holiday machzor, encapsulated in Ki Anu Amecha, We Are Your People, which reads: "You are our Shepard, we are Your sheep." "I'm not a sheep." Jessica never traveled too far from Judaism, staying connected to family ritual and, after moving to Minneapolis in 2007, organizing seders and finding a synagogue community. Today, Ki Anu Amecha is her favorite prayer in all of the High Holiday liturgy, because she feels deeply held by the metaphor of God as a shepherd.

In 2009, meeting anti-Zionist Jews and learning about the occupation of Palestine forced Jessica to ask big questions about Jewishness and everything she'd been taught about Jewish history. At the same time, she was learning from Black, Indigenous, People of Color and white anti-racist healers about healing justice. This included a call to learn about one's own traditions and cultures, and root in our own ancestral lineages, as part of building the world to come. In 2010, attending the Assembly of Jews Confronting Israeli Apartheid and healing justice sessions at the US Social Forum back-to-back over one overwhelmingly influential week clarified and deepened her commitments. In the coming years, she started keeping Shabbat, relearning Hebrew, going to weekday morning davening, all the while wrestling with and reflecting on how these practices related to organizing for justice and movement building. This, and reading *Medicine Stories: Essays for Radicals* by Aurora Levins Morales,[12] pointed her toward rabbinical school. She decided to attend the Reconstructionist Rabbinical College out of a desire to learn and gain skills for transmitting untold Jewish histories, as part of healing collective and historical traumas, and because it was, in many ways, coming home.

Ariana was one of the only people dancing in the pews at the Conservative synagogue down the street from Jessica in suburban Philadelphia, a swath of deep gold and maroon velvet, stained glass windows, and ornate abstract two-story wrought iron Torah ark doors. The foreboding Judaism that was practiced at shul and taught in the Jewish day school that she attended for twelve years was at odds with the joy she felt for it. But at home, Ariana's family debated religion and politics, told each other midrash (מִדְרָשׁ—exegesis on Torah, which she refers to as fan fiction) and asked questions about the Torah. They talked about sexual health and bodies, and ate Moosewood vegetarian food around a table that was the site of kitchen-table Judaism: practical, joyful, silly, serious Judaism. Hanging over her parents' Shabbat table were her great grandparents' ketubah and immigration papers from Poland and a huge poster of a painting of Abraham banishing Hagar and Ishmael, with Sara peering on from the background. Ariana's mother has wrestled with Sara her whole life, so why not put her front and center in the home? Ancestors were felt to be sources of challenge and comfort, and through her parents Ariana found permission to be imperfect, to be brave, and to innovate.

When she went to college in Boston, Ariana fell in with anarchists and feminists and learned about convening physical spaces, harnessing student power, and how messy solidarity and identity-based organizing is by design. She made home and community in one of the only all-student-run women's and gender centers in the country, and organized with a small collective to pressure the university to create a sexual assault response center on campus. Ariana taught in religious school for the duration of her time in college, but her life felt "not that Jewish"—meaning she felt her disconnection with Jewish community. In relationship with incredibly patient Arab and Persian organizers and friends in school, she began the long, painful unraveling of the lies she was told about Palestine in over a decade of formal Jewish education. She started learning about the Nakba,[13] the role Hasbara[14] had in her life, and the warped hawkish worldview put forward in day school. After graduation she attended the lecture that was the impetus for the founding of Open Hillel,[15] and asked a question. An organizer for Jewish Voice for Peace organized her into a coffee date, and she began to understand that her non-Zionist self and Jewish self could exist in one body—and still find places to be in community. Ariana realized she could study Torah, teach, and organize all at once, and applied to rabbinical school, where she met Jessica.

In 2014, toward the end of our first school year together, we walked around Fairmount Park in Philadelphia and first talked about Zionism, our experiences organizing for justice in Palestine, and our school's requirement for students to spend time studying in Palestine in order to become rabbis.[16] This grew into many years of ongoing organizing, friendship, and creative partnership. In our last year of rabbinical school, we went to mikvah and immersed ourselves in water every Rosh Chodesh. Sometimes we went to the Conservative shul's recently renovated mikvah, with dinner at the Jewish deli. Other times, we immersed in the ocean, at a Korean spa, or at a swimming hole. Every time, we reflected on the month that was and what we hoped for in the month ahead, blessing each other and the new moon.

In the years since that first friend-date-nee-organizing meeting, we were ordained side-by-side by the Reconstructionist Rabbinical College in 2018. We have collaborated on projects, including the Radical Jewish Calendar, Jews for Standing Rock, and in the Jewish Voice for Peace Rabbinical Council. We have cheered one another on: Jessica's work with incarcerated Jews and writing and teaching on Jewish histories, trauma, healing and resilience, and combating Christian Zionism, and Ariana's work founding a synagogue in Baltimore, funding and supporting abortion access and care, and podcasting for the Jewish Left.

We come to this book and our work with much in common—the ground that raised us, much of our owning class identities, shared experiences of being cisgender queer femme white women, and our commitment to transformative justice and liberatory solidarity. Within this book, we are called toward different corners of the same room. Ariana finds that the rhythm of parashiyot (Torah portions), halacha Jewish law, and rabbinic teaching on the astrological signs open up a portal into each month. Jessica focuses on the political resonances and opportunities in holiday observance and new rituals that connect past to present. We support each other in our different struggles with the rough places where our tradition and our embodied lives and values conflict.

In cowriting this book, we became chevruta (חַבְרוּתָא) sacred-life-work-study-wives, on all of the challenges, joys, and deep discoveries embedded in the yearcycle. In our chevruta, we attempt to deepen our understandings of Judaism through asking hard questions, pushing each other to go deeper at times when we might want to give up. Our chevurta builds awareness, through practices of self-reflection and loving feedback. We reflect together on our particular perspectives, especially the limits of our understandings that are shaped by experiences of privilege in our Jewish lives and the wider world, as white, class-privileged, currently able-bodied Ashkenazi Jews, with two Jewish parents, ordained as rabbis. We challenge each other to ask bigger questions, learn from more teachers, and hypothesize bolder answers.

Chevruta and cowriting has made it possible to have much deeper pleasure in our learning and writing. We kvell (rejoice) over each others' insights, creativity, and brilliance. We cheer each other on, revel in our partnership, and each feel stronger to work on our own and in other creative collaborations, with the magic of this chevruta inside and between us. Chevruta also made it possible to write this book over the course of five wildly tumultuous years. Ariana was among the people present when Jessica's father died. Jessica officiated Ariana's first child's bris. Our partnership is beyond what either of us could have dreamed up. We hope that our love comes through in our writing, and, perhaps, that it inspires more collaborations. We can be, we know, better together.

We write this book without any attempt at objectivity; we are not academics studying religion, ritual, and culture from outside of it; we are practitioners who are deeply embedded in the movements we are describing. We write this book with a complex relationship to rabbinic authority. We are humbly grateful for the learning and skill-building we've been able to do and the teachers from whom we learn; and we acknowledge the power, privilege, and responsibility of the training and title. Finally, we believe that we must earn respect through our teaching, our organizing, and how we live and work. Ordained as Reconstructionist rabbis, we are in a lineage of a century of rabbis who are not poskim (deciders of Jewish legal authority). Instead, Reconstructionist rabbis developed methods for facilitating individuals, families, and communities through processes of discernment about what meaningful Jewish life and practice looks like for them. This is the rabbinic voice we seek to bring to this book: teaching what we've learned, yes, but most importantly, opening the doors wide to all who want to come and learn.

In This Book

This book embodies our commitments to building Jewish communities of active solidarity, to a Judaism beyond Zionism, and to our ahavat Yisrael (אַהֲבַת יִשְׂרָאֵל), love of Jewish tradition and Jews. As we wrote this book, the introduction grew and grew. We realized that the frameworks underpinning this book are not self-evident; this is part of what excites us about leftist Jewish life at this time: there's a lot up for grabs. The first section is our offering to flesh out some of the theory that undergirds our practice, organized roughly into categories shaped for us by Rabbi Mordechai Kaplan, the founding thinker of Reconstructionism, who talked about Jewishness in terms of Behaving, Belonging, and Believing. Jews were unusual among faith communities, he posited, in that Behaving and Belonging are paramount to Believing. That is–faith is not the beginning point for many Jews, nor is it required in order to have access to Jewishness. We offer an exploration of all three b's, knowing they overlap and feed into each other for many of us.

In each chapter, we begin by laying out the spiritual offerings of the month, and how each month flows in the seasonal arc of the year. Within Jewish mystical tradition there are astrological signs,[17] body parts, letters, combinations of the four-letter name of God, plants, and so much more, associated with each month.[18] In each month, we offer historical context, grounding in sacred text, and an overview of the halacha and minhagim for each holiday. We've included the brachot (blessings) unique to each holiday and given overviews of rituals associated with each holiday. Both halacha and minhag vary widely across Jewish time and place. We've worked to name the origins of rituals, and to include holiday and yearcycle practices from a myriad of Jewish communities. We celebrate and are inspired by Jewish secular and cultural history and traditions. We've gathered the minhagim of our leftist Jewish communities and our recent predecessors, to record how anti-Zionist, anti-racist, feminist, queer Jews are doing Judaism in our times. We offer guides for celebrating each holiday, and for how to align Jewish practice with our liberatory commitments. We know that, as much as we've included, it is only a small taste of the vast array of what can unfold in the Jewish year.

Each month begins with words of intention written by Dori Midnight, held inside adornment created by Sol Weiss. These words are incantations, enchantments, spells, and poems. They are inspired by prekantes and tkhines, women's vernacular prayer practices from Dori's Sephardic and Ashkenazi ancestors. Prekantes and tkhines (תְּחִנּוֹת) are words that women had access to while for centuries they were kept out of the academy and synagogue. Prekantes and tkhines speak of the material issues of their lives and the prayers of their hearts. They are home-based practices, spontaneous, and often connected to an embodied ritual, using the everyday magic of the kitchen and the garden: salt, honey, water, plants. We invited Dori to write these words as she has been one of our primary teachers of the magic of the months, bringing plants and spells to our tables. We invited Sol to weave visual art around the words to bring them to life in a different way, as they have illuminated the seasons and Torah for our movements. We are so unbelievably grateful they said yes.

These spell-poems are here as an offering to connect readers with the kavvanah and spirit of the month, and align with the season and symbols. Since these incantations are rooted in personal, spontaneous prayer practice, you are invited and encouraged to make them your own. Thkines and prekantes always directly address or petition the Divine in an intimate way. Dori has chosen to connect with multiple names and aspects of the Divine in each spell, as well as switching between "I" and "we," "me" and "us," in the tradition of being one connected to many, personal intentions as part of a mycelial web of collective longings. This range of pronouns and names for God is offered in the spirit of many doors, many access points to relate to our experience of source, mystery, life itself. We invite you to exclaim or chant these words at your Rosh Chodesh circle, write them in your journal, place it on your altar, and read them after the announcing of the new month on Shabbat.

We hope that there will be much in this book that will be meaningful to Jews with a wide range of identities and relationships to the tradition. Our communities include secularists and theists, and we see the relationship between secular, cultural, religious, and halachic Judaism shifting in our lifetimes. We know there is so much more Jewish custom and culture creation happening than we could ever describe in this book; in our short dozen years in this work, we've seen the relatively fast-paced ramp up of more and more of our leftist comrades engaging with Judaism and Jewishness. As we try to describe what is happening in living rooms, online, and in the streets, we know this is just a small sample of the vibrant and growing Jewish Left. We offer this book as an introduction to millennia of Jewish tradition, as it intersects with broad and diverse leftist movements for justice in our moment and context. We hope that you will be inspired by something in this book, and we hope that you will see parts of your practice reflected in it. Whether you are new or seasoned in your Jewish practice, your political education, or integrating the two, we anticipate there will be familiar parts of this book and new learnings. We hope, most of all, that this book sparks questions for further study.

In the third part of the book, where we've summarized every Torah portion, or parshah, read in each month, we offer a few words of drash (דְּרַשׁ), explanation, inquiry, or unpacking. When people say Torah (Hebrew for teaching or instruction) they are sometimes referring to general Jewish learning and all knowledge, and sometimes specifically to the first five books of the Hebrew Bible: Beresheet (בְּרֵאשִׁית), Genesis; Shemot (שְׁמוֹת), Exodus; Vayikra (וַיִּקְרָא) Leviticus; Bamidbar (בְּמִדְבַּר), Numbers; Devarim (דְּבָרִים), Deuteronomy; Nevi'im (נְבִיאִים), Prophets; and Ketuvim (כְּתוּבִים), Writings, and is referred to in Jewish tradition by a word made from the acronym of the three parts: Tanakh (תָּנָ"ךְ).

The first five books are separated into parashiyot (portions) that are read as part of weekly prayer services. Most weeks, one parshah is read; in some years there are weeks when there is a double portion. There are parshah divisions as far back as the Dead Sea Scrolls, dating to the third century BCE. The current parshah division was standardized by Rambam in the Mishneh Torah. This means that almost any Jewish community you enter today will be reading the same Torah portion, the same week, all year round. In Jewish tradition, Torah is more than a book, it is a holy text: it is revered as sacred origin and unifying cultural story, and the jumping-off text for halacha and Jewish lifeways. The texts of Torah are filled with violence, misogyny and patriarchy, conquest and war, ableism, and so much that runs counter to our values and political commitments. Why did we include Torah in this book? More to the point, how do leftists read Torah?

We include Torah here because we are in a lineage of text wrestlers, and hope that what we offer here is a useful reference and provocative jumping-off point for further study. Every parshah, verse, word, every letter and flick of the scribe's pen of Torah has been explored for millennia, and has infinite meanings waiting to be discovered by those who are drawn to study.

The Hebrew calendar and living Jewish time in leftist communities, infused with revolutionary vision, are incredible gifts for our lives. We love being seasonally, weekly, daily, pulled out of the calendar controlled by Christian empire, white supremacy, and capitalism, and rooted into different stories and relationships to time. There are abundant challenges in the Hebrew calendar; we love them as ours to wrestle with. We offer no final word on the right or wrong way to do anything, just an invitation to join us in the creative struggles of ever evolving Jewishness.

We invite you to use this book any way you want. Read the chapter for the coming month before Rosh Chodesh, anticipating the holidays and season ahead. Pull it off the shelf as you prepare for your Passover seder, or as you feel the summer shift toward Elul and the New Year. Read it cover to cover to connect with the yearcycle for the first time or to find your renewed place in the Jewish year. Write notes in the margin about ideas, what you tried and loved, what needs reworking. Tuck handouts and text sheets inside this book and leave them for your future self. Bless this book with wine drops and lipstick stains.

The Future

In every generation, yearcycle books like this are published. *The Jewish Catalog* (Richard Siegel, Michael Strassfeld and Sharon Strassfeld), first published in 1971, was a "do it yourself kit" for Judaism, and this book is part of its legacy. We have been sustained by *Seasons of Our Joy* (Rabbi Arthur Waskow), and were gifted the *Guide to Jewish Practice* (ed. Rabbi David Teutsch) in rabbinical school, returning to it often. We've kept Rabbi Jill Hammer's *The Jewish Book of Days* by our bedsides. *The Book of Customs* by Scott-Martin Kosofsky, inspired in its design by the minhogimbukh (Yiddish, "custom book"; מנהגים-בוך) dated earliest in the sixteenth century, teaches us that in every generation, Jews have been wondering how to "do Jewish." We humbly offer this yearcycle book as a part of this lineage.

This book is a snapshot in time of the rituals and practices, fears and joys that our communities hold close today. We are excited for more year-cycle books, from our brilliant community and from the next generations. We believe we will be successful in this endeavor when this edition is surrounded by commentary and questions, full of additions and what we missed. The mysteries and offerings of our calendar wait for us to make meaning of them, to connect to ancestors. It is incumbent upon us in every generation to connect and understand them anew. May you find medicine in the rhythms of our years, and may we find ourselves in the cycles of time.

FRAMEWORKS

As anti-Zionist, queer, ritually practicing Jews engaging with Judaism and Jewish traditions, we have spent a lot of energy carving out space just to exist, be, and be Jewish together. With this book, we claim our space to deepen into nuance, to unpack challenges and untangle contradictions. We dream and organize, pray, celebrate, and mourn at the intersections of spiritual mysteries and material conditions. We explore millennia of tradition across continents while living firmly connected to the here and now and dreaming of a transformed future. Articulating what we're doing, how we're doing it, and why is a holy creative challenge that we are so grateful to have the time and space to explore.

Who We Are ~ What We Do (Belonging)

NO MAINSTREAMS, NO MARGINS, NO ALTERNATIVE, EVER CHANGING

We wrote this book out of our commitment to leftist Jews and Jewish movements, synagogues, organizing, and community. For many years, we've heard and occasionally said that we are part of an "Alternative Judaism," in contrast with "Mainstream Judaism" and the "Mainstream Jewish Community." We understand the temptation to identify as oppositional; we know the harmful impacts of those who wield power, money, resources, and the loudest microphone claiming to speak for and define what is Jewish. We've been told that our commitments to justice in Palestine equate to seeking the destruction of Jews and Judaism. We've seen friends and comrades lose jobs and livelihood for their commitment to justice and raising their voices. We know Jews of Color who have been questioned and attacked for stepping foot into a synagogue, trans Jews who have had their existence interrogated, disabled Jews who cannot even get into the building, and poor and working-class Jews who cannot afford the exorbitant expense of participation in Jewish communal life. There are many people who experience all and more of these harms at the same time. Given the shape and makeup of most of the institutions of Jewish life, we understand identifying as alternative.

And yet, the power of those institutions is transient and variable. When it comes to what it means to be a Jew, to live a Jewish life, to love HaShem,[1] to study Torah, and to work for the world to come, we reject the idea that there is a "norm," and that what deviates from this is "other." We won't cede our power in this way. In *every* generation, in *every* place, Judaism has been "what Jews do."[2] When it comes to living a Jewish life, there has always been a diversity of practices across places and communities, and transitions over time. There has always been innovation and boundary pushing; what is in one moment deemed heresy becomes over the centuries what everyone is doing. Rabbinic Judaism's origin is the example par excellence: reimagining Israelite Temple worship into diasporic prayer life.

What is now just referred to as "Judaism" can historically more accurately be called Rabbinic Judaism. Rabbinic Judaism evolved over centuries, before and after the fall of the Second Temple in 70 CE. The transition from Temple worship to Rabbinic Judaism was a massive upheaval in identity, community, and practice that we now narrate as seamless and inevitable. While the culture surrounding halacha, Jewish law, purports it to be immutable, the entire rabbinic enterprise is built on evolving practice with changing times.[3] The idea of Judaism as a religion, practicable separate from a halachic life, is only a few centuries old.[4] Change, in Judaism, has been constant. Our time is no different, except that now the marginalized and the heretics have easier access to publishing platforms.

Against the backdrop of the ever-changing nature of Jewishness and Judaism, we have been deeply shaped by (and very literally schooled in) two particular approaches to transforming Jewishness and Judaism: Reconstructionism and feminism. One of the core concepts of Reconstructionist Judaism, the movement that Jessica was born and raised in, and where both of us were ordained, is that Judaism is an "evolving religious civilization." As developed by Rabbi Mordechai Kaplan, this concept describes Jewish-

O
R

T
I
M
E
S

S
U
C
H

A
S

T
H
E
S
E

ness's ever-changing nature. The phrase "religious civilization" tries to communicate an expansive relationship to divinity and community: Jewishness has always been more than a singular set of practices, and encompasses multiracial, multicultural, multiethnic people. Kaplan and succeeding generations of Reconstructionists have put the changing nature of Jewishness at the center of our relationship to the tradition, and developed theories and methods to thoughtfully and deliberately relate to when, where, why, and how to make change to Jewish practice. We bring this framework to our engagement with Jewish tradition.

We are also indebted to the lineage of feminist Jewish theologians and organizers, many of whom we are incredibly blessed to have directly learned from and be in relationship with. When we listen we can hear millennia of women and queer, trans, and gender nonconforming people whose voices push through Judaism's male-dominated tradition. For the last sixty years there has been a movement explicitly expanding Jewishness and revolutionizing Judaism's misogynist and patriarchal foundations. We have been shaped by more people than we can name, and many more names than we know: feminist and queer Judaism has been shaped by countless people in Rosh Chodesh groups, song circles, protest encampments, and Torah study chevrutot. It is their vision, risk taking, and experimentation that created the Jewishness we are stepping into.

In the introduction to her 1991 *Standing Again at Sinai: Judaism from a Feminist Perspective*, Judith Plaskow chronicles her development, writing:

> the process of coming to write this book has been for me a gradual process of refusing the split between a Jewish and a feminist self. I am not a Jew in the synagogue and a feminist in the world. I am a Jewish feminist and a feminist Jew in every moment of my life. . . . When Jewish feminists allow Judaism and feminism to be defined by others in oppositional ways, then we are stuck with two "givens" confronting each other, and we are fundamentally divided. When, however, we refuse to sever or choose between different aspects of our identity, we create a new situation. If we are Jews not despite being feminists but *as feminists*, then Judaism will have to change—we will work to change it—to make a whole new identity possible. This change, moreover, may lead to new life for us and for the tradition.[5]

We gratefully acknowledge that we were raised up in the new life and new tradition that Plaskow and so many others worked to create, Jewish communities shaped by foremothers and transparents who insisted on their wholeness within Judaism.

In this book we seek to continue these legacies, and to expand them. Reconstructionist Judaism and Jewish feminist movements have, as in other white, cisgender, middle- and upper-class-led movements, perpetuated harmful dynamics of racism, transphobia, and classism, within ourselves, our communities and our organizations. As U.S.-based Jewish movements of the last century, both Reconstructionist Judaism and Jewish feminist movements have perpetuated Ashkenazi dominance. Jewish feminist spaces have often replicated the unquestioning Zionism of the broader Jewish world and Reconstructionist Judaism maintains an explicit commitment to Zionism. We put ourselves in the lineages of Reconstructionist and feminist Judaisms in order to name where so much of our shaping has come from, acknowledge the transformative power located there, and be accountable for the limitations of those movements. We commit to creating leftist Jewish communities that apply the methods of both movements toward embodying Judaism that honors all life and works to end all oppression, hopefully transforming both movements in the process.

We credit our expanded minds and visions, including learning of the limitations of the movements we were raised in, to Black feminists, Jews of Color, Sephardi and Mizrahi Jews, poor and working-class Jews, trans Jews, disabled Jews, and all those who've experienced marginalization within movements for justice and Judaism. We are committed to building Jewish spaces where all people can thrive, and we know that identity politics of inclusion are insufficient. In the Judaism and Jewishness we are building, we and the tradition are transformed by the commitments that flow from valuing all people in our communities. We are committed to bringing pro-Black anti-racism, gender justice and disability justice, abolition, wealth redistribution, reparations, and land back to Judaism and Jewish tradition. As with other systemic transformations within Jewish history, we root these politics in the heart of inherited tradition, while being open to radical change, as we will explore in this book. We work to dismantle and build new at the same time. While we acknowledge that these commitments put us, today, in a numerical minority among the loudest voices emanating from Jewish institutions, we also claim that these are the values that benefit most Jews, and people, on the planet. From this knowledge, we claim a new center, rather than accept anyone else's margins.

OUR ECOSYSTEM

This new center, while still numerically small, is dynamic and thriving. The leftist Jewish center has houses of study, farms, scribes, musicians and poets, organizers, caregivers, artists, and educators. We hope to take a snapshot of the leftist Jewish world as we understand it, knowing there are pieces outside our periphery, and brilliance still emerging. Our context is of the United States Jewish communities, so that is what we'll describe. We are grateful to be connected to this radical Jewish civilization around the world, and hold that many of these trends expand beyond our specific context. While some of these communities gathered online before the COVID-19 pandemic, online access to radical Jewish communities expanded greatly in the pandemic's wake.

Justice-minded Jewish learning communities and batei midrash (houses of study) are blossoming and growing each year. We have spaces centering on Jews of Color, queer and trans Jews, and anti-Zionist Jews that allow us to teach and learn from unique perspectives. These spaces offer introductory-level classes for those kept out of traditional places of learning that create deep healing through access. They offer rigorous advanced study, creating new midrash, commentary, halacha, drashot, and ritual practice. These places of progressive Torah study are not just creating a new cannon but adding more understanding to the existing library.

Every year, we see more and more leftist students enrolling and graduating from rabbinical schools. The Jewish Left is also nurturing diverse kinds of spiritual and communal leadership: Kohanot (Hebrew priestesses), song leaders, teachers of Torah. We have seen an explosion of fellowships, cohorts, and classes serving a generation of Jews who grew up with little access to, or chose not to engage with, Jewish learning. These include groups of Jews who want to study traditional Jewish text and prayer, for the first time, in politically aligned spaces, and classes outside of the traditional text canon, on Jewish plant medicine, magic, diasporism, embodiment, healing, art, and more. Jewish leftist student and youth organizing is happening in high schools and on college campuses, in communities for young adults, and in spaces where teens gather. Youth power can shape our communities in important ways, as the next generations bring vibrant strategies and new dreams for transformation.

In every generation, Jews start new synagogues and havurot to better reflect their values. In some generations we can start to notice patterns in what's starting, and why. For example, originally started as gay and lesbian synagogues, Congregations Beth Chayim Chadashim was founded in Los Angeles in 1972, Beit Simchat Torah started in New York City in 1973, Beth Ahavah in Philadelphia was founded in 1975, and Sha'ar Zahav in San Francisco started in 1977. In the years we've been writing this book, we've seen a similar growth of new synagogues and havurot, by and large defined by their resistance or opposition to Zionism.

As with everything else on the Left, there are debates about strategy and tactics: some communities are explicitly anti-Zionist, some describe their commitments to solidarity with Palestinians and justice in Palestine. Some, often dependent on the political ecosystem in their local contexts, take political action together, and some focus on being a prayer, ritual, and communal space. Some actively work to engage Zionist and non-Zionist community members and family, some focus on nourishing anti-Zionist Jewish life, and some are revolutionary simply because they are a place where anti-Zionists can be welcome in larger Jewish community. While we often have sharp critique for our proximate, similar but different ways of being, all of these Jewish communities are an extremely exciting and powerful turn from the previous synagogue spectrum of hard Right militant Zionist to liberal Zionist.

Among leftist synagogues and havurot, there is a wide spectrum of Jewish observance and prayer practice. Radical politics don't need to determine anything about the style of davening that moves you. Left communities are following similar trends toward postdenominationalism, as is the rest of the Jewish world, both because of the commitment to Zionism in all the mainstream movements and because of the broader trend away from denomination affiliation. The COVID-19 pandemic at one point transformed our communities to becoming much more accessible, and we're seeing a range of commitments to upholding and furthering accessibility, as well as some backsliding that contradicts our espoused values. As leftists who love organizing but oppose hierarchies and struggle with institutions, we have a complicated relationship with creating governance structures in the communities we start. Organizing synagogues has similar and unique challenges to organizing any group; we look forward to the coming years being a time of learning, experimentation, and growth in this area.

We are in a time of incredible growth of spaces and organizing by and for Black Jews, Asian Jews, Latine Jews, Sephardi Jews, Mizrahi Jews, and coalitional spaces of Jews of Color (JOC), Black, Indigenous, Jews of Color (BIJOC), and Black, Indigenous, Jews of Color, Sephardi and Mizrahi (BIJOCSM). The term BIJOCSM is used by BIJOCSM to build cross-identity solidarity and community together. Jews of Color are creating caucuses within existing organizations, and birthing new formations. These spaces run the gamut of Jewish Left organizing: prayer spaces, batei midrash, art collectives, film festivals, political organizing, and more. BIJOCSM leaders are creating funding mechanisms and taking the reins of research and education, building powerful counterforces to white, Ashkenazi-led Jewish communal organizations' decades of undercounting and underfunding BIJOCSM work. Black, Indigenous, Jews of Color, Sephardi and Mizrahi spaces are creating connection and community, healing and home, necessary Jewish homespace. It is incumbent on all of us to support and resource these holy spaces and this life-giving work.[6]

Leftists and organizers know that the world we are dreaming of is beautiful and bedazzled. Jewish Left artists are creating movement posters, siddurim, ketubot, household Judaica, Torah mantles and synagogue art, tallitot and tzitzit, calligraphy and safrut, poetry and prose, and theater both new and reimagined. New music for liturgy as well as original compositions are flowing from songcircles, singing retreats, and fellowships, deepening and expanding the sound and expression of Jewish life. We're reporting on it, and so much more, in online and print publications specifically focused on Jewish leftist thought, in podcasts, and in journals. Jewish Left artists are curating museum shows and zine collections, publishing books, and starting their own publishing houses. These creative endeavors are blooming from specific lived experiences and identities and as cross-community projects united around politics and aesthetics.

In recent years, increasing numbers of leftist Jews are bringing together centuries of ancestral wisdom with contemporary questions about how we relate to land, live in the seasons, and fundamentally change our relationship to the earth, in the context of human-made climate catastrophe. Following the lineage of Jewish summer camps, retreat centers, and socialist chicken farms,[7] Jewish farms and land projects are rooted in political commitments to justice in the food system, Indigenous land back, and Black land sovereignty and are experimenting with new kinds of collective living and organizing. These formations explore how to embody diasporist and anti-colonial politics, intertwined. Seeking to live in more interconnection with the earth, more Jews are exploring herbalism, plant magic, farming, and food, in urban and rural contexts. As more people wake up to the interconnection of all living beings on our rapidly changing planet, this essential knowledge and these practices must become increasingly integrated into our lives and our Jewishness. Jewish leftists are building dynamic organizations and projects and creating culture and art to explore and expand this work.

Jewish leftists are organizing and mobilizing around countless issues: housing justice, access to health care, immigration justice, prison abolition and movements to defund police, abortion access and reproductive justice, worker power, wealth redistribution, Indigenous land back and reparations, trans liberation, voting rights, anti-militarization, solidarity with Palestine, environmental justice, fighting white nationalism and rising facism, and more. We do this by bringing a range of Jewish experiences to broader movement organizations, in multifaith coalitions and in Jewish-specific organizations.

In short, the Jewish Left is thriving. There are so many different ways to be a radical Jew, and so many beautiful and powerful projects, creations, communities, and institutions growing in support of this. We excel in creativity—when we need something that doesn't otherwise exist in the world, we make it. More and more teachers and practitioners are bringing frameworks and practices of healing and resilience to organizing Jewish communities and living nourishing Jewish lives; Jewish leftists are staying curious about and working to disrupt behaviors shaped by trauma. There is a profound spirit of experimentation in the Jewish Left, engaging deeply with tradition and taking on ancient practice, and a commitment to creating newness where it is needed. We carry the old along with the new, and inherited tradition and innovation have the same legitimacy. The Jewish Left on the whole understands that these are not new ideas or practices, and is committed to finding the stories of our forebears in Jewish time. There is a reclaiming of traditions that is done to bring honor to our ancestors and gifts to our lives. We know that leftist Jewish movements reach back through the generations in labor organizing, anti-colonial organizing, anti-war organizing, and Black freedom movements, as well as within the Jewish world to create the nonhierarchical, feminist, queer, anti-Zionist Torah and community that we build on today.

In this thriving ecosystem, we have work to do, to better align our values and actions, address harm we cause to one another, and create communities of care that can take and embolden powerful action in the world. As we will explore, we have work to do dismantling white supremacy, embodying disability justice and radical accessibility, and making spaces and organizations that include the full range of relationships to Jewishness in our communities.

Oftentimes owning, professional, and managerial-class Jewish leftists, in working to be accountable to privilege, and in negligence and ignorance, erase poor and working-class Jews. This happens conceptually and verbally, in how we think about and describe who Jews are, and structurally, in how much things cost and how much time and what kind of resources we assume people in our communities have. This also shapes what political struggles Jewish leftists take on: for example, expansion of WIC and SNAP, universal health care, encampment defense, and tenant organizing are rarely talked about as issues impacting Jews. This can become a self-fulfilling prophecy, as many poor and working-class Jews find no reason to join explicitly Jewish leftist organizations. It is deeply insufficient to be anti-capitalist in rhetoric while functioning with the assumption that Jews are middle and upper class. Building an analysis of class identities and struggle is essential to making organizations where poor and working-class Jews can participate fully, not having to constantly remind everyone else of their existence, and lead in organizing for economic justice and systemic wealth redistribution.

The work of dismantling white supremacy in our Jewish leftist communities is one that is sometimes enacted, but often only paid lip service to. White supremacy is the water we are all swimming in, and it impacts at every turn how we organize ourselves, whom we listen to, and what we value. On the Jewish Left one trend we have seen from white Jews is the tokenizing of Jews of Color—having JOC leaders absolves the mostly white Jewish organization from having to look further at itself, or despite knowing that JOC should not be responsible for educating white Jews on racism, it happens anyway. Majority white and Ashkenazi communities can homogenize the experiences of Jews of Color and take advantage of terms like BIJOCSM to create an "other" category opposite white Ashkenazim. Commitment to diaspora culture looks like Ashkenazi Jews decentering Eastern European Jewish experience and resourcing BIJOCSM cultural, ritual, and organizing work. One of the perils of self-defining as "other" than the norm is that it is possible for us to put every condemnation on the mainstream and not have to interrogate ourselves for reproducing the same harm. This is intentional work that has to be embedded in everything we do together.

There are theological and ritual elements that need to be addressed and expanded, like examining relationships to chosenness and the place in community of Jews by Choice. Chosenness is the idea that the Jewish people are the Chosen People, a "light unto nations,"[8] the closest ones to the Divine at the expense of all other peoples. While many of our leftist Jewish communities reject this idea, it continues to show up in insidious ways in anti-convert bias. While according to halacha someone who chooses Judaism should never be interrogated about their Jewishness, we have heard some leftists be surprisingly anti-convert. This can stem from trauma, the inability to believe that anyone would want to be Jewish, and the feeling that Jewish pain is what defines us inherently and therefore without experiencing oppression as a Jew one cannot truly understand what it means. We understand that there is no singular story about what it means to be Jewish. We can honor the many pathways Jews take to Jewish community; one does not invalidate the other.

In our eagerness, creativity, and enthusiasm to meet unmet needs in our lives and communities, the Jewish Left sometimes falls into the same commodification that we experience in mainstream Jewish life. Spurred on by nonprofit-culture tendencies toward grass-top organizing and rapid scaling up, new projects can quickly move from ideation to widely public. New projects too quickly apply for foundation funding before exploring community need and resource, and rush to do public-facing programs and offerings before creating the infrastructure needed to support sustainable organizing and care for people. We know that we could gain so much power from collectively slowing down and building reflection, landscape mapping, and strategically assessing needs and capacity into our dreaming and organizing.

In Jewish Left organizing, we often wrestle with questions around positionality and articulating a specifically Jewish stake in a struggle, especially given Jews as a multiracial, cross-class people; different Jews are positioned very differently on these issues, and frameworks of "Jews in solidarity with XYZ" often erase Jews directly impacted by these issues. Across the Jewish Left, we are socialists, communists, anarchists, and more. This political diversity could be a strength, but much like in the rest of the U.S. Left today, many of our organizations are politically underdeveloped, with little practice articulating a coherent political vision or strategy. Indeed, reflecting broader movement trends, for years explicitly Jewish Left organizing trended toward nonprofitization, liberal electoral and legislative campaigns, and one-off direct actions focused on media narrative. But when we zoom out, both through looking back in history and outside of the formal Jewish nonprofit landscape, we can see the wide range of ways of being vibrantly Jewish in political movements and bringing our Jewishness to our political organizing. We hope that the coming years see a renewal of political education on the Jewish Left, more clear articulations of political vision and strategy, and an expansion of kinds of formations, strategies, and tactics.

When we imagine the Jewish leftist future, it is welcoming and confident. In order to grow and thrive we must not default to the cliques or in-groups so often synonymous with subcultures. Litmus tests that require newcomers to prove their political education or commitments replicate the harm we wish to heal and distance from. We must truly believe that what we are doing is an authentic expression of Judaism, or else we will project this insecurity on one another. We are here to stay, powerful, and growing.

EREV RAV, *THE MIXED MULTITUDE*

We are grateful to be in community with Jews of diverse Jewish practice and no practice, people in the process of becoming Jewish, and family, friends, and comrades who have no intention of becoming Jewish. Our Jewish communities have always looked this way—we are in a lineage with multifaith families dating back to Joseph and his wife, Asnat bat Potifar.

Yetziat Mitzrayim (יציאת מצרים), the Exodus, is the central narrative of the Jewish people, the story of our liberation movement. The group that left the Narrow Place together was an erev rav, a mixed multitude, Jews and our non-Jewish partners and neighbors, all together. We celebrate that Jewish community has always had non-Jews in it, partners, family, friends.

There are some roles and practices that non-Jews who are in Jewish relationships and communities are welcome to take on, and some that are distinct for Jews, that for non-Jews to do is appropriation. Confusingly for non-Jews, different communities and different Jews will have different feelings about what is appropriate and what is appropriation. Building genuine relationships for these conversations is key. We know and love that non-Jews in Jewish community often develop their own relationship to Jewish life—feeling connection to the weekly rhythm of Shabbat, having meaningful experiences of prayer in services, celebrating holidays along with Jewish loved ones. This is a wonderful thing, and one that can happen only when there is trust. We also acknowledge that non-Jewish family have been treated in some communities with suspicion and hostility, and excluded from familial ritual observance (for example, not being allowed to come to the Torah for their children's b'nei mitzvah). In order for our Jewish communities to thrive as a mixed multitude, we must be attuned to how non-Jewish community is welcomed and integrated into communal practice.

Simultaneously, non-Jews who enter our communities are encouraged to practice humility and patience—as in any cross-cultural encounter, Jews have no obligation to step into the role of educator when they are going about their Jewish lives. Though many Jews are available to, in some contexts, answer questions, non-Jews entering Jewish space are encouraged to do their own research before and after, build relationships, watch attentively and learn from context clues, and check in with people before launching into questions. Especially for those raised Christian or in Christian hegemonic communities, non-Jews entering our communities have significant work to do unlearning antisemitism.

In our generation, we are feeling the impacts of the Holocaust and of centuries of antisemitism that have separated so many from Jewish practice and community. At times we experience complicated relationships between Jews and non-Jews. In this vein, we see regular struggles within Jewish Left communities about how to hold the range of relationships to Jewish practice, and traverse the differences between us with mutual respect and care. Collectively, we can do better. We can create communities where we greet each other with curiosity instead of suspicion, where we are secure enough in ourselves to affirm all of the genuine ways there are of engaging with Jewishness.

Jewishness predates and does not fit neatly into the category of religion. While there is a robust history and present of Jewish secularism, it does not fit neatly into Christian ideas about the secular: Jewish secularism is distinct from assimilation; Jewish secularists by and large maintain Jewish identity and communal ties and create Jewish cultures. Our Jewish lives, even before we look at how they intersect with our political lives, already break the Christian-dominant bounds of culture and spirituality. Embracing the range of ways of being and doing Jewish can look like nurturing our movement spaces local ecosystems, and Jewish cultural spaces outside of synagogues, and creating events and spaces that don't assume a ritual or prayer practice as the correct way of being Jewish.

People in the process of conversion often have questions about which Jewish practices are appropriate to take on, and how to relate to Jewish community. Converting to Judaism is, in and of itself, a unique cultural practice and sacred tradition. There is no one detailed formula for conversion. In the process, people are required to learn Jewish tradition, to try on Jewish practice, to live Jewishly, and to build a robust and holistic relationship to Jewishness. No one converts in isolation; conversion requires a beit din (בֵּית דִּין), a rabbinic court, and thus a relationship to Jewish community. Before going to beit din and mikvah and formally converting, people in the process of converting aren't yet considered Jewish. Traditionally this means one can't serve on a beit din, be a witness to a ketubah or other legal document, read from Torah, or lead prayers for other Jews. Most of Jewish practice, however, is not only appropriate but encouraged for a conversion student to try on. Behaving and belonging is how a person becomes Jewish.

People in the process of converting in leftist spaces will encounter a range of reactions from people raised with a relationship to Jewishness, including welcoming enthusiasm and excitement, suspicion, doubt, confusion, and straight-up hostility. We seek to transform inhospitable responses to conversion, while also giving people in the process of conversion tools to understand and withstand these positions and the feelings underneath them. Antagonism to conversion can come from suspicion of converts as appropriating Jewishness; lack of understanding about the process of conversion; people's own negative experiences of Jewishness and Judaism; and a lack of understanding about why anyone would choose Jewishness. In the specific context of converts in the Jewish Left, there may be antagonism stemming from deep grief that sometimes is expressed as jealousy of people raised without Jewishness getting to access Jewish learning, practice, community, and identity without needing to unlearn conservative Jewish politics and practice. All of these complex feelings are the result of and are threaded through with the impacts of antisemitism and assimilation.

People born into Judaism deserve space to explore these feelings with each other. Jews who have converted and people in the process of conversion deserve to be welcomed as full members of our communities and to not have their motives interrogated or their status invalidated. All of us deserve to be in process, learning, growing, and changing.

As we build Jewish communities that reflect and push our leftist politics, they must also celebrate the wide range of relationships to Jewishness present in Jewish leftist lives and families. We are, as usual, stronger and more powerful coming together and celebrating our different experiences.

JUDAISM BEYOND ZIONISM

One of the central, animating questions of the Jewish Left today is resistance to, and Jewish life in the context of, Zionism and the ongoing occupation of Palestine. We are living 126 years after the first World Zionist Congress, 107 years after the Balfour Declaration,[9] and 75 years after the first wave of the Nakba. Modern political Zionism has twisted Jewish longing for spiritual wholeness, repair, and safety from ongoing persecution and attempted genocide into the systemic and ongoing displacement of Palestinians, the subjugation of Palestinian rights and freedom, and the erasure and negation of Palestinian histories. It is in this context that we seek to create Judaism beyond Zionism, rooted in a political commitment to anti-Zionism and solidarity with Palestinian struggles for justice.

Zionism refers to Jewish nationalism: movements for Jewish sovereignty, to create a Jewish nation-state. As a political movement, Zionism originated in late-nineteenth-century Europe. Prior to that time, Judaism included theological strands and cultural practices that expressed a belief in the sacredness and significance of Eretz Yisrael (אֶרֶץ יִשְׂרָאֵל) the Land of Israel. Since early Rabbinic Judaism, there have been prayers for kibutz galuyot (קִבּוּץ גָּלֻיּוֹת) ingathering of the exiles, included in the Amidah, the central prayer of every service, said while facing Jerusalem to pray three times a day. Alongside these theologies and practices, there was for most of Jewish history an embrace of diaspora: Jewish communities making homes in all of the places they lived, intermingling with the people and cultures of those places. With few exceptions, Jews did not return en masse to Eretz Yisrael; spiritual and communal leaders did not encourage it, and people didn't do it. Instead, they created complex cultures and traditions that included longing for spiritual home and an end to exile—a theological relationship to longing, while making material homes where they lived. This included making a home in historic Palestine, without, for many centuries, attempting state building projects. This was changed only very recently in the span of Jewish history, with the growth of Zionism, the modern European political movement to build a Jewish nation-state, modeled after other European nation-building and colonial projects. In recent years, Jewish historians and theologians have even challenged the historicity of the narrative of biblical civilization as centrally located and exile as the dispersion of a people as a singular event and cataclysmic change.[10]

None of this denies the importance of Eretz Yisrael and the longing for return as a spiritual concept in Judaism. When we refer to ourselves as anti-Zionist, and talk about building Judaisms beyond Zionism, it is this modern political movement to which we're referring. When we talk about building Judaism beyond Zionism, we are describing the complex project of being open to and up front about multifaceted Jewish relationships to land and place, while being unequivocal about our opposition to Israel as an ethnic nation-state that continues to displace Palestinians and perpetrate apartheid. In this book, we will explore how, throughout the Jewish year, we have opportunities to detangle the millennia-old relationship to Eretz Yisrael from the modern political project of Zionism. We will offer specific examples where the yearcycle invites exploration of these questions (for example, how do we mourn the destruction of the Temple at Tisha b'Av as anti-Zionists?) and discuss rituals when we know there is confusion among anti-Zionists about the roots of a practice and its relationship to Zionism (for example, why is it traditional to observe one day of festival at the beginning of Pesach and Sukkot in Eretz Yisrael, and two in diaspora?).

Fighting for justice for Palestine is a core commitment of our lives. This is intertwined with, but separate from, our work to build and live Judaism beyond Zionism. That is because we understand that the ongoing colonization of Palestine continues primarily because it serves supremacist Christianity, U.S. militarism, and the economic interests of corporations that profit from the domination of life and land. We fight this through broad-based, multiracial, multifaith, intersectional campaigns in line with the Palestinian-led Boycott, Divestment and Sanctions (BDS) Movement[11]; through land defense and solidarity; and through supporting revolutionary Palestinian organizing. Meanwhile, the story that Zionism is a path of safety and liberation for Jews is one that props up and fuels the colonization of Palestine, one that we are called to counter. We do not believe that building Judaism and Jewish communities beyond Zionism will end the occupation of Palestine, and so our anti-Zionist commitments extend beyond our work with Judaism. And, at the same time, we think building Judaism beyond Zionism contributes to ending Zionism's harmful impact on Palestinian lives, and is one piece of a larger movement. How big a piece, and how best to do that, are important questions that we wrestle with regularly.

We build Judaism beyond Zionism for the sake of Jews and Judaism. In addition to the violence against Palestinian people and land, modern political Zionism's hegemony has crept into every aspect of Judaism and Jewish life. Zionist ideology creates and inflames racialized hierarchies within Jewish community that harm Sephardi and Mizrahi Jews, and Jews of Color.[12] Taking the millennia-old spiritual relationship with Eretz Yisrael, the land of Israel, and conflating it with a modern nation-state undermines centuries of theology and culture. Part of the work of our lifetimes, and this book, is claiming relationships to Jerusalem and Eretz Yisrael that center justice and safety for all people who call that land home.

We build Judaism beyond Zionism because deploying millennia of tradition as a weapon in a violent, nationalist, colonial project is a form of cultural violence. We know very well that as Jews we are not the primary targets of Israeli military violence. And, at the same time, our hearts break again and again to see our sacred holidays be turned into times of fear for Palestinian communities. We see Israel's erasure of Mizrahi histories, violently repressing or manipulating Jews' lives in the land. We are by now familiar with the waves of grief and rage when Israel wages war against Gaza and names those military operations after verses from our sacred texts.[13]

We build Judaism beyond Zionism to resist this violence. We claim Judaism before modern political Zionism, not as a romantic, flawless, static tradition but as a treasure trove of dynamic traditions and cultural pathways that are ours to claim and infuse with our visions. It is not up to us as U.S.–based Jews to determine the political future for Palestinians and Israelis. We can, however, work to change culture, hearts, and minds, and organize. Zionism is predicated on, among other things, a belief that antisemitism is neverending, that Jews need an army to keep us safe. We work for the safety and thriving of all people in the land, and an end to antisemitism, Islamophobia, and anti-Arab racism around the world, while organizing for the dismantling of state and military apparatuses that privilege Jewish lives over non-Jewish lives. We are fueled by and every day seek to live a Judaism that opposes ethno-nationalism and Jewish supremacy and turns, in every moment, toward solidarity.

DIASPORISM

As we articulate Judaism beyond Zionism, one of the core concepts that leftist Jews have been buoyed by is diasporism. Diasporism is being actively defined by many of our comrades as we write; the bounds and implications of diasporism are ours to determine and cocreate. At its simplest and broadest, Jewish diasporism is a set of ethical, political philosophies and creative expressions that embrace, rather than shun, Jewish dispersion around the globe, outside of the land of Yisrael. Diasporism is an important rejoinder to Zionist philosophy and the practice of "shlilat ha'golah," negation of the diaspora, which claims that Jewish life outside of Eretz Yisrael and without political sovereignty over a nation-state is inevitably and perpetually dangerous. It is also a counter to lachrymose Jewish history, that says that Jewish life in exile was completely and indelibly an experience of violence and suffering. Diasporism points to centuries of Jewish thriving around the globe, Jewish resilience and creativity, and intermingling with people and cultures in all the places we've lived. And yet, diasporism raises as many questions as it answers: about relationships to land, in the places we live and in Eretz Yisrael; about Jewish peoplehood and theology; and about relationships to other diasporic peoples. There is a robust history of Jewish thought wrestling with galut (גָּלוּת), exile and diaspora. We are influenced by thinkers from across Jewish history, and by the robust ecosystem of Jewish Left explorations of diasporism today.

In much of Jewish tradition, exile is portrayed as the great tragedy and trauma of the Jewish people. In the rabbinic mind, diaspora means distancing from sacred sites, loss of freedom of expression, inability to bring offerings to the Temple in the closest way humans can encounter God. Yearning for kibutz galuyot, the ingathering of exiles, is in our central Amidah prayer, the cornerstone of the grief of Tisha b'Av. Jews have experienced real, deep grief and yearning for safety, place, and stability. And yet, our earliest texts include discussion of dispersion in divergent terms. In Beresheet 26:2–3, Isaac faces famine and is prepared to travel to look for help. But God appears to him and says:

וַיֵּרָא אֵלָיו֙ יְהֹוָ֔ה וַיֹּ֕אמֶר אַל־תֵּרֵ֖ד מִצְרָ֑יְמָה שְׁכֹ֣ן בָּאָ֔רֶץ אֲשֶׁ֖ר אֹמַ֥ר אֵלֶֽיךָ:
גּ֚וּר בָּאָ֣רֶץ הַזֹּ֔את וְאֶֽהְיֶ֥ה עִמְּךָ֖ וַאֲבָרְכֶ֑ךָּ כִּֽי־לְךָ֣ וּֽלְזַרְעֲךָ֗ אֶתֵּן֙ אֶת־כׇּל־הָֽאֲרָצֹ֣ת הָאֵ֔ל
וַהֲקִֽמֹתִי֙ אֶת־הַשְּׁבֻעָ֔ה אֲשֶׁ֥ר נִשְׁבַּ֖עְתִּי לְאַבְרָהָ֥ם אָבִֽיךָ:

יהוה had appeared to him and said, "Do not go down to Egypt;
stay in the land which I point out to you. Reside in this land, and I
will be with you and bless you; I will assign all these lands to you
and to your heirs, fulfilling the oath that I swore to your father
Abraham."

Then, when our ancestors again are faced with famine, God appears to Jacob, Isaac's son, to tell him it is time to go to Egypt in Beresheet 46:1–2:

וַיִּסַּ֤ע יִשְׂרָאֵל֙ וְכׇל־אֲשֶׁר־ל֔וֹ וַיָּבֹ֖א בְּאֵ֣רָה שָּׁ֑בַע וַיִּזְבַּ֣ח זְבָחִ֔ים לֵֽאלֹהֵ֖י אָבִ֥יו יִצְחָֽק:

וַיֹּ֣אמֶר אֱלֹהִ֣ים ׀ לְיִשְׂרָאֵל֮ בְּמַרְאֹ֣ת הַלַּ֔יְלָה וַיֹּ֖אמֶר יַֽעֲקֹ֣ב ׀ יַֽעֲקֹ֑ב וַיֹּ֖אמֶר הִנֵּֽנִי:

וַיֹּ֗אמֶר אָֽנֹכִ֤י הָאֵל֙ אֱלֹהֵ֣י אָבִ֔יךָ אַל־תִּירָא֙ מֵֽרְדָ֣ה מִצְרַ֔יְמָה כִּֽי־לְג֥וֹי גָּד֖וֹל אֲשִֽׂימְךָ֥
שָֽׁם:

So Israel set out with all that was his, and he came to Beer-
sheba, where he offered sacrifices to the God of his father
Isaac's [house]. God called to Yisrael in a vision by night: "Jacob!
Jacob!" He answered, "Here." "I am God, the God of your
father's [house]. Fear not to go down to Mitzrayim, for I will
make you there into a great nation."

When is it the right time to stay in the land, and when is it time to travel? When is exile a result of ethical behavior, and when is it the tragic result of geopolitical machination? Our texts and histories have nuanced relationships to these questions.

In fact, Susanna Heschel points out that most Jews have been living in diaspora since the sixth century—but exile, as it is understood in the liturgical imagination, was not the cause of this diaspora; instead, it never happened.[14] In *A Traveling Homeland: The Babylonian Talmud as Diaspora*, Daniel Boyarin makes the case that the Talmud became a portable, functional homeland for Rabbinic Jews because of exile. Indeed, the rabbis of the Talmud have differing perspectives on exile. In Ketuboth 111a, there is discussion of the text of Jeremiah 27:22, which reads:

בָּבֶלָה יוּבָאוּ וְשָׁמָּה יִהְיוּ עַד יוֹם פָּקְדִי אֹתָם נְאֻם־יְהֹוָה וְהַעֲלִיתִים וַהֲשִׁיבֹתִים אֶל־הַמָּקוֹם הַזֶּה:

> They [the Israelites] shall be brought to Babylon, and there they
> shall remain, until I take note of them—declares HaShem—and
> bring them up and restore them to this place.

As with all Talmudic debate, there is a range of interpretations of this text. One of them is that it is divinely intended for Jews to stay in the diaspora until God's messianic intervention. Medieval commentators affirm God's presence with the Jewish people in diaspora, implicitly rejecting negation of the diaspora. In his commentary on Beresheet 28:15, Sforno[15] writes:

> When I said that after the exile you will expand in all directions
> of the globe, know no boundaries, this is possible only because
> even during the long years of exile I did not abandon you, as
> stated explicitly in Vayikra 26:44 "I will not have rejected them,
> nor will I have abhorred them."[16]

Many Jewish leftists take inspiration from the legacy of the Algemeyner Yidisher Arbeter Bund in Lite, Poyln un Rusland, the General Union of Jewish Workers in Lithuania, Poland, and Russia, known simply as the Bund. Formed in 1897 to organize Jews into the revolutionary cause, they developed a political articulation of doikayt (hereness). Countering Zionist ideology, doikayt affirmed the legitimacy of Jewish life in the places they lived. Bundists committed to struggling for revolution in those places rather than mass movement to Palestine. Most Jews throughout history theorized diaspora through living in it, creating robust, creative, dynamic cultures in all the places they lived.

Ella Shohat's work in *On the Arab-Jew, Palestine, and Other Displacements* illuminates Mizrahi experiences and identities, and puts Mizrahi experience in conversation with other people resisting colonization. This snaps us out of the false binary that simple formations of diaspora may, intentionally or inadvertently, create. In Melanie Kaye/Kantrowtiz's 2007 book, *The Colors of Jews: Racial Politics and Radical Diasporism*, she examines questions of Jewish identity, racialization, and collective formation, explores the racial and cultural diversity of Jews, and shares stories and voices of anti-racist Jewish organizers. She offers a theory of Jewish radical diasporism that embraces the diversity of Jewish life while contextualizing Jews in history and connecting Jews in solidarity with other diaspora peoples.

> One step beyond these [wishes of citizenship] is valuing the margins; not wanting danger or instability—who would?—but not wanting either to surrender the perspective that diaspora can yield. I name this commitment Diasporism to challenge two related notions. First, that living in diaspora is an unfortunate nameless lapse, unchosen and without value. Second, that true home and safety are to be found in the nation state.[17]

Kaye/Kantrowitz's exploration is still extremely relevant to us today, as we are living in many of the same questions and struggles.

How do we configure radical diasporism today? First, as Jewish leftists claiming, celebrating, and making home in the diaspora, most of us are rejecting the Zionist "right of return" to Israel that is afforded to us because of the country's Jewish supremacy. We must, in the same breath, affirm Palestinian right of return in the face of nearly a century of forcible displacement. Jewish diasporism need not be a blanket embrace of diaspora as the preferred condition for all peoples; as Jews, we must be specific in articulating *Jewish* embrace of diaspora and not inadvertently making claims about diaspora for any other peoples. We insist on a diasporism that does not erase Mizrahi histories and cultures; this is to say, our diasporism

FOR TIMES SUCH AS THESE

38

must not, in attempting to reverse negation of the diaspora, negate Jewish life in Palestine over millennia. When we embrace diasporism, it must be while actively naming that many of us are living as settlers on stolen land, and challenging any uncomplicated embrace of diasporism that is inadvertently complicit with settler colonialism. In resisting the weaponization of authentic Jewish experiences of longing for spiritual home and safety, radical diasporism doesn't need to erase or invalidate those feelings. Our radical diasporism must not become a way to turn away from or wash our hands of the violence to which we are proximate, in Palestine or the U.S. We understand theft of land, the displacement of masses of people, the labor of enslaved people who built the lands on which we live, and the imposition of borders to be violence against which we struggle. This is the context in which we form radical diasporism.

For diasporism to be most useful, it needs to not only say what we are rejecting but help to shape the contours of the politics we're embracing, not only for individualized Jews but for Jewish peoplehood. Our radical diasporism must be shaped around a vision of the world and the movement of people around it as it more accurately is: continuously ebbing and flowing, to and from many places of temporary and more permanent homes. We embrace Jewish histories and cultures in all the places Jews have called home, including the land between the river and the sea. This kind of diasporism melts state boundaries and shifts us toward more earth-based practice.

Today, we are surrounded by ever-growing explorations and expressions of radical diasporism.[18] Rather than provide one answer or static definition of diasporism, these projects create space for ongoing learning and new articulations of radical diasporism. This, too, is our commitment: continued exploration of how to live in more right relationship with all the places we call home.

This radical diasporism is made possible by a critique of settler colonialism and the state. Radical diasporism understands that empires and borders, and not the movement of people, are the problem. Jewish radical diasporism must affirm that as we, in the words of Kaye/Kantrowitz, "make home where we are."[19] Making home, which we celebrate, is not making a nation-state. Making home looks like fighting back against the state's hoarding of resources and policing of lives, supporting Indigenous land back and sovereignty, offering and asking for solidarity with other oppressed peoples, and finding new ways of relating to the places where and the peoples with whom we live. As Jews, we have an incredible inheritance of culture and history in diaspora. Naming the marginalization and hostility of governments and elites to Jews in the places we've lived can help us unearth and celebrate our ancestors' ways of organizing ourselves outside of and separate from the state. We can bring these strategies to our broader organizing. Radical diasporism commits us to the project of creating forms of governance and resource sharing outside of the state. Radical diasporism insists we get to know the land on which we live, honor the original inhabitants, and understand ourselves as interdependent parts of the ecosystems in which we dwell. Radical diasporism understands that, in the words of Black Elk as taught to us through the poetry of Ursula K. Leguin, every land is the holy land.[20] We know all land is sacred, and we strive to act accordingly.

How We Do (Behaving)

JUDAISM IS WHAT JEWS DO

As we've named, Judaism and Jewish culture are what Jews in any given generation are doing. That is forever and always changing across generations, and in each generation there is far more diversity of practice than those in power want to acknowledge.

In fact, halacha (Jewish law, literally "the way") was built to change and evolve. On one hand, halacha is rooted in and traces back to Torah, and it is considered by halachic Jews to be the lineage of revealed instructions from God. Within halacha, however, there is a distinction between mitzvot d'oraita (מִצְוֹת דְּאוֹרַיְיתָא), commandments from the Torah, and mitzvot d'rabbanan (מִצְוֹת דְּרַבָּנָן), commandments that the rabbis admit to having constructed in order to, as the saying goes, make a fence around the Torah,[21] or, in other words, create a ring of protection to keep us from violating any Torah commandments. There is also a tradition as old as rabbinic Judaism itself of teshuvot, responsa literature: Jews asking questions from rabbis. This is predicated on the understanding that there is no halachic question under the sun on which all rabbis agree; halacha is multivocal.

This is part of why there is a range of relationships to halacha among politically left Jews. Some (Jews and non-Jews alike) may find this surprising, and it is not without reason that seemingly strict religious observance and leftist, radical politics appear at odds. But halacha is not a single set of laws. It is a way of relating to Jewish practice, a commitment to a set of processes about how that practice is determined, and the tradition in which Jewish practice is rooted. While much of Jewish Left organizing in the last centuries has been vibrantly secular, there have always also been halachic Jews across the contemporary political spectrum.[22] Svara's Trans Halakha Project demonstrates the incredible potential of the halachic process, bringing trans Jewish scholars together to "Develop new halakhic literature that addresses the needs and experiences of trans Jews authentically and without reservation."[23] This gathering of scholars coming together to consider halacha in the light of changing lived realities is how halacha has always changed.

Today, commitment to halacha is one way to be in relationship to Jewish behaving, to doing Jewish. In this book we begin from the belief that there is no one right way to be Jewish, and no one right way to determine Jewish practice. We were raised and trained in the lineage of Reconstructionist relationship to halacha. In traditional halachic discourse, all argumentation flows from and must be coherent within Jewish text tradition; while there is debate and legal reasoning, Torah and Talmud are the first and primary voices. The resulting mitzvot are understood as divinely commanded and obligatory. In Reconstructionism, one of Kaplan's core innovations was the articulation of a relationship to halacha where "the past has a vote, but not a veto."[24] In this approach, we give Jewish text tradition a seat at the table, sitting next to Jewish customs and inherited ritual and practice; our ethics, values, and political commitments; contemporary teachers and wisdom from other cultures and traditions we're a part of and in relationship to; and our body's wisdom, our embodied knowing that we are learning to listen to. We practice putting these voices in conversation with each other. Many of us are doing this all the time without articulating the process. In this book, we are arguing for a more conscious and active engagement with this kind of wrestling, in many ways inspired by and not so different from halachic discourse.

For some, halacha is divinely inspired and a binding obligation. For others, it is a rich resource of ancestral wisdom. Many of us will traverse this spectrum across our Jewish lives. There are no "bad Jews," and none that are "not Jewish enough," and something being in accordance with halacha is not a decider of its goodness or correctness. While often said in a self-deprecating or playful way, these ideas communicate real shame that so many people feel, and underlie deeply harmful hierarchies and exclusion people experience within Jewish space and in the wider world in regard to their Jewishness. We know this is one of the results of separation from Jewish tradition and culture due to antisemitism and the pressure to assimilate into white supremacy's cultural emptiness. We are working to create ever more spaces where all people who desire it have access to learning about and experimenting with the beautiful range of Jewishness. In those spaces, every Jewish way of being, every way people do Jewish, is Jewish enough, and we take on new Jewish practices through following our desires and curiosities. As we build liberatory Jewish communities, we declare that all of our ways of practicing and relating to practice are glorious and sacred.

THE SPIRITUAL IS POLITICAL, THE POLITICAL IS SPIRITUAL

Our feminist teachers taught us that the personal is political. Our engagement with creating wholehearted, values-aligned Jewish lives has shown us that the spiritual is political, and the political is spiritual. Being politically left and traditionally Jewish has often been seen as contradictory because of the Jewish supremacy, chauvinism, misogyny, patriarchy, and religious nationalism in the text and tradition. Indeed, many leftists have been raised in or encounter Jewish tradition that is so antithetical to their values that they leave and never come back. One of the gifts of Jewishness is that rejecting parts of the tradition does not necessitate leaving the culture and community, as the vibrant secular Jewish Left demonstrates.

However, we who feel drawn to theism, prayer, ritual, and spiritual engagement feel no separation between our political commitments, our Jewish selves, and our spiritual lives. We understand that ritual spiritual lives must be infused with our values to be meaningful. We do not deny the harm and violence embodied in and perpetuated through Judaism. As with all cultures shaped by human hands, Jewish tradition bears the imprints of human fragility and fallibility, and, thus, is shaped by and can transmit the oppressive systems humans have created. We, however, have felt the power of Jewish rituals, and of living a life immersed in Judaism and Jewish tradition, and know that the ritual has magic beyond the oppressive forces that formed it and that it forms.

Some argue that leftists should refuse to relinquish the terrain of religion and spirituality to the right out of a strategic organizing imperative: religious affiliation and spiritual communities are where people gather, and it is unwise and shortsighted to give up on such a massive location of collected people and power. We agree with this argument, but it's not where we root our theory or practice. It's not objectively easier or harder, more or less strategic in the abstract, to organize religious people than it is to organize people by block and neighborhood, workplace and trade, impacted issues, and terrain of struggle. Organizing is very hard, and every configuration of people has its unique opportunities and challenges to being organized. We shouldn't give up on organizing religious people because we shouldn't give up on organizing anyone, but we don't make a case for left political engagement with Jewish tradition and spirituality because it is strategic. Instead, we explore how and why spiritual practice and leftist political organizing are so compatible for us, with the hope that we can give language to, mirror, and amplify others' experiences. With others for whom this is meaningful, we know we will be lifelong comrades in organizing in our religious and spiritual communities and in moving people to the left. For leftists unmoved by religious tradition, ritual, or spirituality, don't worry, there is plenty else to do. No one needs to join a congregation to organize it; in fact, we've never seen salting work in religious and spiritual contexts.

The foundation of our belief that Jewish tradition and revolutionary political commitments for liberation and justice go hand in hand is that we are living it. We have experienced Jewishness as the reinforcing and deepening of our values and political commitments, and we have felt our political commitments drawing us closer to community, tradition, and ancestry. We feel it, and then we have to create lives in which these aspects of ourselves are in harmony. When, as Plaskow teaches, "we refuse to sever or choose between different aspects of our identity, we create a new situation."[25] We apply this wisdom of feminist Judaism to all of our leftist politics. In doing so we are refusing to walk away from millennia of deep and nuanced cultural traditions. We claim all of Jewish tradition as our own, not to follow by rote without question but to celebrate and wrestle with, to be transformed by and to transform.

We are in good company across many communities and traditions. Over the last decade, we have seen an incredible growth of leftist movements engaging with spirituality, culture, ritual, and healing. We are indebted to Indigenous-led organizing and Black, women of color organizing for groundbreaking work articulating and creating spaces for practice in this area.[26] Concepts of healing justice and the frequency of leftist organizers engaging in spiritual, cultural practices are growing in popularity. But by and large in the popular imagination, the Right still has a hold on "religion" and "tradition." So it makes sense that many on the Left refer to themselves as "spiritual but not religious." In this context, it is important to articulate more about how we understand ourselves as politically left and Jewishly traditional, to open up the hood of the car and investigate its innerworkings. In doing so, we hope to develop more clarity about what we're doing as spiritual and religious leftists, how, and why. While our exploration is rooted in Jewish tradition, we hope it has applications for people in other communities and lineages, wrestling with other traditions.

This explanation, and this whole book, is rooted in our lived experiences. We got to where we are and how we live, practice, and organize from following our desires, and being in community with countless others who live lives of praxis. We think, read, and talk about our Jewishness and our politics; create spaces and take actions that embody our desires and ideas; and reflect, dissect, and debate what worked and what didn't, the surprising successes and newfound contradictions. We bring it all into the next experiment. We know we can bring radical politics and Jewish tradition together because we do it.

When we slow down to talk about how we are able to bring Jewish tradition and leftist politics together, their mutuality feels deeply unsurprising. Our political commitments are to ending oppressive systems, transforming relationships between people, and transforming the relationship of people to the rest of creation to be one of care and reverence. We seek to repair interpersonal and collective harm and to create ways of tending to harm that heal rather than perpetuate cycles of violence. As leftists, we want to find ways to structure our communal relationship and organizations in ways that sustain life and well-being. All of these commitments are deeply in alignment with what we experience as the foundational and foremost teachings of Jewish tradition over the millenia: reverence for life, attention to and appreciation of interdependence and the connection between all things, and deep concern for justice and communal well-being.

While we find the theoretical frameworks of left politics and the core of Jewish tradition to be in alignment, we also find the day-to-day operationalizing of our politics with our inherited tradition to have many opportunities for mutual reinforcement. As we will explore, Jewish tradition provides structures for strengthening our relationships to the earth and seasons, in deep alignment with the profound calling of our time for environmental justice. Jewish holidays provide opportunities for us to come together as communities outside of capitalist modes of exchange—something rare and precious in our day—with revolutionary potential. Daily, weekly, and seasonal Jewish prayer and holiday ritual offer set times and prompts for personal and collective self-reflection that can aid us in living our values. This list could, and will, go on and on.

The places where we find conflict between our inherited traditions and our political commitments are dynamic opportunities to reflect on and sharpen both. Mikvah, the ritual immersion in water, has been used over the centuries to control and demean menstruating bodies. Some of our holidays assume and celebrate Jewish supremacy. Many of our original texts portray a violent, patriarchal deity and celebrate militarism and colonization. This list, too, could and will go on and on. We believe the work of studying, unpacking, bringing ourselves to, experimenting with, and transforming these texts, traditions, and rituals has the potential to heal some of the harm that they have caused, and, in doing so, be one part of building the world that we, as people committed to organizing for justice and liberation, are fighting for.

The compatibility of revolutionary politics with inherited traditions should be seen as an asset to both. Those of us who seek to transform the world toward liberation for all people must insist that people can and should bring all of themselves along, including ancestors with whom we disagree, complex cultural traditions, and rituals whose power we cannot fully put into words. In doing so, we affirm that the world we seek to build leaves no one, and no part of ourselves, behind.

As we will show in this book, we are part of a thriving Jewish Left that encompasses people across a wide range of relationships to and participation in Jewish tradition and practice, all of whom have their own lived experiences and articulations of integrating these pieces of themselves. How, we will now explore, do all of us, with our varied ways of being Jewish and left, organize ourselves?

Jewish leftist practice can take infinite shapes, and we see patterns and tendencies in how the Jewish Left is organized. Leftist political groups (Jews for Racial and Economic Justice, Jewish Voice for Peace, If Not Now, etc.) acknowledge and lean into their organizations' meeting of members' need for Jewish community. Celebrating Jewish holidays together is one of the primary shapes this can take. We also see spiritual homes (congregations and havurot) that are made up primarily of people who are politically aligned with each other, who, for a range of reasons, take political action together. These tendanices are by no means a binary: many people participate in both, many political organizations and spiritual homes collaborate, and we see people across the Jewish Left bringing ritual, prayer, song, and tradition into campaigns, political organizing, and direct action. Walking in off the street to a leftist Jewish Channukah party, it's unlikely that you'd be able to tell right away what brought people there or what kind of organizational space you're entering. As students of revolutionary histories and liberation struggles, this is by no means surprising. We take inspiration and guidance from Black freedom movements, the American Indian Movement, abolitionist organizing across the centuries, and more, to remember the intuitive interweaving of the Left with tradition, culture, and spirituality.

Just as there are dynamic points of tension and struggle when bringing our leftist political commitments to our inherited tradition, there are also points of struggle when, in our organizations, we take action that, while synergistic, are not what the organizations were originally intended and designed for. This is to say, while celebrating Jewish holidays with our political groups and taking political action with our Jewish ritual homes comes very naturally to many of us, there are tensions that will likely never be completely resolved. Some people chafe at certain points of overlap, saying things like, "My political group is getting too religious, doing too much singing, devoting too much time to holidays"; "My spiritual home is talking about politics too much. I organize all day every day, here I want to sing and get some relief from organizing strategy"; "This action has too much singing"; or "This action wasn't moving at all. We should be singing!"

We don't think these tensions can or should be resolved. Instead, we acknowledge that in both political organizing and spiritual life, there is a wonderfully wide range of what people desire and are nourished by, and what is strategic and effective at meeting peoples' needs, organizational vision, and goals. We can seek to be more clear about the components of what we can do together, so people can have more clarity about what works for them and what they understand to be strategic, and create organizations that reflect those desires and beliefs.

In broad terms, we see both our political organizations and our spiritual homes being spaces where people:

* Build relationships and create community.
* Study, learn, and grow.
* Try to change the world, through embodying a set of specific values and/or organizing for those values to be more widely held in the world.
* Mark seasonal change and lifecycle events together. Create containers for joy and grief, and the range of human emotion in responding to what's happening in the world.
* Meet each others' material needs for food, clothing, shelter, and resources.
* Experience, marvel at, and wonder about the universe and Divinity.
* Make and experience creative expression: song, dance, storytelling, food, poetry, visual art and crafts, philosophy, and more.

Looking at this list, we think it's powerful that we form organizations where people can meet more than one of these needs; it's unrealistic that people organize in one space, learn and skill-build in another, celebrate seasons in yet another, take in art and get to be creative in yet another. The fracturing of these needs into isolated experiences that each person is required to seek out on their own is a reflection of the alienation of capitalism.[27]

And yet, it is unsurprising that different people have different preferences for ways of being together, and want to participate in organizations that prioritize certain activities over others. There is no strict recipe to follow when forming political organizations that also are places of community building, learning, and meaning making, or spiritual organizations where we take political action together. One opportunity for growth in the Jewish Left is a more clear articulation of what people are doing together and why, and rigorous development of strategy and skills for the points of tension that we know emerge in seeking to balance our needs.

What is paramount is that we refuse to constrain or hand over any part of ourselves. We who dream of and struggle for a transformed world, like all people, deserve nourishing, creative, meaningful lives, in community and with connection to ancestors, ritual, and beauty. In fact, we challenge the contemporary delineations of religion, spirituality, culture, community, and ethics. Treating these as distinct and isolated elements is rooted in Christian hegemony and European, Enlightenment-era conceptions of modernity. For most communities across time and around the globe, what people believed about the world, creation, life and death, Divinity, how they lived, how they celebrated and mourned, how they honored ancestors, how they treated each other, and membership in a lifelong community were all intertwined and interdependent elements of life. In articulating and living politically left Jewish lives, we are able to integrate parts of ourselves that need not be in tension. This internal cohesion is just one aspect of the potential for our Jewishness to facilitate individual and collective healing.

YEARCYCLE AS HEALING ~ HEALING THROUGH LIVING JEWISHLY

As we create rituals that embody our values, they grow in their potential to not only be spiritual spaces and political events but, in fact, sites of healing.[28] This happens more powerfully with attention to ourselves, our communities, and what each holiday holds, and intention about the particularities of ritual as a tool of healing, with awareness of its limitations and possibilities.

Trauma is harm that leaves an impact beyond the time, place, and individuals to whom it occurs. Trauma is experienced in the way those impacts reverberate throughout our bodies, minds, spirits, relationships and interactions, worldviews and theologies, and whole lives. Today, there are a wide range of modalities for processing trauma and the impacts of trauma. Ritual, prayer, and spiritual practices are arguably one of the oldest sets of tools humans have for building resilience and healing trauma. Our Jewish traditions include millennia of wisdom that speak to commemorating and moving through grief and loss; transforming hurt and harm; cultivating gratitude, joy, and connection; marking liminal moments and transitions; being present in the current moment; connecting to the seasons, the earth, and our ancestors; asking for help; and more.

While embodied practices are relatively new to the field of psychology and mental health care as ways to address trauma healing, such practices have been an inherent dimension of ancient ritual for millennia. Making ritual is taking a story, goal or hope, value, or vision and making it into a series of actions, embodied and enacted. Ritual provides a container and a spiritual context in which people can express and embody big feelings and have transformative healing experiences through movement, dance, song, and breath practices, without necessarily understanding logically how the healing occurs. In this way, ritual has the power to transform our internal experience of the world, shift our stories, and change our moods and emotional responses, both in the present moment and over time. There are risks to be aware of: ritual space can be incredibly vulnerable, and introducing a ritual as engaging with trauma and healing has the potential to bring up even more difficult and overwhelming emotions to which the group or ritual leader may not be prepared to responsibly tend.

We can bring healing frameworks to all kinds of ritual: personal and daily practice, lifecycle and special occasions, moments of celebration and grief in our political organizing. In this book, we will bring our attention to the healing potential of Jewish holidays and the yearcycle.

The healing potential of Jewish holidays is as infinite as the people who create rituals in celebration of them. Within the wide range of possibilities, we find it helpful to look toward the layers of meaning within the yearcycle as a starting point and guideposts. Each holiday in the Jewish year has at least three general things happening: a relationship to the earth and place in the seasonal cycle (i.e., planting at Pesach, firstfruits at Shavuot, harvesting at Sukkot, marking the solstice at Channukah, and the sap rising at Tu b'Shvat); a story of the origins and developments of the Israelite and Jewish collective narrative (i.e., liberation from enslavement at Pesach, receiving

Torah at Shavuot, wandering in the Wilderness at Sukkot); and invitations to specific forms of reflection, personal transformation, and spiritual growth (i.e., reflecting on our relationships with each other and with the Divine, in specific and nuanced ways, with every holiday from Tisha b'Av through Sukkot). Some holidays have more tradition and cultural content about one aspect than another, and some people like to live more in one aspect of the holidays than another. Each aspect (earth and seasons, collective story, and personal transformation) holds potential for our individual and collective transformation.

Living in times of climate chaos, one of our primary tasks is to learn to listen to, and live in better awareness of our interconnection with, the earth and all living things. Our disconnection from ourselves as deeply a part of nature and made up of millions of living things is, in fact, one impact of the trauma of capitalism, white supremacy, and colonization, that mechanizes the earth and sees humans as outside of nature. Living in Jewish time and celebrating Jewish holidays can be part of our reawakening to ourselves as part of earth. The aspect of each holiday that invites focus on our spiritual selves, our relationships with each other, and cultivating connection with the Divine offers us tools of self-reflection that are invaluable in healing processes. Relationships are both the source of our wounding and often the site of our healing; Jewish holidays offer us tools for reflecting on and taking steps to transform our relationships.

Finally, the layer of Jewish holidays that tells parts of the story of Jews as a people holds incredible potential for shifting and healing historical trauma. Dr. Maria Yellow Horse Brave Heart defines historical trauma as "the cumulative emotional and psychological wounding over the lifespan and across generations, emanating from massive group trauma."[29] Historical trauma happens when the impacts of collective traumas, unresolved in one generation, are passed down to future generations of the community. Much like familial intergenerational trauma, historical trauma can be passed down through behavior patterns and values. Much like the collective traumas from which they emerge, historical trauma can also be passed down through culture: story, art, ritual, law, theology, and more.

Most people live at the intersections of and embody multiple legacies of ancestral trauma. As a multiracial, multicultural, many-historied people, within Jewish communities we find multiple threads of historical traumas. We must therefore challenge any essentializing of "Jewish trauma" as a singular story, wounding, or patterning. There is, however, a dominant narrative of Jewish history, classically named by Salo Whitmayer Baron as "the lachrymose view of Jewish history,"[30] that claims that Jewishness is first and foremost an experience of oppression, that Jewish history is primarily characterized by the experience of anti-Jewish violence. This framework of Jewish history feeds and is fed by a contemporary framing of antisemitism as inevitable, cyclical, and never ending. While antisemitism is real and present, to frame it as out of time, inevitable, and never ending is an impact, perpetuation, and manipulation of trauma. There are many ways that this and other impacts of historical trauma get transmitted across and through generations. Jewish holidays are one place where we can perpetuate trauma narratives, or, with intention, shift them.[31]

Each holiday offers an opportunity to be intentional about what story we are telling about Jewish history, how we frame what happened to us, and what meaning we make of it. Each holiday offers an opportunity to interrupt the calcified stories shaped by historical trauma and offer life-giving, generative, values-aligned, and creative stories of our resilience, survival, and thriving. Do we tell the story of Jews as perpetual and inevitable targets of violence, isolated in the world? Or tell stories of resistance to empire, cross-community solidarity, and surviving and thriving with creativity and strength? Antisemitism tries to kill Jews, convert us to Christianity, assimilate our cultures, and collude with the empires that are trying to kill and convert us. Refusing, reversing, and healing from the violence of assimilation can come from retaining and growing diverse Jewish cultures and being actively, visibly Jewish together on our holidays.

How do we create Jewish holiday celebrations that resist assimilation and isolation, that embody the kind of transformation of historical traumas we want to live? There is no prescription for healing historical trauma. Instead, we ask ourselves reflection questions to, each year, each season, be in a process of discernment about what will serve our specific communities in that specific moment. Some questions we ask are about:

* The room you'll be in: Who is this for? What do they need? What are the divisions within the community? Within people's selves?

* The time we're in: What's happening in the world? How is that impacting the people you'll be with, the ones they're paying attention to? Ignoring?
* Relationship to Jewishness: What stories do the people you're in ritual with hold about where Jews come from? What is their relationship to Judaism and Jewishness? Ritual? God? History?
* Future dreaming: Where do I see hurt in my/this community? What's my vision of the future? The Jewish future? Where is the hurt?
* This holiday: What is the medicine that our ancestors found in this holiday? What medicine is resonating with me? What is the ritual technology offers our bodies? What excites me? What makes me angry, sad, alienated, shut down? What gives me life? What stories do I want to tell?[32]

Embedding frameworks about trauma and healing into our Jewish practices and holiday celebrations is one set of tools for creating rituals that reflect our values and further our visions for the world we want to see. We will continue to layer and weave together more questions about how to embody our values and dreams in our ritual lives. How, in concrete ways, do we bring our political commitments into ritual?

POLITICIZING RITUAL, RITUALIZING OUR POLITICS

We wrote this book as part of our work intentionally infusing politics into Jewish ritual, and Jewish ritual into our politics. Yet still, at times, we struggle with *how* to do this, and how to do it well. In this section we will explore how our rituals can better articulate our political commitments in ways that don't shut down the creativity of our ritual craft, or undermine the spiritual experiences of our Jewish lives; how we create ritual that flows from and serves all the different sets and settings where we make them; and the essential task of creating ritual that reflects our power and privilege analysis while engaging in traditions created in very different times and places.

One frequent challenge we've experienced in intentionally bringing our political commitments to Jewish tradition is didactic ritual, where political headlines take precedence over craft. This can lessen the impact of attempted political education and blunt the religious ritual, spiritual, embodied experience, and healing potential.

Why is this a problem? Our Jewish tradition and calendar calls us to connect with what is happening to the earth, not in intellectual abstraction but in material reality. We are called to go outside, count the barley sheaves, and bless the buds on the fruit trees. We are asked to engage with the vulnerability and interdependence of our lives and the necessity of shelter through sleeping outside. We stop time and celebrate liberation and mass movements for freedom through eating the foods our ancestors ate on their journeys. We create communal gatherings to internalize the stories of our ancestors. We sing, sit in silence, move our bodies. In ritual, we use signs and signifiers that carry suitcases with thousands of years of meaning, and part of the power of ritual is in not explaining everything, instead trusting the practice of ritual to create an experience that is beyond and more than words. At times, in the quest to create ritual that reflects our political commitments, our ritual spaces become borderline teach-ins, with poor pedagogy at that: ritual leaders and participants reading long bodies of text, frontal performances, and one-note, emotionless, awkward spaces.

Where does this problem come from? Didactic ritual often emerges from a place of distrust: this ritual, and the people here, won't be able to hold the values and politics of the space unless we explain and repeat them. There are, indeed, some characteristics of ritual as a modality that seem to challenge ways of being we most value in politically left spaces: rituals can be spaces of liminality and mystery, whereas in our political space we often seek to turn complex problems into their simplest components, in order to force people to choose a side. Ritual deals in the ineffable: as much as we try to put words to things, the potency of a ritual space is often in creating experiences that are powerful precisely because they cannot fully be explained. In our political education and organizing, we seek to clear away the voicelessness that systems of oppression create for the masses of people, and describe those systems in very clear language: part of challenging the hegemony and pervasiveness of white supremacy, capitalism, colonization, and patriarchy is in explaining them so that they can be dismantled. Given these very real challenges, the fears that drive didactic political ritual make sense.

We are committed to finding ways to infuse our political commitments into ritual in ways that not only preserve but actually enhance what ritual does best: show, not tell. Describe, yes, but then practice, embody, enact. Creating wholehearted, nondidactic political ritual means that we integrate our political commitments into rituals in ways that flow from and enhance the potency of each. The anecdotes, we believe, are in the process more than the content. Once again we say that we will not, in this book, offer a prescription or set of guidelines. We know there is no single right way to create embodied political ritual; no correct ratio of sacred text to breakout groups or songs to speeches. It is in the process of engaging with the tradition, while holding our politics and contemporary struggles, that the most powerful ritual, and organizing, can emerge.

As we discussed in exploring politicized spirituality and religion, we start from a place of recognizing the congruity of what is often seen as in contraction, and deepening our understanding and trust of their alignment. We must build our core strength of knowing that our political organizing will not disappear when we put down the clipboards and light the candles, and let our ritual flow from that confidence. We proudly commit to throwing down hard for strategic campaigns, powerful actions, transformative relationship building, and political education; we sing loudly, eat a lot, pray with intention, laugh hard, and weep freely and copiously. Our political organizing and our emotional and spiritual lives coexist in the same days and lifetimes. We are not soft or politically sloppy because we enter into ritual space. In fact, ritual, when we can immerse in it, can be a space of expanding the capacity of our bodies and neshamot (נְשָׁמוֹת), souls to feel, think, pray, dance, weep, laugh, sing, and connect with each other. In addition to being a core human need that we all deserve, ritual and the spiritual emotional exploration it brings enhance our ability to organize. We begin by trusting ourselves and our desires.

From there, we examine the offering of the season, digging into the histories and stories, texts and traditions of the specific holiday and paying attention to what emerges. We listen for what that specific ritual moment has to teach us as it coincides with our specific political moment and contexts. Sometimes we come to a holiday and the focus is completely evident, such as observing Tisha b'Av while Black Lives Matter uprisings fill our streets or making Sukkot while water protectors put their bodies on the line at Standing Rock.[33] We work to pay attention to the nuance, creativity, and centuries of wisdom in our holidays, and to bring a deep engagement with the specificity of the political moment we are in. The more genuine the connection between the holiday ritual and the political moment, the less work we have to do to make those connections for ritual participants, and the more powerful the ritual will be.

In this process, it is essential to engage with the contradictions between our rituals and our commitments. Our tradition includes plenty of harmful ideologies and ritual embodiment of those ideologies. It is up to us as ritual leaders to decide, in the planning process, what needs to be altered or discarded, and how we want to show our process in the ritual space. This can look like, for example, at a Passover seder, naming why we are saying Mitzrayim (מִצְרַיִם), literally, the narrow place, rather than Egypt: as a tool to combat Islamophobia and anti-Arab racism. As with the questions of trauma and healing in Jewish ritual, how we do this will fluctuate wildly depending on set and setting.

In fact, a key part of the process of creating nuanced politicized ritual with the potential to transform is deciding, and being intentional about, where it's going to happen and who it's for. Ritual and spiritual practice are not one size fits all, they are not performances with an audience. They are transformative tools that are intended to meet and be for specific moments, places, and people. This is especially important in the context of bringing ritual and symbols of Jewishness as one tool in direct action and engaging in public displays of Jewish holidays as political theater. Oftentimes didactic ritual occurs when we are so used to practicing our leftist Jewish ritual in the streets, as part of direct action, and forget or don't know how to shift it when we bring it home.

We find it helpful to think about ritual in three different spaces: at home, with close comrades and chosen family; in community, with generally aligned though not deeply connected extended networks; and in the streets, as part of creative direct action. Home rituals are hopefully within intimate spaces where we can be vulnerable, and even lean into that vulnerability. We ask hard questions that we don't know the answers to, and we have the rare and precious chance to be messy and unfinished. We hope to experience big joy and big grief. We make space to explore sensitive aspects of personal transformation: how have we changed, where have we missed the mark, how have we hurt ourselves and each other, and how do we want to change?

Ritual in community, with our congregations, political organizations, and allied friends and organizations, can also be a chance to experience joy and grief. We might have less space to explore our individual experiences, with the trade-off of getting to feel we are part of something, surrounded and connected in the best ways: hearing many voices singing, seeing many faces across our screens, knowing we are not alone in our feelings. This is also where we can establish communal norms about what we believe and how we enact those beliefs: we give voice, for example, to our commitments to justice in Palestine, ending anti-Black racism, and fighting for abolition, land back, and reparations. We generally assume in these spaces that people are coming together with broad political alignment or a willingness to engage with the political commitments of the space. We often build education into these spaces from a place of exploring and deepening, and not trying to convince or persuade.

Finally, when we create ritual in the streets, as part of creative direct actions, we can also experience big joy and big grief. More often than not, we are doing ritual in the streets when we are experiencing overwhelming rage; we hope to do more ritual in the streets at moments of big wins and movement victories. While ritual in actions can have incredibly transformative power for the participants, it also has a dual and usually primary role of sending a message. This kind of ritual tends to have very little nuance: this is where we bring our clarity about right and wrong and about what must be changed.

Jewish ritual can be powerful in many kinds of action, and raises specific challenges. Often in the case of Jewish organizing in solidarity with Palestine, ritual in direct action is a way of demonstrating Jewish opposition to Zionism in a way that hopes to throw a wrench in the narrative that Israel's violent actions are justified for the sake of Jewish safety. Over the years, we have more and more questions about this strategy. Given the overwhelming weight of Christian Zionist support for Israel, how important is it to bring Jewish ritual into direct action? We've experienced the way bringing Jewish ritual into political actions opposing the occupation of Palestine, which primarily harms Palestinians, can recenter the action and conversation on Jews and Jewish feelings. As with all ritual, and all political action, we believe in thinking strategically about the what, where, when, how, and why. We can make plenty of Jewish ritual space that grieves and counters Zionist narratives; when we bring the ritual into the street, it must be done strategically and in partnership with Palestinian-led organizing.

As we engage with the creative and political challenges of creating values-aligned ritual and bringing ritual into political action, we can affirm that this process will always be an experiment. The Jewish year, campaigns and movements, and our lives move in cycles, change over time, and offer lifelong learning. Part of the essential process of creating politically aligned ritual is the debrief: what worked and what didn't, why, and what do we want to do differently next time? There will always be a next time.

Sometimes, when we create political ritual, part of what gets expressed in didactic and heavy-handed ways is coming out of discomfort with power and privilege dynamics within the space, to counter how oppressive systems are playing out in our groups, and to overcompensate for undealt with accessibility issues. As we think about who any specific holiday ritual is for, we have to think about accessibility, power, and privilege, in vast and specific ways. In the next section, we will unpack these dynamics head-on.

JEWISH LIBERATION MEANS DISABILITY JUSTICE

Accessibility is often talked about in terms of who can physically get into a room. That is an essential question. And we believe that in order to have spiritually nourishing, politically aligned, collectively healing, revolutionary Jewish spaces, there is so much more to accessibility. As Rabbi Julia Watts Belser writes in "God on Wheels: Disability and Jewish Feminist Theology,"

> I fear that by conceptualizing disability primarily as an access
> problem to be solved, we fail to invite in the vibrant, transgressive
> potential of disability culture: of a "crip" sensibility that
> celebrates disability as a way of life, a radically different way
> of moving through the world. . . . Disability culture is marked by
> a lively spirit of adaptability, creativity, and resilience—not to
> mention a vibrant sense of delight.[34]

Jewish spaces, including Jewish Left spaces, will, by default, reflect all of the ableism, fatphobia, and ageism, racism, and white supremacy of the world. In "The Needy for a Pair of Sandals: Jacob's Unsettling, and Our Own," Jess Belasco, director of the Disability Justice Torah Circle at Svara, writes,

> When I've suffered greatly, it's usually been at the hands of communities that were created by others who had suffered in their previous communities, and left them to form new spaces where their humanity and Jewish practice could be more fully celebrated.[35]

Belasco lovingly incites us to consider the harm and hierarchies that are perpetuated in progressive communities, in particular the ways the COVID-19 pandemic has revealed the profound and abiding ableism at play in Jewish communities and organizations. She points out the risks and harm of settling: believing our spaces are inclusive and diverse enough, and that there's no further we can go.

Thinking of access as a problem to be solved, and settling into "good enough" are two common pitfalls we experience in Jewish Left spaces. A few more: In Jewish Left spaces, as in left spaces in general, we often move at a speed that doesn't allow for a real accounting of accessibility, putting product or output ahead of a process that leaves no one behind. When we are challenged to do better, we respond with defensiveness rather than curiosity. There is deep and real conditioning about ignoring our bodies and suppressing our needs; it can be profoundly overwhelming to try to take in the scale of what disability justice requires of us. At times people have conflicting accessibility needs (for example, someone needs a particular scent to settle their nervous system, while someone else is scent-sensitive and needs a space to be fragrance free). There will be real material limitations of time, space, and resources. Sometimes when we are being hurt and left out, disregarded in a space, for the eighteenth time this week and thousandth time this lifetime, we communicate in loud and direct ways that challenge the deferential mode of asking for things that able-bodied people are used to from disabled people. All of this is happening in contexts where we rarely make time to slow down and work through conflict. All of this is happening in the context where more and more of us are tired, sick, hurting, without access to affordable, competent health care. The struggle is real, and is likely to increase in our lifetimes.

Sins Invalid is a "disability justice based performance project that incubates and celebrates artists with disabilities, centralizing artists of color and LGBTQ/gender-variant artists as communities who have been historically marginalized."[36] Their 10 Principles of Disability Justice[37] are powerful Torah to spark and guide us:

1. Intersectionality: "We do not live single issue lives." —Audre Lorde. Ableism, coupled with white supremacy, supported by capitalism, underscored by heteropatriarchy, has rendered the vast majority of the world "invalid."

2. Leadership of the Most Impacted: "We are led by those who most know these systems." —Aurora Levins Morales

3. Anti-Capitalist Politic: In an economy that sees land and humans as components of profit, we are anti-capitalist by the nature of having non-conforming body/minds.

4. Commitment to Cross-Movement Organizing: Shifting how social justice movements understand disability and contextualize ableism, disability justice lends itself to politics of alliance.

5. Recognizing Wholeness: People have inherent worth outside of commodity relations and capitalist notions of productivity. Each person is full of history and life experience.

6. Sustainability: We pace ourselves, individually and collectively, to be sustained long term. Our embodied experiences guide us toward ongoing justice and liberation.

7. Commitment to Cross-Disability Solidarity: We honor the insights and participation of all of our community members, knowing that isolation undermines collective liberation.

8. Interdependence: We meet each others' needs as we build toward liberation, knowing that state solutions inevitably extend into further control over lives.

9. Collective Access: As brown, black and queer-bodied disabled people we bring flexibility and creative nuance that go beyond able-bodied/minded normativity, to be in community with each other.

10. Collective Liberation: No body or mind can be left behind—only moving together can we accomplish the revolution we require.

We will spend our lifetimes deepening into each of these principles. Taken as a whole, they have the potential to truly transform how we treat ourselves and each other. Disability justice affirms that, while our spaces and cultures have been designed with certain assumptions about how our bodies and minds move, in fact there is no static or normal body.

Liberatory Judaism means committing to lifelong engagement in the joyful, revolutionary creative project of valuing all of our bodies, in the myriad ways we are shaped, move, sound, and feel, as integral to what we know Jewish community must be. Access can be a holistic framework that doesn't end at who knows about and can come to a space. It can shift how all of us, all of our marvelous and unique body-mind-spirits, are able to participate, be present, and be relatively safe in spaces and organizations. Because of ageism and ableism, babies, youth, caregivers, and elders are excluded from leftist spaces, and our Jewish Left spaces are often age segregated. Being intentional about access is one tool to counter that and create the intergenerational spaces we all need.

Access will not come with just a checklist or training. We must look to the work of disability justice, as formulated and forwarded by queer and trans Black and brown disabled people, to guide our way to everyday transformation, to make Judaisms and Jewish spaces that we can all bring ourselves to and in which we experience our own and each others' divinity. Disability justice looks like affirming that sick and disabled people do not need to hide or minimize in order to participate in Jewish life. In fact, we can shape all of our spaces and organizations by designing for diverse and ever-changing access needs. As usual, the process is as important as what we do. Disability justice looks like building in frequent checks for access needs, welcoming interruptions as those needs shift and change, and following up (how did we do, what can we do better next time?). Embracing the process of disability justice can help us release our (ableist, white supremacist) perfectionism. We will truly never be done, because our bodies are always changing.

Disabled people have existed since Creation, and Jewish tradition offers us so much technology to build communities of care and curiosity for each other. Of course, Judaism has embedded within it deeply harmful text and ritual. We take what is life affirming, offer interpretation to others, and leave the rest.

Hiddur mitzvah (הִדּוּר מִצְוָה), beautifying the commandments, is a value that weaves its way through this book and our year (it is one of our favorites). It underlines that it is not enough to do the letter of the law; instead we must adorn and delight in observance and Jewish life. Sure, a Torah could be wrapped in a plain muslin cloth, but why do that when we can be extra? Get that Torah a mint velvet and purple leather garment covered in seashells that clang when it is carried! Judaism tolerates the bare minimum, but reaches for delight. So too, it is not enough for the dominant nondisabled Jewish institution to tolerate accessibility, to do just enough begrudgingly; we must delight in disability, and in the ways considering disability transforms our days and relationships, and the centrality of disabled people to Jewish life. Hiddur mitzvah understands that quiet prayer is fine, but cacophonous stimming during the "silent" Amidah is better. Hiddur mitzvah begs us to not make ourselves smaller to fit into "good enoughs" of attempts at event access. Hiddur mitzvah understands that a ramp at the back of the building that leads a wheelchair user to roll through a musty dusty basement to get to the meeting room is not enough. By adorning our crutches or those of our neighbor, we adorn the Divine. Liberatory Jewish community cannot check access off at the bare minimum.

Embedded into the flow of Jewish life is the mitzvah of bikur cholim (בִּיקּוּר חוֹלִים), visiting the sick. We model our behavior after the facet of God that is, and acts with, chesed (חֶסֶד), lovingkindness. In *Care Work: Dreaming Disability Justice*, Leah Lakshmi Piepzna-Samarasinha writes about care webs:

> The care webs I write about here break from the model of paid attendant care as the only way to access disability support. Resisting the model of charity and gratitude, they are controlled by the needs and desires of the disabled people running them. Some of them rely on a mix of abled and disabled people to help; some of them are experiments in "crip-made access"—access made by and for disabled people only, turning on its head the model that disabled people can only passively receive care, not

give it or determine what kinds of care we want. Whether they are disabled only or involve disabled and non-disabled folks, they still work from a model of *solidarity not charity*—of showing up for each other in mutual aid and respect.[38]

Midrash teaches that when we visit the sick, we behave like God. We would expand on that to say that the sick as well as the friend who visits them are both exhibiting God-like behaviors. Everybody gets sick, and in community we take turns caring for one another and receiving care. When Avraham is recovering from his brit milah, God visits him in the form of three messengers, for whom Avraham drops everything to wash their feet and feed them.[39] This is the origin of both the commandment of bikur cholim (visiting the sick) and offering hachnasat orchim (הַכְנָסַת אוֹרְחִים) hospitality. We offer reciprocal care to one another. These few verses challenge ableist ideas of one-way charity, who is the helper and who needs care.

Admitting failure and mistake is fundamental for liberatory Jewish communities to be accessible. Teshuvah is our model of repair that requires personal reflection, interpersonal amends making, and public repair for public harm. All too often in Jewish community, people with disabilities are overpromised or gaslit—"we never said captioners were guaranteed," "events are only physically accessible when we're in xyz building," or "we just couldn't ask people to keep masking for another High Holy Day season." Disabled people are used to this behavior from nondisabled people. Jewish community must be ready to practice teshuvah when mistakes are made, instead of further causing harm atop harm.

The COVID-19 pandemic continues to shine a spotlight on our communities' profound lack of commitment to and practice of disability justice. In the quest to "return to normal" many communities dropped or significantly decreased COVID precautions and ended online or hybrid offerings, in ways that left sick and disabled people behind and put all of us at unnecessary risk. As Leah Lakshmi Piepzna-Samarasinha, quoting Alice Wong, titled her most recent book: *The Future Is Disabled*.[40] In the Exodus story, Moses led the Israelites with the support of a communication partner, his brother Aaron. Judaism's greatest liberatory Jewish community was led by a disabled person—the past was disabled, too. Liberatory Jewish community must follow the leadership of disabled people and grow with disability justice as a core framework.

BUILDING JUDAISM AGAINST WHITE SUPREMACY

Our Judaism is fundamentally invested in liberation, and thus is fundamentally opposed to white supremacy. White supremacy targets people of color (often in specific ways for different groups) and benefits people who are considered white (which in the U.S. has included most European-descendant Jews). The legacy of white supremacy in the U.S. was formed within this country's specific history of enslavement of African people, genocide of Indigenous people, Jim Crow, imperialist wars, and a wide range of laws and social policies that excluded various groups of people of color from the rights, protections, and benefits afforded to people racialized as white.

To transform white supremacy in ourselves and the world, we look to the Torah of Black feminists, including so many in our Jewish communities today. We study the 1977 Combahee River Collective statement, which articulated a Black feminist socialist politic, weaving together experience and analysis of race, class, and gender oppressions and demanding a struggle that leaves no one behind, asserting that "If Black women were free, it would mean that everyone else would have to be free since our freedom would necessitate the destruction of all the systems of oppression."[41]

Black feminist scholar Kimberlé Crenshaw gave us the term *intersectionality* to describe the ways that systems of oppression are overlaid on our bodies and identities, how they affect, magnify, and change each other to become more than the sum of their parts. The many identities we each hold—our gender, sexuality, class status, disability, and more—influence the ways we experience oppression and privilege regarding our racialization. White Jews and Jews of Color are both targeted by antisemitism; within white supremacy, whiteness may have a mediating/buffering effect for white Jews, whereas the ways that Jews of Color are racialized may magnify and create a specific form of antisemitism. Intersectionality also shows us how all of our liberation is bound up together.

White supremacy and other systems of oppression are pervasive and insidious, including in Jewish Left spaces. We know that in many Jewish communities, as in the world, there is still work to be done in moving white people to understand and make the commitment to combat white supremacy. There is also so much work needed in moving this commitment from intention to sustained action. As a multiracial, multiethnic, multicultural

multicultural people, our commitments to ending white supremacy come from a range of relationships to histories and contemporary manifestations of it. We begin, again and again, from a place of centering an unwavering commitment to ending racism and white supremacy, in all its forms: in ourselves, in our interactions, and in our organizing.

Anti-Black racism describes the specific ways that race-based hatred particularly targets Black people and Blackness, and the way the U.S. was constructed on anti-Blackness. In building and growing leftist Jewish spaces, we are committed to not only countering white supremacy but celebrating Blackness. We must study Black-led movements, honor Black teachers, and organize for justice in ways that center Black liberation. We are committed to doing this in nontokenizing ways that challenge oversimplified identity politics. As the Jews of Color Initiative writes, we must "work for structural change, not superficial inclusion."[42] This means bringing all of our political commitments to the work of fighting white supremacy, integrating gender and economic justice and everything else we care about and are fighting for. For white people, paramount to this work is the commitment to be in it long-term, not looking for easy checklist solutions but building resilience to try things, receive feedback, and keep going. Just as we continue to learn Torah every year, remeet the same holidays every year, pray the same prayers every day and find new meanings, we will enact the practices of anti-racism again and again, deepening and growing over our lifetimes.

While Jews of Color have been organizing for decades, in the last few years we have witnessed the proliferation of conversations about racism within Jewish spaces, and increased visibility of BIJOCSM organizing and spaces. JOCSM, or Jews of Color, Sephardim and Mizrahim, much like People of Color or Black Indigenous and People of Color, is a politicized term. That is to say, there is, of course, extreme diversity among people who are Jews of Color, all the more so among BIJOCSM. Sephardim are descended from Jewish communities in what is now Spain and Portugal; Mizrahim are Jews of Southwest Asia, North Africa, Central Asia, and the Balkans. Some Black and brown Jews of Color are Ashkenazi; some Sephardi and Mizrahi Jews identify as white.[43] Jewish community includes Ethiopian and Igbo Jews, Cochin Jews in India, the Jewish community in Kaifeng, China, and on and on. Jews of Color, Sephardi and Mizrahi Jews organize together in resistance to the ways European-descended Jews who have assimilated into whiteness perpetrate and perpetuate racism and white supremacy, and the ways Ashkenazi cultures and traditions have become hegemonic in Jewish spaces. BIJOCSM organizing is needed because of the way white Ashkenazi Jews hold power in Jewish communities and institutions, and because of the work that is needed to challenge both white supremacy and Ashkenazi dominance, which are distinct but so often mutually reinforcing.

Ashkenazi Jews have work to do challenging Ashkenazi dominance. Ashkenazi dominance often shows up as assuming Ashkenazi traditions are equivalent to Jewish tradition, *the* norm or right way to be Jewish. Sometimes this looks like erasing all other Jewish cultures and traditions, treating Sephardi and Mizrahi traditions as marginal or exotic, and tokenizing non-Ashkenazi Jews. Ashkenazi dominance blends with white supremacy and anti-Arab racism in particular to erase Mizrahi Jews, holding up a wildly inaccurate and harmful "Jewish/Arab" binary used to prop up the occupation of Palestine. At other times, this can look like co-opting Mizrahi identities and histories of pre-1948 life in Palestine to reinforce Zionist land claims.

An essential part of the work to challenge Ashkenazi dominance is learning Jewish geographies to more accurately understand our histories. For much of Jewish history, the vast majority of Jews lived in what would now be considered Sephardi and Mizrahi regions; all of Tanakh and Talmud was created before Jews had organized communities in Europe. Ashkenazi, Sephardi, and Mizrahi each contain endless cultural diversity, and challenging Ashkenazi dominance is just barely the beginning of creating Jewish communities that celebrate the multiplicity of Jewish expressions. As we do this, we must wrestle with cultural appropriation within the Jewish community.

For many Jews today, who grew up assimilated, or who have little knowledge of the Jewish cultures of their lineage, it's upsetting and confusing to learn Jewish practice, and we wrestle with coming as a novice to something that we feel was supposed to be homegrown. Adding to that uncertainty about which Jewish practices come from where, lack of information about our own lineages, and how hard it can be to learn the source of a particular tradition, it can be deeply intimidating to know where or how to start. This is also why finding our way, trying and learning and trying some more, is so powerful and has so much potential for healing. We are in a relatively unique generation in Jewish history, where people with so many cultures and traditions are mixing in Jewish communities. We have work to do to learn how to make vibrant multitradition Jewish communities that respect and honor the breadth and depth of Jewish expression.

The core principles we bring to learning about and practicing new-to-us Jewish rituals and traditions are relationship and context. We try to learn the cultural contexts and histories of rituals we are engaging with, and transmit those contexts and histories interwoven with the rituals. We name our own backgrounds, as much as we know and the holes that we don't, when we are engaging with new-to-us traditions. We seek out places and sources to learn from people who are steeped in a tradition, who are choosing to be teachers, and know their context. When we learn and pass on those traditions, we name our teachers. Pirkei Avot 6:6 teaches the principle of b'shem omoro, בְּשֵׁם אוֹמְרוֹ, literally, "in the name of," saying:

. . . שֶׁכָּל הָאוֹמֵר דָּבָר בְּשֵׁם אוֹמְרוֹ מֵבִיא גְאֻלָּה לָעוֹלָם.

Everyone who says a thing in the name of the one who said it,
brings deliverance into the world.

From this we learn that, for thousands of years, people have worried about stealing one another's wisdom, and a simple protection from it is to say from whom we learned a teaching. We can also name our relationships to the tradition we're passing on and why it's meaningful to us.

We are committed to learning and taking action to challenge racism and Ashkenazi dominance, for the sake of ending the harm and violence of supremacy, and to building vibrant multiracial Jewish communities where all of our people can thrive. We do this because of our ethics, how we want to treat people and be treated, and because of our spiritual and theological commitments: we understand all bodies are holy, and that all life is interconnected. Next we will explore these theological commitments: what beliefs undergird all of our actions? How do we cultivate theologies that meet the moment we're in?

Why We Do (Believing)

Like so many Jews and leftists before us, we spend most of our time behaving and belonging, organizing, making, and doing. In the previous sections, and in our forthcoming exploration of the Jewish months, we share what we're seeing and what we hope to see on the Jewish Left. We aim to describe some of the boundless creativity, the diverse breadth and depth of what's happening across the movement, which we hope will continue to grow and influence Jewish communities and futures. Now, as we turn to explore belief, we make no such claims of perspective. Instead, we are sharing a taste of our personal, specific theologies. They are deeply rooted in and feed our leftist politics. We hope this exploration is supportive to many more leftist Jews exploring and articulating experiences of and perspectives on mysteries of life and the universe, the nature of God and holiness, and what we believe about why we are here. We look forward, in years to come, to being in robust dialogue that creates more Jewish leftist theologies.

We will always resist theological conformity. In addition to being boring and dangerous, it's deeply not Jewish. There have always been diverse understandings of God: God is incorporeal, and yet we find numerous descriptions of God's body parts in Torah. The Rambam attempted to create unified and consistent theology in his 13 Principles of Faith, yet there has always been critical engagement with these principles, and they have never taken on a position of doctrine within Judaism or Jewishness.

In our times, Christian theologians have usefully given name to what they call "constructive theology." In contrast to dogmatic and systematic theologies that are "attempting to express in human words and concepts what the divine King had objectively and authoritatively given the church or synagogue in revelation," constructive theologians embrace "the theological enterprise as explicitly and essentially imaginative construction."[44] This understanding, that theologians are making stuff up, and that we are deeply rooted in and influenced by our contexts, not describing objective truth, frees up theology to speak much more directly to challenges of a given time and place. To ask what theologies speak to these moments and our specific questions.

In this vein we offer our Jewish constructivist theologies: rooted in Jewish lives, histories, stories, texts, worldviews, traditions, and lineages and speaking to our time and the challenges we face. As we joyfully embrace the knowing that no one can, will, or should have the last word, we are freed up to get creative and aggressively imaginative. We turn inward, to our deepest knowing, we look around us at the magnificence of the world, and we gaze at each other in wonder.

Like so many revolutionaries before us, our theological commitments express themselves, first and foremost, as love. We explore our love of the Divine, love of our people, love of all people, and love of the Earth. These commitments are mutually reinforcing; they all require each other.

AHAVAT HASHEM ~ אַהֲבַת הַשֵּׁם

HaShem, literally, the Name: In Hebrew, the letters י-ה-ו-ה, the unpronounceable name of the Divine Creator, point to millennia of diverse and at times contradictory beliefs about God. In English, we use ever-changing metaphorical names and pronouns for the Source of Change, Sacred Breath, Oneness. Between the two of us, and inside of ourselves, we also contain diverse and at times contradictory beliefs about God. Our Torah and our teachers do not present a consistent or logical theology or understanding of God; different qualities are emphasized and deemphasized depending on the narrative, ethical, or historical moment. Throughout this book there is an understanding of the world as Interconnected, Alive, and infused with Goodness, Magic, and Mystery beyond human understanding and capabilities, so powerful and humbling that we capitalize the names out of respect. We declare our love for that Interconnection, Aliveness, Goodness, Magic and Mystery.

As we write about our experiences of God, we are very aware that religion is pretty good at saying that God agrees with whatever it is the humans speaking seem to think. If anyone says they know exactly what God wants, they're either lying or profoundly misguided. How can we possibly know?!

Engagement with Jewish life does not necessitate ahavat HaShem, something that Christian dominance claims to be true. Judaism is a system of tinkering, timekeeping, languages, political movements, families and communities, art and culture, and foodways, all of which can operate without a belief that the way we live is necessitated by a Creator. Faith is one facet of Jewish identity, and the entire mountain does not crumble without it. We are proud to be part of a long tradition that includes Jewish nonbelievers, secularists, agnostics, atheists, and humanists.

It would be disingenuous, however, to fully separate Judaism on the whole from theology. And it would be similarly disingenuous to claim that "Judaism believes it is okay to not believe in God," because, well, who is speaking on behalf of Judaism? Just ask Elisha ben Abuya, the daddy of all apostates, renamed "Acher," the Other, for not believing in Divine power of Torah.[45] Both, and.

Both, And is, in fact, one of our experiences of God. Divine wholeness, that gathers the broken and whole parts of our world, that understands contradiction and contains multitudes of possibilities, that rejects binaries. God is the presence of understanding, compromise, completeness.

We know and love our God of the Second Naivete: the anthropomorphic God of Beresheet speaks to ancestors in dreams, is deeply invested in the goings-on of human life, receives every prayer, wraps us up in tallitot under the wings of the Shechina, has inside jokes with humankind. We double back on this emotional connection through the concept of "second naivete," a reapproaching of a simplistic understanding of theology that accepts information at face value, then, after maturing and seriously considering the information and understanding the depth beneath, continues to connect with the surface-level emotions and words with greater nuance.[46]

The theology of God is Change, as taught by fictional character Lauren Olamina in The Book of the Living,[47] exemplifies process theology, that change is itself what God is. That when justice happens, that is God. God is not the One who causes justice, God is Justice. Transformation, inspiration, passion, connection—those are God.

God is Interconnection, Interdependence, Mutuality. None of us can exist without each other. We literally breathe each others' breaths, and we are made of and interconnected with all life on earth. The ways in which we are made of and shaped from each other: this is God. We are blessed to feel some of our deepest joy when we become aware of that connection: this is one way we know it is holy.

God is Nature, Ruach ha'olam, (windbreath of the world) the animating force that causes rivers to run and the planets to spin and the wind to blow.

We feel Divine presence in the beauty and neutrality of the natural world, and our rituals express that awe and vulnerability in the presence of nature.

Living in the cycles of nature through Jewish time and making Jewish holiday rituals are one set of practices that help us to feel closer to, uncover deeper understanding of, and, most importantly, embody and experience holiness. The Jewish yearcycle weaves us into tighter networks of care and reciprocity with our communities, with the earth, with the wider world: from here we experience so much more of the beauty, joy, heartbreak, and grief of life. This, to us, is holy. Jewish concepts of divinity as reflected in all of creation remind us to take care of others, ourselves, and the earth, and infuse all of the practices with specialness. Jewish theologies of Divine oneness help us experience interconnection and practice interdependence. One strand of our yearcycle is constructed on the Exodus journey and asserts a liberation theology: that the Source of Holiness in the world wants us free. Living in Jewish time helps us live into experiences of holiness that give our lives momentum, magic, and meaning. This is one part of our Ahavat HaShem, affirming and loving holiness in the world.

Understanding that there are so many different ways to engage with the Divine, how do we engage with sacred text that is so often attributed to God? Torah miSanai (תּוֹרָה מִסִּינַי), Torah from Sinai, posits that the five books of Moses, or perhaps also the Prophets, Writings, and Oral Torah were all whispered from God into Moses' ear. In this telling, they were then brought down from the top of Mount Sinai, a fully factual telling of events that really happened and passed down through the generations. Divine inspiration understands the words of Torah to be written by human beings with inspiration from God, a blend of myth telling and historical events. Human authorship understands Torah to be a collection of really good stories told by human beings for centuries before they were written down, inspired by real events like famine, empire, family fighting, and awe of wide open skies. We believe different things about Torah on different days. We engage with the sacred nature of a text told from generation to generation. We know its holiness does not just come from the One/s who wrote it but has accrued over the years the longer it has been told.

Finding Torah holy doesn't mean we have to accept everything that it says—or every interpretation. Torah miSinai theology presents specific challenges when we read the violence of conquest, assault, and slavery in the text. It is hard to love Torah when it is used as a weapon against queer people, disabled people, women, non-Jews, multifaith families, and the list goes on. We've heard the accusation of and struggled with "cherry picking": how can you pull only the parts of the text that you like, or that agree with you? And yet, emphasizing certain texts over others is as old as Rabbinic Judaism itself: the rabbis wrestled with some parts of Torah until they could deactivate its power. We classically see this in rabbinic disagreement with the commandment in Devarim 21:18–21 that gives parents permission to stone a rebellious son. Other texts, like the beauty of tehillim (psalms) and the inspiration of the Exodus story, are picked out of Torah and put in the liturgy for us to sing everyday. Jews have, while leaving the Torah intact as a sacred text, in some ways taken what they've liked and left the rest. It is impossible to find a consistent logic in Torah, so we are invited to find the places where we can find footholds, find wisdom that enriches our life and spurs us to just action. We wrestle with the rest, choosing to reinterpret or discard what we cannot abide.

As Jews, we are blessed not only to inherit the text but to inherit a text tradition founded on asking questions. One of the fundamental building blocks of the project of Rabbinic Judaism is to revere the text as holy, engage in text study as a sacred practice, while, in the same moments, debate, question, and draw new understandings, some of which seem to run counter to the plain meaning of the text. The Talmud is full of stories affirming that people get to make new meanings of Torah.[48] Torah and Talmud are canonical and authoritative texts that are, in that spirit, often used to perpetrate harm and oppression. And, at the same time, they contain inside of them frameworks that we use to engage them toward liberation. We do not include Torah or any Jewish text in this book to cover over the violence of the text, or to claim them as inherently aligned with our own values. Tanakh was created over many centuries, divinely inspired, transmitted and shaped by many human hands, minds, and hearts, in completely different cultural, social, economic, and political contexts than our own.

In Devarim 6:5 we are instructed:

$$\text{וְאָהַבְתָּ אֵת יְהֹוָה אֱלֹהֶיךָ בְּכָל־לְבָבְךָ וּבְכָל־נַפְשְׁךָ וּבְכָל־מְאֹדֶךָ:}$$

You shall love your God יהוה with all your heart and with all your soul and with all your might.

This text commands us to remember the God that drew ancestors close and made promises of greatness, despite the odds. To remember the God that freed ancestors from enslavement and drew them out of narrow places. For those who feel ahavat HaShem, that love manifests in different ways—through following mitzvot and halacha to the letter, binding it as a sign on their arms and heads in tefillin (Devarim 6:8). For others it is through learning, struggle, and debate, teaching that Torah was given to be wrestled with by the generations that come after them (Devarim 6:7). For still others it is through behaving in God-like ways, acting to end oppression, hear the voices of the suffering and take action, and do what is right and good (Devarim 6:18).

These theologies feed and are fed by our radical politics. They teach us to live life and fear no man, to be strong and have courage.[49] These theologies teach us to struggle for more holiness in the world and that the world is worth struggling for. These theologies teach us to honor the wisdom of the ones who came before us; to live in service of the ones who will come after. We declare "one God, no masters!"

AHAVAT YISRAEL ~ אַהֲבַת יִשְׂרָאֵל

We wrote this book because we love Jews and Judaism. We love the infinite expressions of Jewishness pouring forth from Jews in every time and place. We love our people. We cultivate this love as a spiritual practice, even when we don't like or agree with, and even actively oppose and work to transform some of those expressions of Jewishness. Jews throughout time have called this love ahavat Yisrael. In doing so we understand ourselves as descendants of Yisrael, the one who wrestles with the Divine. As klal Yisrael (כְּלַל יִשְׂרָאֵל), we are the community of those wrestlers.

Indeed, we declare our love of Jews and Jewishness knowing full well how much harm has been done or accepted in the name of "chosen people" theology, loving Jews above all others. We are living in a time when the spiritual practice of love and care of our own people has been channeled into an exclusive ethno-nationalism that has literally pushed Palestinian people out of their homes and off their lands. We know every religious tradition has chauvinistic expressions that claim our way is the way, our understanding of divinity is the correct and true understanding of divinity, and thus we are the best. We know the risks of loving.

Yet as we strive to live aligned with our values, as we seek to open ourselves, again and again, toward participating full-heartedly in the world, we learn again and again the value of ahavat Yisrael (אהבת ישראל), the love of Jewish collectivity. We see part of our task as making repair, where and when needed, for the harm that religious institutions and Jewish communities have done. And we do this while living a vibrant Jewish life that is committed to, but not subsumed by, the work of repair.

In these times, we feel the persistent pull toward having loving relationships with ourselves and our bodies, and with land, earth, animals, and all of creation. We have experienced being in relationship to tradition, community, and ancestors as deeply necessary to thriving, and toward building the new world. From this awareness, we have let ourselves feel the joy of loving our people, loving Jews and Jewishness. We believe we can love our Jewish people specifically and specially without loving Jews exclusively or more than we love others. This mirrors the intimate loves in our lives: loving an array of friends, comrades, and family, uniquely and specifically, not necessarily more or less. This is a theological expression because we don't believe in a God that chooses some people over others, we believe in manifold expressions of holiness. And we believe that Jewishness is one of those expressions of holiness, and ours to wrestle with, and to love.

Given the way ahavat Yisrael has been misused to perpetuate violence, it is a powerful, sacred act to claim and redefine ahavat Yisrael in nonhierarchical ways. We believe ahavat Yisrael can be a practice that births deeper solidarity with other peoples: self-loathing, for ourselves and our people, gets in the way of genuine relationships and consistent, values-aligned action. Explicitly claiming ahavat Yisrael is a method of being intentional about how that connection is expressed, and how it is inextricably linked and balanced with ahavat Olam, love of the world.

AHAVAT OLAM ~ אַהֲבַת עוֹלָם

We have come to see these as intertwined strands: ahavat Yisrael must be an immovable part of ahavat Olam. And, if we are committed to ahavat

Olam, a healthy, nonchauvinistic sense of ahavat Yisrael is a part of that. By ahavat Olam, we mean a love of the world and all people in it, a love of people's individual humanness and collective humanity. People are complex and messy, full of contradictions, special and beautiful and weird and capable of amazing acts of love. We name our love of all creation as ahavat Olam.

When we practice ahavat Olam, we can take powerful pleasure in our love of our people, organizers, and movements. We love our creative instincts, and our lust to live, survive, and thrive. In movements where cynicism and analytical thought are sometimes used as a protective shield, we want to shine light, care, song, joy, laughter, delight, and beauty. We understand and often feel rage and cynicism, deep disgust and despair at what humans are capable of doing to one another. We make space and time for those feelings. And we cultivate love because we can, because love supports us in caring for each other and receiving care, and because love feeds pleasure. We want our organizing and Judaism to be infused with fierce love, the possibilities of trust, and the vulnerability to dream. We know this will make our movements and our lives stronger, more transformative, more sustainable.

AHAVAT HA'ADAMAH ~ אַהֲבַת הָאֲדָמָה

We close with a commitment to a kind of love that, while interconnected with all of the others, feels in many ways paramount: we are committed to ahavat ha'adamah, loving the earth. In traditional halacha, we have the commandment of bal tashchit, to not destroy. Taken from Devarim 20:19, it is based on the instruction to not destroy the trees when making war against a city. Much like millennia of rabbis and decades of organizers before us, we find this instruction insufficient on its own to meet this moment. More than not destroying, we feel and are committed to the obligation to actively love the earth and all of creation. When we slow down enough to listen, our love of God, our love of the world, every cell in our body calls out to us to answer to this love.

If you're reading this book, you likely need no convincing that the climate crisis is here and now. You likely know it is disproportionately impacting Black, brown, and Indigenous people, poor people, disabled and sick people. We know that capitalism, which necessitates alienation from the land and presupposes wealth hoarding, and colonization, which perpetrates theft and destruction of people and land, are responsible. We know that massive change is needed, at every level, yesterday. We know this can be incredibly terrifying and overwhelming.

What do Judaism and Jewishness have to offer this moment and the struggles we face? Jewish tradition, as with anything, can be co-opted by capitalism, used to prop up the status quo. But if we allow it, Jewishness can force us to look up from what we're doing, going about our days woefully unresponsive to the crisis at hand, and it can throw a wrench in the gears of business as usual. Jewish tradition invites us to declare the interconnection of all life. This is medicine for the separation from the earth that most of us live in most of the time. Jewishness provides a way of making community and living in relationship to each other and the earth in ways that are older than capitalism. Jewishness provides ways of relating to people, place, and labor, in fundamentally different ways than we are used to now. Jewish prayer provides songs to sing when we are afraid, and ways of asking for help. Orientation toward the earth's aliveness is built into the rhythm of the Jewish day and year. Every day, multiple times a day in prayer, we marvel at and give gratitude for creation. Every holiday, every time we say kiddush we honor the holiness of creation. When we turn to Jewish histories, we see that our people and their communities have been destroyed many times over. Ways of life have been decimated. We keep going. When we turn to Jewish tradition, we find ways of living in relationship to land and labor that celebrate human creativity while also valuing sustainability. In biblical stories and rabbinic law, we see practice that begins and ends with gratitude, that instructs living within the earth's limits, and that reminds us that our actions have consequences.

Throughout this book we will explore some of the specific ways Jewish holidays, as we described above, can be part of transforming our relationships to earth and healing the false separation in which we live. We also know that Jewish organizations, as is true of all groups of people, have power to leverage in organizing for climate justice, work that is thankfully being taken up more and more every day. One of our other key tasks is to flesh out theologies, philosophies, and the practice of active love for the earth. Our ahavat ha'adamah must be guided by, and offer something to, the conditions we are living in, and the rest of our spiritual and political commitments.

As with all of our theologies, the theology of ahavat ha'adamah and our Jewish lives are mutually reinforcing: we feel called toward greater interconnection with the earth in our bodies, we look toward our tradition to resource and affirm those feelings, and we see love of and interconnection with the web of life in our tradition and inherited wisdom and that feeds the feeling in our bodies. Humans are not, we know, superior life forms. Jewish tradition knows we were created last, and we know we have much to learn from the rest of creation. Our bodies are made of and will return to earth, and we wouldn't be able to stay alive without trillions of microbial creatures inside of us, without the trees our breath, without the earth our food, and without the sun and rain that feed us all. We are not superior; we are not even separate. God, who is and is in everything, is one, we declare multiple times a day. Jewish tradition, just like the rest of the world around us, is loud and clear in directing our attention to the earth.

We root in a place of ahavat ha'aamah first and foremost because we believe all people must bring what they can to this struggle, and spiritual frameworks are one of our offerings. We also believe we have a responsibility to create climate justice–centered theologies because we know some of the ideas fueling the destruction of the earth and the ensuing climate crisis are based in biblical interpretation. Right-wing Christian readings of the creation story in Genesis use the idea that man has dominion over all of the earth and all of the creatures of the earth to defend and fuel climate catastrophe. We believe there is no one single ideological culprit behind the climate crisis, but seeing our sacred texts being used for this, we feel called to respond. Besides, many of us, whether or not we were raised reading Torah, were raised with the implicit and explicit ideology of human superiority, which we must uproot in ourselves and collectively transform.

While in Beresheet 1, the first human is given control over the earth, in the next chapter, Beresheet 2:15, God rests the first human in Gan Eden with instructions to לְעָבְדָהּ וּלְשָׁמְרָהּ, to serve and to protect her, a very different relationship of responsibility. What would it look like for every human to understand that the core relationship between us and the earth is to be in service to it? This is just one example of the deep sea of wisdom available to those of us who look to our texts and traditions for inspiration. Many parts of Tanakh say that the earth belongs to God and is sacred and beyond any human ownership and control. When we look to our tradition, we experience an abundance of texts and practices that declare the holiness of creation and the interdependence of humans with and as part of creation. Again and again, God is understood as water, as land, as place; God speaks through fire and is revealed on a mountain; God's power is seen in and through creation.

Judaism and Jewishness, as with every culture and tradition, grow and change to meet the moment, because they are made and remade by humans, all of us growing and changing in each time. The moment that we are in and the time to come is going to be shaped by climate catastrophe and, we pray, by a just transition away from capitalism and extractivism to economies of care, sustainability, and regeneration. Our inherited Jewish traditions, as is true with every tradition, have so much to offer us. Whether the wisdom in our tradition that can best serve this moment can come forward is up to us: are we listening? Whether the parts of our tradition that need to be put down by the wayside because they are no longer serving us will be put down is up to us: can we let go? We will need as many expressions of ahavat ha'adamah as there are creatures in creation.

Becoming

We've explored frameworks in which this book is grounded: belonging (who we are, what we do); behaving (how we do what we do); and believing (why we do what we do). From here, we head into the months and holidays. Jewish time, we often say, is a spiral. The wheel of the year comes back around to meet us. We are changed, our lives change, the world changes. We know how we are changing by remeeting the anchors in time that the Jewish yearcycle provides. In many ways, we know what we offer here is nothing new: people engaging with our inherited traditions, bringing our lives to meet the cultures of the time, reshaping ourselves and received wisdom in constant, dynamic processes. Much of what we personally find most inspiring, comforting, and sustaining from Jewish traditions are the parts that most simply remind us of our humanity and our holiness: singing, cooking for people, eating with people, asking questions, telling stories, noticing the seasons. Nothing so new. And we have dedicated our lives to being in this tradition in ways that birth new possibilities, that meet each new moment of creation. In our lifetimes, we see and hope to see current systems breaking down, and we desire and organize to live in more of the world to come. As empires crumble, we bring our communities, traditions, cultures, and spirits with us. We let the world change, change us, and change our traditions. We go there together.

PART 2

THE JEWISH YEAR

Honey,
   drip through the days of my life
    sweetening everything
     healing even the most ancient of wounds
    pour forth from my tongue
   golden rivers of kindness

Rock,
steady me as I come undone
teach us what you know about time
about star bodies and scattering dust
about no beginnings and no endings
about what to put down and what to pick up

Waters,
wash me away
carry me home
soften and dissolve this exhausted husk
take the crumbs of our lives out to sea
let me ride the tides of this turning year

Rain,
return me to life
bearing a cup of collective responsibility in my hands

   Ancestors,
    we remember
    we're listening

   You of Many Names, of Many Doors, of Many Paths,
    open the gates of forgiveness
    open the way to a year drenched in justice
open my lips
open our hearts
untangle me
and braid me back into life

WELCOME TO תשרי TISHREI

Who and what in your life supports and nurtures you? Who do you feel most excited about supporting and nurturing? What is the state of your relationships with these people whom you love, and what do you want it to be? What kind of attention and care would improve the quality of your connections with the people who thrill you, show up for you, and invite you into their lives?

What communities support and nurture you? What is your commitment to them? What communities do you want to offer your gifts to this year? What do you want to receive from community? How will you ask for that?

Introduction to Tishrei

רַבִּי אֱלִיעֶזֶר אוֹמֵר: בְּתִשְׁרֵי נִבְרָא הָעוֹלָם, בְּתִשְׁרֵי נוֹלְדוּ אָבוֹת, בְּתִשְׁרֵי מֵתוּ אָבוֹת . . . בְּרֹאשׁ הַשָּׁנָה נִפְקְדָה שָׂרָה רָחֵל וְחַנָּה, בְּרֹאשׁ הַשָּׁנָה יָצָא יוֹסֵף מִבֵּית הָאֲסוּרִין. בְּרֹאשׁ הַשָּׁנָה בָּטְלָה עֲבוֹדָה מֵאֲבוֹתֵינוּ בְּמִצְרַיִם, בְּתִשְׁרֵי עֲתִידִין לִיגָּאֵל.

Rabbi Eliezer says: In Tishrei the world was created; in Tishrei the Patriarchs were born; in Tishrei the Patriarchs died . . . on Rosh HaShana Sarah, Rachel, and Hannah were remembered by God and conceived; on Rosh HaShana Joseph came out from prison; on Rosh HaShana our forefathers' slavery in Egypt ceased; and in Tishrei in the future the Jewish people will be redeemed in the final redemption with the coming of the Messiah.

—*Talmud Bavli* Rosh HaShanah 10b–11a

Tishrei: We begin again. This month holds renewal, reflection, repair, rest, rain, and rejoicing in an interlocking cycle. Tishrei is like going to a spiritual car wash. It has the potential to help us transform and deepen on personal, communal, and global levels, setting the tone for the year ahead. And Tishrei can be exhausting. So many holidays, the highest of highs, and the deepest of depths—*who designed this?!* We ask every year, about a week in.

Within the cycle of Jewish time, Tishrei ties together the year that was with the year that is, creating a portal through which to move. While there are four new years in the Jewish year,[1] Rosh Hashanah marks the start of the new calendar year, and the fullness of the month reflects its importance. We enter into the new year with Rosh HaShanah, followed closely by Yom Kippur, in that order to remind us that annulling vows and being wiped clean does not allow us to pretend that the past never happened. Rather, it helps us bring the work of the last year into the new one. From Yom Kippur, we head speedily into Sukkot, Shemini Atzeret, and Simchat Torah; a wild ride that keeps us alert, engaged, and interacting with each other.

Tishrei is a month where we embody the spiritual and political practice of hope. Amidst everything we have experienced in the past year, looking toward everything we know and don't know about the year ahead, how can we gather the koach כֹּחַ (strength) to envision things being different? We do it in community. Doing the work of transformation in community and as a community is in stark contrast to the value of individualism that is so prominent in white supremacy culture, Christian hegemony, and capitalism. Our tradition gives us holidays to enable us to move through this time collectively. What would it look like if, instead, we were able to bring the communitarianism of the Tishrei cycle to our commitments to transform collectively and to transform the world?

While the work of self-reflection in Tishrei might seem individual, when we travel through the holiday cycle of Tishrei in community, we have the potential to be transformed as a group. During the Rosh Hashanah Musaf service we recite ve'asu lachem agudah echat (וְתֵעָשׂוּ לְכֶם אֲגֻדָּה אֶחַת), "make yourself a united group," and in many ways the rituals of the holidays accomplish this. The people we prayed Selichot (סְלִיחוֹת), penitential prayers, with before Rosh Hashanah are the same people we squeeze and pass apples to, the same people that we beat our chests and press our cheeks to the ground next to on Yom Kippur, and the same people we explode into dancing with at the neilah (נְעִילָה), the closing service.

The language of teshuvah (תְּשׁוּבָה), repair, return, repentance, is in the first person plural; we admit that "we" have missed the mark in a variety of ways, listing harms we know we have not personally committed, because others in the kahal (קָהָל), the community, may have, and we are holding all of our misdeeds and mistakes together. These are the same people we huddle with in our sukkahs as the air gets crisper and we celebrate all we have harvested, the same people with whom we pray for abundance as we make willows rain down on Hoshannah Rabbah, the same people we linger with through Shemini Atzeret, and the same people we come undone in story and song with and unroll the Torah scrolls with as we sing and dance on Simchat Torah. By the end of the complete circuit of holidays, we are transformed as a group. We have become something different. We don't have to, and we can't, do it alone.

Tishrei is a month when inhabiting the holidays, getting through the fire hose of Judaism and Jewish community life, is a collective venture. We strive to live in the season in ways that are purposeful and meaningful, connected to our political commitments and communal obligations, and that also allow us to feel the transformative power of this time and our ancestors' offerings.

The parashiyot in Tishrei are Ha'azinu, V'zot haBracha, and Beresheet. We finish reading Devarim, then we begin again with Beresheet! This month calls us to notice endings and beginnings. We read Torah without end—each year V'zot haBracha blends into Beresheet, the ending of the Torah and beginning blending together. Moses' death, on the cusp of making it into the land but not being allowed to enter, gives us space in this season to name disappointment, loss, betrayal. Beresheet gives us opportunity to begin again, call in hope, or even begin a new practice of study. Destruction and creation are inherently interconnected.

Tishrei in Action

ROSH HASHANAH

In the final month of the year, we reflect on the year that was. Elul is about returning to ourselves, and recommitting to the lives we want to live. On Rosh Hashanah, we bless our ability to transform. The holiday is a two-day gateway into a new year, and, we hope, newness in ourselves. It is also a celebration: the birthday of the world. In the midst of personal reflection on harm and transformation, and before the deep repentant work of Yom Kippur, our ancestors gifted us with a day to celebrate. We celebrate that we are alive, that the world exists, and that the world and everyone in it has made it to a new year. How can our Rosh Hashanah practices embody the experience of celebrating a birthday party for every single particle of life on the planet?

Some of us will spend time in a synagogue building or virtual prayer space. Some of us will spend time in the deep woods, in the wide desert, or by moving water. We will cook and eat big, delicious meals. Some will spend time alone, with the Divine, with family of origin, with family with whom we struggle, or with family we have chosen. We will spend the day alone and in crowds, with loving animals and plant friends. There will be song, poetry, and silence. And, with practice, there might be the vibrations of centuries of ancestors making this day separate and sacred, a gateway forward, backward, and sideways in time. On Rosh Hashanah, we try to crack open the door to a new year and imagine new and evolving selves, individually and collectively.

As leftists, we spend so many days of the year feeling the burden of the world as it is, weighed down by the slow grind of oppressive systems that have infiltrated so many of our daily lives and interpersonal interactions. On Rosh Hashanah, we reach for the belief that change is possible, even inevitable. We try to celebrate as we will when the change we seek is won and the new world is here.

Rosh Hashanah Prayer and Liturgy

Rosh Hashanah services begin at sundown on the twenty-ninth of Elul. As befitting such a significant event, we have two jam-packed days to enter the new year. The basic flow of the days mirrors the service order and structure of any other festival day. For the holiday, there is added liturgy and piyyutim (פִּיּוּטִים), liturgical poems that are read, chanted, or sung during the liturgy, often of specific holidays; special nusach (the musical mode of a specific region and service); and particular Torah readings for each of the days. There is a special Rosh Hashanah Musaf (additional) service and, if it's not also Shabbat, a shofar service. We cap it all off later in the day with the ritual of tashlich (תַשְׁלִיךְ) ("to cast away," the special ritual of release in this season).

The many hours of ark opening and closing, rising in body or spirit, singing, chanting, silence, reading, talking, singing more, more silence, "turn to page 732 in your machzor" (מַחְזוֹר), the special prayerbook used on High Holidays: this can be both uplifting and exhausting, moving and boring, empowering and agitating. It takes work, practice, and magic that we may or may not feel year to year to be able to access this experience. Services might not be the place that creates the gateway into and celebration of the new year that you need. What is all of this *for*, anyway?

The intensity of Rosh Hashanah services is not an accident. We believe the marathon is, in and of itself, an embodiment practice. Jewish practice holds the wisdom of embodiment—in feasting and fasting, in dynamics of sound and silence, in prostration and rising and orienting our bodies up and down and up and down. In this context, the content of the prayers can move us out of our daily routines and into a space of reflection; take us from a tight intellectual grip on static right and wrong, and open us to the possibility of transformation. Dance parties can also do this. Bike trips, walks in the woods, lying still by the water, plunging into water; with intention these can, we believe, create parallel energy to what is happening in the synagogue. Getting the body exhausted, worked up, warmed, to see what flows from the heart and spirit, is really old technology, and humans find ways to do it in all times, places, and bodies.

Many in our communities, after years of finding spiritual embodiment outside of Judaism, are now seeking it in synagogue, curious about what might be unlocked in very old words and melodies. We will explore some of the special prayers of the services to support more meaningful understanding of the key themes of the liturgy. We hope this will make services more meaningful and accessible, as we try to comprehend the gifts and burdens our ancestors transmitted to us through these texts. And, the most seasoned davener (prayer) will still, every year, get lost or tune out at some point in the service. All of us can, every year, remeet High Holiday rituals with curiosity.

We strive to interact with these rituals in ways that are not rote, but instead lift us out of one year and move us into the next. We can engage in meaningful ways, whether we are in or out of a physical synagogue, with a siddur open or closed; whether we are singing or listening, meditating or journaling, dancing, laughing, crying, and all of the above.

Shacharit[2]

The morning begins similar to Shabbat morning davening, with Birchot HaShachar (בְּרְכוֹת הַשַּׁחַר), morning blessings, and psukei d'zimra (פְּסוּקֵי דְזִמְרָא), songs of praise. From there, we shift out of the gentle morning into specifically Rosh Hashanah Shacharit, recreating an ordination ritual. Though it is a part of the morning liturgy during the entire year, a shift into High Holiday nusach (נוסח), tonal and musical theme, calls our attention to the *HaMelech* verses: "The sovereign one, presiding on your lofty and exalted throne!" In Elul, the last month of the year, we declare that the king is in the field.[3] In Tishrei, on Rosh Hashanah morning, we seat the king on a high and exalted throne, kiseh ram v'nisa (כִּסֵּא רָם וְנִשָּׂא). How are those of us who spend our lives challenging oppressive hierarchies supposed to chant this? Some of us just can't, and won't. Some of us will hear the chant and wrestle with it. How might we make meaning of our tradition's insistence on God as king?

To begin, we notice that in our yearcycle, this king does not receive their throne simply by birth and mechanics, but through relationship. God spent the past month with us in the field, watching us labor, toil the earth, weed the garden. Sometimes, when we make space, God is helping us lug dirt and dig and water. God has participated in the work. Now that we know one another, have an intimate relationship and some mutual understanding, it is permissible to ordain the Holy One of Blessing in the High

Holy Day liturgy. Unlike with earthly rulers, declaring HaMelech means we enter into a consensual relationship, again and again. Maybe this means literally with Divinity. Maybe we are chanting to Jewih tradition, time, and practice. What we learn from this cycle is that Elul is for introspection, and Tishrei is for commitment and ordination of whatever is holy to us.

HaMelech, both in this first call, and throughout the many references to God as Sovereign of the Rosh Hashanah service, can also be a doorway into reflecting on sovereignty. Sovereignty is the power to self-govern, to have full governing rights over oneself without outside interference. Our ancestors, having been conquered and subjugated, were making a powerful claim in naming God as the one true Sovereign. In a cultural context where human kings were to be deferred to as all-powerful, as sovereign, our ancestors defiantly stated that human kings could not compare to God.

There are infinite ways to reconstruct and create a new meaning from HaMelech as a concept in the Rosh Hashanah liturgy. We can begin by asking: Who or what is it that we believe is all powerful? To what power in the world do we defer? What theologies—the Earth as Sacred, God as the Web of Life, God as Benevolent Healer—let us declare in full voice that God is sovereign? We can also take this moment to investigate political sovereignty as a site of struggle. Who and what currently has sovereignty in our world, the ability to self-govern? What work are we willing to do toward sovereignty? In our commitments to supporting Indigenous sovereignty and the rights of all people to have a voice in the decisions that impact their lives, we declare that this vision is holy, that no one individual person may rule over another.

The Torah service for Rosh Hashanah tells dramatic stories from the Torah and Prophets. As with all holiday readings, the selections are outside of the linear cycle of parashiyot and instead are selected to be read at the holiday.

ROSH HASHANAH, DAY 1
Beresheet: 21:1–21:34: Sarah gives birth, and Abraham names the child Isaac. Sarah demands that Abraham cast out Hagar and her son Ishmael, which he does. Hagar and Ishmael go into the wilderness and run out of water. God hears Ishmael's cries, speaks to Hagar, and reveals a well to her so that they are able to survive. Abraham makes a treaty with Abimelech, and continues to live in the land of the Philistines.

Bamidbar 29:1–29:6: On the first day of the seventh month, we are commanded not to work, but instead to observe a "sacred occasion," and make offerings. These are the instructions for what we've come to mark as Rosh Hashanah.

Haftorah: I Samuel 1:1–2:10: Hannah, who has been childless for many years, goes to the Temple at Shiloh to pray. Eli, the priest, mistakes her weeping for drunkenness, but God answers Hannah's prayer and she gives birth to Samuel, whom she commits to serving in the Temple. The reading closes with the text of Hannah's prayer.

ROSH HASHANAH, DAY 2

Beresheet 22:1–22:4: God tells Abraham to sacrifice Isaac as a burnt offering, and without question, Abraham sets out to do it. They head up the mountain, Abraham lays out wood, builds an altar, ties Isaac to it, and raises his knife. Just then, an angel of God calls out to stop him and reveals a ram for Abraham to sacrifice in Isaac's place. The angel blesses Abraham and his descendents. This story is referred to as the Akedah, meaning the binding.

Bamidbar 29:1–29:6: We read the same section of Bamidbar as the Musaf reading. See above.

Haftorah: Jeremiah 31:1–31:19: Jeremiah prophesied that God will save, rescue, and bless the people of Israel.

Midmorning Rosh Hashanah the shofar service takes place. For some, this is the main event of the whole kit and kaboodle. After having read the story of the Akedah ("binding" in reference to the binding of Isaac), we honor the sacrifice of the ram by bringing a ram's horn to our lips and making a great noise. Rambam[4] summarized the call of the shofar and purpose of the special shofar service in Hilchot Teshuvah 3.4:

עוּרוּ יְשֵׁנִים מִשְׁנַתְכֶם וְנִרְדָּמִים הָקִיצוּ מִתַּרְדֵּמַתְכֶם . . .

וְחַפְּשׂוּ בְּמַעֲשֵׂיכֶם וְחִזְרוּ בִּתְשׁוּבָה וְזִכְרוּ בּוֹרַאֲכֶם . . .

Awake, you sleepers from your slumber.

Examine your deeds, make teshuva, and remember your Creator.

There are many interpretations of the order of the blasts of the shofar. Rabbi Isaiah Horowitz teaches that the different blasts can be imagined as mirroring the process of teshuvah: moving us from wholeness (the long blasts) through breaking (many short blasts) and back to wholeness (the longest blast of all). Some hear the shofar blasts, others feel the reverberations in our bodies, and all of us take this journey through breaking down and repairing many times during the spiritual work of Tishrei.

After the shofar service, we go directly into the Musaf service. The special Musaf Rosh Hashanah Amidah has three parts, each focused on one of the key themes of the day: Malchuyot: sovereignty; Zichronot: remembrance; Shofarot: the sounds of the shofar. These are three of the top themes of Rosh Hashanah, and so in this Musaf Amidah we get a concentration of the major foci of the holiday. Each section has unique blessings and hymns and concludes with a shofar blast. Many communities infuse this section with creative readings and poetry, ways to make new meaning of these three themes. Every year we must ask ourselves: What is sovereign to us? What do we want to remember? And what will wake us up, over and over again?

During the Malchuyot section, the Grand Aleinu is chanted. Every other recitation of the Aleinu throughout the year, is a reference to this Aleinu, the original Aleinu, in the Musaf Amidah. Today, many communities make a full prostration: in body or spirit, getting on our knees and then lying face down. This is one way to embody malchuyot: physically taking the position of being fully on and of the earth and trusting our congregation enough to close our eyes while vulnerable on the ground. This position and practice will not work for all of us every year. We can take it as an invitation to ritually embody humility. We might ask ourselves if there are other positions that remind us, safely, of our humanity and vulnerability, and allow us to give over control to the forces of care, compassion, understanding, and creation.

As part of the Kedushah blessing in the Rosh Hashanah Musaf, we say Unetaneh Tokef ("let us speak to the awesomeness"). This central piece of High Holiday liturgy includes the proclamation that "on Rosh Hashanah all is written and revealed, and on Yom Kippur the course of every life is sealed." We then recite a range of fates that could befall people in the year to come, affirming that God is controlling and decreeing it during the ten days between Rosh Hashanah and Yom Kippur. The prayer continues: "But teshuva (repair), tfillah (prayer), and tzedakah (just giving)" (return, prayer, just giving) make the decree, and living in the world, easier to bear.

Some years, we have raged against or rolled our eyes at this theology; other years we are struck by the accuracy of the complete lack of human control that the prayer declares. In the year to come, yes, there will be death and illness, loss and grief. We pause in the doorway to the new year, setting our intentions, casting forward our hopes, prayers, and dreams, and yet affirming that we have no idea and very little control over what will happen. We remind ourselves that, no matter what is happening, we can make choices every day about how we want to live. Our ancestral offerings of transformation (teshuvah); prayer, ritual, song, and breath (tfillah); and engaging in the work of justice (tzedakah) can accompany, uplift, and guide us throughout the year. In this prayer, Jewish tradition affirms that no one tool will work for everyone all the time; we could spend a lifetime exploring how to live teshuvah, tfillah, and tzedakah. This prayer embodies the struggle many of us feel between releasing into our powerlessness at so much of the mystery of life and death, and embracing the agency that we have, every day, to live.

The Talmud[5] cites that Joseph, eleventh child of the patriarch Jacob, was freed from prison[6] on Rosh HaShanah. In 2020, a group of organizers, friends and family of incarcerated people, and Jewish chaplains came together to form Matir Asurim: Jewish Care Network for Incarcerated People. In contrast to the primarily Orthodox Jewish prisoner support organizations, Matir Asurim creates Jewishly diverse resources and builds Jewish community across prison walls. Matir Asurim is inspired by many incredible organizations that bring abolitionist principles to prisoner support: penpal projects, newsletters, books through bars, and organizing to change conditions and get people out. Rosh HaShanah is a powerful time to rededicate our work to end prisons, and to build relationships across prison walls, with family, friends, in community, and through mutual aid and prisoner support organizing. We know that our celebrations of the new year will be complete only when all can celebrate, in freedom, together.

Tashlich

The afternoon of the first day of Rosh Hashanah is one customary time for the ritual of tashlich, the physical embodiment of casting off sins by throwing breadcrumbs into moving water. This practice was not devised by the rabbis and is not mentioned in Torah or Talmud, though texts, such as Micah 7:19, are now connected to it:

תַּשְׁלִיךְ בִּמְצֻלוֹת יָם כָּל־חַטֹּאותָם

You will cast their sins into the sea.

Instead, this was a popular custom in Medieval Ashkenazic communities. Religious authorities of the day were opposed to it, thinking that people would substitute the physical act of throwing away their metaphorical sins for the real work of deep personal transformation and actually moving away from wrongdoing. Today, we know tashlich as one of the ways of taking all the journaling, singing, praying, talking, and thinking about change and embodying our intentions. It is also a practice of coming to the water's edge, possibly the same place every year, and collectively committing to let go of that which is no longer serving our visions and dreams of a transformed world. What might returning to the same place each year teach?

Tashlich is a powerful ritual, whether done alone, with friends and family, or with organizations and collectives. The ten days between Rosh Hashanah and Yom Kippur can be a time to experiment with different tashlich rituals.

Many of our organizations and much of our work organizing for a transformed world can, at times, become permeated with guilt and shame. There is so much work to be done, and no one person or group can ever do it all. But, through the ritual of collective tashlich, we can transform our individual burdens into collective responsibility. When we come together to name the harms of the Israeli occupation, settler colonialism on Turtle Island,7 racism and white supremacy, mass incarceration and policing, climate degradation, and wealth hoarding, it becomes clear that none of us can possibly hold all of this on our own. We do collective tashlich to take collective responsibility for the overwhelming hurt and harm in our world. We commit, together, to working to avoid the practices, patterns, and worldviews that constrict and harm. We publicly commit to, in the new year, striving lovingly to practice something different.

Philadelphia Jews for a Just Peace and Jewish Voice for Peace-Seattle are among the many local groups with over a decade of gathering publicly to wrestle with casting off the sins of Israeli occupation and apartheid while also taking personal responsibility for our obligations to work to stop the displacement and dispossession of Palestinians. JVP Seattle's first tashlich ritual was in 2006. That summer, in which Israel escalated violence against Gaza and Lebanon, a shooter entered the Jewish Federation in Seattle, killing one person and wounding five, saying he was "angry at Israel." The group and community came together to make sense of the overwhelming loss and grief. Jews present at the ritual acknowledged the acts of the Israeli government done in their name and took responsibility for the transgressions of the Israeli occupation. Non-Jews took responsibility for antisemitism and Christian dominance. Everyone committed to working for a different world in the coming year.[8]

Creating tashlich can involve sharing a collective list of sins that the group is casting off, or framing the ritual by looking back over the year and giving people time to reflect on and share what they want to cast off. Tashlich is powerful in that it invites us to practice casting off both individually and collectively.

Rosh Hashanah Foods

On erev Rosh Hashanah, and on the afternoon and evening of both days, we gather for festive meals. Just like on Shabbat, we begin erev Rosh Hashanah with candles, wine, and challah (חַלָּה). We say a special, holiday-specific blessing over the wine. On Rosh Hashanah, we shape the challah into our visions and intentions: a round challah, symbolizing the full circle of the year; crowns, symbolizing the coronation of the Divine; ladders, symbolizing spiritual striving as in Jacob's dream. There are traditions of challot shaped like animals of places Jews lived. From Ukraine, for example, we might find a challah shaped like a bird, symbolizing the wish for our sins to be carried away as if by a bird, and our prayers to be carried up to heaven.[9] We often add more honey, sugar, or raisins to our challah as we wish each other a sweet new year. We dip apples in honey to bring more and more sweetness to our lips. We set our table with pomegranates and let their seeds burst out, symbolizing the 613 mitzvot of Torah and all the fertile potential of the new year. Ashkenazi tradition includes eating fish heads, symbolizing a striving to be "the head, not the tail" in the year to come, and the power of swimming together as a school, a powerful collective.

Dating back to the Babylonian Talmud, and practiced by Iranian Persian Jews for centuries, many Mizrahi families and communities today continue the ritual of a Rosh Hashanah seder. The meal is filled with the recitation of biblical verses, and blessing and eating symbolic foods, replete with layers of meaning. Dates can symbolize an end to our enemies and to ignorance; pomegranates stand for fullness and mitzvot; apples are for a sweet year; string beans mean abundance; pumpkins or gourds remind us to ask God to rip up any evil decrees against us; spinach or beet leaves represent the hope that our enemies will depart; leeks, chives, or scallions symbolize our wish that those who want to hurt us will be cut off; and a fish or sheep's head or a head of lettuce stands for leadership.[10]

In this season of ritualizing our interdependence, Rosh Hashanah and Yom Kippur both provide important opportunities for community meals. Dinners on erev Rosh Hashanah and the first day of the holiday, as well as meals to end the Yom Kippur fast are excellent times to bring together your household, your neighborhood block, your affinity group, your book group, or your political organization for a collective meal. On Rosh Hashanah you can look back at the year that was and forward at the year that will be; on Yom Kippur you can eat and revel. This is as essential for our collective transformation as all of the liturgy.

There are many ways to navigate the epic new year's ritual that is Rosh Hashanah, whether over meals, in or out of synagogue, with journaling or singing, alone or with community, at the beach or in the forest. We know our practice will grow, change, and shift throughout our lives. Some years we will want a lot of time for quiet reflection; other years we will want boisterous noise. Some years the liturgy might land like powerful poetry; other years it will ring hollow. However we find our way into and experience the rituals of the new year, we can take comfort in our lineage as Jews who, year after year, return to greet the new year, to bless the majesty of creation, and to recommit to transformation, doing our powerful part in the sacred creation of the world.

Just as Elul stretches out before Rosh Hashana and gives us an on-ramp to the new year, the aseret yamei teshuvah (עֲשֶׂרֶת יְמֵי תְּשׁוּבָה), the Ten Days of Repentance, creates a spiritual bridge between Rosh Hashanah and Yom Kippur. During these days we cull from everything that was awakened on Rosh Hashanah, and weave it into our preparations for Yom Kippur. On Yom Kippur, we turn to the Divine for forgiveness, but before we approach the Holy of Holies, we must turn to other people and make teshuvah, repentance and amends, for the harm that we've done to each other. The aseret yamei teshuvah gives us spiritually supported time for those conversations, blessed with all of the hope and potential of a new year.

During this time, our daily prayers continue to include Psalm 27, which we've been saying since the beginning of Elul and which will continue through the end of Sukkot. We insert a plea to be inscribed in the Book of Life in the Amidah, before the closing line of the first, second, and last two blessings. The traditional liturgy refers to God as King during this time. Before the morning service, Selichot prayers are said, and Avinu Malkeinu is added to the morning and afternoon prayers, except on Shabbat. If traditional liturgy isn't part of your practice, you can choose poems, songs, and meditations that will elevate this time for you. If your theology doesn't include a God who can write you in a book of life, you might think about who or what you turn to for support to do the work of transformation.

Shabbat Shuva is the Shabbat between Rosh Hashanah and Yom Kippur. A time of extra attention to teshuvah, in many Ashkenazi communities this was traditionally one of only two Shabbatot of the year (Shabbat Shuva and Shabbat Ha'Gadol, the Shabbat before Pesach) when rabbis gave sermons. This is an invitation to us to think about the role of the rabbi, and how often rabbis are on the mic today. Shabbat Shuva helps us imagine transitioning back to a two-sermon-a-year rabbinate, alongside diversifying and democratizing whose voices are leading us in prayer and teaching Torah.

This liminal Shabbat between Rosh HaShanah and Yom Kippur is a beautiful time to make rituals to honor in-betweenness. Some have the custom of having a mikvah, ritual bath, to honor this Shabbat. Some will gather by a lake or the sea, making tashlich, eating honey on challah, and running screaming into the ocean naked, solo or with friends, to wash off what remains of the year that was.

YOM KIPPUR

We barely catch our collective breath from Rosh Hashanah, and before we know it Yom Kippur is at the door. Vayikra details the Temple rituals: the high priest puts the sins of the community onto a goat and sends it off into the wilderness in order to purify the people. In Vayikra 16:29–31, we read:

וְהָיְתָה לָכֶם לְחֻקַּת עוֹלָם בַּחֹדֶשׁ הַשְּׁבִיעִי בֶּעָשׂוֹר לַחֹדֶשׁ תְּעַנּוּ אֶת־נַפְשֹׁתֵיכֶם
וְכָל־מְלָאכָה לֹא תַעֲשׂוּ הָאֶזְרָח וְהַגֵּר הַגָּר בְּתוֹכְכֶם: כִּי־בַיּוֹם הַזֶּה יְכַפֵּר עֲלֵיכֶם
לְטַהֵר אֶתְכֶם מִכֹּל חַטֹּאתֵיכֶם לִפְנֵי יְהוָה תִּטְהָרוּ: שַׁבַּת שַׁבָּתוֹן הִיא לָכֶם וְעִנִּיתֶם
אֶת־נַפְשֹׁתֵיכֶם חֻקַּת עוֹלָם:

> And this shall be to you a law for all time: In the seventh month,
> on the tenth day of the month, you shall practice self-denial; and
> you shall do no manner of work, neither the citizen nor the alien
> who resides among you. For on this day atonement will be made
> for you to cleanse you of all your sins; you shall be clean before
> The Divine. It shall be a sabbath of complete rest for you, and
> you shall practice self-denial; it is a law for all time.

Shabbat Shabbaton, a Shabbat of Shabbats, the holiest day of the Jewish year. Traditionally, Yom Kippur is spent in synagogue all day. It is also one of the holidays with the most embodied practices, all designed to bring us face-to-face with the possibility of individual and collective accountability. There are many ways to experience the wisdom of this day, to bring ourselves into practices of vulnerability for the sake of transformation.

Yom Kippur is described as a day that is a rehearsal for our deaths. We wear all white, evoking the traditional Jewish burial shroud, as well as angels.[11] If we can do it without harming ourselves, we abstain from food and water for twenty-five hours. We also abstain from bathing, anointing ourselves with oil, wearing leather shoes, and sexual activity. We are invited to consider the questions: What embodied practices bring us closer to a felt sense of our own mortality? What is revealed when we push closer to our fragility? How might our actions, especially in relationships, be transformed by an awareness of life's transience?

Yom Kippur puts our actions under an intense microscope. Many people have had experiences of Yom Kippur services, Jewish and other religious spaces, that are berating and shaming. This is not, we believe, in line with the inherited wisdom of the holiday. Yom Kippur offers us a container to rigorously, but gently, consider actions we've done that have caused harm, and aspects of ourselves we want to change. We do this from a place of love, and with community and Divine support. Prayer leaders, and all of us cocreating this holiday, have a responsibility to be aware of the context in which we practice Yom Kippur: a majority culture of Christian hegemony, which has a different understanding of sin, reward, and punishment. In rabbinic Judaism's formulation of harm, missing the mark is an action that, while requiring accountability and repair, does not alter the basic nature of our souls, our selves as b'tzelem Elohim (בְּצֶלֶם אֱלֹהִים), created in the Divine image. Every year on Yom Kippur, we have the opportunity to do the essential work of shifting culture around harm, accountability, and shame. When we practice this in our self-reflection, relationship repair, and Jewish rituals, it can ripple out and strengthen us for the work of transforming communities and culture.

Yom Kippur Prayer and Liturgy

Yom Kippur begins at sundown with the Kol Nidre service, the one evening service a year when a tallit (טַלִּית), a prayer shawl, is worn, since Yom Kippur is seen as one long day. On the tenth, we pray Shacharit, Musaf, Mincha, and the special Yom Kippur Neilah service, all incorporating prayers and readings that are unique to the holiday liturgy.

The recitation of Kol Nidre ("all vows") is as iconic a piece of Jewish liturgy as there is. The evocative music and dramatic recitation call us to attention. We stand, in body or spirit, and two people holding Torah scrolls stand on either side of the hazan chanting the Kol Nidre, creating a spiritual beit din, a court of three.

Not truly a prayer in the traditional Jewish formulation (without the Baruch atah, Blessed are You ending), we recite, three times, a legal formula, declaring that:

All vows, prohibitions, oaths, consecrations, restrictions, or equivalent expressions of vows, which I may vow, swear, dedicate, or which I may prescribe for myself or for others, from this Yom Kippur until the next Yom Kippur, which comes to us for good, we regret them all; all shall be hereby absolved, remitted, canceled, declared null and void, not in force or in effect. Let our vows not be considered vows; let our prohibitions not be considered prohibitions; and let our oaths not be considered oaths.

Kol Nidre's origins are unknown; it may date from the Gaonic period of the sixth to the eighth centuries in Babylon, now Iraq. Through the centuries, Kol Nidre has had a controversial place in the Yom Kippur liturgy. At times, rabbis condemned it as pagan and superstitious; at other times it was seen as making Jews seem untrustworthy.

What does it mean to start Yom Kippur having annulled our vows? Doesn't that mean that the commitments made throughout the year have no meaning? Why does the year not begin with Yom Kippur, rather than Rosh Hashanah, so that we can step into the New Year with a clean slate?

Tishrei is a critical feedback sandwich. Rosh Hashanah provides a warm-up, giving us hope for relationships and the year ahead. It can fortify and prepare us for the work of Yom Kippur. After Yom Kippur, Sukkot comforts us in the arms of community care: whatever harm we are repairing, we still belong, together. Yom Kippur, in between, asks us to confront the harm we have caused and the harm we are holding and healing. We cannot leave our problems in the old year, says Yom Kippur. Instead, the first act of the new year brings us to account for our actions from the year that has just passed and our commitments for the year ahead. Kol Nidre can open up blocked places. The annulment of vows can bring our attention to impermanence: once vows are annulled in the heavenly realm, it is possible to concentrate on making needed changes in the earthly world. Kol Nidre can be a pathway into the humility of Yom Kippur that we so vividly need in our political organizing. In our work we seek to enact lifelong commitments to working for justice; at the same time we know we must always reflect and be open to growth and change. Kol Nidre believes in our ability to begin again, year after year.

Confessional Prayers

Yom Kippur offers many liturgical moments of naming where we've missed the mark. Doing so in song, chant, and poetry, in a mix of languages, can make it more possible to explore the felt sense of missing the mark without getting stuck in blame and shame. The viddui (וִדּוּי), confession on Yom Kippur mirrors the viddui that is both part of the nightly Shema, and recited on the deathbed. Ashamnu (אָשַׁמְנוּ) is an acrostic prayer that lists transgressions from aleph to tav, through the whole Hebrew alphabet. The congregation rises as a whole and we each pound our chests with each word, as we collectively, and personally, repent. We recite all together to acknowledge collective accountability that enables harm to happen. Recited ten times throughout Yom Kippur, during the Al Cheit (עַל חֵטְא) congregants continue to tap or pound their chests with each line, collectively repenting with statements such as: "For the wrongdoing that we have done before you through the prompting of the heart, and for the wrongdoing that we have done before you through the influence of others." Some congregations solicit personal Al Cheits and read them aloud anonymously. The refrain comes like a balm: "and for them all, God of Forgiveness, please forgive us, pardon us, help us atone!" This liturgy is spread throughout the day, and interwoven with the festival liturgy of gratitude and celebration of divine goodness and miracles, helping us remember for the sake of what we are doing all of this repentance.

Avodah Service

Immediately following the Musaf Amidah, we come to the Avodah service. This service is primarily text from Torah, Vayikra 16, and Mishnah Yoma 1–7, describing Yom Kippur during Temple times, surrounded by piyyutim (פִּיּוּטִים), liturgical poems. We read very detailed stage directions: the preparation for the ritual, where everyone from the High Priest to the collected congregation would be, cleansing baths, and the enactment of the literal scapegoat in Vayikra 16:21–22:

וְסָמַךְ אַהֲרֹן אֶת־שְׁתֵּי יָדָו עַל רֹאשׁ הַשָּׂעִיר הַחַי וְהִתְוַדָּה עָלָיו אֶת־כָּל־עֲוֹנֹת בְּנֵי יִשְׂרָאֵל וְאֶת־כָּל־פִּשְׁעֵיהֶם לְכָל־חַטֹּאתָם וְנָתַן אֹתָם עַל־רֹאשׁ הַשָּׂעִיר וְשִׁלַּח

בְּיַד־אִישׁ עִתִּי הַמִּדְבָּרָה:וְנָשָׂא הַשָּׂעִיר עָלָיו אֶת־כָּל־עֲוֺנֹתָם אֶל־אֶרֶץ גְּזֵרָה וְשִׁלַּח אֶת־הַשָּׂעִיר בַּמִּדְבָּר:

Aaron shall lay both his hands upon the head of the live goat and confess over it all the iniquities and transgressions of the Israelites, whatever their sins, putting them on the head of the goat; and it shall be sent off to the wilderness through a designated agent. Thus the goat shall carry on it all their iniquities to an inaccessible region; and the goat shall be set free in the wilderness.

As Jews who do not pray for a literal Third Temple to appear, this can be a difficult service and ritual to connect to, millennia away from the smoke-filled Holy of Holies. At high holy day services at the Tikkun Olam Chavurah in Philadelphia, they spend the Avodah service with the actual goats of the Philadelphia Goat Project at Awbury Arboretum. Rabbi Linda Holtzman explains:

I have always been curious about the experience of ancient Israelites, feeling completely forgiven after they placed all of their misdeeds on a goat and sent it away. Something about the embodied nature of that experience seemed powerful to me. I had assumed that when we were with goats, it would just feel silly. I knew that we would enjoy them, but I wondered if the actual experience would have any of the power of the ancient rite of forgiveness. It did. Both times. When we placed our hands on the goats and had them walk away with all that we wanted to be rid of that we did during the past year, we felt as if it was all lifted. We were able to move into the year more freely than we were before we laid our hands on the goats. I heard one of the handlers say to the goats "OK. Shake off whatever it is they put on you." Only then could they move ahead. Something real and visceral took place. I want us to do it again. And it was a lot of fun. Goats are terrific![12]

Unetaneh Tokef

The Unetaneh Tokef is a key part of the Yom Kippur morning Musaf service. "On Rosh HaShanah it is written, and on Yom Kippur it is sealed" goes the refrain. "How many will pass on and how many will thrive, who will live and who will die. . . ." In years when smoke from forest fires keeps people from shul or coming in respirators, "who by fire" cries out loudly. In years when a loved one survives a terrifying illness, "who will live" shocks our systems. Unetaneh Tokef is a container for our greatest fears and our deepest yearnings, as it declares:[13] But t'filah, teshuvah, and tzedakah can revert the harshness of the decree. Prayer, return, and justice work, the liturgy promises, can have an impact on what is written. Even in the midst of our deepest fears, when we feel most at the mercy of fate, we are reminded that we can still love, we can still repair, we can still fight.

Martyrology

The Eleh Ezkerah ("these I remember") is a section of the Yom Kippur service that follows the Avodah service. The traditional text speaks of Jewish martyrs who chose death instead of denying the Torah and their Jewishness. Over the centuries, material was added to the martyrology service to include Jews who did not choose to die, who were killed in the Christian-perpetrated Crusades, pogroms, and the Nazi Holocaust.

This is a service that many of us are not very at home in. We struggle with the detailed descriptions of violence, and the valorization of martyrdom, choosing death over conversion. At the same time, we sit with and try to understand the layered reasons our ancestors had for making these choices in the face of incredible violence. We try to learn from subsequent generations honoring these lives, and these deaths, through placing this intense ritual in the center of one of the most important days of the sacred year.

The martyrology service is one of the times in our ritual year where we are confronted very directly with the imprints of collective violence and historical traumas on our culture and tradition. We are working to create a living Judaism that is not solely focused on reenacting trauma and living in fear. In that context, this service can create a contained ritual time to be with our collective grief at anti-Jewish violence, in ways that honor our pain and open possibilities for healing. What can we learn from this ritual about collective grief? Our tradition teaches us to use texts and songs to explore our ancestors' feelings of fear and vulnerability, alongside honoring their dedication to their beliefs, and the community that they fought for.

One way that many communities open toward healing during the martyrology service is by expanding our focus beyond anti-Jewish violence. We know that many peoples have experienced, and survived, racist, genocidal violence. During the martyrology service, we can remember, grieve, and honor Black lives lost to police violence, Palestinian lives lost to Israeli occupation, Indigenous lives lost to European and U.S. colonization, and so many lives lost to hatred and state violence in our times. This can make the service feel like an even heavier load to bear. It can also communicate that we, as Jews, are not alone in the violence we face. This service can, as we make our way through Yom Kippur, point the way toward mutuality and solidarity. We remember, we grieve, and we dedicate ourselves to creating a world where no one faces this kind of violence.

Grand Aleinu

The Aleinu is part of the Yom Kippur Musaf service, notable because of the choreography. Throughout the year we bend from the knee to bow, and on Rosh HaShanah we are invited to lower to the earth and bow from our knees; during the Aleinu on Yom Kippur we are invited to fully prostrate, lowering our bodies flat onto the earth. Whether or not this embodied practice is physically or emotionally available to you, this moment of prayer invites an exploration of a spiritual posture of supplication. Perhaps, from this position, you more fully experience the love radiating out from the Earth, closely connecting to the land that sustains you and offers you love that you return in caretaking. Perhaps, from this position, you experience your smallness, your vulnerability, your temporary time in this world, more deeply imagining your own death, more deeply surrendering to the care that you need. Perhaps you pause to be stunned by your surroundings, people spread out on the ground. Perhaps we realize the high stakes of this moment. There is no room for pretenses, no time for composure, just the intensity of the day.

Torah Readings for Yom Kippur

SHACHARIT

Vayikra 16: The traditional Torah reading on the morning of Yom Kippur describes the ritual of atonement made by the *Kohen Gadol*, the high priest, in the Holy of Holies. This involves the ritual of taking two goats, dedicating one to HaShem, and sending one into the wilderness for Azazel. The parshah details the ritual of the slaughter of the sacrificial goat.

Isaiah 57:14–58:14: In the haftorah for Yom Kippur morning, God chastises the people through the prophet Isaiah, expressing the desire for a true and full accounting of their behavior and righteous deeds, rather than performative ritual fasting without personal transformation. God asks: "Is this the fast that I delight in?"

MINCHA

Vayikra 18: The traditional afternoon Torah reading is also from Vayikra, the chapter of Achrei-Mot that details forbidden sexual relations. Due to the homophobia and misogyny of this text, some congregations substitute a different reading; many instead read Devarim 29:9–30:20, from parshat Nitzavim, about teshuvah, God's anger, and forgiveness.

Jonah: During the afternoon of Yom Kippur, the Book of Jonah provides a compelling narrative exploration of one man's journey to try to escape accountability and his divinely proscribed purpose.[14]

YIZKOR

The Yizkor memorial service is recited four times a year: Yom Kippur, Shemini Atzeret, Pesach, and Shavuot. Yom Kippur's Yizkor, while not liturgically different than the others, carries with it a heavier mode. At the New Year, when we remember with particular sadness those who are missing from our tables, and when we spend long times in contemplation, the Yom Kippur Yizkor service is deeply felt. The service centers around silence and the recitation of the Yizkor prayer, said for individual loved ones. El Malei Rachamaim ("God full of compassion") is chanted. Some communities invite speakers to share reflections on loved ones, and phys-

ically enact remembrance through placing a stone or sharing a picture. Yizkor concludes with the Kaddish prayer.

While Yizkor is traditionally said for family members, it is a time to remember all of our collective beloved dead, known and unknown to us. It can be powerful for ritual leaders to name movement ancestors, and invite people to share remembrances of ancestors who've shaped our communities, and to remember all those who have no one to say Yizkor for them. In creating communal Yizkor services, it's essential to make a container where all who wish to have a chance to share, to try to hold our layered grieving collectively. Yizkor will, of course, not work for everyone. We can take the placement of Yizkor in our traditional festival liturgy as teaching to be intentional about creating space for remembrance in all of our seasonal rituals, experimenting with all the ways it can look, and trusting that our bodies and spirits will know what they need, year to year.

Memorial candles, known as ner neshamah (literally "soul candle") or yahrtzeit candle in Yiddish, are lit before the Yom Kippur holiday candles. Yiddishist, Kohenet, and historian Annie Cohen writes of the practice of making memorial candles for Yom Kippur with wicks measured around the circumference of a cemetery or an individual gravestone:

> In the early 18th Century, Jewish women in Lithuania, Belarus and elsewhere in Eastern Europe would perform the rituals of *feldmestn* and *keyvermestn*. Often created during Elul, the women measured the perimeter of cemeteries and graves with candle wicks. These wicks would then be used to make memorial candles to be lit during Yom Kippur. This was a special time of year when the boundary between the worlds of the living and the dead seemed to be thinning and the ancestors were called for support in prayer.
>
> As the women wove the threads through the cemetery, they would recite a *tkhine,* or personal prayer, generally said in Yiddish. You can adapt the traditional *tkhine* by making specific requests for protection in the coming year, and bringing in the names and special characteristics of your ancestors.[15]

The machzor pulls no punches. We're talking death, we're talking harm, we're talking shame, bodies, relationships, God as a King. We embody our own deaths and publicly confess to harm we have enabled or done to others. Yom Kippur attempts to call up our deepest pains. You may, or may not, be ready to sit in services and look deeply into your soul. Maybe you slip a favorite book in your bag, perhaps you take long breaks outside or in the hallway, volunteer with kids' programs or setting up the room for breakfast. Maybe you don't go to shul at all, but spend it on a mountaintop or floating in the water. There are as many ways to be in this season of deep reflection as there are Jews in the world.

Yom Kippur Balls

Yom Kippur is a whole lot of holiday. After a lifetime of being told that this is the "most important day" of the Jewish year, a creative and vibrant culture has grown up around what we must do, or not do, on Yom Kippur. For many, it is the one day a year to go to synagogue, the day to be blessedly anonymous and lost in the crowd. It is a day you can do on your own, fasting and recounting the year's hurts and harms from the quiet of your home or wherever calls to you.

Yom Kippur is a day with so much meaning and power that intentionally *not* observing it is more meaningful than not observing any other holiday. In the 1890s, Yiddish anarchists in London, New York, later the United States and Canada held Yom Kippur balls, festive public meals and dances intentionally scheduled for Yom Kippur to disrupt and counter repressive religious culture.[16] In recent years, Jewish leftists in London and Glasgow have brought back the Yom Kippur ball, organizing queer dance parties and rowdy punk shows.[17]

Yom Kippur is for us and by us; Yom Kippur is what we make it. The invitation is there, every year, to be with ourselves, our lives and choices, and our people. Any way that we interact with that invitation is Jewish culture because we make it Jewish culture. See you at shul, and at the ball.

SUKKOT

> Find one person with whom you made repairs over the ten days.
> Invite them to your fort, if you made one ~ to your house, if
> you didn't. Prepare a meal for them, with your own hands, in
> whatever form that takes ~ digging the potatoes yourself, or
> opening the box. Serve your guest. Offer them the best you
> have. Say: Welcome. Say: Thank you. Say: This is only the
> beginning. Celebrate the work of connection and repair.
>
> —"Ritual: Sukkot" in *The Social Justice Warrior's Guide
> to the High Holy Days*, by Dane Kuttler, p. 48

There is a minhag at the conclusion of Yom Kippur services: go home and start building a sukkah. We may have spent all day in synagogue, some of us have been fasting, we as a people have collectively been immersed in the holiest twenty-five hours of the year. And yet—rush home and get ready for the next holiday?

This rush is an opportunity to begin the new year by practicing our new commitments. All day on Yom Kippur we reflected on what we could do differently, how we could show up more, ways to build and rebuild relationships that are in need of attention, and the work we want to do to bring more justice into the world. Sukkot, five short days after Yom Kippur, invites us to dwell in the insight we've harvested, for the whole week of the fifteenth until the twenty-first of Tishrei. So after Yom Kippur ends, we show our readiness to dig even deeper by laying the first beams that night.

The last day of Sukkot, on the twenty-second of Tishrei, is also Shemini Atzeret, followed by Simchat Torah on the twenty-third of Tishrei. Sukkot is the first holiday in the calendar year—followed by Pesach and Shavuot—with roots in biblical pilgrimage festivals whose opening and closing days are observed as chag (חַג, festival) or Yom Tov (יוֹם טוֹב, literally, a good day). These are days like Shabbat when no work is done. The days between are known as chol ha'moed (חוֹל הַמּוֹעֵד), the weekdays of the festival.[18]

Early rabbinic sources established, and many still today practice, observing one day of chag in Eretz Yisrael and two days of chaggim outside the land. At first glance, this seems to be part of Jewish tradition designating spiritual differences between Eretz Yisrael and diaspora. In fact, this tradition grew out of necessity during a time when there was not a fixed calendar. The Mishnah, in Tractate Rosh Hashanah, describes how months were declared based on witnesses seeing the new moon, and communicated across great distances by bonfires and smoke signals. Runners, we learn, had to travel far distances to proclaim the moon,[19] and Samaritans were intentionally lighting fires on different days to confuse the calendar.[20] In this context, two-day chag served to make sure Jews living further away from the center of rabbinic authority were, on some day or another, observing the holiday on the correct day.

What is the purpose of the two-day chag now that we can be confident about the calendar? How does it feel to observe two-day chag as an anti-Zionist? For some, two-day chag will be a meaningful connection to an era with different relationships to time, and a way to embody that time. For others, it is hard enough to take one day of chag while living embedded in mainstream culture shaped by Christian hegemony and capitalism. Two days of chag can feel like we are aligning with centering Eretz Yisrael, *or* it can feel like we are celebrating how Jews in rabbinic tradition have *always* been dispersed. As with all of our Jewish lives, what we do, and how we feel about it, is sure to change over our lifetimes. How many days we observe is never as important as our engagement with the tradition, and finding community in exploring these questions together.

Historically, Sukkot is a place, first named when Jacob traveled there after his encounter with Esau.[21] During the Exodus, the Children of Israel journeyed to Sukkot before crossing the sea. "Sukkah" refers to the temporary structures they used while traveling in the desert, and "Sukkot" is both the name of the festival and the plural of sukkah. The holiday is called Z'man Simcheteinu (זְמַן שִׂמְחָתֵנוּ), "the season of our joy," acknowledging joy at the abundance of the harvest. It is also called Chag HaAsif (חַג הָאָסִיף), "the gathering festival," honoring the harvest and the gathering of the community in the sukkah. We pray for rain during the Hoshanot recited each morning during Sukkot; on Hoshannah Rabbah, the seventh day of the festival; and even nightly at Simchat Beit HaShoevah celebrations.[22]

As we eat, or even sleep, in a sukkah, we remember our ancestors wandering in the desert, dwelling in temporary huts. We recall the biblical pilgrimage festival to the holy Temple; we honor the changing season and the incoming harvest. We acknowledge the abundance that God provided for the Israelites in the Wilderness, for the farmers in their fields, and for us in this moment of festival.[23] Blended through these layers are embodied practices of vulnerability, as we linger with each other in community, having journeyed through Rosh HaShanah and Yom Kippur together, making teshuvah and having difficult conversations. We ask for the Divine to וּפְרֹשׂ עָלֵינוּ סֻכַּת שְׁלוֹמֶךָ (ufros alienu sukkat shlomecha), spread over us Your shelter of peace. The temporariness and openness of the physical structure of the sukkah is designed to help us experience divine and communal protection.

Build a Sukkah

The Torah commands that we build and dwell in sukkot for seven days:

אַךְ בַּחֲמִשָּׁה עָשָׂר יוֹם לַחֹדֶשׁ הַשְּׁבִיעִי בְּאָסְפְּכֶם אֶת-תְּבוּאַת הָאָרֶץ תָּחֹגּוּ אֶת-חַג-ה' שִׁבְעַת יָמִים בַּיּוֹם הָרִאשׁוֹן שַׁבָּתוֹן וּבַיּוֹם הַשְּׁמִינִי שַׁבָּתוֹן:

Mark, on the fifteenth day of the seventh month, when you have gathered in the yield of your land, you shall observe the festival of the Divine [to last] seven days: a complete rest on the first day, and a complete rest on the eighth day.

—Vayikra 23:39

The sukkah evokes memories of Abraham, stationed outside his tent waiting to welcome visitors in Beresheet 18, or even, according to midrash, building sukkot in celebration of the angels' good news.[24]

The ceiling of the sukkah should be made from skhakh, branches and foliage that grew from the earth, and there are very specific measurements and specifications for a halachic sukkah.[25] It cannot be placed under a tree, for example, they must be detached. Many people use bamboo mats for the ceiling, which should provide more shade than light, but also, according to folk tradition, be open enough to see the stars. A beautiful passage in the Gemara that claims that the roof of a sukkah is modeled after the clouds of glory in which God appeared in the desert.[26] And in the world to come, it is said, the righteous will have sukkot made for them from the skin of Leviathan![27]

When we can't build a halachic sukkah, there are still many ways to experience hut life. One friend weaves a canopy of yarn across her New

York City apartment living room and tucks foliage and fruit into it, to create a canopy for Sukkot. Pillow forts are a beloved way to honor the festival at home when a sukkah is out of reach. We can visit friends' sukkot, or go to community sukkot at synagogues, parks, and college campuses. Many Jewish intentional living communities and farms, like Isabella Freedman, Pearlstone Farm, and Urban Adamah, host Sukkot celebrations, bringing us back and forward to the harvest festival pilgrimage roots of the holiday. At Linke Fligl, a queer Jewish chicken farm and cultural organizing project that was based in upstate New York from 2016 to 2022, queers from across the diaspora gathered to mark sacred time in a round sukkah under the stars. They prayed three times a day, escorted the Torah under her chuppah (חֻפָּה), wedding canopy, through a field of goldenrod, and at night embodied raucous Simchat Beit Ha'shoeva celebrations, as it is described in *Talmud Bavli*, Sukkot 51a: singing, dancing, and burning priestly undergarments.

Whatever sukkah we dwell in, we have the opportunity to bless, saying:

בָּרוּךְ אַתָּה יהוה אֱלֹהֵינוּ רוח הָעוֹלָם אֲשֶׁר קִדְּשָׁנוּ בְּמִצְוֹתָיו וְצִוָּנוּ לֵישֵׁב בַּסֻּכָּה

Baruch atah, Adonai Eloheinu, Ruach ha'olam, asher kid'shanu b'mitzvotav v'tzivanu leisheiv basukkah.

Blessed are You, Adonai our God, Sovereign of all: who hallows us with mitzvot, commanding us to dwell in the sukkah.

While the sukkah has walls and a ceiling, it is vulnerable to the elements. We engage in an embodied way with our individual and collective vulnerability by eating, singing, sleeping, and learning in a sukkah for a week, in a way we did not even during Rosh Hashanah and Yom Kippur. Sukkot is all about hospitality. Host friends and neighbors in the sukkah for meals. But don't stop there—have your organizing meetings in the sukkah, sleep there, join virtual classes from your sukkah, host your own teach-ins. If you are making a community sukkah, hanging informational signs about the structure and how to use it, who is welcome (everyone!), and the condition that guests should leave it in when they're finished makes it more welcoming.

Ushpizin are honored guests that we metaphorically invite into the sukkah each night. This practice is based on a text in the Zohar. As a reward for dwelling in sukkot, we are blessed with welcoming God's presence and seven honored ancestors: Abraham, Isaac, Jacob, Moses, Aaron, Joseph, and David.[28] Jewish feminists began the practice of adding Sarah, Rebecca, Rachel, Leah, Miriam, Deborah, and Ruth. Solomon and Esther are added for those who eat in the sukkah on the eighth night. Some follow chronological order, while the Zohar's not bound by a linear nature of time. In Sephardi tradition, a chair is set aside for the visiting ushpizin each evening, and sacred books and food are sent to those in need with a note that says "this is a share of the ushpizin." The ushpizin are invited each night with a short liturgy, often said before the meal. At Hinenu in Baltimore, the community brings pictures of its own ancestors, biological and chosen, to hang on the walls of the sukkah.

Sukkot is an opportunity to fulfill the queerest of the mitzvot, hiddur mitzvah. Usually translated as "beautifying the commandments," we like to think of it as "making the necessary beautiful." Queer aesthetics make life beautiful for its own sake, and for the sake of our survival. Queer aesthetics beautify that which is sacred, and the things that shelter us—our homes, each other. On Sukkot we bust out our maximalist selves to adorn shelter. The sukkah is traditionally decorated with fruit hanging from the roof, and the blessings may be framed and hung on the walls. Whatever makes the space beautiful to you is spot on: twinkly lights, paper chains, pennants or banners, your favorite pages from the Radical Jewish Calendar, pictures of your ancestors or other ushpizin you plan to invite, a community calendar of events in your sukkah. Every wall can be a different kind of fabric. Long bolts of canvas can be painted with a mural, showing the brachot for dwelling in the sukkah, invited ancestors, the plants we are harvesting; anything that inspires and delights.

Sukkot is a holiday with incredible potential for interwoven political action. A sukkah symbolizes shelter, community, collective vulnerability, and protection, and can be built anywhere, from a public square, to an encampment, to a protest camp. A week of eating outdoors, while we are commanded to invite people to join us, instructs us on building community. We gather our comrades and allied organizations, learn together in the sukkah, while feasting and feeding each other as resistance. From 2006 to 2014, Great Small Works, New York's community pageant and puppet theater, created The Sukkos Mob, a portable show that moved around the city streets performing in English, Yiddish, and Spanish.²⁹ A sukkah is an invitation to many types of community collaboration and creativity.

Chasidic Rabbi Hayyim Halberstam of Sandz is credited with teaching that "If the poor are not welcome, none of the ushpizin will come to the sukkah."³⁰ Building temporary structures outdoors, vulnerable to the elements, calls on us to pay explicit attention to houselessness and housing instability in our communities. How will you share resources during this week? How can you welcome those in need of shelter into your sukkah, beyond just this week? If you are building a sukkah in a public place, how might it provide shelter for those who sleep outdoors all year. What commitments to creating home and shelter all year round do we make when we remove it after a week?

On Sukkot, we can take action around housing, learning about and joining a movement in our community advocating for housing for all, against eviction and gentrification. Sukkot is a time to join or strengthen our relationships to encampment support and mutual aid organizing. Sukkot, as a harvest festival that puts us in close contact with the earth and her seasons, is a time to reflect on the land and land sovereignty, and to take action on Indigenous sovereignty and movements for returning land back. If your community does not currently pay meaningful rent to the original inhabitants of the land you're on, Sukkot can be the time to learn how to do this and begin.³¹

Lulav and Etrog

וּלְקַחְתֶּם לָכֶם בַּיּוֹם הָרִאשׁוֹן פְּרִי עֵץ הָדָר כַּפֹּת תְּמָרִים וַעֲנַף עֵץ־עָבֹת וְעַרְבֵי־
נָחַל וּשְׂמַחְתֶּם לִפְנֵי יְהוָה אֱלֹהֵיכֶם שִׁבְעַת יָמִים:

On the first day you shall take for yourselves the product of hadar trees, branches of palm trees, boughs of leafy trees, and willows of the brook, and you shall rejoice before HaShem your God seven days.

—Vayikra 23:40

A lulav, a wand of palm, myrtle, and willow held together with a holder made of palm leaves, is used each day of Sukkot. An etrog (a citron, which is like a large lemon) is held with it, completing the four species. This is the fruit claimed by midrash to have been that which grew on the Tree of Knowledge in the Garden of Eden,[32] called "pri etz hadar," fruit of a beautiful tree. The four species are said to represent different objects, such as parts of the body, according to Kabbalah.[33] Myrtle represents the eyes, willow stands for the mouth, the palm is the spine, and the etrog reminds us of the heart. They can also represent four kinds of people.

> Taste represents learning. Smell represents good deeds. The etrog has both taste and smell. The lulav has taste but not fragrance. The myrtle has smell but no taste. And the willow has neither. Each represents a different type of [person]. Some have both learning and good deeds; some have one without the other; and some have neither. Real community is found in their being bound together and brought under one roof.[34]

The lulav, like all of Sukkot, is unmistakably old magic that pre-dates rabbinic Judaism. This classic wand of bundled live materials that together describes unity, is shaken in six directions in the hope that it will bring rain. There is much discussion that, to truly fulfill the commandment of ulkachatem lachem, "to take to yourself," one cannot borrow another's lulav on the first day.[35] This defines the importance and financial priority of the holiday, but also communicates the uniqueness of every person's lulav, and the magic of the festival.

The willow, myrtle, and palm are bound together in the Sephardi tradition with knotted palm leaves, and in the Ashkenazi tradition with a woven holder. The Gemara explains that the lulav should be "positioned in the manner of growth," with the bottom of the branches facing down.[36] The lulav is held with the willow on the left side and myrtle on the right. In Ashkenazi tradition, the etrog is held with the pitom (fragile stem) pointed down before the blessing and turned to face up afterward. Some people pick up the etrog first, as it symbolizes the heart, and because it is mentioned first in the verse. In Sephardi tradition, the etrog is picked up after the blessing is said entirely. The etrog is held in the left hand and the other species bundled in the right, held together as a single unit.[37] The blessings for taking lulav are said:

בְּרוּכָה אַתְּ יָהּ אֱלֹהֵינוּ רוּחַ הָעוֹלָם אֲשֶׁר קִדְּשַׁתְנוּ בְּמִצְוֹתֶיהָ וְצִוַּתְנוּ עַל נְטִילַת
לוּלָב

Brukhah At Yah Eloheynu ruakh ha'olam asher kid'shatnu
b'mitzvoteha v'tzivatnu al n'tilat lulav.

Blessed are you, Divine, Breath of Life, who sanctifies us with
Your commandments and has enjoined upon us the mitzvah of
the lulav.

The first time upon taking lulav:

בְּרוּכָה אַתְּ יָהּ אֱלֹהֵינוּ רוּחַ הָעוֹלָם שֶׁהֶחֱיָתְנוּ וְקִיְּמַתְנוּ וְהִגִּיעַתְנוּ לַזְּמָן הַזֶּה

Brukhah At Yah Eloheynu ruah ha'olam sheheheyatnu
v'kiy'matnu v'higiatnu lazman hazeh.

Blessed are you, Source, Breath of Life, who has kept us alive,
sustained us, and enabled us to reach this moment.

As with all of our ritual objects, where they come from and how they
are made is as important as how the object is used. Gemara teaches that
materials that were stolen, dried, or from a "condemned city" cannot be
used in the mitzvah of taking lulav and etrog.[38] We honor that tradition
when we question the sources of lulav and etrog. The species of the lulav
and the etrog are based on plants that grow in the land of Palestine. For
those of us who live on a different continent, with different seasons, and
who oppose the occupation of Palestine, foraging our own lulav and etrogs
helps us celebrate this earth- and plant-based practice in ways that uplift,
rather than undermine, our political commitments. Lulav and etrog can be
made from anything that evokes the symbolism of the holiday.

In 5778, Rakia Sky Brown, Gabi Kirk, Noah Rubin-Blose, and Miriam
Saperstein published *The Book of Lulav*, wrestling with how to source lulav
and etrog in the contexts of capitalism, consumerism, and colonization, in
Palestine/Israel and on Turtle Island.[39] In addition to examples of diaspora
lulav sourced from many places and contexts, they offer these questions to
guide the process of lulav making:

1. How do we collectively relate to rituals around harvest and a learned memory of agricultural connection of our ancestors when many modern Jewish communities have been forcibly separated from land and cultivation?
2. How do we relate to harvest rituals when very few of us have ever participated in a harvest?
3. How do we harvest on land that is not our own?
4. How can we celebrate harvest as one part of a beautiful process?

They then explore the meaning of each traditional species, and detail how to find a symbolically related species in different landscapes. As important as the objects are the ways in which they are harvested. Learning about the land we are on and the plants we are in relationship to and harvesting them in rituals of reciprocal care are an opportunity to think about our relationship to the lands we are on.

Sukkot takes preparation, which we often don't see coming, given the packed first half of Tishrei. If you are ordering a lulav, Judaica shops and congregations that do group orders have cutoff deadlines. We love a leisurely foraging walk to a special place, and we've made beautiful lulav and etrog from what we've found on our blocks. However we make it, we're grateful for the opportunity to hold something that connects us, mindbodyspirit, with land, the season, and the sacredness of it all.

Sukkot Prayer and Liturgy

Hallel is an energetic, joyful singing of psalms of praise, included in the Shacharit service on special occasions. For all of Sukkot and Hanukah, on the first two days of Pesach, and on Shavuot, full Hallel is said: Psalms 113–18. On the last six days of Pesach and on Rosh Chodesh, half Hallel is said, omitting the first halves of Psalm 115 and 116. On Sukkot, lulav and etrog are waved during Hallel.

Today, many congregations say Hallel on Yom HaAtzmau'ut (Israeli Independence Day) and Yom Yerushalayim (Jerusalem Day, commemorating the end of the 1967 War), demonstrating that we leftists aren't the only ones bringing together Jewish ritual practice and politics. We look forward

TISHREI

113

to creating a new Hallel to celebrate a free Palestine. Today, we can experiment with singing selections from Hallel for campaign wins and other moments of communal joy.

The Torah readings for Sukkot Day 1 and 2 are Vayikra 22:26–23:44 and Bamidbar 29:12–16: On the first two days of Sukkot, the Torah readings are the instructions for observing the festivals, including Pesach, Shavuot, Rosh Hashanah, and Sukkot, from both Vayikra and Bamidbar.

On chol ha'moed Sukkot, the intermediate days, we read the verses of Torah from Bamidbar 29 that describe the burnt offerings and libations made on the specific intermediate days of Sukkot.

On Shabbat chol ha'moed Sukkot, when Shabbat falls in the middle of Sukkot, Shemot 33:12–34:26 is read. Hashem agrees to partially appear to Moses, passing by so that Moses may see God's back. God then commands Moses to carve the second set of tablets, and we read the thirteen attributes of God.

Either on the Shabbat during Sukkot, or, if there is not an intermediate Shabbat during Sukkot, on Shemini Atzeret, we read Kohelet, the book of Ecclesiastes. Similarly to reading Megillat Esther on Purim, Song of Songs on Pesach, Ruth on Shavuot, and Lamentations on Tisha b'Av, we read Kohelet on Sukkot or Shimini Atzeret, perhaps because it was the last remaining megillah without a specific holiday on which to read it.[40] Rabbinic authorities over the years, and we in our time, can find thematic connections. "To everything there is a season," declared King Solomon, who is traditionally credited with authoring the book.[41] On Sukkot, known as the "season of our joy," Kohelet brings us to earth, dealing with the difficult realities of life and death. When we read Ruth in the spring, there is mention of firstfruits; when we read Kohelet in the fall, as we gather the last harvest, we read about aging and death. After the heights of the Yamim Noraim, reading Kohelet during Sukkot or Shemini Atzeret begins pulling us back down to earth.

HOSHANOT

Following the Torah service, the community opens the ark and recites Hoshanot, a liturgy singing "hoshiah nah," "please save us." The Hoshanot is a prayer specifically for rain. The hakafot (circling) are repeated on Simchat Torah. On Sukkot, we have come together to dwell in our vulnerability together. Where so many of the words in a prayerbook feel cold and abstract, walking in a circle, waving lulav, and singing "hoshiah nah!" can unlock the reality of our fears and yearning. In our times, there is plenty to connect to when we call out for help. Hoshanot are an opportunity to reflect: What are we crying out about, and who, or what, are we imagining will save us? What do we do when we hear each other's calls?

HOSHANA RABBAH

Hoshannah Rabbah is the seventh day of Sukkot. While it is still considered a part of the Sukkot festival and chol ha'moed, it is also a unique celebration.

Seven hakafot are made using the Hoshanot liturgy. Core to Hoshannah Rabbah is the beating of the aravot (willow branches.) At the end of the seven hakafot, the aravot are removed from the lulav bundle and beaten against the ground. The ritual is described with great detail in the Mishnah[42] but without a specific explanation. Perhaps this symbolizes rain as the leaves fall to the ground. Perhaps it releases anxiety about harvest, or remaining feelings from Yom Kippur. The rabbis attempt to connect this to Temple practices, but can't really explain this ritual and this is unsettling to them. It feels like very old magic indeed. On Hoshannah Rabbah we pray for water for the coming year.[43] It is no coincidence that near the end of the outdoor festival we begin to pray for rain—not at the beginning.

Some stay up all night reading Torah (specifically the book of Devarim, which serves as a repetition of the Torah), or reciting psalms. Some Sephardi communities recite Selichot, petitionary prayers. Some stop sitting in the sukkah and using the lulav when Hoshannah Rabbah ends, while some continue through Shemini Atzeret.

SHEMINI ATZERET

Shemini Atzeret, the eighth day of the Assembly, can be confusing. It is considered both the last day of Sukkot and its own independent festival. But what is it marking?

In Vayikra 23:36 we read:

שִׁבְעַת יָמִים תַּקְרִיבוּ אִשֶּׁה לֵי״ה׳ בַּיּוֹם הַשְּׁמִינִי מִקְרָא־קֹדֶשׁ יִהְיֶה לָכֶם וְהִקְרַבְתֶּם אִשֶּׁה לֵי״ה׳ עֲצֶרֶת הִוא כָּל־מְלֶאכֶת עֲבֹדָה לֹא תַעֲשׂוּ:

Seven days you shall bring offerings by fire to HaShem. On the eighth day you shall observe a sacred occasion and bring an offering by fire to HaShem; it is a sacred gathering: you shall not work at your occupations.

In his commentary on this verse, Rashi[44] writes:

עצרת הוא. עֲצַרְתִּי אֶתְכֶם אֶצְלִי; כְּמֶלֶךְ שֶׁזִּמֵּן אֶת בָּנָיו לִסְעוּדָה לְכָךְ וְכָךְ יָמִים, כֵּיוָן שֶׁהִגִּיעַ זְמַנָּן לִפָּטֵר, אָמַר, בָּנַי בְּבַקָּשָׁה מִכֶּם עַכְּבוּ עִמִּי עוֹד יוֹם אֶחָד, קָשָׁה עָלַי פְּרֵדַתְכֶם:

A sacred gathering: I keep you back with Me one day more. It is similar to the case of a king who invited his children to a banquet for a certain number of days. When the time arrived for them to take their departure he said, "Children, I beg of you, stay one day more with me; it is so hard for me to part with you!"

Traditionally, Shemini Atzeret is understood as a last chance to share the intimacy of Sukkot with HaShem. In practice, this looks like holding on to some of the rituals of Sukkot, while introducing additional observances particular to the day. We continue to eat our meals in the sukkah, but without the blessings for dwelling in the sukkah. Shemini Atzeret also marks a transition point between the fall festivals and the winter season. Shemini Atzeret is the last call of Sukkot, a chance to squeeze in our last taste of Sukkot simcha, while also mentally, emotionally, and spiritually preparing for the transition from this special time.

The Talmud enumerates the ways in which Shemini Atzeret is similar to and different from Sukkot. Many of the differences have to do with the kohanim (priests) and the Temple offerings, while some practical differences remain. Yizkor, the special memorial service for the dead, is said on Shemini Atzeret, as it is a festival when people are gathered together in community, yet with a different, more restrained feel, more appropriate for Yizkor than Sukkot.

Shemini Atzeret Prayer and Liturgy

The Torah reading on Shimini Atzeret is Devarim 14:22–16:17. This includes laws of kashrut and of the festival offerings. In between, we read one of the passages that explains shmita (שְׁמְטָה) and tithing, two practices of land and wealth redistribution that strive to keep the community in sustainable, balanced relationship with the land and each other.

Finally, Shemini Atzeret is the day when we begin saying Tfilat HaGeshem (תְּפִלַת הַגֶּשֶׁם) the prayer for rain, for the winter months. This prayer was originally designated for Sukkot, but delayed, possibly so as not to spoil the sukkah experience. Before or during the Musaf Amidah, the shaliach tzibbur, (שְׁלִיחַ צִבּוּר), prayer leader, recites an extended prayer for rain, including a series of piyyutim (פִּיוּטִים) sacred poems. From this point until Pesach (Passover), the second blessing of the Amidah includes thanking God because God causes mashiv ha'ruach umorid ha'gashem (מַשִּׁיב הָרוּחַ וּמוֹרִיד הַגֶּשֶׁם), the wind to blow and the rain to fall. This blessing is based on the seasons and agricultural needs of our ancestors who lived in Eretz Yisrael and the Babylonian Diaspora. For those of us not oriented toward the growing seasons in those lands, this blessing can remind us of the many places our ancestors have lived. We can talk to local farmers and ask what they pray for at different seasons and write locally specific blessings. As climate change makes for unpredictable and chaotic weather around us, this blessing can orient us toward our own power to work with God for ecological healing. After many months of individual and collective reflection and a week of dwelling in a sukkah, we take Shemini Atzeret as an offering to orient toward the material and living world around us. We acknowledge life, death, and the power that moves us between them.

SIMCHAT TORAH

At the end of this holiday cycle in this jam-packed month is Simchat Torah, the celebration that today marks the conclusion of reading every parshah in the Torah and beginning again. Now a popular grand finale to the season, Simchat Torah is a relatively late addition to the Tishrei cycle. Simchat Torah is not mentioned as such in the Talmud; Shemini Atzeret is named as a two-day festival.[45] At some point in the Gaonic period (600–1000 CE), the custom of Babylonian Jewish communities reading the whole Torah in one year gained widespread favor over the triennial reading system (taking three years to read the whole Torah) in Eretz Yisrael. From there, traditions of celebrating the completion and rebeginning of reading grew over the course of the Rishonic period (1100–1500 CE).

With all of these major festivals in such close contact, Simchat Torah can sometimes feel like the odd one out. What does ending and restarting the Torah have to do with reflection, repair, and vulnerability? It's true that the modalities we've been steeped in throughout the month look different from Simchat Torah. Here we embody the jubilation of Torah learning in raucous dancing and music, sweets and liquor, dancing in the streets and leaping off of ceiling rafters. Children parading with flags for the Torah and holding stuffy Toraot, all while we dance with the scroll around and around in circles. Simchat Torah teaches us about a kind of joy different from that of Purim or Passover, a kind of embodied practice that gives us space to collectively sigh and release.

The wisdom of the timing of Simchat Torah is that we are at the end of a long and intense cycle: We have spent most of this month of Tishrei in our heads and hearts. Before that, we spent Elul in reflection and the difficult work of interpersonal repair. And, if we can remember all the way back to the summer, we began this journey months ago, with the grief and collective wail of Tisha b'Av. At the conclusion of this long cycle, Simchat Torah grounds us in our bodies and closes the circuit.

How can those of us who wrestle with the violence and harm in the text of Torah all year round dance with it at this festival? Even when we find ways to honor and learn from the text, we read the same words every year. How can there be something new to learn? Pirkei Avot 5:22 tells us to "Turn it, turn it, everything is in it," which Jewish tradition understands to refer to Torah: study it, unpack it, take it apart and put it back together, and, our ancestors believed, we will find all the questions we need to ask, and all the learning we need in this lifetime. Simchat Torah is an invitation and a challenge, that there is always something new to learn, that there is medicine in retelling your stories. Simchat Torah invites us to listen to the elders in our communities, to learn movement history from the people who lived it, and to allow ourselves to wrestle with the ways those stories are transmitted, without discarding them. By showing kavod, honor, to our elders, wrestling with the stories we've inherited, we can be transformed.

Torah Reading

The Torah has no beginning or end. On Simchat Torah we read the final verses from the book of Devarim, and we immediately start again from the beginning. One custom is to unroll the scroll completely around the room, demonstrating the cyclical nature of Torah, and placing our youngest community members in the center to find themselves in the text. We then break into song and dance, moving in rotations around the room in seven hakafot, embodying the cyclical nature of Jewish time, and of Torah.

Public Judaism

It can be customary for some communities to take the party outside; Simchat Torah dancing sometimes pours out into the streets, or even starts there. Sometimes we plan in advance and permit the block for a Torah Block Party. Sometimes we take a block, separating when a car comes. The Torah, usually kept safe inside in the Aron HaKodesh (אֲרוֹן הַקֹּדֶשׁ) ark, reverently taken out to gently kiss and caress, is now being hoisted high overhead on a busy intersection.

Being this Jewish in public, in the context of Christian hegemony and antisemitism, can bring up a range of feelings. Defiance and pride, embarrassment and discomfort, joy and power, the whole range, or a confusing mix of them all. Even when it feels like a stretch, on Simchat Torah, we are encouraged to transform our vulnerability into bravado, to embody a kind of joy that says to each other "get in here and get on some of this good sweet Torah!" Together, and aided by our most sacred ritual object, we can practice being Jewish in public in a big way on Simchat Torah, in ways that can strengthen us to celebrate being visibly Jewish all year round. When we dance on Simchat Torah, in the streets, synagogues, homes, and clubs, we embody a powerful finale to a month of exploring vulnerability in community.

Chattan v'Kallah haTorah (חֲתַן וְכַלָּה הַתּוֹרָה) is a custom in many communities to honor members of the community who have given generously of their energy and resources during the year. The bride and groom of the Torah are sometimes a married couple but sometimes not, and are called up for aliyot on Simchat Torah during the Torah reading.

In Baltimore, Hinenu synagogue has turned the tradition on its ear. Who doesn't want to marry Torah?! In lieu of the Chattan v'Kallah haTorah, a group aliyah is called for "reim haTorah" (רֵעִים הַתּוֹרָה), beloveds of the Torah. This aliyah includes anyone in the community seeking to bring in more love, whether love of text and study, romantic love, familial love, or friendship. Coming forward publicly and saying that you want to increase love in one's life in the coming year is a very vulnerable act. Yet it has become a powerful minhag (custom) in our community—and deep friendships and a relationship or two has blossomed after such an aliyah.

As the month of megaholidays comes to an end, we remember that Tishrei will return again. The more we deepen into the anchoring power of the holidays, the greater the potential to feel the rhythms of the Jewish year in its cyclical nature: seasons like these autumnal High Holidays of repair, mirrored in the spring freedom journey, will always come back around. Challenging linear notions of forward time and progress, the Jewish yearcycle invites us to move in a spiral, and move with the spirals of time flowing around us.

ALL TOGETHER NOW

The Yamim Noraim is both the best of times and the worst of times to get in front of a Jewish crowd, or to try to get a Jewish crowd together to do an action. On the one hand, many of us are gathered together already. On the other hand, many of us are already very busy preparing for the holidays. As organizers, when we work within the flow of the holidays, and lean into the specific spaces and shapes of our local communities, there are ample ways to create Jewishly meaningful political spaces. This can happen both by bringing our organizing to where the Jews already are gathered, and by gathering Jewishly in line with our political commitments and what each year calls for.

If you live in a community with synagogue or havurah that takes political action together, there might be a High Holiday planning team that is figuring out many days of programming, including study sessions on Yom Kippur afternoon, speaker series in the sukkah, or talks spread throughout the holiday. These teams will likely start planning in May or June; reach out to them early and pitch political education that you want to see in your community. Then, offer to organize it.

In this chapter, we journeyed through the most intensely packed month of the Jewish calendar, with the most synagogue-heavy observances of the year. For those who live in a community without a synagogue or havurah that is aligned with your politics and Jewish vision, who have been harmed by synagogue communities, or who just don't enjoy synagogue services, it can be extremely overwhelming to know how to access this month. At the same time we are told that it is somehow the *most* important time of year to be Jewish. Tishrei can be lonely.

In this chapter, we offered the traditions of Tishrei, as we will with the whole year, as our ancestors' collective gift to us; ours to open and explore whenever and however we desire it. The season will turn and the new year will be born, no matter how much of the traditional liturgy we say. If you are someone who longs for more Jewish community of practice in your place, there are very likely others with that same desire. This is a powerful time to create new spaces, invite each other to Jewish practice, try new things, and build new communal spaces. A meal, gathering for tashlich, a song or poetry circle with any melodies or words that move you, a discussion of harm and repair, a celebration of newness: this is all Tishrei. More important than what we do is how we do it: breaking the patterns of isolation that white supremacy and capitalism normalize, reweaving communities of connection and care.

Holy Breath,
let me catch mine
in the quiet that comes after
the deluge of song

Rain of Justice,
fill our mouths and rivers
with prayer and protest:
may all waters run free and clear
from the Cannonball River to the taps of Flint,
Michigan
from Gaza to the Ganges
from the River Jordan to the Mississippi delta

this month,
may our tears be a salt offering coursing toward the
altar of sea
may our breath be an air offering received by the
green ones as a hushed thank you
may our resting bodies be in deep conversation with
moss and stone

gathered under a canopy of stars
   may we lay down the rush, the urgency, the
   busyness
   even though we know what time it is
   even though there is so much to do
   even though it never feels like enough

please
lay us down, Sheltering Peace,
tuck us into the thickening dark
and let us rest

WELCOME TO חשון CHESHVAN

What happened for you and to you during the month of Tishrei? Where or when, and how, did you experience turning, returning, newness, change, or stagnation? What was unearthed that you want to bring forward into the rest of the year?

What practices feed your attention and awakeness every day? What practices do you want to try on this day, this week, this month, this year? What support will you get to cultivate awakeness, attention, and intention in your daily life?

Introduction to Cheshvan

Resting is a connection and a path back to our true nature.
We are stripped down to who we really were before the terror
of capitalism and white supremacy. We say no to the systems
that see us as simply machines. We resist the lie that we aren't
enough. We are enough! We are divine. Our bodies don't belong
to these toxic systems. We know better. Our Spirits know better.
—Tricia Heresy, *Rest Is Resistance*

Cheshvan is the month equivalent of weekly Shabbat and every seven years shmita,[1] and can be a time to intentionally practice rest. Within white supremacy and capitalism, rest can be an escape, or rest can be a generative, active part of the cycle of transformation. Artist and theologian Tricia Hersey, founder of the Nap Ministry, teaches that Rest Is Resistance, "deeply influenced by Black Liberation Theology, Womanism/Womanist Theology, Afro Futurism, Reparations Theory, Somatics and Community

123

Organizing."[2] In multiracial, anti-racist Jewish communities, we must be intentional about rest. We know that all people need and deserve rest. We also know that life in white supremacist capitalism puts consistent and specific burdens on People of Color in general, and Indigenous people and Black people specifically. We are working to create spaces and relationships where conversations about rest are regular and spacious, where power dynamics are named, and where support for rest can be offered and asked for without shame or fear. Let us create Cheshvan as a potential gateway, every year, for deep and renewing rest.

Cheshvan is our monthlong exhale. After all of the intense activity of Tishrei, Cheshvan is a month without rabbinic holidays, a time for spacious spiritual, emotional, and physical recovery. Like maintaining silence after a song to feel it resonate in the air and our bodies, Cheshvan is when we get to settle in and see in the stillness the results of the last month's activity and energy. We can literally and figuratively get our houses, minds, and hearts in order (the chaos of the season leaves little room for housekeeping!) and restock the cupboards, preserving, pickling, and putting up the food we harvested in Tishrei. We have the space and time to nurture the relationships that we hopefully gave attention to during the Elul-Tishrei teshuvah cycle.

Cheshvan is referred to as Marcheshvan in rabbinic texts.[3] The most common explanation is to translate this as "Bitter Cheshvan," a reference to the rabbis' sadness that they had no holidays this month, and mourning the deaths of biblical matriarchs Sarah and Rachel during the month. "Mar" can also be translated as "a drop of water," and understood as a reference to the upcoming reading of parashiyot Noah and the beginning of the rainy season in Eretz Yisrael. It's also possible that "Marcheshvan" is a holdover from the Akkadian names for the month, translating to the eighth month, counting from Nisan.

Rav Kohenet Jill Hammer cites 1 Cheshvan as Noah's birth,[4] based on when we read parshat Noah in the year cycle. A midrash[5] explains that before he was born, "people did not reap what they sowed. They would sow wheat and reap thorns and thistles, but when Noah was born, the world reverted to normal: Wheat was sown and wheat was reaped; barley was sown and barley was reaped." Noah's birth and the beginning of Cheshvan start a season of matching the labor we have to do to what we hope to harvest. There is a generative interplay between our sadness at saying goodbye to the frenetic energy of the High Holidays for another year and the openness of Cheshvan. We have the space to begin thinking about how to match our words with our deeds—how can we make good on the teshuvah we promised in Elul and Tishrei? By relaxing into Cheshvan we also have the opportunity to reap the benefits of space for a month of feelings to emerge. We take our time noticing what's uncovered.

In our organizing, we know it's important to not jump from action to action, campaign to campaign, without time for reflection and learning in between. Cheshvan gives us that time, and we aspire to open to it. Tishrei is: big sexy direct action energy. Cheshvan is: how did that go, what did we win, where do we go from here? And the sometimes unsexy work of implementation. In Tishrei we studied Indigenous land rights; in Cheshvan we figure out how to pay the land tax. In Tishrei we talked about transformative justice; in Cheshvan we discern who will be trained in accountability process facilitation. In Tishrei we made repair; in Cheshvan we try to embody change. Part of our political work is learning to live differently, and to do so when no one is watching. In Tishrei we beat on our hearts; in Cheshvan we try to keep our hearts open, every day. In Cheshvan we work to embody our intentions for the new year. In Tishrei we worked to create Jewish spaces that embody the world we want to see. In Cheshvan we ask, are there people who wanted to be there who couldn't make it in the door this year? Why? What did we do differently this year that we want to repeat? What else do we want to practice?

In contrast with the restful invitation of Cheshvan, but deeply resonant with the bitterness of the month, U.S. elections often fall during Cheshvan. Whatever our relationship to electoral organizing, the Jewish calendar in general, and this month in particular, offers us tools for staying afloat during the choppy waters of uncertainty, fear, and disappointment that pervade U.S. elections. Living in Jewish time helps us anchor in systems older than capitalism and collective organization older than nation-states. We know that elections are not the be-all and end-all of how transformation to more just systems and humane ways of living happens; we know we need new forms of governance where actual democracy can be practiced and people can have meaningful say in the material conditions of their lives. Coming out of the visionary power of Tishrei, Cheshvan offers us spaciousness to interact with elections as one of many tactics to bring people into deeper political engagement. Elections in this month must never be the end point of organizing, but a beginning. There is so much room to be and to grow in Cheshvan, and the year is still so fresh.

The autumn equinox traditionally lands in Cheshvan, layering one of our core ancestor stories onto this transition between seasons. According to Machzor Vitry, an eleventh-century High Holiday prayerbook, the Akedah (binding of Isaac) happened on the autumn equinox.[6] Rav Kohenet Jill Hammer brings a midrash and connection to this season[7]: the Torah describes that following the Akedah, Abraham returns home without a mention of Isaac.[8] Midrash Rabbah[9] offers an explanation for where Isaac went, saying that he descends the mountain after this profound moment of violence and trauma, and instead of going home, heads to the yeshiva of Shem and Ever, Noah's son and grandson. This midrash is delightfully anachronistic: what were they studying at this yeshiva long before Torah would be given at Sinai? It also speaks to the redemptive power of taking space to heal from trauma. Placing this story on the equinox, in Cheshvan, points us toward the power of this month for rest.

The parashiyot of Cheshvan are Noach, Lech Lecha, Vayera, Chayyei Sarah, and Toldot. Cheshvan comes like a release in so many ways, with space to process all that Tishrei brought. The narratives at the beginning of Beresheet that we read this month are easier to follow but bring deep ethical challenges: the destruction of the world and its recreation with Noah's ark, the dissolution of connection at the Tower of Babel, the creation of the Jewish people with Abraham and Sarah and the violence against Hagar and Ishmael, the covenant and the near-sacrifice of Isaac, visiting angels and Sodom and Ammorah. Newly reinvigorated to reflect on our behaviors and relationships, we dig in to the parashiyot of Cheshvan to consider just action and right relationship in practice.

Cheshvan in Practice

SIGD

As Cheshvan comes to a close, Ethiopian Jews celebrate Sigd. Coming fifty days after Yom Kippur, on the twenty-ninth of Cheshvan, Sigd means "prostration" or "supplication" in the ancient liturgical language Ge'ez. The celebration marks Moses' coming down from communing with God on Sinai. Traditionally, Sigd is marked by ascending to mountaintops, praying, and reading Torah. Sigd is a fast day that ends with a collective feast.

Sigd goes unmentioned in many Jewish yearcycle books and resources, and unknown in many Jewish communities. For those raised and acculturated primarily in Ashkenazi and/or Rabbinic Judaism, this can be a time to learn Ethiopian Jewish culture and history, without tokenizing or appropriating it.

COLLECTIVE CHESHVAN REFLECTION

As the bridge from the intensity of summer activity and the High Holiday cycle into the winter season, Cheshvan offers us an opportunity to take a breath and survey how far we've journeyed. This month invites us to process the teshuvah work we did interpersonally and communally, and to deepen in the learning we engaged in, our commitment to resolutions we made, and our understanding of encounters with the Divine. We can do this individually, and also collectively in our Jewish communities and political organizations: Whose needs were met in the year that passed, and Tishrei in particular, and whose were not? Who was elevated in leadership, and who was missing? Who do you want to center in the year ahead?

Cheshvan is a reminder that we cannot last long when we string high-intensity moments together. Pausing to reflect is a fundamental part of the rhythm. Often in our organizing, we might feel pressure to jump to the next task and work to make it bigger, flashier, and better than the last. The high drama of the High Holy Day season in our spirits and communities might compel us to think "how do we keep getting those butts in seats?," "How do we keep mobilizing donation dollars?," or "How do we keep this level of volunteer and organizer engagement going all year?" Cheshvan teaches that learning and reflecting are fundamental to responsible organizing. Jumping from campaign to campaign without time to pause, breathe, care for one another, and process is ableist white supremacy culture in action.

On the other hand, it is important to ensure that our learning and processing is in the service of self and community care, not a means to

CHESHVAN

avoid showing up and doing the work. We strive to turn resolutions into actions, lest we return to Tishrei each year making the same commitments without movement. The Rambam teaches that teshuvah is only complete when we have an opportunity to do the same harm again, but choose not to.[10] For the harm caused by action and inaction alike, it is critical to both reflect and mobilize.

How do we hold these tensions, if either making space to deepen or making time to mobilize feels unfamiliar? We make space to reflect, and for accountable action planning; we cannot have one without the other. This is how Cheshvan becomes the bridge from Tishrei to the rest of the year.

In your community, congregation, and collectives, make time to reflect: What conversations moved you? What dreams emerged for your year? What commitments did you make? What learning do you want to do together in the year to come?

Make plans to act:

What political commitments were clarified during Tishrei, or the year that passed? What learning do you want to do in the coming months? Who are the teachers in your communities from whom you can learn? What is already happening around you in this work that you can support and follow? What are you being called to do? What support will you need to do this?

We can expand the restful reflection of Cheshvan into all aspects of our lives. Gather your collective and make a six-month plan to learn together and show up together. Sit down with your house- and lifemates and make a budget that allows you to spend money in a more values-aligned way. Talk with a therapist or healer about focusing energy on yourself in the year ahead. Get support in the often arduous task of find a trusted therapist or healer. Ask a friend or comrade to be an accountabilibuddy for the year, a chevruta for the ongoing questions and struggles.

Above all, in Cheshvan, we let the time be, and let be.

light me up,
Eternal Flame,
and let me burn bright hot
sparks dancing in the eyes of my lovers
and comrades

fire, fists, heels, bricks,
chants, spells, seed bombs, bodies:
we throw everything we've got
at forces of domination
at border walls and prisons
at armies of occupation

but tonight, we play
tonight, we are all gold honey and oil
tonight, we sing in the velvet dark
tonight, we tuck dreams into the pockets of our
hearts
tonight, we kiss by the light made by bees and
radical Jews
tonight, we place our candles in the window as
radiant defiance
 tonight, we sneak into the army camp and heads
  will roll!
    tonight, we burn it down!

    every day we make these miracles with each
    other

what is a miracle
if not this:
resistance and love,
kindling in your hands

 # WELCOME TO כסלו KISLEV

What does resistance to injustice look like in your life? What do you need in order to strengthen your resistance muscles? In what spaces do you feel powerful?

What has been the role of assimilation in your Jewish life? How does it impact you today? What does resistance to assimilation that supports feminist, anti-racist, anti-nationalist values look like?

Where do you find hope? What practices, people, art, music, and spaces cultivate hope? What kind of time and space allows you to dream?

What do you want to let go of as the days get shorter? What do you want to invite in as the nights get longer?

Introduction to Kislev

לפי שראה אדם הראשון יום שמתמעט והולך אמר אוי לי שמא בשביל
שסרחתי עולם חשוך בעדי וחוזר לתוהו ובוהו וזו היא מיתה שנק־
נסה עלי מן השמים עמד וישב ח' ימים בתענית [ובתפלה] כיון שראה
תקופת טבת וראה יום שמאריך והולך אמר מנהגו של עולם הוא
הלך ועשה שמונה ימים טובים לשנה האחרת עשאן לאלו ולאלו ימים
טובים הוא קבעם לשם שמים והם קבעום לשם עבודת כוכבים

When Adam the first man saw that the day was progressively diminishing, he said: Woe is me; perhaps because I sinned the world is becoming dark around me and will ultimately return to chaos and disorder. And this is the death that was sentenced upon me from Heaven, as it is written: "And to dust shall you return" (Beresheet 3:19). He arose and spent eight days in fasting and in prayer. Once he saw that the season of Tevet, i.e., the winter solstice, had arrived, and saw that the day was progressively lengthening after the solstice, he said: Clearly, the days become shorter and then longer, and this is the order of the world. He went and observed a festival for eight days. Upon the next year, he observed both these eight days on which he had fasted on the previous year, and these eight days of his celebration, as days of festivities. He, Adam, established these festivals for the sake of Heaven, but they, the gentiles of later generations, established them for the sake of idol worship.

—Avodah Zarah 8b

After the restful retreat of Cheshvan, Kislev is a journeying month. For those of us in the Northern Hemisphere, Kislev lights the path forward into the darkness of winter. Kislev teaches about darkness and light, how they are both necessary and illuminate each other.

Kislev is a month in which we work to unlearn the white supremacist culture that says that darkness is something to be feared. In hegemonic Christianity, darkness and blackness are associated with sin and negativity. As Jews, we have our own specific inheritance to unpack around darkness and night. In the above Gemara, Adam ha'Rishon (the first human) navigates the first winter. In this story, Adam at first fears the night, experiencing the long nights as punishment. Yet, this fear is portrayed as uninformed, a childlike response to never having experienced winter before. Once he observes the days getting longer, he learns not only not to fear the winter and long nights but to celebrate them with a festival. "This is the order of the world," with its contrasts and seasons. The winter, the nights, the darkness are meant to be, are necessary, are a gift from the Divine. Our earliest ancestors and storytellers marked the solstice. For those who long for a Jewish practice that comes close to the rhythm of the seasons, Kislev and Channukah are robust invitations.

Kislev is understood as a powerful month for dreaming. Longer nights, with hopefully more sleep, give our unconscious a larger canvas on which to paint. Most of the Torah portions that reference dreams, and the power of dreams as divine conduit, are read in Kislev—nine out of ten. This interplay between the Torah and the season is an invitation to notice our dreams, and to dream with intentionality. As we tunnel deeper into winter, as we slow down and bundle up in the Northern Hemisphere, Kislev can be a time to send up sparks of imagination. The fall was for harvesting, and now, the winter is a time to draw sustenance from the abundance of our emotional and physical, individual and collective storerooms, to dream and to scheme.

The symbol of this month's mazal, star sign, is Sagittarius, the constellation of the bow. Keshet is the Hebrew word for bow (and arrow) as well as rainbow. The rainbow is the symbol of the covenant between God and Noah, the promise of the continuation of the generations, the protection of the world as long as it abides. In Kislev we honor generations of queer ancestors with the promise of the rainbow and reading the stories of Joseph. We locate ourselves in a chain of transmission from the generations, and our responsibility to the earth as long as it abides.

The spirit of Channukah, a celebration of resistance and miracles, permeates Kislev. In this way, Kislev becomes a month not only about individual dreams and finding our singular light in the darkness. It is also a month of collective dreaming, collective candle lighting, and the victories that are possible from persisting to find each other in the dark. In Kislev, we feed each other foods full of fat, a beautifully Jewish love language.[1]

In Kislev, as much as any other month of the year, it is easy to feel the intrusion of the Christian calendar. Christmas music is all around; Christmas and the Gregorian New Year, and their accompanying baggage must be navigated, with the decision of what to reply to "Merry Christmas" and "Happy holidays!" when, in some years, Channukah ended weeks before. There are as many relationships to the presence of Christmas as there are Jews under the sun and moon: for some it is joyful, familial, restful, and a part of our multifaith family celebrations. For others it is fraught, annoying, painful, and depressing. For most of us it is a mix. As a mixed multitude of Jews coming from and living in many civilizations, the essential practice for navigating this time is to hold the true diversity of experiences with and relationships to this season. Our communities, lovingly built and tended with care, can hold all of the complex energy and emotion of Kislev, and, in this season of physical hibernation, we can spiritually expand. We can create Kislev as a month that, as the nights lengthen, makes space for song, connection, and magic.

The parashiyot of Kislev are Vayetzei, Vayishlach, Vayeshev, and Miketz. We follow the continued growth of the Jewish family, the second generation of covenanted relationship with HaShem. This month we see family dysfunction continue, yearning for connection in so many forms—parental approval, romantic partnership, peace between siblings, conception, affirmation from family, and healing in family after violence. Amidst all this tumult is the presence of dreaming, the force that connects humans to the Divine and gives them insights to navigate earthly relationships. As winter looms larger in the Northern Hemisphere, Kislev invites us to reach toward the gifts of dreaming—to have imagination and inspiration to break out of hopelessness, cycles of cruelty, and generational harm.

Kislev in Practice

CHANNUKAH

The literal highlight of Kislev, Channukah is a holiday with more complexity than is immediately apparent as we eat fried foods and light candles. We read the origin story of Channukah in the two Books of Maccabees, which are part of the Apocrypha: books that were considered part of the biblical canon by the Jews of Alexandria during the Second Temple period, but that were not included in the Tanakh as it currently exists.

The Book of Maccabees takes place during Greek rule in Jerusalem, during the Second Temple period. Greek king Antiochus Epiphanes made Jewish rituals illegal and instituted worship of Greek gods, a process known as Hellenization. At the time, the Jewish community was split, with many people assimilating into Greek culture, and others violently resisting. In 169 BCE, Mattathias, an elderly kohen, killed a Jew who was preparing to ritually slaughter a pig. He and his five sons fled to live then the hills and organized resistance to Greek rule. In 164 BCE, this group, known as the Maccabees, retook Jerusalem. Seemingly because they could not celebrate Sukkot on time, they marked an eight-day festival beginning on the twenty-fifth of Kislev. They installed themselves as rulers; the son of the last surviving Maccabee brother, John Hyrcanus, established the Hasmonean dynasty.

The Hasmonean dynasty, which survived until 37 BCE, has a fraught legacy in Jewish history, and we as leftists would be well served to wrestle with it, and to complicate our Channukah celebrations. The establishment of a non-Davidic kingship in Judea was seen as illegitimate by the rabbis; fighting between two of the Hasmonean descendants over the kingship is what is often seen as opening the door to Roman rule. The Maccabees were anti-assimilationists who violently dictated what other Jews should and shouldn't do. As progressive Jews, many of us struggle with a holiday celebrating people who were killing Jews that, in their time, were a lot like us. So did the rabbis. Channukah is one of the only festivals that is not mentioned in the Mishnah, the earliest layer of the Talmud. There is no rabbinic exploration of Channukah until the Gemara, which is where, in Shabbat 21b, the story of the miracle of the oil is found. The telling of Channukah in the Gemara includes only the briefest mention of the Hasmonean dynasty established by the Maccabees, and focuses on Channukah as a springboard for Hallel.

Rabbi Arthur Waskow hypothesizes:

> The rabbis were not happy with the Maccabean approach to Jewish life. They were writing in the period when similar revolts against Rome, seeking to win the Jews' political independence, to turn Judea into a rocky fortress, and to toughen the Jewish people had been systematically and brutally smashed by the iron fist of Rome.[2]

Out of this discomfort with the military thrust of the Maccabee story, the rabbis transitioned Channukah into a spiritual holiday focused on God's power and people's faith and dedication. To drive home this message, the haftorah we read on Shabbat Channukah is Zechariah 2:14–4:7, where we read in Zechariah 4:6:

. . . זֶה דְּבַר־יהוה אֶל־זְרֻבָּבֶל לֵאמֹר לֹא בְחַיִל וְלֹא בְכֹחַ כִּי אִם־בְּרוּחִי אָמַר
יהוה צְבָאוֹת:

> This is the word of Hashem to Zerubbabel: Not by might, nor by power, but by My spirit—said HaShem of Hosts.

Today, Channukah is an opportunity to reflect on the nuanced political struggles of our time, refracted through the centuries-old resistance movements of our ancestors. Alongside the resonances of light and dark, solstice magic, and deep winter nights, we wrestle with the complexities of our histories. Assimilation, conflicting Jewish responses to empire, collaboration with those in power, violence and uprising, nationalism and diaspora; all are questions raised by the story, history, and layers of observance of Channukah. Through eight days and nights, we have space during Channukah for the multitude of meanings. Channukah is sturdy enough for us to include acknowledgment of likely Maccabean ancestral disapproval of all the ways we're observing it and living in our celebrations. At times we can even delight in the irony of Channukah being one of the most resilient holidays of the yearcycle, extremely compatible with assimilation in our contexts. This is the power of being part of a living tradition.

FOOD

Channukah food uplifts two key symbols of the Channukah story: oil and dairy. Fried foods honor the rabbinic miracle of one day's kosher oil lasting for eight days. Dairy food honors the strategy of Judith, who seduced the Assyrian general Holofernes with dairy food and wine before murdering him, leading to the Maccabees' victory over the invading army. While potato latkes, bimuelos, sufganiyot, and dosa are some of the popular foods, anything fried in oil is a festive treat. Try a deep fryer party, where one person provides the hot oil, and everyone brings something to fry. Sephardic cassola (sweet cheese pancakes) or Ashkenazi cheese blintzes (crepes stuffed with farmer's cheese) bring it all together.

DREIDEL

The dreidel (Yiddish), or sivivon (Hebrew from the word "spin"), is a spinning top with the letters נ (nun), ג (gimel), ה (hey), ש (shin), or פ (pey) on the four sides. The letters can stand for נֵס גָּדוֹל הָיָה שָׁם, nes gadol hayah sham, "a great miracle happened there," or nes gadol hayah po, נֵס גָּדוֹל הָיָה פּוֹ "a great miracle happned here." Dreidels printed in diaspora say שָׁם, sham, there, whereas dreidels printed in Israel say פּוֹ, po, here. In

Yiddish, before the letters told a story of Hannukah, the dreidel was a list of instructions for how to play the game: nun for נישט (nisht, "not," meaning "nothing"), gimel for גאַנץ (gants, "entire, whole"), hei for האַלב (halb, "half"), and shin for שטעל אַרײַן (shtel arayn, "put in.")

A common folk story about why we play with the dreidel on Channukah is as a cover for the Jews studying Torah in Greek-controlled land. When the Greek guards would come to make sure no one was studying Torah, the Jews would hide their scrolls and pull out dreidels and coins, claiming, "No studying here! We're just gambling." Another explanation says that the total numerical value for the letters on a נגהש dreidel equals 358, the same number as the word Messiah.[3] Or, the four letters represent kingdoms that tried to exterminate the Jews. In reality, the dreidel game existed as early as 1500 in England, with four letters on the sides indicating the rules of how much to take out or put into the "pot." The chocolate coins, called gelt, Yiddish for money, are delicious. Some people play with real gelt, too.

LITURGY

The liturgy for Channukah includes the addition of Al HaNisim (On the Miracles), which is recited on Channukah and Purim, during the Amidah during the three daily prayer services, and after Birkat haMazon (the prayer after a meal). The version for Channukah describes the miracles of the military victory, not the oil. Rabbi Elisha Friedman teaches that this is purposeful, in that our daily prayer practice asks us to notice the mundane miracles of life, rather than just the supernatural. The prayer provides an opportunity to grapple with the violence of war, alongside gratitude for surviving conquest.

In addition to the Al HaNisim addition to the Amidah, a full Hallel is recited every day (see Sukkot Liturgy on page 113 to read more about Hallel). The Torah is read every day of Channukah, from Bamidbar 7:1–8:4, describing the consecration of the Temple and the offerings brought there by various tribal leaders. No doubt this reading was selected because of the desecration of the Temple and its subsequent rededication in the Channukah story.

The lighting of the Channukiah happens at home,[4] and the following blessings are recited:

בָּרוּךְ אַתָּה יְיָ אֱלֹהֵינוּ מֶלֶךְ הָעוֹלָם, אֲשֶׁר קִדְּשָׁנוּ בְּמִצְוֹתָיו וְצִוָּנוּ לְהַדְלִיק נֵר שֶׁל חֲנֻכָּה.

Baruch atah Adonai, Eloheinu Melech ha'olam, asher kid'shanu b'mitzvotav v'tzivanu l'hadlik ner shel Hanukkah.

Praised are You, Our God, Light Bringer of the universe, Who made us holy through Your commandments and commanded us to kindle the Hanukah lights.

בָּרוּךְ אַתָּה יְיָ אֱלֹהֵינוּ מֶלֶךְ הָעוֹלָם, שֶׁעָשָׂה נִסִּים לַאֲבוֹתֵינוּ וְאִמּוֹתֵינוּ בַּיָּמִים הָהֵם בַּזְּמַן הַזֶּה.

Baruch atah Adonai, Eloheinu Melech ha'olam, she-asah nisim la'avoteinu bayamim hahem bazman hazeh.

Praised are You, Our God, Source of the universe, Who performed wondrous deeds for our ancestors in those ancient days at this season.

On the first night only:

בָּרוּךְ אַתָּה יְיָ אֱלֹהֵינוּ מֶלֶךְ הָעוֹלָם, שֶׁהֶחֱיָנוּ וְקִיְּמָנוּ וְהִגִּיעָנוּ לַזְּמַן הַזֶּה.

Baruch atah Adonai, Elohenu Melech ha'olam, Shehecheyanu, v'kiyimanu, v'higiyanu la'zman hazeh.

Praised are You, Our God, Miracle of the universe, Who has given us life and sustained us and enabled us to reach this season.

LIGHTING

A Channukiyah is a candelabra that holds nine lights,[5] one for each night of Channukah plus the shammash, the "helper" candle. The shammash is lit first, and used to light the other candles, as it is taught in the Gemara: "Rava said: One must kindle another light in addition to the Hanukkah lights in order to use its light"[6]

As with most things, there is a debate in the Gemara about how to light: Should the Channukiah start filled with all eight candles, with one being removed each night? Or should a candle be added each night?

אָמַר עוּלָּא: פְּלִיגִי בַּהּ תְּרֵי אָמוֹרָאֵי בְּמַעְרְבָא, רַבִּי יוֹסֵי בַּר אָבִין וְרַבִּי יוֹסֵי בַּר זְבִידָא. חַד אָמַר טַעְמָא דְּבֵית שַׁמַּאי כְּנֶגֶד יָמִים הַנִּכְנָסִין, וְטַעְמָא דְּבֵית הִלֵּל כְּנֶגֶד יָמִים הַיּוֹצְאִין. וְחַד אָמַר טַעְמָא דְּבֵית שַׁמַּאי כְּנֶגֶד פָּרֵי הֶחָג, וְטַעְמָא דְּבֵית הִלֵּל דְּמַעֲלִין בַּקֹּדֶשׁ וְאֵין מוֹרִידִין.

Ulla said: There were two amora'im in the West, who disagreed with regard to this dispute, Rabbi Yosei bar Avin and Rabbi Yosei bar Zevida. One said that the reason for Beit Shammai's opinion is that the number of lights corresponds to the incoming days. The reason for Beit Hillel's opinion is that the number of lights corresponds to the outgoing days. And one said that the reason for Beit Shammai's opinion is that the number of lights corresponds to the bulls of the festival of Sukkot: Thirteen were sacrificed on the first day and each succeeding day one fewer was sacrificed. The reason for Beit Hillel's opinion is that the number of lights is based on the principle: One elevates to a higher level in matters of sanctity and one does not downgrade.

The prevailing decision to add a candle each night came from Rabbi Hillel, who said the candles in the Channukiah represent the number of each day, as well as from an elder who taught that one does not "downgrade" in matters of sanctity.[7] Jewish tradition preserves the minority opinion, and some households now side with Rabbi Shammai, who gave the contrary opinion, light the Channukiah with the most candles on the first day and count down to one.

Oil Channukiyot are a beautiful and classic style, with wicks laid in the small vessels or cups for each night. Channukiyot can be DIY'd (like all Judaica!) with eight places to put candles (or eight tea lights) and a ninth candle, the shammash, a little taller.

One should place the Channukiah in the window, in order to observe the mitzvah of pirsumei hanes, "publicizing the miracle."[8] The iconic image of a Channukiyah in a window with a Nazi flag in the background calls to mind the mitzvah, and the danger alluded to in the Gemara. The picture was taken by Rachel Posner in Kiel, Germany, in 1932, a month before Hitler rose to power. Her husband, Rabbi Dr. Akiva Posner, was the last rabbi of Kiel. On the back of the picture, she wrote in German:

Chanukah 5692
(1932)
"Death to Judah"
So the flag says
"Judah will live forever"
So the light answers[9]

Despite the complexities of the holiday, Channukiah is a symbol of hope in the long, cold nights of winter, a sign of bravery, and an illumination of a history of miracles wrought by God and humans acting in divine ways. Placing a Channukiyah in the window is a symbol of resilience and pride.

KWANZAKKAH

In 5780/2019, Black Yids Matter (BYM), a national organizing project of Black Jews, released a guide for celebrating Kwanzakkah, created by Shoshana Brown, Jess Valoris, Leah King, Dr. Tarece Johnson, Megan Madison, Graie Hagans, Kyle Rocco, Autumn Leonard, and Rachel Faulkner, and edited by Erica Walker. Kwanzakkah is "a holiday integrating rituals and values of Kwanzaa and Hanukkah." Rereleased by the Black Liberation Collective in 5781, Kwanzakkah invites Black Jews to light the kinara[10] next to the Channukiyah, pour libations and ask for blessings of unity, tell stories, sing songs, and cook African soul fried rice and green slaw with Dijon dressing.

Kohenet Shoshana Akua Brown writes:

For us, Kwanzakkah is the not-so-secret note to all young Black Jews to remind them of COMMUNITY. It's meant to inspire

COURAGE to continue boldly stepping into the world as their full selves, unapologetically. I'd like to imagine this Kwanzakkah guide as a love letter to my younger self: everything I wanted and dreamed of and knew could exist—because if I was dreaming this up by myself, others must also be having this same dream.[11]

SINGING

Following the lighting of the Channukiyah, we sing special songs. "Hanei-rot Halalu," reminds us of the miracles and prohibition against doing anything but gazing upon the light and remembering. "Maoz Tzur" ("Rock of Ages,") blesses God's saving power and great miracles.

Many other songs have been composed to celebrate the holiday, like the Yiddish "Drey Dreidel" composed by Moyshe Oysher, Flory Jagoda's "Ocho Kandelikas," "Hanuka Dance" by Woody Guthrie, "8 Nights of Hannukah" by Sharon Jones and the Dap Kings, "I Had a Little Dreidel," written by Samuel E. Goldfarb, and, most recently, "Puppy for Hannukah" by Daveed Diggs. There are many silly and sweet songs because the festival is a celebration of miracles and light, but, perhaps, also there is a prevalence of Hannukah music because of the efforts to elevate Hannukah to a status of greater importance than it merits religiously.

HOW MANY Ns? Ks? Hs?

There are countless ways to spell the name of the Festival of Lights in English. Each transliteration of the Hebrew חֲנֻכָּה follows different rules, and there is no wrong way to do it. Hanukah, Channukah, Chanukkah, Chanuka, Chanike (Yiddish), Hanuká (Ladino), or even Rabbi Lynn Gottleib's Hanooka. Be as consistent, or inconsistent, as you like!

THE "DECEMBER DILEMMA"

In the United States, Channukah is often assumed by the secular, aka Christian, world to be the most important Jewish holiday. Silver and blue decorations hang next to (or on) company Christmas trees, Channuki-yot are displayed next to public Christmas displays, and ugly Channukah sweaters are now popular at big box stores. Christian hegemony uplifted Channukah out of the desire to create a Jewish equivalent to Christmas at the same time of year, without having to learn anything about Judaism. The Channukiyah quite literally becomes a prop for Christmas celebrations.

This has also transformed how Jews celebrate Channukah. Gifts used to be exchanged at Purim, but in the nineteenth century gift giving shifted to Channukah so that it would be more like Christmas. Dreidel is also a popular game played at Christmas, appearing as early as the sixteenth century. And if the public display was accurate to the story, it would be a diorama of an Aron HaKodesh, holy ark where the Torah is stored, or a miniature campus of the Second Temple, not a Channukah menorah.

While there can be power in the visibility of Channukah being respected in Christian hegemonic culture, at times we chafe against and resist randomly attaching Channukah to things to make them "interfaith" or "multifaith." As little as is known about Channukah and Judaism by non-Jews, there are many other religious and spiritual traditions that respond to the season where night gets longer with light kindling activities, like Diwali and the Solstice, that are even less visible and understood.

According to 2013 research, 72 percent of Jewish families that are non-Orthodox are multifaith.[12] The elevation of Channukah because it is at the same time of year as Christmas can be an incredibly sweet opportunity to celebrate multiple family traditions at the same time. When Channukah and Christmas overlap, multifaith families can light the Channukiah in the glow of the lights of a Christmas tree. Chosen family may make latkes in the glow of an Advent wreath. Like the classic 1996 holiday song dreams,

> Finding faith and common ground the best that they were able,
> Lighting trees in darkness, learning new ways from the old, and
> Making sense of history and drawing warmth out of the cold.[13]

The institutional Jewish world is terrified of this, fearful that being near Christmas or in-family with Christians endangers the Jewish future. That is not true. Making people feel guilty about who they love and how they blend traditions is a sure path to disengagement and alienation, much more than any half-baked program about a "December dilemma."

Individual connection and meaning-making is something Jews and the people who love us have been doing for as long as there have been Israelites schlepping around the desert. It is the disproportionate societal uplift of Channukah above all other Jewish holidays that erases the reality of its religious significance, and shoehorns a Jewish holiday into a Christian mold. Whether one is waging a war on Christmas or reveling in all the light the season can offer, Channukah, like every Jewish holiday, is as meaningful and powerful as we make it.

PUBLIC CHANNUKAH ACTION

Channukah *is* collective action. As a holiday centered around organized struggle and resistance, Channukah calls us together. As with every Jewish holiday, Channukah can take place in the streets to broadcast our voices and amplify our campaigns, or we can create home-based and inward-facing containers for community connection and weaving. With eight nights, we can take our time with Channukah, and organize different gatherings to support different important formations in our lives, spending some nights at home, some nights with comrades, some nights in the streets.

Public Channukah actions have so much to offer in terms of visual language. This is, for better or worse, the most recognizable holiday to non-Jews, but that means that a giant cardboard menorah immediately communicates that we are creating Jewish space (unlike, for instance, during Sukkot). Organizers have taken advantage of this to create powerful public actions. The ritual shape of eight nights, with a candle for each night, provides a scaffolding on which to move through different ideas, concepts, and dedications.

In 5775/2014, Channukah fell soon after grand juries failed to indict Darren Wilson and Daniel Pantaleo, white cops who murdered Michael Brown in Ferguson and Eric Garner in New York. As part of national uprisings and resistance, a group of Jews created 8 Nights, 8 Actions: A Channukah Dedicated to the Spirit of Resistance and the Movement to End Police Violence.[14] For each night, there was a different spiritual dedication and invitation to action, in line with demands from Black-led Fer-

KISLEV

guson Action, and resonating with the themes of Channukah. Each night, a Black person killed by the police was honored.

> 1st Night: Public Observance ~ We remember Michael Brown
> 2nd Night: Generate Light ~ We remember Yvette Smith
> 3rd Night: Not by Might ~ We remember Aiyana Mo'Nay Stanley Jones
> 4th Night: Kindling Hope ~ We remember Rekia Boyd
> 5th Night: Give Gelt ~ We remember Tamir Rice
> 6th Night: In Our Times ~ We remember Tarika Wilson
> 7th Night: Fuel the Fire ~ We remember Dante Parker
> 8th Night: Dedication ~ We remember Eric Garner

Jewish Voice for Peace's 5776/2015 Chanukkah Ritual Companion offers "eight Channukah gifts, one for each night, eight little sparks of renewal to help sustain us for the long road. We might wish to reflect on these, either in our own hearts, with our family and friends, or in actions in the streets—while our faces are reflecting the lights of the Hanukkiah."[5]

> 1st Night: Not by Might, Not by Power, but by Spirit
> 2nd Night: Religious Freedom
> 3rd Night: Sacred Joy
> 4th Night: Celebrating Light and Dark
> 5th Night: Abundance
> 6th Night: Being open to Change
> 7th Night: Steadfastness/Sumoud
> 8th Night: Honoring our Ancestors

During Channukah 5777/2016, in the wake of Trump's election, JVP's Network Against Islamophobia organized public actions in twenty-six cities, holding public commitments to fighting Islamophobia, anti-Arab racism, and white supremacy. Their stance: "We refuse to be silent about anti-Muslim and racist hate speech and hate crimes. We condemn state surveillance of the Muslim community. We fight anti-Muslim profiling and racial profiling in all its forms. We call for an end to racist policing. We protest the use of Islamophobia and anti-Arab racism to justify Israel's repressive policies against Palestinians."[16]

With eight nights, candles can be lit in the streets one night, in the intimacy of our living rooms with beloveds the next night, and at a raucous party the night after that. Channukah is powerfully accessible: It is the holiday, along with Pesach, that many Jews have enough basic knowledge of to feel comfortable with and included in. With a few candles and a few blessings we can transform a winter night into a magical space of connection and miracles.

Living in at least two calendars, Jews know the end of the Gregorian year is coming when Channukah arrives. It is a great time to bring your core team or organizing collective together to reflect on and celebrate the year. The eight nights and the theme of rededication create space to articulate individual and collective visions of the year to come. Bringing together the people you organize with in the weeds every week, and the people from other formations who you usually only see at actions, can knit the fabric of our movements closer together. This strengthens our ability to show up for each other all year round.

Preparing for winter and the time of inward-turning in the Northern Hemisphere makes Channukah, and all of Kislev, a time to find each other and ask about each other's needs, reminding ourselves who we can call on when the cold comes and the nights lengthen. Just as it feels like time to hunker down and hole up, Channukah calls us out to come closer to each other. Channukah is an occasion to ask each other what is needed to survive the winter. Kislev is a month to dream of, and embody, our thriving.

LANDBACK

deep calls to deep
dark calls to dark
all of creation echoes:
Blackness is Beloved

on the longest night
leviathan rises from the salty depths
a monstrous roar
restoring balance in the sea

rise up in us, Holy Anger,
let our rage ripple and wave
a collective tsunami
furiously washing the world into mutual flourishing

we wait in the dark,
so let the waiting be the thing itself

we are made of stars and sea,
so let us swim in the relief of being mystery

Ocean of Becoming,
        Luminous Darkness,
            G!d of Sacred Monsters,
let us remember how before we became people of the book
        we were people of the moon

WELCOME TO טבת TEVET

How will you bring the light you created in Channukah forward into the next month? The rest of winter? Your year?

What creates a cocoon for you? What aspects of yourself emerge when you feel most sheltered and protected? What will you do to nurture, feed, and warm yourself, your loved ones, and your communities this season?

Many of us organize in campaign and movement cycles that both have times of action and times of rest, and yet fight against the cycles of the season and try to override earth's time of rest. What rest does your movement need? What reset do your collective and your comrades need? What practices of pause, reflect, and reset can you try on this Tevet?

Introduction to Tevet

Soils are the most biologically diverse places on earth. Three quarters of our planet is covered with a layer of sea water, two miles in depth. Providing a deep dark habitat to the greatest number of organisms on Earth, and the blackness of night is one of the most important influences on the biological world.

Artificial light at night disrupts the livelihoods of nocturnal species, confuses our circadian rhythms, plays havoc with sea turtle navigation, alters how insects pollinate and animals reproduce, interrupts our sleep patterns, and is downright bad for our health—just like white supremacy.

So love your Blackness, respect your shadow, tend to your womb and gut and blood and bones. Even more than your skin and what we can see. Let your eyes adjust to the dark. Therein

lies the miracle of starlight, of fireflies, of bioluminescent firefly on
a moon-dappled night in the moist oak woods.

How can you protect the Blackness within and around you?

How do you value darkness? What makes it possible?

—Naima Penniman, "Concentric Memory: Re-membering
Our Way Into the Future," *A Darker Wilderness*

Tevet moves fully into the depths of winter in the Northern Hemisphere. The celebrations of Tevet fall at the beginning of the month, while the end of the month is filled with the quiet that winter brings. Opening with the festival of Chag ha'Banot, the first two days of the month are illuminated by the shining Channukiah: the gift of light and warmth as we move into the long nights ahead. Some years Channukah ends before the winter solstice, while in others it happens very close to it. In the classic midrash about Adam ha'Rishon that we learned last month, it is in Tevet that Adam saw the days growing longer and light returning. His fears that the world was ending because the nights had been growing longer were assuaged. In our lifetime, we know the fear of the world's imminent ending being upon us. Tevet gives us the seasonal embodied practice of the words' endless cycles. The light will return, whether or not we're here to see it.

On the first of this month, Noah, Na'amah,[1] and their children see the peaks of mountains from inside their floating ark and celebrate their relief that the waters are beginning to recede, even if it will be months before they will disembark the ark.[2] They offer sacrifices and nourish the glimmer of hope that we tend in the depth of winter.

In Tevet, there is movement toward comfort with each other, and with Torah. In Megillat Esther, Esther is taken to King Achashverus's palace in the month of Tevet.[3] Rashi explains that this is in the cold season, "when one body enjoys [the warmth of] another body." B. Megillah 13a explains that the Holy One of Blessing "designated that cold season in order to endear her to him."

A story about Hillel the Elder tells of a time, one Friday in Tevet, that he did not have enough money to enter the study hall. He climbed onto the roof to hear the Torah being taught inside. A snowstorm came and covered Hillel in three cubits of snow. The next morning, the beit midrash was still dark. The great teachers realized a frozen Hillel was on the skylight, brought him in, and cared for his frostbite. They claimed that this proves that poverty is no excuse for the failure to attempt to study Torah.[4] We read this story as a reminder that economic structures that keep people out of batei midrash must be dismantled. In the cold of Tevet, we are called to share resources so no one is, literally, out in the cold, and to organize for safe housing, and access to Torah, for all.

This month is not all peaceful. Tevet carries with it deep pain that we mark with a fast on the tenth of Tevet. The tenth of Tevet commemorates the breaching of the walls of the First and Second Temples, and, in the days prior to it, the forced translation of the Torah into Greek, and the death of the great Ezra the Scribe who brought Torah back to the people. This month is replete with feelings of being exposed, disconnected, and vulnerable. The winter season calls on us to bundle up, nourish ourselves and each other with root veggies and thick soups, and share resources to make it through this often isolating time.

The parashiyot of Tevet are Vayigash, Vayechi, Shemot, and Vaera, which complete the story cycle of Joseph and his brothers and bring the people from Canaan into Mitzrayim. We begin the book of Shemot this month, the enslavement of the Jewish people, and the beginning of the Exodus story starting with some of the plagues. In one month of parashiyot our ancestors become climate refugees, then are enslaved, and then are redeemed from slavery. How powerful that this descent and ascent happens in only one month, that the most embittered moments of the Torah are contained and do not bleed over into another month. Another prophetic text written to help humans survive environmental disaster and human cruelty is the medicine written by Octavia Butler in Lauren Olamina's The Book of the Living. She reminds us that "the only lasting truth is Change. God Is Change." Tevet contains within it descent and ascent to remind us of this fact.

Tevet in Practice

CHANNUKAH . . . CONTINUED

The first two days of Tevet are the last two days of Channukah. What is, overall, a quiet month begins with the fullest expression of the menorah's power, perhaps offering enough light to last through the long nights of Tevet.

CHAG HA'BANOT / ROSH CHODESH LABANOT / EID AL-BANOT

Every Rosh Chodesh has been traditionally associated with and celebrated by women; Rosh Chodesh Tevet, the one Rosh Chodesh that falls in the middle of a holiday, holds a bonus festival, specifically for the Jewish communities of Tunisia, Libya, Algeria, Morocco, Greece, and Turkey. Rosh Chodesh Tevet is known as Chag ha'Banot (חַג הַבָּנוֹת) the "festival of the daughters."

Chag ha'Banot celebrates Judith's triumph over Holofernes. Sefer Yehudit, the Book of Judith, is a apocryphal[5] text that became a midrash closely associated with Channukah. Judith, a widow living in the time of Antiochus IV, lures the Assyrian general Holofernes to her tent, feeds him cheese and wine until he falls asleep, and then beheads him. In Tunisian tradition, Judith's righteous act took place on Rosh Chodesh Tevet, and so women would celebrate Judith and throw feasts in her honor. Esther is also celebrated on Chag ha'Banot,[6] as Tevet is the month when Esther came to King Ahasuerus's palace and was crowned queen.[7] Rabbi Jill Hammer teaches that Chag ha'Banot was a time when women, mothers, and daughters were celebrated:

> One tradition was that women would come to the synagogue, touch the Torah, and pray for the health of their daughters. Mothers would give their daughters gifts, and bridegrooms would

give gifts to their brides. Girls who were fighting were expected to reconcile on Chag haBanot. Old women and young women would come together to dance.[8]

As a women's festival, there are no traditional rabbinic text sources (i.e., no reference in the Talmud or rabbinic responsa) to Chag ha'Banot. We are grateful to be living Jewishly in a time of cross-pollination and amplification of truly oral traditions, women's and queer minhagim (customs), and diaspora Judaism. May Chag ha'Banot weave us closer in with our foremothers' dreams, spells, and magic.

ASARAH B'TEVET (TENTH OF TEVET)

Asarah b'Tevet is a minor fast day, one of four alongside Tzom Gedaliah, Ta'anit Esther, and the seventeenth of Tammuz. Asara b'Tevet primarily commemorates the beginning of Nebuchadnezzar's siege on Jerusalem in 588 BCE. It is connected, in the wheel of the year, to the seventeenth of Tammuz and Tisha b'Av six months later, when we mark the breaching of the walls of Jerusalem and the destruction of the Temple. Asarah b'Tevet was first marked in II Kings, and named as a fast day in Zechariah 8. Asarah b'Tevet also came to be associated with the death of Ezra the Scribe, on the ninth of Tevet, and the creation of the Septuagint, the forced translation of the Torah in 476 BCE, on the eighth of Tevet.[9] As the story goes, first told in the apocryphal Letter of Aristeas, King Ptolemy of Egypt forced seventy scholars into separate rooms and demanded they translate the Torah into Greek.

Minor fasts last from sunup to sundown, and work is permitted. Liturgical changes for the day include adding Avinu Malkeinu after the morning Amidah, and Selichot liturgy for Asarah b'Tevet is added during Tachanun. Specifically, Asarah b'Tevet is a fast day marking times when layers of separation that served as protection between Jews and non-Jews have been threatened. For those of us who read the Torah in translation and do not long for a return to Temple times, how do we mark this day? Perhaps we don't mourn that the Torah was translated, but our own challenges to read it in the original, and to speak each other's languages. We can mourn the death and destruction inflicted on Jews by various empires over the centuries, and the ways in which fear of such violence has shaped so much of Judaism. Coming so close on the heels of Channukah, Asarah b'Tevet provides an opportunity for a more staid reflection time on the complexities of the Maccabean revolt. And if none of the ancestral invitations are resonating, all of the minor fast days that have traditionally commemorated tragedies are opportunities for ritual space to the grief that can be so pervasive in life in late-stage capitalism. We can experiment with fasting from food, certain speech or actions, and other embodied practice changes, we can make space for prayer, song, silence, and poetry, we can invite in mourning alongside our ancestors, and see what arises.

THE OTHER NEW YEAR

After Channukah's grand finale, Tevet provides a relative lull on the Jewish calendar, and usually coincides with the Gregorian New Year. While living in two calendars is often a struggle, we like to take all the new years we can get. Tevet's Jewish holiday lull, layered on a time when the Christian dominant world might want less from Jews, offers some of us more open time. This can be an opportunity for the personal work of reflection, the inward community work of relationship building, and collective big picture dreaming.

Tevet, the fourth month since Rosh Hashana, can be an excellent time for a gentle first quarter of the year check-in. It is an opportunity to look back on intentions set at the New Year and see what has stuck and what has fallen away, and to gently return to practice and intention where possible. Coming out of Tevet, we will head into a rollicking span of months that includes Tu b'Shvat, Purim, and Pesach, so Tevet can be a time to look ahead and begin planning. As the Torah portions of this month tell the heart of the Exodus story, there is an invitation and an opportunity to look deeply into personal and communal origin and liberation stories in an expansive, curious way.

But at the end of the day, we can let Tevet's long nights and few holidays be a chance for real sleep and rest. It is not necessary to create more work for ourselves. The rhythm of the Jewish year invites us to hibernate, turn inward, and cuddle up. In the measured process of the year, Tevet permits, and even invites, us to slow down. Let's.

LANDBACK

an upward bound song of sap:
sweetness rising toward light

every day we practice being trees:
all life breathing an exchange of praise and gratitude
sharing gossip and survival strategies in root and canopy
leaning toward each other, making boundaries, changing,
dying
trying to stay alive
and make more life

it is the new year of trees:
we set our ritual tables
on stolen land

our tongues wrestle with this pleasure and this grief
as we feast on soft yielding flesh, husked and pitted, seeds within and without
tiny pink rivers running down our chins
teeth sunk into the fruiting bodies of poisoned fields and extractive labor

what are the blessings we say
for the trees whose seeds were carried by kidnapped kin across the Atlantic
for the ghost groves of ancient olive in occupied Palestine
for the forests full of defenders perched in protest
for the birches with their witnessing eyes
for the ceiba, the live oak, the baobab, the coast redwood

Tree of Life, we are trying to hold fast to you,
striving to be worthy to be called *trees of the field*

when we are quiet enough to listen to the rustling of Your leaves,
when the grasses and weeds, flowers and mosses join in chorus,
there is no prayer but this:
return all lands to Indigenous hands

WELCOME
TO שבט
SHVAT

What places nourish your soul? How? What are your commitments to caring for those places as they care for you?

   Whose land are you on? Where are the original inhabitants now? What did the original inhabitants of the land you are on call this place? What were their names for God? How did they care for the land? What can you do this month to honor the original inhabitants of the land, and to nurture the land?

Introduction to Shvat

כִּי־תָצוּר אֶל־עִיר יָמִים רַבִּים לְהִלָּחֵם עָלֶיהָ לְתָפְשָׂהּ לֹא־
תַשְׁחִית אֶת־עֵצָהּ לִנְדֹּחַ עָלָיו גַּרְזֶן כִּי מִמֶּנּוּ תֹאכֵל וְאֹתוֹ לֹא
תִכְרֹת כִּי הָאָדָם עֵץ הַשָּׂדֶה לָבֹא מִפָּנֶיךָ בַּמָּצוֹר:

When you besiege a city for a long time, in making war against it to take it, you shall not destroy its trees by forcing an axe against them: for thou may eat of them, and you shall not cut them down; for is the tree of the field a man, that it should be besieged by thee?

—Devarim 20:19

In Shvat we get busy. The inward focus and incipient hibernation that mark the season have turned a corner at the winter solstice. In Shvat, we remember that there is growing, creating, and blossoming ahead, and celebrate the passage through Shvat by marking all that bubbles beneath the surface, and having faith that fruit is coming. By the next month, it will be time to explode from introspection into collective joy, made possible because we have sunk our roots deep into learning about ourselves and what the darkness can teach. On the first day of the eleventh month, Rosh Chodesh Shvat, the final book of the Torah Devarim begins. We read in Devarim 1:3:

וַיְהִי בְּאַרְבָּעִים שָׁנָה בְּעַשְׁתֵּי־עָשָׂר חֹדֶשׁ בְּאֶחָד לַחֹדֶשׁ דִּבֶּר מֹשֶׁה אֶל־בְּנֵי יִשְׂרָאֵל כְּכֹל אֲשֶׁר צִוָּה ה׳ אֹתוֹ אֲלֵהֶם:

It was in the fortieth year, on the first day of the eleventh month, that Moses addressed the Israelites in accordance with the instructions that God had given him for them.

This month marks the time of mattan Torah (מַתַּן תּוֹרָה), recieving Torah, when Moshe began his recitation of the Mishnah Torah, the repetition of the most important parts of the first four books of the Torah.[1]

Tradition teaches that, during this month, great insights into the Torah are uncovered. The students of Chiddushei HaRim[2] report that he taught that "all the chiddushei Torah (new insights on the Torah) that a person is going to develop in the course of the entire year are presented to them from Heaven during Shvat."[3] All the insights a person will come to know, all the big ideas, all the inspiration, are coming this month. They will sit below the surface, waiting to blossom.

In our movement work, Shvat often falls in a season that tends toward internal work and strategy. In many places it is too cold to sustain street actions, there are no major elections, and we are between the end of the Gregorian year and the external action that spring can bring. This can be a month that we cultivate receiving and uncovering new and deeper insights into the Torah of organizing: individually and collectively we can open toward the questions that need our attention: What longing is beginning to sprout under the surface? What strategy, if we pay attention to it, can grow?

Shvat is also the People's Month! Rashi teaches in his commentary on Devarim 1:5 that Moshe took great care to teach the Torah in "all 70 different languages," taking a positive initiative to make the Torah available to people no matter what language they spoke. The constellation for this month is Aquarius. Its constellation is the pail, a vessel that collects water and brings it to the people, animals, and plants that need it. Shvat is a month where "Living Water," Torah, is collected and brought to nourish the collective.

The parashiyot in Shevat are Bo, Beshalach, Yitro, and Mishpatim. This month the Israelites cross the sea and on the other side begin to learn how to become a free people. We learn that that entails celebrating victories with song, distributing responsibility and asking for help, feeling awe, making collective commitments for the future, and agreeing upon norms and behaviors. How can receiving rules make us free? We learn in Shvat that entering into agreements, choosing how we want to be treated and to treat others, is a mark of liberated people. This glimmer of freedom starts moving in Shvat, preparing to blossom in the spring.

Shvat in Practice

TU B'SHVAT

Shvat finds many of us curled up at home, deep into the slog of winter and the isolation it can bring, or unfurling into creative dreaming and making things indoors. Shvat, the middle of winter in the Northern Hemisphere, brings with it the celebration of the New Year for the Trees. How can this be? Tu b'Shvat sanctifies that change can start small and private and still be celebrated. The sap begins to rise, and while we cannot see it, growth is coming.

Tu b'Shvat comes when the rains have finally saturated the earth,[4] and tree sap begins to move. Trees prepare to end hibernation, and eventually bud and grow in the spring and summer. Sustenance, planning, and inspiration build up during this month, and though the fruits of the labor may not be obvious just yet, we celebrate what is to come. The movement we bless in Shvat will be the blossoming of fruits in Nisan. As the holiday of Tu b'Shvat teaches, much begins to flow beneath the surface.

NEW YEAR OF THE TREES

The first mention of Tu b'Shvat is in Mishnah Rosh Hashanah 1:1, which lays out four new years: Nisan for kings and for festivals; Elul for the tithing of animals; Tishrei for counting years, shmita,[5] and jubilee; and Shvat, the new year for the trees. Why do we need a new year for the trees? In Vayikra we are instructed:

וְכִי־תָבֹאוּ אֶל־הָאָרֶץ וּנְטַעְתֶּם כָּל־עֵץ מַאֲכָל וַעֲרַלְתֶּם עָרְלָתוֹ אֶת־פִּרְיוֹ שָׁלֹשׁ
שָׁנִים יִהְיֶה לָכֶם עֲרֵלִים לֹא יֵאָכֵל: כדוּבַשָּׁנָה הָרְבִיעִת יִהְיֶה כָּל־פִּרְיוֹ קֹדֶשׁ
הִלּוּלִים לַיהוָה: כהוּבַשָּׁנָה הַחֲמִישִׁת תֹּאכְלוּ אֶת־פִּרְיוֹ לְהוֹסִיף לָכֶם תְּבוּאָתוֹ אֲנִי
יְהוָה אֱלֹהֵיכֶם:

When you enter the land and plant any tree for food, you shall
regard its fruit as forbidden. Three years it shall be forbidden for
you, not to be eaten. In the fourth year all its fruit shall be set
aside for jubilation before the Divine; and only in the fifth year
may you use its fruit—that its yield to you may be increased: I
HaShem am your God.

—Vayikra 19:23–25

In order to eat the fruit of a tree, we need to be able to count the years from when a tree was planted. Anything planted before the fifteenth of Shvat is counted in a group during the current year, while anything planted after the fifteenth of Shvat is counted with the next year's trees. Originally an agricultural counting method, Tu b'Shvat's resonances have been expanded over many centuries to mark sacred relationships with earth, land, trees, and fruit.

There are no halachic obligations on Tu b'Shvat, no mitzvot to fulfill. Yet Jews have, for many centuries and in many parts of the world, found deep spiritual resonance and meaning from the invitations of Tu b'Shvat. Today, there are myriad ways to engage Tu b'Shvat in spiritually, politically integrated, and inspiring ways.

KABBALISTIC SEDER

The Kabbalistic Tu b'Shvat seder is accredited to Rabbi Yitzak Luria of Safed and other Kabbalists of sixteenth-century Palestine. The seder follows a pattern similar to the Passover seder with four cups of wine, and includes the seven fruits of Eretz Yisrael. The seder is organized around the "Four Worlds." In each, there is a glass of wine or juice in certain combinations of white and red, and a category of fruit. That structure is:

Asiyah (עֲשִׂיָּה), action:
> White wine
> Fruit and nuts with shells and peels

Yetzirah (יְצִירָה), formation:
> Half white and half red wine
> Fruit with inedible pits and seeds

Briyah (בְּרִיאָה), thought:
> Three-quarter red wine with one-quarter white wine
> Entirely edible fruits

Atzilut (אֲצִילוּת), spirit:
> Red wine with a drop of white wine
> Only smell

Alongside each world, we can sing songs, read poetry, and discuss how we are in, relating to, and grappling with that world. For example, in the first world, Asiyah, fruits and nuts with shells and peels are eaten, and a glass of all white wine or juice is blessed, then drunk. We discuss the material world of action in our lives. How are we taking action, how are we blocked from action, what are the kinds of actions we seek, and how can this sacred meal in community move us toward action? As with all centuries-old offerings, we can probe the framework. Do these four worlds resonate for us today? Are there different worlds that new fruit invites us into?

SHVAT

OVER THE CENTURIES, AROUND THE WORLD

Around the world, Jews eat fruit to celebrate Tu b'Shvat. The symbolism of different fruits is ripe for ritual, like Kurdistani Jews who pray for an abundant fruit season by putting sweet fruit around trees,[6] or some European Jews who eat fifteen different kinds of fruit on Tu BiShvat (perhaps because of the date of the holiday on the fifteenth of Shvat),[7] or some Persian Jews who lower baskets of fruit into one another's homes through chimneys.[8] Many will make sure to eat a new piece of fruit, in order to get to say the Shehecheyanu blessing over it. The Shehecheyanu is said when doing something for the first time in a year, such as lighting Hanukah candles, beginning the Passover seder, welcoming new life, wearing a new piece of clothing, or hanging a mezuzah in a new home. Savoring a mouthful of new fruit brings the Shehecheyanu experience onto our tongues.

TU B'SHVAT TODAY

The spiritual invitations of spring and rebirth during Tu b'Shvat are powerful metaphors and invitations in the arc of the journey through the year. But Tu b'Shvat also brings up hard political questions: How is it possible to celebrate a holiday that celebrates trees in the land of Israel/Palestine, when the Israeli government weaponizes trees and planting to steal Palestinian land? How is it possible to celebrate a holiday that acknowledges the sacredness of land and our relationship to it, while Indigenous people are still being actively exiled from their land on Turtle Island and while many of us live as uninvited settlers? How is it possible to mark a holiday about the cycles of the earth when human destruction is so violently, and likely irreparably, damaging the earth's cycles, body, and future?

Everything that is fraught and challenging about Tu b'Shvat is also what can open up new places of meaning. We can turn toward the historical and political challenges of Tu b'Shvat, and transform the festival's relevance for our lives and times.

We can root into this present moment, rife with contradictions, with a tradition that pushes right on what is most painful, and forces confrontation. Tu b'Shvat is an invitation to learning and collective action. Tu b'Shvat celebrations can be dedicated to the trees and humans of the field, that all may grow in a just world without fear of destruction.

PALESTINE SOLIDARITY AND TU B'SHVAT

Though Tu b'Shvat is older than the modern nation state of Israel, years of work by Zionist organizers have equated Tu b'Shvat with support for Israel. This, coupled with decades-long colonization of the land that weaponizes trees, makes this holiday an important time to challenge the intertwining of Zionism and Judaism, and a crucial time to take action in solidarity with Palestinians resisting the erasure of their histories and the theft of their lands.

The Jewish National Fund (Keren Kayemet LeYisrael) was established in 1901 to collect money to buy property in Palestine. Now, their signature little blue boxes are synonymous with tzedakah in many Jewish homes, and annual Tu b'Shvat tree-planting ceremonies are seen as a normalized part of the holiday. In fact, the JNF has been well documented as planting Israeli forests of non-native and invasive trees to displace Palestinian people and destroy Palestinian property.[9] Alongside of this planting, the Israeli Defense Force routinely uproots thousand-year-old olive trees as part of its campaign of punitive home demolitions against Palestinians.[10]

Digging into Tu b'Shvat can look like remembering a broader history of this holiday, its spiritual lessons, and a relationship to the land before Israel was established as a modern state. It is important to separate what existed before the establishment of the modern state of Israel and what has been warped by it. The contemporary practice of Tu b'Shvat is wrapped up in Zionist mythology, ideology, and colonization. However, like cursive Hebrew, Tu b'Shvat existed before 1948. Solidarity with Palestine does not require the surrender of rich traditions, but instead asks for critical thinking about *how* to practice them. Devarim 20:19 teaches:

כִּי־תָצוּר אֶל־עִיר יָמִים רַבִּים לְהִלָּחֵם עָלֶיהָ לְתָפְשָׂהּ לֹא־תַשְׁחִית אֶת־עֵצָהּ לִנְדֹּחַ עָלָיו גַּרְזֶן כִּי מִמֶּנּוּ תֹאכֵל וְאֹתוֹ לֹא תִכְרֹת כִּי הָאָדָם עֵץ הַשָּׂדֶה לָבֹא מִפָּנֶיךָ בַּמָּצוֹר:

When in your war against a city you have to besiege it a long time in order to capture it, you must not destroy its trees, wielding the ax against them. You may eat of them, but you must not cut them down. Are trees of the field human to withdraw before you into the besieged city?

Elliott batTzedek and Hannah Schwarzschild created *Trees of Reconciliation: A Tu b'Shvat Haggadah* in 2010. The seder has four sections: The Seed, which talks about the traditional Jewish relationships to trees; the Blossom, which discusses early Zionist relationships with and conceptions of land; the Fruit, which is about the JNF's intentional destruction of Palestinian homes and orchards and colonization of the land; and the Harvest, which recounts contemporary violence against people and land today. The seder is filled with songs, poetry, history, and blessings, and closes with the lines: "All land is holy. All people are chosen."

This is one example of using the four-cup structure of the seder to teach, learn, and engage in repair. Other observances could include collecting funds for the Stop the JNF Campaign at Tu b'Shvat seders, screening films about Palestine, telling the story of the JNF, and organizing to support Palestinian land rights in honor of Tu b'Shvat.

Understanding that Tu b'Shvat and its rituals are older than the state of Israel, and creating spiritually meaningful spaces where we engage with the colonization of Palestine, is part of separating Judaism from Zionism. We can make rituals that are both political and personal, tell untold histories, organize for justice in Palestine, *and* connect, as our ancestors did, to the movement of life in the trees.

INDIGENOUS SOLIDARITY ON TURTLE ISLAND

Tu b'Shvat celebrates connection to the land and its sacredness. For settlers living on stolen Indigenous land in North America/Turtle Island, marking Tu b'Shvat is an invitation to pay attention to this land, to learn about and join in action in solidarity with the original people of the land.

On Tu b'Shvat, we can seek out and lift up the voices of Native American Jews. At this season, with the invitation to turn toward Indigenous sovereignty, we ask ourselves:

*Who was displaced from the place/s you live, so that you might
    live there?*

Where are they now?

*What were the specific ways that colonization happened in the
    place where you live? What are the sites of violence woven
    into the land where you live?*

*What are the histories of the Indigenous peoples who steward
    the land you live on? What is the Indigenous community
    invested in now?*

If you don't already know the answers to these questions, Tu b'Shvat is an excellent time to learn about the original stewards of the land, the history of colonization, and what the struggle for indigenous rights and sovereignty looks like today. Tu b'Shvat can be the time to bring the practice of an Indigenous land acknowledgment to the local Jewish community and its ritual practice. In "Beyond Territorial Acknowledgments," Chelsea Vowel writes:

> If we think of territorial acknowledgments as sites of potential
> disruption, they can be transformative acts that to some extent
> undo Indigenous erasure. I believe this is true as long as these
> acknowledgments discomfit both those speaking and hearing
> the words. The fact of Indigenous presence should force non-
> Indigenous peoples to confront their own place on these lands.[11]

Land acknowledgments can be pathways into more knowledge, relationship, and action.[12] Tu b'Shvat's invitation to pay extra attention to the land can be a moment to bring this practice into the local community and maintain it throughout the year.

What would a Tu b'Shvat seder dedicated to Indigenous solidarity and sovereignty look like? Inspired by the order of the four cups in the Kabbalistic Tu b'Shvat seder, this seder moves us through:

Asiyah/action: dedication to first peoples of this land;
Yetzirah/formation: understanding the violence and genocide of
    colonization and attempted genocide;

Briyah/thought: the histories and contemporary acts of resistance, survival, and thriving; and

Atzilut/spirit: the future of decolonization we are working toward.

We want our words and rituals to help us embody and lead to action that is more in line with our values. More and more places have ways to pay reparations in the form of real rent, like the Shuumi Land Tax on traditional Chochenyo and Karkin Ohlone territory, Real Rent Duwamish, and the Manna-hatta Fund to support the American Indian Community House. Since 2019, Jews on Ohlone Land has been answering the call for Indigenous solidarity, explicitly as Jews and rooted in Jewish frameworks and traditions:

> Jews On Ohlone Land invites Jews living in Lisjan territory to join in this healing and transformation in solidarity with the Sogorea Te' Land Trust and the Confederated Villages of Lisjan Nation as we learn to live as good guests on this land. We do this through the practice of teshuvah (relational repair), which calls us to engage with our own experiences of perpetrating and benefitting from colonization, as well as with Jewish experiences of violence, displacement and genocide. Living as whole people in diaspora, fully present on Lisjan Ohlone land and deeply rooting in our own ancestral ways and teachings, we are building beloved Jewish community in alignment with this place and Indigenous people.[13]

In a place where there is no existing land tax, we can mark Tu b'Shvat by moving money to Indigenous organizing, which is happening everywhere. As Tu b'Shvat is, biblically, a tax day,[14] moving money to Indigenous people on Tu b'Shvat is not a donation, or even tzedakah, but a rightful payment to the original protectors of the land we are on.

By continuing to weave commitments to and struggles for justice into the Jewish year, our methods of bringing Indigenous sovereignty and solidarity to all land-oriented holidays will grow and deepen. Tu b'Shvat can create a touchstone, turning and returning to build relationships, and living into the process of decolonization.

ALL LAND IS SACRED: EARTH JUSTICE

Tu b'Shvat is a time to look at our relationship to the earth, and a time to deepen our spiritual and political relationships to movements for environmental, climate, and food justice. This is not a contemporary innovation; this is, in many ways, what Tu b'Shvat has always been about. Tu b'Shvat is, was, and always will be an opportunity to look at relationships to the natural world, find out what teshuvah is needed, and spiritually prepare to take it on.

The Torah communicates a range of relationships and theologies that Jewish people's ancestors had with the earth, the land, and the cycles of planting and harvest. On the one hand, Beresheet asserts a theology of human domination over animals and the earth, ideas that have been used as fuel and source text for centuries of capitalist extractive economy and environmental degradation. Yet, as with every cherry-picked verse of Torah used to prop up oppression and harm, there is so much more in the tradition on which to draw.

Our ancestors understood that our behaviors have an impact on the land. The condition of the earth, the activities of the harvest, and the weather are barometers of whether or not our actions as humans are in right relationship with the rest of Creation. In the second paragraph of the Shema, lines from Devarim 11:13–17, are said daily, multiple times a day:

וְהָיָ֗ה אִם־שָׁמֹ֤עַ תִּשְׁמְעוּ֙ אֶל־מִצְוֺתַ֔י אֲשֶׁ֧ר אָנֹכִ֛י מְצַוֶּ֥ה אֶתְכֶ֖ם הַיּ֑וֹם לְאַהֲבָ֞ה אֶת־יְהוָ֤ה אֱלֹֽהֵיכֶם֙ וּלְעָבְד֔וֹ בְּכָל־לְבַבְכֶ֖ם וּבְכָל־נַפְשְׁכֶֽם: וְנָתַתִּ֧י מְטַֽר־אַרְצְכֶ֛ם בְּעִתּ֖וֹ יוֹרֶ֣ה וּמַלְק֑וֹשׁ וְאָסַפְתָּ֣ דְגָנֶ֔ךָ וְתִֽירֹשְׁךָ֖ וְיִצְהָרֶֽךָ: וְנָתַתִּ֛י עֵ֥שֶׂב בְּשָׂדְךָ֖ לִבְהֶמְתֶּ֑ךָ וְאָכַלְתָּ֖ וְשָׂבָֽעְתָּ: הִשָּֽׁמְר֣וּ לָכֶ֔ם פֶּ֥ן יִפְתֶּ֖ה לְבַבְכֶ֑ם וְסַרְתֶּ֗ם וַעֲבַדְתֶּם֙ אֱלֹהִ֣ים אֲחֵרִ֔ים וְהִשְׁתַּחֲוִיתֶ֖ם לָהֶֽם: וְחָרָ֨ה אַף־יְהוָ֜ה בָּכֶ֗ם וְעָצַ֤ר אֶת־הַשָּׁמַ֙יִם֙ וְלֹא־יִהְיֶ֣ה מָטָ֔ר וְהָ֣אֲדָמָ֔ה לֹ֥א תִתֵּ֖ן אֶת־יְבוּלָ֑הּ וַאֲבַדְתֶּ֣ם מְהֵרָ֗ה מֵעַל֙ הָאָ֣רֶץ הַטֹּבָ֔ה אֲשֶׁ֥ר יְהוָ֖ה נֹתֵ֥ן לָכֶֽם:

If, then, you obey the mitzvot that I enjoin upon you this day, loving the Divine your God and serving God with all your heart and soul, I will grant the rain for your land in season, the early rain and the late. You shall gather in your new grain and wine and oil—I will also provide grass in the fields for your cattle—and thus you shall eat your fill. Take care not to be lured away to serve other gods and bow to them. For the Divine's anger will flare up against you, and God will shut up the skies so that there will be no rain and the ground will not yield its produce; and you will soon perish from the good land that HaShem is assigning to you.

Many of us have complex feelings about an angry God who rewards and punishes for obedience, or even acts this directly in the world. But it is possible to relate to our ancestors' understanding of needing to live by their values, and that the earth is impacted by the values we as humans live by. Tu b'Shvat is a time that calls attention to this relationship.

For decades, Jews have been bringing the Torah of sacred care for the earth to movements for climate and environmental justice, and bringing calls for urgent climate action to Jewish communities. In recent years, there's been a burst of energy in Jewish sustainable food organizing and farm projects. Black- and Brown-led organizing shows the profound ways in which environmental racism has decimated communities of color, poor and working-class communities, and rural communities. This work pushes environmental, climate, and food justice organizing to more intersectional analysis and action, and Jewish action for climate justice must move with it.

As people fighting against environmental racism and for a just transition to a regenerative economy, we bring those commitments to our Tu b'Shvat seder tables. That can look like:

Setting an environmental justice new year's resolution for the New Year for the trees. Sometimes, more than other organizing, getting involved in climate action can be overwhelming: fear of what's at stake can immobilize us. But Tu b'Shvat is an opportunity to disrupt daily routine and shake up our stuckness. Tu b'Shvat can mark time in all of our journeys of cutting our dependence on fossil fuels, learning about the earth in the places we live, and taking meaningful action for climate justice and a just transition. Ask: What is one action to take between this Tu b'Shvat and next? One book to read? One conversation to have?

Organizing a Tu b'Shvat seder focused on local struggles for environmental justice. Inspired by the order of the four cups in the Kabbalistic Tu b'Shvat seder, we can imagine a seder with the following intentions:

Asiyah/action: dedication to the earth; focusing on the mountains, forests, and watersheds of the place your seder is located;

Yetzirah/formation: learning about the human impacts colonization, chattel slavery, extractive capitalism, and industrial development has had on the specific land that you're on;

Briyah/thought: learning about local organizing campaigns and thinking about alternatives to the current land and climate policies;

Atzilut/spirit: dreaming, practicing, and taking into our bodies a reconnection to the earth in the place where we live.

Tu b'Shvat reminds us that the earth has its own new year, and lives in its own time cycles. Tu b'Shvat reminds us that our ancestors had relationships to earth, land, food, and trees that we can call on and learn from. Over the centuries, our ancestors created new ways to spiritually encounter the earth they understood themselves as originating from, returning to, and living in sacred relationship with. In our time, we must find deeper, bolder, and new ways to embody this sacred relationship, so that we all may live.

MAKING TU B'SHVAT

Making your own Tu b'Shvat seder is an opportunity to tap into what you and your community need in the dormancy of winter. What will invigorate you and yours to keep it all growing? Who is it nourishing?

Planning a Tu b'Shvat seder with these questions as your starting place can take you in many directions. Perhaps your organizing collective has gotten stuck in interpersonal dynamics, and needs to reground in shared values and a vision for justice. Maybe your family and friends are weathering the long winter and in need of some reflection and joy. Maybe your synagogue community is ready to engage more deeply with Palestinian liberation or Indigenous sovereignty and could be guided by the order of a seder. Perhaps Tu b'Shvat is the frame by which you can shape a public demonstration, and moving through the four worlds tightens your narrative.

Take a pulse for where you are, what your heart is reaching out for, and how Tu b'Shvat can nourish this moment. Particularly because there are no halachic requirements to make a Tu b'Shvat seder, there is no wrong way to do it! Using the template of the Kabbalistic seder allows for a form for your conversation, but is by no means required. During the seder, the grape juice or wine is blessed and drunk, food is blessed and eaten, readings are shared, and reflections are made.

Haggadah

Every Haggadah, the guidebook for the seder, will offer a different kind of opportunity for reading and reflection. Select a Haggadah that you like, use it in full, add or subtract selections or whole portions, or make your own. Haggadot are the original Jewish zine, so bring in poetry and readings that resonate with you in this moment.[15] Invite everyone who will attend to prepare a teaching about the holiday, trees, or the earth, or to share a plant they feel connected to or are curious about.

Food and Wine

Etrogim, pomegranates, figs, grapes, dates, olives, wheat, pears, carobs, almonds, walnuts, and apples are the traditional first twelve fruits for a seder, but some will add as many fruits as possible. For a seder following the "Four Worlds" pattern, you might use some or none of the above, but find fruits and nuts and herbs that meet the designated categories. Bring in herbs or an etrog from Sukkot for the World of Spirit (marked by smell.) Find local foods that match the categories, or foods that connect in some way to the issue the celebration is addressing. Invite guests to bring a category of food ("someone should bring things with peels and shells, someone bring fully edible foods!") or provide it as host, but be sure to have enough for everyone to eat some of each food.

The fruit of the vine sanctifies Jewish ritual. The Tu b'Shvat seder combines red and white juice or wine in different ratios. Beginning with a glass of all white wine and ending up with a glass of all red wine, the transition from the "World of Action" to the "World of Spirit" is made manifest. It is evocative of the Birkat haMazon recited at a Sheva Brachot (the grace after meals following a wedding). When two glasses of wine are poured together, the combining of the different wines is an invitation to see the ways in which action, formation, thought, and spirit inform one another and are a part of a larger whole.

Particularly on Tu b'Shvat, use sustainable materials for the meal. Hiddur mitzvah, the mitzvah of making things beautiful, invites us to decorate our seder table and home in honor of the holiday. Get out your favorite tablecloth. Put some potted plants right on the table. Have a seder outside under a huge tree. Hang some fruit from the branches! Some Tu b'Shvat seders include a full meal while some are focused solely on ritual foods. This is up to you.

Taking It to the Streets

The messages of Tu b'Shvat lead us to advocate for being in right relationship with the earth, to advocate for the sacredness of all land, and to advocate for Jewish and non-Jewish organizations and institutions to take action for our planet. Make a Tu b'Shvat seder demonstration-performance at the pipeline demo, or bring the foods of Tu b'Shvat to a community hearing on sustainability. Let the millennia-old wisdom of Jewish relationship to trees and earth breathe new life into our urgent work of today.

SHABBAT SHIRAH

Shabbat Shirah, a special Shabbat in honor of Song of the Sea, generally falls on the Shabbat before or after Tu b'Shvat, when we read parshah Beshalach. Shabbat Shirah is observed with special musical services, concerts, and teachings. The Song of the Sea is a song of joy and liberation, and we place ourselves on the other side of the sea and join in raucous song. This is the traditional time to grab your timbrel.

Leftist Jewish communities have had to intentionally work to create singing cultures, in spaces that, for many reasons, often have trouble singing together. One impact of forming communities around shared politics is that we often come from diverse nusachot (נֻסָחוֹת) different Jewish musical traditions, and don't all know the same songs and melodies. Some of us were raised in Jewish communities where cantors and choirs perform, and the congregation rarely, if ever, joins in, and then is drowned out by amplification of those at the front of the room. Many of us were raised assimilated or nonpracticing, and didn't learn Jewish music, prayer, or songs. Today, many of us know the embodied power of singing together, the importance for individual and collective healing and movement building of synching our breath and getting loud together. We are blessed that projects like Let My People Sing, the Rising Song Institute, and countless incredible song leaders, have taken on the holy work of strengthening progressive Jewish communities' singing muscles in this generation. Every community can benefit from intentionally talking about singing, learning new songs, and uncovering the power of song in ritual, as a healing modality, and as part of movements for justice and organizing. Shabbat Shirah is a wonderful time to begin, and to deepen.

Resonating with its proximity to Tu b'Shvat, traditionally birds are honored on Shabbat Shirah for their participation in the celebration of the miracle of the crossing of the sea. Rabbi Judah Loew[16] taught the custom to go out and feed the birds before Shabbat Shirah.[17] "It is said that the importance of singing songs to HaShem is unfathomable, and that singing can open your heart and invoke blessings and prayers that are deep within your heart. The act of feeding birds in the winter for Shabbat Shirah is a practice of Hakarat HaTov, of gratitude, or literally, 'recognizing the good.'"[18] Let this Shabbat encourage us to sing and to listen for the songs of creatures all around us.

As Shvat comes to a close, we can reflect on all we have planted this month. In Adar and Nissan, we will make room for and bless the buds and flowers that will grow. In Shvat, we remember that we are made of, ever returning to, and humbly in service for, holy earth. This awareness, the yearcycle teaches us, comes first.

LANDBACK

Torrent of Delight,
turn us upside down!
shake us like a gragger
until all the ways we take ourselves so
seriously
fall like poppy seeds
into early spring soil,
earth wet with tears and piss
spilled from laughter

tickle us, O River of Bliss,
until we forget who we thought we were supposed to be
and remember who we really are

get us drunk on juice, Vine of Pleasure!
and behold us in all our glittering glory:
in our genderful genderfuckery
in sweaty spiels of freaks
in tulle and spandex, trash and treasure, lipstick, leather, and
lace
in the streets and in our kitchens
in our gayest dazzle camouflage

yes
please
may we frolic toward a liberated spring
riots of dandelions busting out of concrete
unfurling wildcrafted scrolls
full of dew-soaked tales
of upending empire

WELCOME TO אדר ADAR

What inspires you to resist oppressive forces? What does resistance look like, in big and small ways, in your life? Who has your back? Who is your resistance for the sake of?

Where and when do you get to play? How do you feed absurdity in your life? Who makes you laugh? What can you do to bring in more laughter this month?

How can glamour, beauty, and pageantry serve resistance and world building?

Introduction to Adar

My hunch is that joy is an ember for or precursor to wild and unpredictable and transgressive and unboundaried solidarity. And that that solidarity might incite further joy. Which might incite further solidarity. And on and on. My hunch is that joy, emerging from our common sorrow—which does not necessarily mean we have the same sorrows, but that we, in common, sorrow—might draw us together. It might depolarize us and de-atomoize us enough that we can consider what, in common, we love. And though attending to what we hate in common is too often all the rage (and it happens also to be very big business), noticing what we love in common, and studying *that*, might help us survive. It's why I think of joy, which gets us to love, as being a practice of survival.

—Ross Gay, *Inciting Joy*

There is nothing like walking down the street in go-go boots, costume just barely stuffed under your winter coat, trying to get to the Purim party fashionably late but still early enough to make it for the shpil.[1] Adar, the month of mazal,[2] gifts us with reasons to rejoice even in the grayest of wintertimes in the Northern Hemisphere. Adar invites us to find joy: in our lives, in our days, in our movement work. We are called to joy even, or especially, when facing life-or-death moments.

Adar, whose constellation is Pisces, recalls a well-known organizing poster: A big fish chases down a tiny fish, and is about to eat it in one bite. But right behind it, an entire school of fish are coordinated, swimming in the shape of an even bigger fish, and speeding toward that big fish. Luck sometimes occurs by chance, when the stars align, but at other times it comes from coordinated and careful planning in mass movements. Fish, a sign of abundance, are deeply immersed in that which gives them life. Adar reminds us to look around and see who we're swimming with.

This month we mark the seventh of Adar: both Moses' yahrtzeit (anniversary of a death) and his birthdate. The Lubavicher Rebbe[3] teaches that because even Haman, the villain of the Purim story, knew that Adar contained Moses' yahrtzeit and no holidays or celebrations, he chose it as the time to destroy the Jewish people. He did not know it was also Moses' birthdate. And the luck continued.

It is said that as soon as Adar enters, joy increases.[4] This month of joy peaks on the full moon at Purim, and we are encouraged to spread the joy across the whole month. In the arc of the season, Purim is understood in the context of Passover, which arrives next month in Nisan. Purim is youthful, featuring ecstatic expressions of joy over the Jewish people's liberation from annihilation by an enemy through play, costume, and spoof. Passover will arrive with what is often a more mature, staid expression of celebration over the liberation from Mitzrayim, through the seder, talking around a table. The liberation and joy of Purim leads to the liberation and joy of Passover, and Purim's celebrations ritualize that pathway. On Purim, it is a mitzvah to give matanot l'evyonim (מַתָּנוֹת לָאֶבְיוֹנִים) gifts to the poor. This money is explicitly intended to help offset the cost of Passover ritual food and observance. The hustle needed to make it to Passover is a communal responsibility that starts in Adar.

On the wheel of the year, Adar is opposite the month of Av, and there are many ways to tunnel through the year back and forth from Adar to Av, and the High Holiday season. Adar's qualities of abundant joy, luck, and gratitude for being saved from destruction also carry with them a taste of sorrow for the destruction of the Temple that we mark on the ninth of Av, and all of the other times the Jewish people have not been miraculously saved. Later in Av, the fifteenth, Tu b'Av, is known as one of the Jewish people's happiest days, a day of love that recalls the joy of Adar. The trepidation, fear, hope, and deep resounding joy of Yom Kippur connects to Purim; Yom Kippur literally means "a day like Purim." The pairing of Adar and Av can support us when, inevitably, some years Adar is not joyful. Adar contains all the ups and downs, grief and loss, heartbreak and distress, of any given month of our lives. Adar incites us to find moments of simcha in our struggle, and reassures us that simcha will be there for us, whether we feel it or not in any given month or year.

LEAP YEARS

The Jewish calendar is a lunisolar calendar, which means it is calculated in time with the seasons and the sun, as well as the cycles of the moon. In this system, holidays are kept fixed in their seasons (spring and fall), and the new month is calculated by the new moon. In order to achieve this layered time, the Jewish calendar has leap years, in which there is a thirteenth month. Leap years are calculated in a nineteen-year cycle, and seven out of the nineteen years are "embolismic years," years with an additional month. In Jewish tradition, leap years are known as "pregnant years." This ensures that the harvest festivals continue to be celebrated in accordance with the growing year, and Rosh HaShanah is always in the fall. In pregnant years, an additional month of Adar is added, resulting in Adar I and Adar II.

Rav Kohenet Jill Hammer teaches, in the introduction to her work *The Jewish Book of Days*, that the association of each month of the Jewish calendar with a biblical tribe stretches back as early as Sefer Yetzirah, the earliest known text of Jewish mystical tradition, dating from sometime between 200 BCE and 200 CE. Hammer dedicates Adar I in a leap year to Dinah, the only named daughter among Jacob's twelve sons. An extra month of the year, especially in the season of joyfulness, is an invitation to find new forms of joy, celebrate unsung ancestors, and revel in the creativity of our tradition.

ADAR

In a leap year, the first time Adar occurs, Adar I is viewed as the additional month. Thus, Adar II holds all of the month's holidays in a leap year. There is plenty of debate about how to mark birthdays and yahrtzeits in a leap year. This can get confusing! Most scholars agree that:

* If a person dies in Adar I in a leap year, their yahrtzeit is marked in Adar in a regular year, and Adar I in a leap year.
* If a person dies in Adar II in a leap year, their yahrtzeit is marked in Adar in a regular year, and Adar II in a leap year.
* If a person dies in Adar in a regular year, in another regular year, their yahrtzeit is marked in Adar.

What happens when someone dies during Adar in a regular year, then a leap year occurs and suddenly there are two Adars? In which Adar is the yahrtzeit?

There is not rabbinic or cultural consensus on this question. Some reasons to mark the regular Adar yahrtzeit in Adar I are to follow the principle of "rushing to do a mitzvah." For example, on this principle we are taught to, when possible, pay loans back sooner rather than later. On the other hand, there are reasons for marking the regular Adar yahrtzeit in Adar II: Adar I is the "added" month, and the holidays of the month are all observed in Adar II to keep Purim tied in time to Passover. Some sources mark the yahrtzeit in both Adars, while others recommend marking it the first year in Adar I, since the counting is for "twelve months" and not one year, and in later years in Adar II.

This question of yahrtzeits can help illustrate the logic and flow of leap years. At the end of the day, we can mark any and all days that our memory and grief calls for. We can mark a yahrtzeit differently on different years, and experiment with what the rhythm of an ancient calendar, synched with both the sun and the moon, can teach us about time and honoring our beloved dead.

The parashiyot in Adar are Terumah, Tetzaveh, Ki Tisa, Vayakhel, and Pekudei. This month the Israelites build the Mishkan and adorn the priests in the most lush, beautiful creations the Holy One of Blessing can dream up. Aaron and his lineage are named as the high priests, and the craftspeople Bezalel and Oholiab are lifted up to lead the greatest theater build our people have known to that point. The people create the Golden Calf and are punished. The desire for a Golden Calf comes at the time the Israelites are waiting alone at the base of the mountain. Creating a place for God to dwell in the Mishkan gives the Israelites a place to direct their attention and passions. This month's travel through the Torah focuses on the world of aesthetics, and the pride and comfort it can bring.

Adar in Practice

7 ADAR FESTIVAL FOR CHEVRA KADISHA COMMUNITIES

The seventh of Adar marks both Moshe Rabbeinu's birthday and his yahrtzeit (יָארְצֵייט), the anniversary of his death. There is a specific tikkun (תִּיקוּן), a prayer for the day, and it has become a day in which many Jewish burial societies, chevra kadisha (חֶבְרָה קַדִּישָׁא), gather to mark the year, and celebrate each other and the important work they do. When Moshe died, we are taught, the Holy One prepared him for burial. It is on this night, then, that the sacred workers of the chevra kadisha can take a night off to reflect and be together outside of the focused and solemn work of preparing bodies for burial.

At the Community Chevra Kaddisha of Greater Boston, Em Fish reports:

> We get dinner catered at one of the area shuls and we have time to shmooze[5] (because who ever has time to shmooze! I work with these people for hours and hours and don't know much about them! Also it's so strange to see the men . . . like, are they here for a softball league benefit dinner? I've never seen them! But over the years this dinner is the reason why even the men start to look familiar. Anyway . . .) and then there's a speaker (often a prof from Hebrew College or another school in the area) about some aspect of death and dying.[6]

This practice of inversion of what is common and regular for the chevra kadisha resonates with the month of Adar, in which we turn things on their heads. On the seventh of Adar, we blend the care of death work with the joys of communal life. What new traditions do you feel called to create at that intersection?

PURIM

V'nahafoch hu (וְנַהֲפוֹךְ הוּא): the opposite happened. Purim is the holiday where we lift up and lean into reversals of fortune, upending of norms, and revolutionary change. Our ancestors taught us not to just retell this particular story, not only to ritually symbolically honor it but to literally try it on. It is not enough to simply envision winning, it must be acted out. We are encouraged to dress in character and make it live in our current time, place, and political realities. Moreover, it must be fun and funny, full of pageantry, sass, and sex. Our ancestors had, as we sometimes do today, revenge fantasies. They did not all and always fear the pharaohs of their times. They mocked them, came at them sideways, made each other laugh in order to release and relieve the tension and fear that people living under authoritarian rule can come to embody. In our Purim celebrations, we take this lesson to heart in order to ask: What is the resistance story that we want to try on this year? What creative strategies for disrupting power can we embody? How is it possible, for at least one night of the year, to get up the courage to make each other laugh, to flirt, to dance, and to play.

Megillat Esther and the Origins of Purim

The centerpiece of Purim is Megillat Esther, one of the five scrolls of Tanakh that is read publicly on specific holidays.[7] Reading it, it seems that Purim became a holiday in order to celebrate the story of Esther and Mordechai's triumph over Haman and Ahasuerus. However, many scholars believe the opposite happened: During the Persian Period (approximately 550–330 BCE), Jews were in the habit of celebrating a spring equinox timed–festival of revelry and feasting alongside their non-Jewish neighbors, and Megillat Esther was crafted to fill in a Jewish story of spring vs. winter, good vs. evil, Esther vs. Haman.[8]

The Purim story takes place in Shushan, the ruins of which are on the same site as the modern Iranian city of Shush. Observing Purim, we must be aware of the histories and contemporary realities of Orientalism and racist erasure present in Jewish life. Shushan isn't an imaginary place, and Persian Jewish culture, tradition, and communities continue to thrive today. Non-Iranian Jews observing Purim must guard against perpetrating Orientalism and appropriating Persian Jewish culture in costuming, dance, and music.

Zionist reading of Jewish history has understood Purim as yet another story proving that anti-Jewish oppression is inevitable and immutable, and that Jews have never and will never be safe in diaspora. We reject this reading. Purim teaches us that our Jewish inheritance, sacred stories, and ritual culture have always been diasporic, even within Biblical times. Purim teaches about the inherent violence of authoritarianism, the dangers of xenophobia, the responsibility of people to act courageously and collectively, and the power of women and femmes to control their own bodies and save their people.

In Megillat Esther, King Ahasuerus, a classically misogynist monarch, fires Queen Vashti for refusing to dance for him. After an unsurprisingly offensive virgin beauty contest, Hadassah, also known as Esther, becomes queen, while concealing her Jewishness. During her time as queen, comically evil Haman hatches a plot to kill all the Jews in the land. Esther, with moral support from her adoptive uncle Mordechai and the rest of the Jewish community, reveals herself as Jewish to the king and foils Haman's plan. Though the King's Haman-inspired decree to kill all the Jews can't be revoked, Ahasuerus writes a second decree, authorizing the Jews to not only defend themselves but avenge themselves against whoever attacks them. The story ends with a disturbing and heartbreakingly long list of all the places where the Jews got to extract revenge by murdering many thousands of people who had attacked them.

Megillat Esther is a layered story, hilarious and uplifting at times, painful and upsetting at others, with many details often glossed over in our retellings. Clocking in at ten narrative-packed chapters, it's one of the more readable books of Tanakh, and we recommend you check it all out for yourself. From a place of engagement with the text and its legacy, we can craft Purim seasons that encompass the depth and breadth of this holiday and its complicated legacy.

Release and Resistance

Spiritually, Purim is a time of personal and communal release. There are many drashot, stories, on the connection between Purim and Yom Kippur. At first, they seem in stark emotional and spiritual contrast: joy and mirth contrasted with solemnity and grief; collective life-saving contrasted with reenacting our deaths; masquerade, dress-up, acting a part contrasted with baring our souls, to ourselves, each other, and God. But Jewish tradition loves teaching through contrasts, and reminding us of the multitudes contained in all the moments of joy and grief (see also: breaking the glass under the chuppah). Juxtaposing Purim and Yom Kippur helps us tease out the themes of vulnerability and redemption so core to both holidays. Connecting Purim and Yom Kippur can help us take Purim more seriously and Yom Kippur more joyfully. On Purim, we ask: where can there be play, theater, humor, and joy? It is seriously important. On Yom Kippur, we ask: what are our individual and collective responsibilities?

Politically, Purim has much to teach about struggles for justice in the face of overwhelming state-sponsored terrorism. The story reveals the power of using a diversity of tactics: Vashti goes on strike, Esther salts, Mordechai lobbies, and people take on solidarity fasts with Esther. Haman parades Mordechai through the streets in an act of spontaneous political street theater. Mordechai challenges Esther to use her position of power for the greater good, to risk something real, saying: "Perhaps you have attained royal position for just such a crisis" (Esther 4:14). Ahasuerus facilitates the wealth redistribution of Haman's estate to Esther. When attacked, the Jews take up armed resistance.

Alongside and deeply woven into the story of resistance and rebellion, it is essential to confront and be accountable for acts of violence by Jews that this story spawned and encouraged. Not only do Jews take up armed resistance, they enact revenge killings; the legacy of the violence in this ripples through our text tradition and history. Haman is an Agagite, which the text understands means he is a descendant of Amalek. In Devarim 25:19, we read:

וְהָיָ֡ה בְּהָנִ֣יחַ יְהֹוָ֣ה אֱלֹהֶ֣יךָ ׀ לְ֠ךָ מִכׇּל־אֹ֨יְבֶ֜יךָ מִסָּבִ֗יב בָּאָ֙רֶץ֙ אֲשֶׁ֣ר יְהֹוָֽה־אֱלֹהֶ֗יךָ נֹתֵ֣ן לְךָ֤ נַחֲלָה֙ לְרִשְׁתָּ֔הּ תִּמְחֶה֙ אֶת־זֵ֣כֶר עֲמָלֵ֔ק מִתַּ֖חַת הַשָּׁמָ֑יִם לֹ֖א תִּשְׁכָּֽח׃

> Therefore, when Hashem your God grants you safety from all
> your enemies around you, in the land that Hashem your God is
> giving you as a hereditary portion, you shall blot out the memory
> of Amalek from under heaven. Do not forget!

Already, by the time of the Talmud, the rabbis understood that there were no living descendents of Amalek, and that the commandment was already nullified.[9] Rabbinic commentators continued to struggle with how there could be, even if it was impossible to act on, a commandment to destroy a whole people. Some interpret this as permission to act in self-defense, while others interpret it spiritually and metaphorically, that we are to blot out Amalek mentality, to oppose and work to root out any instinct in oneself or others toward violence and oppression.

In our times, extremist Zionist Jews have taken this biblical commandment as instruction to perpetrate terrorist violence against Palestinians, specifically timed around Purim.[10] On Purim 1994, Baruch Goldstein, a U.S.–born Israeli, murdered 29 and wounded 125 Palestinian Muslims in Hebron. Though this massacre was condemned in word by official bodies of the Israeli government, Goldstein's grave in Kriyat Arba became a shrine and pilgrimage site for right-wing extremists.

Today, Jews are still wrestling with how to integrate this devastating reality with how we observe Purim, a holiday traditionally marked by joyful celebration. One way of thinking about this is to go back to Megillat Esther: In Chapter 9, Jews perpetrate extreme violence on non-Jews, and the text is confusing about whether that violence was self-defense or outright aggression. In contrast with centuries of inherited wisdom about mourning the death of Pharaoh's army during the Pesach story, there is no liturgical disruption or ritual mourning of the violence in Megillat Esther.

This text has inspired violence and harm that continues to impact Palestinian lives in our lifetime. We must create new rituals to shine a light on and disrupt this violence. Our tradition's existing wisdom for reading violent texts can help us read Megillat Esther. There are, traditionally, several places in the chanting of the megillah where the music changes from the cantillation for Megillat Esther to the cantillation for Eicha (Book of Lamentations), particularly at certain moments in the story of terror and mourning. Noticeably, however, this does not typically happen in chapters 8–10 when the text describes how the Jews would "attack those who sought their hurt" (Esther 9:2). Instead, this cantillation is reserved for violence against Jews. We believe the Eicha trope is fitting for all acts of terror and violence in the text, including those perpetrated by Jews.

As with making a shiva visit (and when reading Eicha on Tisha b'Av), the community could take on the communal practice of sitting lower to or on the ground (as people are physically able) when reading the violent passages of Megillat Esther. Or, as when reading about the ten plagues during the Passover seder, we can spill out drops of wine to decrease joy. Not just symbolic, Purim, as with all holidays, includes mitzvot of material action. Matanot l'evyonim, traditionally understood as "gifts to the poor," can be an opportunity to make reparations to the Palestinian community in Hebron, which is still terrorized by settler violence, on Purim and throughout the year. In these ways, and more that we will discover every year, Purim can become a holiday of resistance to *all* empires.

Fasting and Feasting

Much like during Pesach, there is a robust tradition of eating foods that represent the story of Purim. Hamantaschen (Yiddish "Haman pockets"), or Oznei Haman ("Ears of Haman"), are delicious triangle-shaped shortbread cookies with jam in the middle, representing the villain of the Purim story. For others, they resemble a vulva.[11] Folares are a Sephardic food, pastry dough flecked with cheese in a cage-like shape representing Haman's hanging noose, holding an egg, symbolizing Haman's head.

For some, observing Purim begins with Ta'anit Esther, the fast of Esther, a dawn to dusk fast on erev Purim, the thirteenth day of Adar (if Purim falls on a Sunday, then Ta'anit Esther is marked on the eleventh day of Adar so as to not fast on Shabbat). This practice is not referenced in rabbinic literature as a way to mark Purim until the eighth to ninth centuries. It resonates, however, with the fast that Esther did to spiritually prepare herself to confront Ahasuerus, and the solidarity fasts that the Jews of Shushan observed with her. Today, some have the practice of dedicating their Ta'anit Esther fast to talking about and organizing against gendered violence in Jewish communities and the world.

Mitzvot and Melachot

There are four signature mitzvot on Purim. Each of these mitzvot have their own robust body of scholarship on how to observe them, and myriad opportunities to make them meaningful and values-aligned in our time.

1. MIKRA MEGILLAH

Reading Megillat Esther preferably happens publicly, in the synagogue or in a collective space. Many traditions exist about how to read the megillah: everyone should have their own scroll or copy in front of them, different trope is used to chant various sections of the story (see above), and pauses and volume changes can be used for emphasis. Even the traditional "straight" reading of the scroll is high drama, and everyone is obligated to hear it. Our ancestors understood the use of compelling theatrics to tell important stories, a teaching tool that can be embodied during Purim and all year round.

Before reading the megillah, the reader traditionally says three blessings:

בָּרוּךְ אַתָּה יהוה אֱלֹהֵינוּ מֶלֶךְ הָעוֹלָם, אֲשֶׁר קִדְּשָׁנוּ בְּמִצְוֹתָיו, וְצִוָּנוּ עַל מִקְרָא מְגִלָּה.

Baruch atah Adonai, Eloheinu Ruach ha'olam, asher kid'shanu b'mitzvotav, v'tzivanu al mikra megilah.

Blessed are You, our God, Creative Source of the world, Who makes us holy through mitzvot, and instructs us to read the megillah.

בָּרוּךְ אַתָּה, יְיָ אֱלֹהֵינוּ, מֶלֶךְ הָעוֹלָם, שֶׁעָשָׂה נִסִּים לַאֲבוֹתֵינוּ וְאִמּוֹתֵינוּ בַּיָּמִים הָהֵם בַּזְּמַן הַזֶּה.

Baruch atah Adonai, Eloheinu Melech ha'olam, she-asah nisim la'avoteinu bayamim hahem bazman hazeh.

Praised are You, Our God, Source of the universe, Who performed wondrous deeds for our ancestors in those ancient days at this season.

בָּרוּךְ אַתָּה יְיָ אֱלֹהֵינוּ מֶלֶךְ הָעוֹלָם, שֶׁהֶחֱיָנוּ וְקִיְּמָנוּ וְהִגִּיעָנוּ לַזְּמַן הַזֶּה.

Baruch atah Adonai, Elohenu Melech ha'olam, Shehecheyanu, v'kiyimanu, v'higiyanu la'zman hazeh.

Praised are You, Our God, Miracle of the universe, Who has given us life and sustained us and enabled us to reach this season.

The traditional blessing after reading Megillat Esther thanks God for supporting and saving us, alongside thanking God for punishing our foes and exacting vengeance, saying:

Blessed are You, HaShem, our God, Source of the universe, Who takes up our grievance, judges our claim, avenges our wrong; Who brings just retribution upon all enemies of our soul, and exacts vengeance for us from our foes. Blessed are You, Adonai, Who exacts vengeance for His people Israel from all their foes, the God Who brings salvation.

Reisa Aviva Mukamal created a brilliantly simple, edited version of this blessing, deleting the vengeance, and preserving the safety. Mukamal suggests reciting instead:

Blessed are You, Adonai, our God, Creator of the universe, Who takes up our grievance, judges our claim, avenges our wrong; Blessed are You, Adonai, the God who brings salvation.[12]

We can experiment, each year, with what we feel moved to give thanks to and bless after hearing megillah read. It might be for the Source of holiness, it might be for other sources of protection and safety. We might give thanks for the blessing of getting to read this challenging text in community, or the blessing of receiving millennia-old inherited tradition.

2. SEUDAT PURIM

The festive Purim meal is a seudat mitzvah, a halachically obligatory meal. We have seudot mitzvah on lifecycle celebrations, Shabbat and chaggim (holidays), to comfort mourners, and in moments of gratitude. The Seudat Purim is an embodiment of celebrating Jewish survival and thriving. Even when Purim falls on a weekday, communal Purim shpils and parties often get scheduled for Saturday nights. While we appreciate the practicality of this, we love a weekday Seudat Purim as a delicious way to mark Purim on the Jewish calendar. It is tradition to drink wine on Purim, to drink until one can "no longer tell the difference between 'Cursed-is-Haman,' and 'Blessed-is-Mordechai.'"[13] Part of creating a truly joyful Purim is having a range of creative spaces, which must include sober events where fun and joy flow.

3. MISHLOACH MANOT, SHALACH MANOS, PLATICOS DE PURIM

Sending gifts is the mitzvah of sending edible gifts. At least two edible "portions" are sent to someone to communicate care and respect for the recipient. This mitzvah is designed as a way to remember the Jewish care and solidarity between Esther, Mordechai, and the Jews of Shushan. We love the obligation to feed each other, to care for each other materially, with deliciousness. To eat and feed each other treats. To remember that in the long struggles we're a part of, we don't only need to work and think, but also to nourish and delight.

4. MATANOT L'EVYONIM

Giving gifts to the poor, along with feasting and giving gifts to friends and comrades, is part of the original instructions in Megillat Esther on how to observe Purim. Rabbinic tradition instructs that this is separate from other tzedakah obligations. Matanot l'evyonim must be given during the day of Purim, in time for someone to be able to use it to celebrate Purim, though without any question about what it will be used for.

In the centuries of rabbinic scholarship and halachic teaching on tzedakah, there is plenty to wrestle with: outdated assumptions about money and power, classist language, and patronizing instructions. There is also robust and, in many ways, countercultural material and practices of wealth redistribution.[14] From the mitzvah of matanot l'evyonim, we learn it isn't possible to celebrate the joy of Purim without materially attending to inequity in both the Jewish and the wider community. This mitzvah points to valuing all people's need and worthiness for joy and celebration, in contrast with so much contemporary charity model money moving that never directly gives people money, and often has extreme stipulations on what it can be used for. Many communities collect money on Purim that is specifically given directly to benefit poor people's lives and needs, without strings attached or overhead taken.

Though Purim is a day of joy and feasting, it is not a biblically instructed festival. Melacha (מְלָאכָה) work is technically permitted, with the strong recommendation that one does it only if it's joyful and in the spirit of celebration. This is not possible for most people under capitalism. Where possible, we recommend late starts and long lunches, and creating Purim-style joy on any day of the week, month, and lifetime that we can reach it.

Until You Cannot Tell the Difference: Drinking on Purim

The rabbinic instruction to drink on Purim comes from Megillah 7b:

אָמַר רָבָא: מִיחַיַּיב אִינִישׁ לְבַסּוֹמֵי בְּפוּרַיָּא עַד דְּלָא יָדַע בֵּין אָרוּר הָמָן לְבָרוּךְ מָרְדֳּכַי.

> Rava said: A person is obligated to become intoxicated with wine on Purim until he is so intoxicated that he does not know how to distinguish between cursed is Haman and blessed is Mordecai.

The raucous celebration of the miracle of Purim and the inversion of reality for some is most quickly done with a strong drink. In some communities even the most dour can be found knocking back a shot on the bimah. Jewish spaces in general have an affirmative relationship with drinking, like on Simchat Torah or on Shabbat.

However, drinking is not required, and when planning a communal

Purim observance, it is important to consider sober people and folks in recovery in your community and how to make spaces safer for them. One of the two traditional megillah readings can be dry, we can always have mocktails available, and people can be encouraged to bring their own drinks of whatever is joyful and delicious to them. Pikuach nefesh, saving a life, supersedes all other mitzvot.

Another traditional way to invert reality, to confuse the hero with the villain, is through napping. It is hard to know the difference between good and bad when sleeping! If you don't drink on Purim, you can observe the mitzvah by slipping into the dreamworld.

Directly following the Gemara quoted above about the obligation to become intoxicated on Purim, we read this story:

רַבָּה וְרַבִּי זֵירָא עָבְדוּ סְעוּדַת פּוּרִים בַּהֲדֵי הֲדָדֵי. אִיבַּסּוּם. קָם רַבָּה שַׁחְטֵיהּ לְרַבִּי זֵירָא. לְמָחָר, בָּעֵי רַחֲמֵי וְאַחֲיֵיהּ. לְשָׁנָה, אֲמַר לֵיהּ: נֵיתֵי מָר וְנַעֲבֵיד סְעוּדַת פּוּרִים בַּהֲדֵי הֲדָדֵי. אֲמַר לֵיהּ: לָא בְּכׇל שַׁעְתָּא וְשַׁעְתָּא מִתְרְחִישׁ נִיסָּא.

Rabba and Rabbi Zeira prepared a Purim feast with each other, and they became intoxicated to the point that Rabba arose and slaughtered Rabbi Zeira. The next day, when he became sober and realized what he had done, Rabba asked God for mercy, and revived him. The next year, Rabba said to Rabbi Zeira . . . "come and let us prepare the Purim feast with each other." [Rabbi Zeira] said to [Rabba]: "Miracles do not happen each and every hour."

From this we learn that our ancestors also struggled with the kind of harm that can happen under the influence of substances, and practiced setting boundaries with each other, not returning to party with someone who'd shown themself unable to observe Purim responsibly in their simcha. We hope to create Purim celebrations where we can learn from this wisdom of our ancestors. We learn from our ancestors that we cannot compromise safety for want of a Purim celebration. We want to create Purim celebrations where we consider our collective safety before harm happens.

ADAR

Revolutionary Theater: Radical Purim Shpils

Dramatic costuming is another way to invert reality, and Purim shpils, skits and plays, are the fantastical, often farcical retelling of the Purim story. Purim offers a release valve, a chance to blow off steam that builds up within a community over the year, or in our larger world.

A shpil has inherent political potential, as it is often an artistic telling of a story by marginalized people that mocks power and marginalized people. Radical Purim Shpils have been created for many years and, for many queer and leftist Jews, the ur-shpil is the Aftselakhis Spectacle Committee, a group affiliated with Jews for Racial and Economic Justice. In their book *Dazzle Camouflage: Spectacular Theatrical Strategies for Resistance and Resilience*, Ezra Berkley Nepon writes:

> Since 2002, Jews for Racial and Economic Justice (JFREJ) has sponsored a radical Purimshpil project founded by Adrienne Cooper and Jenny Romaine in partnership with the Workmen's Circle/Arbeter-Ring and the Great Small Works Theater Company. In the late 2000's, the Afselakhis Spectacle Committee formed as a collective of artists and cultural producers who have continued to work with JFREJ and a long list of other artists and social justice organizations to produce Purim spectacles that bring together 500+ revelers each year for a wild time. This Purimshpil offers a powerful example of what can happen when we use our cultural abundance in our political organizing. The shows have enlivened, enlightened, confused and inspired JFREJ members, comrades, and friends from 2002's *Giant Puppet Purim Ball Against the Death Penalty* to 2004's *Rehearsal for the Downfall of Shoeshine: An Immigrant Justice Purim Spectacular!* to 2007's *Roti and Homentaschn: The Palace Workers Revolt!* to 2013's *I See What You're Doing: Purim, Puppets, Politsey*, and 2015's *Your Roots Are Showing: An Underground Purim Botanical*.[15]

Today, radical Purim shpils that embody leftist political values and explore justice movements in comic and joyful retellings are taking place in an ever increasing number of cities and synagogues.

Costuming

Costumes on Purim range from the traditional (Queen Vashti or Uncle Mordechai), to the topical (a pun on the most recent political uproar), to the fantastic (a glittery explosion meets papier mâché meets strange wigs). Above all is the power to reveal a truth about oneself through concealment behind a costume. Let your freakiest flag fly on Purim. Let your greatest hopes, deepest desires, or strongest fears be interpreted through costume.

Purim is femme magic at its best, the political shaking booties with the beautiful, the grotesque coated in sequins and sitting center stage. Vashti, our non-Jewish ancestor who was too busy at her all-ladies party to dance for her husband, who shouted "No!" in the face of the entitled misogynistic monarchy, gets down only with those she chooses. Purim is a pageant, a revelation, a show.

By concealing our identities, divisions that might exist in a community or between groups of people are lessened, and celebration could, at its most divine and possible, be a communal and horizontal activity.

Purim is also a time when white people's racism, Ashkenazi people's exoticization of Mizrahi people, and cis people's transphobia can get violently expressed through costume. While the holiday is a time for playful reversals, it is never ok for people with material power in the systems in which we live to spoof people who are the targets of violence by those same systems. Blackface and Brownface are never ok.

Meanwhile, some people "cross dress" on Purim in observance of inversions and re-becomings. Rabbi Emily Aviva Kapor has written about the potential liberatory power of this practice, as well as the dangers of transphobia. She writes:

> If you are a trans* person and you enjoy dressing up however you enjoy it on Purim, please, don't stop. Express your truth however you're going to express it. If you're just starting to experiment, do not let anything I've written deter you. Experiment however you're going to experiment, and do what feels right when it feels right to do it. Just because I didn't have great Purim experiences doesn't mean you won't as well. Yours might be fantastic. Don't let me stop you from exploring.

If you are a cis person who is cross-dressing on Purim, please, please think about it carefully. Consider the implications, especially to trans* people. Think about it from the perspective of a trans* person who sees you. What message are you sending to them? Are you supporting them? Demonstrating allyship? What if they're not out yet, and they see you? What might that tell them about being trans*?

Purim is a holiday when the truth is supposed to come out. I hope that we can all do our part to make this truth one of inclusivity and affirmation.[16]

Bringing It Home: Shushan Purim, Purim Katan, and Local Purim

מְבָרֵךְ עַל הָרָעָה מֵעֵין עַל הַטּוֹבָה, וְעַל הַטּוֹבָה מֵעֵין עַל הָרָעָה.

One says the benediction for a calamity apart from any attendant good, and for good fortune apart from any attendant evil.

—Brachot 54a

Shushan Purim is observed within walled cities, now only Jerusalem, on the day after Purim, the fifteenth of Adar. At the conclusion of the megillah when the Jewish people are given free reign to attack their enemies, the mustered Jews who fought in walled cities attack for two days instead of just one.[17] We continue to struggle with the violence embedded into the story of Purim and look for creative ways to embody anti-Zionist principles in our Purim celebrations. Shushan Purim could instead become a day of collective mourning for Zionist violence.

Purim Katan is observed in leap years on the fourteenth of Adar I. Though Purim is not celebrated in Adar I but instead the following month in Adar II, the calendar ensures we mark the fourteenth of the month all the same. Similarly, Shushan Purim Katan is observed on fifteenth of Adar I.

Local Purim observances are established to commemorate the local Jewish community being saved from violence or disaster, evocative of how the Jews of Shushan were saved in Megillat Esther. For example, Purim Edom is celebrated on 4 Heshvan in commemoration of the Jews of Algiers who were saved from destruction in the Spanish-Algerian wars of 1516–17 and 1542. Jews of Leghorn celebrate a local Purim on 12 Shevat to mark when the community was saved from destruction in an earthquake in 1742. Jews in Mstislavl (Russia) mark a local Purim on 4 Shevat to mark when the community was saved from slaughter by the Cossacks in 1744. The custom of local Purims is an invitation for us to learn the specific histories of the places we live today, both to reckon with antisemitism *and* to celebrate our survival. What day would your community celebrate, and how could that celebration be a reminder and source of thriving?

Family Purim, similarly to local Purim celebrations, mark life-saving miracles on a much smaller scale. Povidl Purim ("Plum Jam Purim") is marked by the Brandeis family of Jungbunzlau, in Bohemia, on the tenth of Adar, when David Brandeis and his family were saved from the accusation of having killed non-Jews by poisoning plum jam, in 1731. The Heller family of Prague marks a family Purim on 1 Adar when Yom Tov Lipman, the Rabbi of Prague, was saved from a death sentence, in 1629.[18]

ADAR

Putting on a Purimshpil

Anyone can put on a Purim play. It can be for the city's radical Jewish enclave, a local organization, your family, or your collective housemates. Purim shpils have been happening since the 1500s, and have historically been funny monologues, straight retellings of the Purim story, or plays that integrate contemporary themes with biblical themes and the story of Purim itself. The shpil is an opportunity to make art about liberation, or Jewish farce. It is a chance to find your story in an ancient Jewish story. It is an opportunity to make medicine!

First, think about the audience. Ask: Who is this shpil for? Who is this shpil aiming to nurture, who is it aiming to agitate? What are the political realities in your local/city/state community? What is the audience yearning for in days like these? What has happened in the life of your community this year that needs a release valve (for example: fear, tension, or processing collective work).

Second, consider stories. Think about: what is the story of Purim teaching on a personal level this year? Study Megillat Esther with the shpil writers, and see what emerges. Should the focus be on a particular element or character? What messages of the story are crying out to be told?

Third, find a message, find a gloss. Contemplate: How can the Purim story best be told to one's specific community? What should be lifted up and emphasized that the community needs to hear this year? What is the takeaway message for the shpil?

Is there a larger story frame to set this in, like a well-known musical, or folk story, or news article? By taking community needs and the story of Purim into a third world, it is possible to bring in more play, more creativity, and more exploration of an idea from all sides.

Fourth, get busy! Write a script or a song cycle. Assemble costumes. Rehearse. Make a snazzy invitation and flier. Invite friends and neighbors and make a playlist for post-shpil dancing. Get a band together. Break a leg.

However you tell and wrestle with the story, the exuberance of Purim and the joy of Adar can catapult us across the final sprint of winter months and into spring. As the season begins to turn, we look toward even more liberatory visions of the world to come, and practicing freedom in the here and now.

Illustration © Sol Weiss. Incantation © Dori Midnight.

come upon us, Spring,
with your winds of pleasure and change
with your fireflowers and lilacs and nettles that make us want to be
face down in earth
huffing your holy scent

from the narrows, we cry out
and You answer us with
an expanse of sky and sea,
fields of poppies,
a dream of milk and honey

awaken our tongues, Bitterness,
make us gush
hungry for life itself
compel us to move toward freedom
leaving no one behind

open all the doors!
the prophets are right here, right now—
making ways of no ways, teaching us about collective care, chaining
themselves to trees, dancing in infinite gender, ruining kings, bringing
water, saving seeds, remembering diasporic languages, blockading
pipelines, weaving prayers, walking out, lying down

some days we gather around the kitchen table and plot the
revolution
some days we are sick and tired
we make a plate of beet and bone, saltwater and greens,
orange, spoon, and root
maybe read that one poem
make nonna's soup
dayenu : it is enough

the garden is full of fists of flowers
raised in revolt
toward the growing light,
toward another world
which is also here and now

WELCOME TO נִיסָן NISAN

Where do you see signs of change, big or small, in your life, on the earth, in the world? What can you do to nurture seeds of change?

What stories of revolution are part of your lineage? Who do you want to share your stories with? What lessons have you learned from the stories you've inherited? How do you live out these stories of revolution?

What does freedom mean to you? How do you embody freedom in your life? What would freedom look like in your communities? What strategies for getting free have you deepened or learned about since last Pesach? What do you want to practice more of in the year to come?

Introduction to Nisan

בָּרוּךְ אַתָּה יְיָ אֱלֹהֵינוּ מֶלֶךְ הָעוֹלָם, שֶׁלֹא חִסַּר בָּעוֹלָמוֹ כְּלוּם, וּבָרָא בּוֹ בְּרִיּוֹת טוֹבוֹת וְאִילָנוֹת טוֹבִים, לְהַנּוֹת בָּהֶם בְּנֵי אָדָם:

Barukh atah Adonai Eloheinu Melech ha'olam shelo ḥiseir ba-olamo Klum uvara vo briyot tovot v'ilanot tovim l'hanot bahem b'nei Adam.

Blessed are you, our God, Divine Source, for there is nothing lacking in the world at all, and good creatures and good trees were created in it, through which pleasure is brought to humans.

In Nisan we bless the earth as she begins to sprout, we affirm freedom where we see it blooming, and we bow to the turning of the season. In the

Northern Hemisphere, the month of Nisan is the time when we can say this special blessing for seeing a fruit tree in bloom.

As with all of the Jewish year, the layers of Nisan illuminate and reinforce each other, as our people's stories and rituals are layered on top of and interwoven with the earth's stories and rituals. Nisan is about newness: new growth, new freedoms, and a new year.

EARTH BLOOM

As with so much of the Jewish year, the calendar points to the earth's wisdom, as the seasons point to the Jewish calendar's offerings. In Torah, this month is known as Chodesh HaAviv (חֹדֶשׁ הָאָבִיב). Aviv is the early stage of ripening, evoking greenness, fresh, young, barley shoots, and refers to the spring. All around, in many places Jews have lived, there are new green and growing things starting to peek their heads out. The days are getting longer and the spring equinox is here, or near. The earth calls out for change, newness, revolution. The zodiac sign of Nisan is Aries, the lamb or the ram, present in the month on the seder plate in the form of the shank bone and bringing our attention, all month long, to new life.

LIBERATION STORY

When we picture and feel into spring, it makes embodied sense that our ancestors observed Pesach, a festival of freedom, in this season. In Torah, the Israelite people experienced enslavement in Mitzrayim. Mitzrayim (מִצְרַיִם) is the biblical Hebrew word for Egypt. Its root צער, also means narrowness. When we speak of leaving Mitzrayim, in the context of today's anti-Arab racism and Islamophobia, it is important to affirm that we are not talking about contemporary Egypt.

Instead, in Nisan, we explore freedom struggles from across time, asking what lessons they have to teach us today. We consider what spiritual freedom might be: breaking out of doubt, and releasing constriction that keeps us stuck in narrow places. During Nisan, there is an opportunity to reckon with the overwhelming weight of slavery and dispossession, envision liberation, share strategies to fight smarter, and promise each other to continue on the journey together. During Nisan, we reckon with the weight and velocity of the empires that we live under, and carve out space to speak the world to come into existence.

We often focus on how this happens at the seder meal, when we come together around picnic blankets or piled on couches or scrunched around folding tables. Freedom is embodied in our posture and sung in songs from an unlocked heart. We fill our plates with foods that teach and nourish, and experiment with getting free under the full moon. And the rituals of the freedom journey expand all month long, beginning with cleaning for Pesach leading up to the holiday and incorporating a special Shabbat before Pesach. We learn from our ancestors that moving out of narrowness is not an end but a beginning.

In the cycle of the Jewish year, Pesach is the very beginning of the next journey, or a midpoint in one long journey. On the second night, Jews begin counting the Omer, counting seven weeks of seven days until Shavuot, the celebration of receiving Torah at Sinai. This season is full of spiritual, ancestral, and communal offerings, tools to engage minds, bodies, and hearts. It is a time for reflection on where we've been, where we are going, and the daily attention it takes to create and embody liberation for all.

A NEW YEAR

In Jewish tradition, all of this springing forth, from the earth and from material and metaphorical constriction, adds up to a significant seasonal shift. In Shemot 12:2, God tells Moses and Aaron:

הַחֹדֶשׁ הַזֶּה לָכֶם רֹאשׁ חֳדָשִׁים רִאשׁוֹן הוּא לָכֶם לְחָדְשֵׁי הַשָּׁנָה:

This month shall mark for you the beginning of the months;
it shall be the first of the months of the year for you.

The first of Nisan is one of the new years that the Mishnah teaches about in Rosh Hashanah 1:1, saying:

בְּאֶחָד בְּנִיסָן רֹאשׁ הַשָּׁנָה לַמְּלָכִים וְלָרְגָלִים

The first of Nisan is the new year for kings and for festivals.

Though we count the year change in Tishrei, Nisan is considered the first month. Nisan is often referred to as the "civic year," from which festivals are counted[1] and the reigns of kings begin and end. Telling the liberation story of Pesach this month allows people to imagine even more freedom, and envision a new way of governing our collective lives.

Jewish tradition instructs us that in this season of new growth, it is time to clean out the cobwebs and crumbs from the corners of our home and hearts. We go to the corners of our hearts and clean out that which keeps us stuck in narrow places. We make seders together to notice what is resonating across many bodies and neshamot. In the circle of the year, it is instructive that Nisan is opposite Tishrei. While the work of Tishrei is often focused on personal and interpersonal renewal, Nisan invites a focus on collective revolution and renewal, and an orientation of life and work toward greater visions for collective liberation. The harvests of Tishrei feed what we build in Nisan; the visions dreamed in Nisan guide our personal work in Tishrei. In this way, living in the spiral of Jewish time creates mutually reinforcing processes: our individual bodies' healing and freedom are possible only in the context of collective and communal healing and freedom; our collectives and communities are made up of diverse, holy bodies that deserve liberatory love and care. In the Nisan, we celebrate the ways in which all of our freedom is possible and close at hand.

The parashiyot in Nisan are Vayikra, Tzav, and Shmini. We read of the offerings, the reasonings for them, and the logistics of temple sacrifice. Aaron and his sons are ordained, and then Nadav and Avihu, his eldest, die after bringing an unrequested offering. In the month of Nisan we are called to think about our location in the collective Jewish story of Exodus and find ourselves in this story of freedom. One of the ways we do this is through the minutiae—the cleaning and preparing and obsessing over getting our homes ready for Passover. It is the tension between minute detail and cosmic questions that electrifies the month of Nisan and creates such holiness in bringing sacrifices. It is the swing between mundane and divine where Judaism lives, in this month in particular.

Nisan in Action

PESACH: THE LEFTIST HIGH HOLIDAY

Pesach is, for many radical Jews, the true High Holiday of the year. It is the time when we create intimate, extended gatherings with our closest comrades, and dive into the hardest questions of our organizing, long into the night. It is the time to organize massive community-wide sedarim, and sit around the table with other Jews, non-Jews, family by birth or by choice, comrades, friends, and all those beloved ones who are deep into different campaigns, and cross-pollinate. After the long winter, during which we might have had trouble leaving the house or finding sources of joy and hope, Pesach focuses our attention on newly growing things and old stories of liberation.

Every year there is an opportunity to grow: to start preparing for Pesach in a way that cleans out the nooks and crannies of our hearts and spirits, deepening our seders' magic and purpose. The seder then becomes not only the culmination of a journey of liberation but the beginning of a journey of transformation and redemption.

RE/TELLING THE STORY

The holiday of Pesach is rooted in Torah, which teaches *how* to commemorate the Exodus from Mitzrayim before it actually takes place. In between the announcement of the tenth plague and its enactment, there are a few verses in which God instructs the Israelites both how to escape the tenth plague when it happens and how to observe Pesach in the future.

The Israelites are instructed to roast a lamb from the tenth until the fourteenth of the month, and then put the blood of the lamb on their doorposts, eat the roast offering with unleavened bread and bitter herbs, and burn any leftovers. The blood will keep away the Angel of Death, who will kill every firstborn child of their enslavers, the tenth plague, and spare their households. In this day is called a זכרון (zikaron), a remembrance. And so, in Shemot 12:14–16, Passover is established:

וְהָיָה֩ הַיּ֨וֹם הַזֶּ֤ה לָכֶם֙ לְזִכָּר֔וֹן וְחַגֹּתֶ֥ם אֹת֖וֹ חַ֣ג לַֽיהוָ֑ה לְדֹרֹ֣תֵיכֶ֔ם חֻקַּ֥ת עוֹלָ֖ם תְּחָגֻּֽהוּ׃ שִׁבְעַ֤ת יָמִים֙ מַצּ֣וֹת תֹּאכֵ֔לוּ אַ֚ךְ בַּיּ֣וֹם הָרִאשׁ֔וֹן תַּשְׁבִּ֥יתוּ שְּׂאֹ֖ר מִבָּתֵּיכֶ֑ם כִּ֣י ׀ כָּל־אֹכֵ֣ל חָמֵ֗ץ וְנִכְרְתָ֞ה הַנֶּ֤פֶשׁ הַהִוא֙ מִיִּשְׂרָאֵ֔ל מִיּ֥וֹם הָרִאשֹׁ֖ן עַד־י֥וֹם הַשְּׁבִעִֽי׃ (טז) וּבַיּ֤וֹם הָרִאשׁוֹן֙ מִקְרָא־קֹ֔דֶשׁ וּבַיּוֹם֙ הַשְּׁבִיעִ֔י מִקְרָא־קֹ֖דֶשׁ יִהְיֶ֣ה לָכֶ֑ם כָּל־מְלָאכָה֙ לֹא־יֵעָשֶׂ֣ה בָהֶ֔ם אַ֣ךְ אֲשֶׁ֧ר יֵאָכֵ֛ל לְכָל־נֶ֖פֶשׁ ה֥וּא לְבַדּ֖וֹ יֵעָשֶׂ֥ה לָכֶֽם׃

This day shall be to you one of remembrance: you shall celebrate it as a festival to HaShem throughout the ages; you shall celebrate it as an institution for all time. Seven days you shall eat unleavened bread; on the very first day you shall remove leaven from your houses, for whoever eats leavened bread from the first day to the seventh day, that person shall be cut off from Yisrael. You shall celebrate a sacred occasion on the first day, and a sacred occasion on the seventh day; no work at all shall be done on them; only what every person is to eat, that alone may be prepared for you.

The establishment of Pesach within the story of the killing of the first-born children is only one of the disturbing and confusing aspects of how we relate to the Exodus story. In observing Pesach and retelling the Exodus story, we are confronted with the task of interrupting cycles of violence that come down through the millennia in this narrative.

We also wrestle with how to tell the story of the Exodus, living in a time and context with different relationships to story and history than those of past generations. We are told in Shemot 13:8 to tell the Exodus story in the first person:

וְהִגַּדְתָּ֣ לְבִנְךָ֔ בַּיּ֥וֹם הַה֖וּא לֵאמֹ֑ר בַּעֲב֣וּר זֶ֗ה עָשָׂ֤ה יְיָ֙ לִ֔י בְּצֵאתִ֖י מִמִּצְרָֽיִם׃

And you shall explain to your son on that day, 'It is because of what the Divine did for me when I went free from Mitzrayim.'

As part of observing Pesach, Torah commands the recitation of a statement, also stressed in the Mishnah,[2] that describes the Exodus journey into expansiveness as a family affair. In Devarim 26:5 we read:

וְעָנִיתָ וְאָמַרְתָּ לִפְנֵי ׀ יְיָ אֱלֹהֶיךָ אֲרַמִּי אֹבֵד אָבִי וַיֵּרֶד מִצְרַיְמָה וַיָּגָר שָׁם בִּמְתֵי מְעָט וַיְהִי־שָׁם לְגוֹי גָּדוֹל עָצוּם וָרָב:

> You shall then recite as follows before the HaShem your God:
> "My father was a fugitive Aramean. He went down to Mitzrayim
> with meager numbers and sojourned there; but there he became
> a great and very populous nation."

Many of us were either taught, or assumed, that while some elements of the Exodus story were exaggerated for dramatic effect, it still told some kind of verified history. In this context, it can be upsetting to learn there is very little academic consensus upon extrabiblical evidence for the Exodus, as it is told in Torah.

There are, however, histories of the people who came to be the Israelites, who told the stories that became Torah, who struggled under overwhelming material oppression, who experienced and resisted empires, who dreamed of freedom. They came from a culture without the concepts of "fact" and "fiction" that we have today, and with very different relationships to story.

When we retell the Exodus story in the first person, we are not making a claim to its historical veracity, or celebrating the violence in the story. Instead, we are communicating that we, in complicated and ever-shifting ways, accept the complex legacy of this story, in all of its nuance. We take upon ourselves the responsibility to ask the questions raised by this story, year after year.

CHAMETZ

Passover arrives in spirit long before the first seder on the fifteenth of Nisan. Preparing for the holiday can be as meaningful as the celebration itself. Torah says, in Shemot 13:3:

וַיֹּאמֶר מֹשֶׁה אֶל־הָעָם זָכוֹר אֶת־הַיּוֹם הַזֶּה אֲשֶׁר יְצָאתֶם מִמִּצְרַיִם מִבֵּית עֲבָדִים
כִּי בְּחֹזֶק יָד הוֹצִיא יְהֹוָה אֶתְכֶם מִזֶּה וְלֹא יֵאָכֵל חָמֵץ:

And Moses said to the people, "Remember this day, on which you
went free from Mitzrayim, the house of bondage, how HaShem
freed you from it with a mighty hand: no leavened bread shall
be eaten."

This instruction is repeated in Devarim 16:4:

וְלֹא־יֵרָאֶה לְךָ שְׂאֹר בְּכָל־גְּבֻלְךָ שִׁבְעַת יָמִים וְלֹא־יָלִין מִן־הַבָּשָׂר אֲשֶׁר תִּזְבַּח
בָּעֶרֶב בַּיּוֹם הָרִאשׁוֹן לַבֹּקֶר:

And there shall be no leaven seen with thee in all the borders
seven days; neither shall any of the flesh, which you sacrificest
the first day at even, remain all night until the morning.

Chametz is any food made from five prohibited grains, combined with
a leavening agent, and left to rise for longer than eighteen minutes. Most
translations of the five prohibited grains understand them as wheat, barley,
oat, rye, and spelt. Clearing chametz out of the home and out of one's possession happens until the night before Passover. In some homes, cabinets
are cleared out and wiped down and Passover dishes are carried up from
the basement. Closets containing pots not kosher for Passover are locked
or taped off, and all food not kosher for Passover is put away. Chametz can
be carried out of the house entirely and sold or given away to mutual aid
and food redistribution organizations.

This cleaning offers an opportunity to think about what spiritual chametz needs clearing out. Parallel to the month of Tishrei, this is the mid-
way point of the year. What commitments, hopes, and agreements did you
enter into during the Yamim Noraim? It is human to accrue chametz, and
there is nothing wrong with it. The wheel of the year provides opportunities to reflect and restart.

It can be easy to lose track of the reasons for cleaning. Part of the
challenge of cleaning for Passover is focusing on the spiritual preparation
and not becoming fixated on scrubbing. It is so easy to feel pressure to

clean every corner of the house, and, as each day ticks closer to Passover, to become more and more burdened by the cleaning and cooking left to do.[3] In many homes, this becomes gendered labor, the bulk of the work needed to make Pesach done by women. A refrain we love, "Dust isn't chametz and your children are not the Passover sacrifice," is a reminder that the anxiety and stress of cleaning creeps in easily, but Passover cleaning has a specific goal. It is chametz, not dust, we are obligated to remove from our homes. How can you connect to the ritualized cleaning without offering up your well-being to the anxiety of kashering the house?

There's a ritual for that.

On the night before Passover, each Jewish household performs bedikat chametz (בְּדִיקַת חָמֵץ), a final search for chametz in the house. This closes the door on the need to clean and marks a transition between unready and ready. The searchers gather first to make a blessing:

בָּרוּךְ אַתָּה, יְיָ אֱלֹהֵינוּ, מֶלֶךְ הָעוֹלָם אֲשֶׁר קִדְּשָׁנוּ בְּמִצְוֹתָיו, וְצִוָּנוּ עַל בְּעוּר חָמֵץ.

Baruch ata Adonai Eloheinu melech ha'olam asher kid'shanu b'mitzvotav v'tzivanu al bi'ur chametz.

Blessed are You, Adonai our God, Source of the universe, who has sanctified us through commandments, and has commanded us concerning the removal of chametz.

With a feather, spoon, and candle, the searchers move about the house checking corners and behind furniture to find any spots where chametz may still be hiding. There is a custom to hide an additional ten pieces of chametz, wrapped in something flammable, and find them, too. The chametz is gathered and set aside to be burned the next morning. The ritual ends with the recitation of the below text, kol chamira, in a language they understand perhaps as many as three times to strengthen the point:

SEPHARDIC TEXT

כל חמירא דאיכא ברשותי,
דלא חזיתיה ודלא בערתיה,
אעראד ארפעכ יוהלו ליטבל

All chametz in my possession that I
have not seen,
and have not destroyed,
shall be nullified like the dust of
the earth.

ASHKENAZI TEXT

כל חמירא וחמיעא דאיכא ברשותי,
דלא חזיתיה ודלא בערתיה,
לבטיל ולהוי הפקר כעפרא דארעא

All chametz or leaven in my
possession that I have not seen,
and have not destroyed,
shall be nullified and become
ownerless,
like the dust of the earth.

The next morning, all remaining chametz should be burned. Some communities will have huge bonfires going the morning of Passover, where chametz can be destroyed. The text to recite during the burning is:

SEPHARDIC TEXT

כל חמירא דאיכא ברשותי,
היתיזח אלדו היתיזחד
היתרעב אלדו היתרעבד
אעראד ארפעכ יוהלו ליטבל

All chametz in my possession that
I have seen and that I have not
seen,
that I have destroyed and that I
have not destroyed,
shall be nullified like the dust of
the earth

ASHKENAZI TEXT

כל חמירא וחמיעא דאיכא ברשותי,
היתיזח אלדו היתיזחד
היתרעב אלדו היתרעבד
אעראד ארפעכ רקפה יוהלו ליטבל

All chametz or leaven in my
possession that I have seen and
that I have not seen,
that I have destroyed and that I
have not destroyed,
shall be nullified and become
ownerless,
like the dust of the earth

In addition to burning chametz, the practice of selling chametz to non-Jewish neighbors began as early as the late second century.[4] Texts of contemporary halachic contracts sell all the chametz owned by a person, or sold by one person on behalf of their community, to another for a period of a certain number of days. After the end of Passover the chametz can be bought back. We often are asked "what about my multifaith household?" This opens beautiful opportunities to explore various practices in one's family/group house system. What does owning chametz signify? How are the members of the household moving through Passover together? Are you all eating the same way, or are some keeping a dietary restriction for Passover and not others?

This practice is an opportunity to focus on the interdependence between faith communities for religious observance. Mimouna, the North African festival on the evening and day following the end of Passover, is celebrated with neighbors, often Muslim. Interdependence is crucial to the Jewish story of liberation, and these bookending festivals recall that fact. In addition to, or instead of, temporarily selling chametz, it can be donated. Part of cleaning for Pesach can include bringing unopened, nonperishable food to a local food bank. We can organize a food drive in our neighborhoods and Jewish communities, and build collective culture that regularly, embodied in our rituals, practices food redistribution.

However we go about removing leavened grains from our homes and kitchens, bedikat chametz offers a spiritual invitation alongside the physical task. What are we ready to let go of on the way to liberation?

TA'ANIT BECHOROT

Ta'anit Bechorot (תַּעֲנִית בְּכוֹרוֹת), the Fast of the Firstborn, is observed by the eldest child in a family on the day of erev Passover, in memory of the tenth and final plague that killed the eldest Egyptian children and precipitated the Exodus. During the preparation for a seder, this fast marks a mythical time and the interplay of joy at Jewish liberation and grief at another people's destruction. However, fasting on an incredibly busy day might be too burdensome, so there is a practice of making a siyyum (סִיּוּם), concluding celebration, the morning of Passover. Finishing even a section of something one is learning is a joy that overshadows a fast, and eating to celebrate a siyyum breaks the fast.[5] Therefore, eldest children who observe Ta'anit Bechorot may make a siyyum the morning of Passover and be able to eat the rest of the day.

In addition to not eating chametz, the five prohibited grains, Ashkenazi and some Sephardi observance prohibits eating kitniyot (קִטְנִיּוֹת), legumes that historically were often stored with or are easy to confuse with chametz. They include rice, corn, soybeans, peanuts, sesame seeds, and lentils. Mizrahi and many Sephardi communities permit kitniyot.

Whether you grew up eating kitniyot or not, whether this Pesach or next you decide to eat kitniyot or not, whether you lay off the chametz for a eight days, eight hours, or eight minutes, Pesach's food prohibitions are embodied ways of recalling our ancestors' experiences of slavery and struggle. Taking on such a practice can root one in that collective memory.

Pesach is not only about what we don't eat; it is also about what we do eat. The same five grains that, if left too long, become chametz, are the ones that are required to make matzah. The commandment to eat matzah comes from the Torah, in Shemot 12:39:

וַיֹּאפוּ אֶת־הַבָּצֵק אֲשֶׁר הוֹצִיאוּ מִמִּצְרַיִם עֻגֹת מַצּוֹת כִּי לֹא חָמֵץ כִּי־גֹרְשׁוּ מִמִּצְרַיִם וְלֹא יָכְלוּ לְהִתְמַהְמֵהַּ וְגַם־צֵדָה לֹא־עָשׂוּ לָהֶם:

And they baked unleavened cakes of the dough which they brought forth out of Mitzrayim, for it was not leavened; because they were thrust out of Mitzrayim, and could not tarry, neither had they prepared for themselves any victual.

From the time that water is added to the wheat flour, no more than eighteen minutes may pass before it is put into the oven, not giving it time to rise. The dough is also punctured in order to keep it from rising.

Shmura matzah is matzah made from water and wheat that, from the time it is harvested, is watched and guarded to ensure that water does not come in contact with it. Some people's practice requires eating shmura matzah at the Passover seder, or for the first seven days. It is extremely costly, considering all the labor that goes into it, and is considered a way of observing hiddur mitzvah, beautifying the mitzvot. Shmura matzah was not widely used on Passover until Rabbi Menachem Mendel Schneerson encouraged its use.[6] In 1838, Isaac Singer invented a machine to roll out matzah dough. In 1959, Rabbi Solomon Kluger decried machine-made matzah, while his brother published a defense of the invention.[7] The debate is still unsettled in some Orthodox communities. From the beginning of Passover observance to today, Jews also make matzah at home, and it is surprisingly easy to do. Just clean out your oven, set it to high heat, heat a pizza stone covered in foil, and set a timer for eighteen minutes. Then combine flour and water, roll out and stipple the dough with a fork to keep it from rising, and chuck it in the oven.

Passover is a festival, which means feasting! Shulchan Orech, the festive seder meal in the middle of the seder, is often many courses long. Ancestral recipes and new innovations alike incorporate rich delicacies, spring vegetables, and enough leftovers to sustain you through at least the first few days of Pesach.

The afikomen, the piece of matzah that is hidden and found during the portion of the seder called Tzafun, the searching, is the last taste of food one eats at a seder meal. Perhaps this is to reconnect us with the "Bread of Affliction and Liberation." Perhaps it is a rabbinic stricture to ensure that feasters would not travel from house to house all night long, feasting and carrying on. Perhaps both.

SEDER

While the festival is observed for eight days outside of Eretz Yisrael, the focal point of the Passover observance is the seder. In diaspora, it is customary to make two seders, on the first and second nights of Passover. A seder is a feast-meets-ritual service-meets-storytelling circle-meets-strategy session, and while there are set customs for it, each seder looks different.

One of the many joys of Passover is welcoming family and friends, neighbors, and comrades to the seder table. The Pesach seder is organized around asking questions, making it especially joyful to invite people who have never been to a seder before. Instead of being an annoyance or burden, this beginner's mind is a gift to everyone else at the seder. "All who are hungry come and eat," declares the Haggadah. Extending hospitality to your community and beyond your regular circle is one of the special gifts of Passover.

The seder table itself is an altar, adorned with symbolic foods to link the participants with the story of freedom. It is modeled after the Greek symposium, where diners literally laid around the table drinking wine, eating delicious foods, and discussing important questions for hours. Being able to recline, feast, and converse are hallmarks of freedom.

The traditional symbolic foods include: karpas (parsley or fresh green veggie), beitzah (hard-boiled egg), maror (bitter herbs), charoset (fruit and nut mixture), chazeret (bitter lettuce), and zeroah (shank bone or a non-meat alternative like a beet). The table should have saltwater for dipping the karpas, and lots of matzah (three set aside in a bag for the ritual separation and creation of the afikomen).

Like all Jewish rituals, our symbols on the seder plate are not static. Today we are the inheritors of many decades of leftist Jews adding to the plate. In her 1997 book, *Like Bread on the Seder Plate: Jewish Lesbians and the Transformation of Tradition*, Rabbi Rebeca Alpert opens with the layered origin story of what has become the ritual of putting an orange on the seder plate to symbolize inclusion of LGBTQIA people in Jewish life.

> In the winter of 1979 the Jewish Women's Group at the
> University of California Berkeley Hillel invited the rebbitzin
> from the campus Chabad House, Hinda Langer, to speak on the
> subject of "Women and halakha." Out of simple curiosity, one of
> the organizers asked Langer for her opinion about the place of
> lesbians in Judaism. Langer treated the issue as a minor matter.
> She suggested that it was a small transgression, like eating bread
> during Passover. Something one shouldn't do, but for which there
> would be few consequences.[8]

The story continues, of organizers deciding to put a crust of bread on their seder plate that spring, "in solidarity with lesbians who were trying to find a place in Jewish life." This practice made its way into lesbian Haggadot in the early 1980s.

> While not all groups felt comfortable placing bread on the seder
> plate . . . the story itself served to make the point. At the Oberlin
> seder, they decided to leave an open space on the seder plate
> that was marked makom. This term literally means space, but it
> is also a word used in Jewish tradition as a name for God that

is without gender. This "space" would leave room for Jewish lesbians, and others who have felt alienated, to enter.

But the story does not end there. Moved by the ritual, but too uncomfortable with the symbolism of bread on the seder plate, Jewish feminists substituted an orange for the bread and began placing it on the plate. . . . The transgressive nature, both of the symbol and of the act, was again removed. But over the years the legend changed. The story began to be told about a Jewish feminist who, speaking in Florida, was upbraided by a man who said to her that women rabbis had as much of a role in Judaism as oranges did on a seder plate, or alternatively that women had as much place on the bimah as oranges on the seder plate. Putting an orange on the seder plate to represent women's roles in Judaism seemed to appeal to many people, and the practice has been incorporated into seders. . . .

And so a contemporary legend was born. Like any evocative story, it was not often told the same way twice. The complex variations of this story resonate with the complicated ways Jewish lesbians have been dealt with by the Jewish community. This process of transmission also made it clear that Jewish lesbians saw our treatment in the Jewish community quite differently from the way others, from the Chabad rebbitzin to the Jewish feminist, saw it.[9]

This story helps us to think about what we're putting on our plates, why, and how we tell the stories about how they got there. It also teaches us about ritual development, and helps us imagine the complex processes by which all of the items got to the seder plate.

In recent years, we've seen seder plates with many new and powerful symbols: Olives as a symbol of solidarity with the Palestinian people, reminding us of the Palestinian olive trees that are systematically and repeatedly destroyed by the IDF. Artichokes to represent the inclusion of multifaith families, a lock to represent prison abolition, tomatoes to represent the fight for fair farm working conditions, chocolate to represent fair trade.

It can be incredibly meaningful to see the movements that you are invested in, or issues you want your gathered seder guests to learn more about, reflected on your seder table. Others might find a seder plate heavy with new foods to be overcrowded. We think there's a balance. When adding food and items to the seder plate, remember they are tools to deepen our conversations and learning around the seder table. When you add an item, ask yourself, where in the seder will you make time to learn about it and honor it?

"Seder" (סֵדֶר) means order, and the seder itself has a prescribed order, a road map laid out. It is divided into fifteen distinct steps:

1. Kadesh (קדש): Sanctification of the wine
2. Urchatz (ורחץ): Hand washing without saying a blessing
3. Karpas (כרפס): Eating green vegetables
4. Yahatz (יחץ): Breaking the middle matzah
5. Maggid (מגיד): Telling the Exodus story
6. Rachatz (רחצה): Hand washing before meal
7. Motzi (מוציא): Blessing the matzah as a food from the earth
8. Matzah (מצה): Blessing the matzah specifically
9. Maror (מרור): Eating bitter herbs
10. Korech (כורך): Eating matzah and maror together
11. Shulchan Orech (שלחן עורך): Eating the festive meal
12. Tzafun (צפון): Eating the afikomen
13. Barech (ברך): Reciting Birkat haMazon, the blessing after the meal
14. Hallel (הלל): Singing songs of praise
15. Nirtzah (נרצה): Concluding the seder

Every step of the seder contains multiple layers of meaning. There is its spring seasonal significance, the symbolism of the Exodus story itself, the layers of meaning added by our ancestors over the centuries, and new meanings we discover every year that we create a seder. The Haggadah, "the telling," is the guidebook for the seder, and there are myriad gorgeous Haggadot that tell the story in overlapping but nuanced ways. In every generation, Jews will find new ways to tell stories of liberation and embody the themes of the Exodus.

MIMOUNA

As Pesach ends, Moroccan and North African Jews gather to celebrate Mimouna. The feast celebrates the end of Pesach and highlights our interdependence: Jews need to sell their chametz to non-Jews in order to observe Passover, and when the holiday is over and chametz returns to its original owner, neighbors gather to share food. Mimouna is often a celebration between Jewish and Muslim neighbors, which flies in the face of Islamophobic and xenophobic Jewish ideas about where Jews are safe and with whom. The meal is filled with chametz-centered delicacies like mofletta, a Moroccan pancake.

In 2019, the Mizrahi & Sefardi Caucus of Jews for Racial and Economic Justice in New York hosted a Mimouna celebration alongside the Arab American Association of New York and Desis Rising Up and Moving, partners in their organizing against Trump's Muslim Ban, the NYPD's discriminatory surveillance of Muslim communities, and white nationalist hate violence.

> It was an evening that can only be described by sheer abundance: an abundance of people; an abundance of sweet desserts; an abundance of joy, of solidarity, of livelihood, of connection; and an abundance of firmly rooted Jewish culture and ritual alongside our beloved Arab, Muslim, and South Asian neighbors in the diaspora.[10]

In years when Passover and Ramadan intersect, there are beautiful opportunities for Jews and Muslims to feast together, breaking Passover and the day's fast with a chametz-filled iftar meal. As Pesach brings us together to talk about liberation, we can set our tables as sites of solidarity and cross-community building.

NISAN

LAYERS OF PESACH ~ EXODUS FOR ALL ~ THE MIXED MULTITUDES

Who is Pesach for? Torah makes it clear that commemorating the Exodus through eating the Pesach offering is a community-specific ritual, in Shemot 12:43:

וַיֹּאמֶר יְהוָה אֶל־מֹשֶׁה וְאַהֲרֹן זֹאת חֻקַּת הַפָּסַח כָּל־בֶּן־נֵכָר לֹא־יֹאכַל בּוֹ:

God said to Moses and Aaron: This is the law of the Passover offering:
No foreigner shall eat of it.

Traditionally, Rosh Hashanah is the birthday of the world, and Pesach is the birth of the liberation of the Jewish people. Beresheet is the creation of all peoples; Pesach is understood as the creation of the Jewish people through the miracles at the sea and the Covenant at Sinai.

And, yet, we also read that the children of Israel were not alone on their journey. As it says in Shemot 12:37–28:

וַיִּסְעוּ בְנֵי־יִשְׂרָאֵל מֵרַעְמְסֵס סֻכֹּתָה כְּשֵׁשׁ־מֵאוֹת אֶלֶף רַגְלִי הַגְּבָרִים לְבַד מִטָּף:
וְגַם־עֵרֶב רַב עָלָה אִתָּם וְצֹאן וּבָקָר מִקְנֶה כָּבֵד מְאֹד:

The Children of Israel moved on from Ra'amses to Sukkot, about six hundred thousand on foot, menfolk apart from little-ones, and also a mixed multitude went up with them. . . .

Over time, the Exodus story became a cornerstone in liberation theologies throughout history, especially Black Liberation Theology. This deeply resonates with our reading of the text: the erev rav, or mixed multitude, says to us that it was not a single group leaving Mitzrayim; we left as a multiethnic liberation movement of enslaved people seeking freedom together. We are called back, year after year, to the intertwined lineages of people telling freedom stories, whispering and shouting about how to get free.

In "Rethinking 'Go Down Moses' at the Passover Seder" Shekhiynah Larks at Be'chol Lashon writes about the experience of being at an overwhelmingly majority-white seder where "Go Down Moses" was sung. She teaches the history of the spiritual to unpack why it was so uncomfortable to be with a table of white Jews singing this:

> All culture, history, ritual, and spirituality on the plantation were passed down by elders orally, m'dor l'dor, from generation to generation. This sacred inheritance provided a source of comfort amid strife and served as a means for coded communication. 'Go Down Moses' served as one such allusion to indicate an exodus from plantations. To cite Cantor David Fair, "Spirituals were sung not just for gratification and general fun, but often to save lives."
>
> Out of context, it becomes easy to use this song to center our pain on someone else's story. We lose an opportunity to practice radical empathy for the historical and continued fight for Black liberation. The biblical story of Moses and the Exodus is our collective Jewish heritage. Still, it stands apart from the relatively recent history of enslaved Black Americans and the ongoing legacy of the brutality of racism.
>
> Renditions of 'Go Down Moses' at Passover Seders often problematically compare cultural memory and mythos of the Jewish people to the historical and contemporary trauma of Black people. . . .
>
> Too often Negro Spirituals are exploited as entertainment by the white gaze. These songs lament bondage and injustice. The people in attendance misinterpreted hopeful yearning as joy. They didn't understand the code, but how could they? It wasn't intended for them to understand. Seeing the smiling faces and hearing the remarks of glee after the song was sung at the Freedom Seder deeply wounded my soul.[11]

NISAN

When we gather for Pesach today and dramatically tell the Exodus story through the seder, we bring an awareness of the layers of history, and of our bodies, identities, and experiences of power and privilege. We wrestle with how to tell a particular Jewish story, given the multiracial, multicultural, multiethnic nature of Jews as a people, and in the context of many people's freedom stories and the universal resonances of the Exodus. How do we welcome all of our people to the seder, with all of our histories?

We ask these questions, again and again, every year. We begin to answer by noticing that the seder table is crowded with many offerings. Leeks and roasted beets and saltwater and goblets of wine and wind-up matzah ball toys share this precious space. The story of Exodus is most true when being told by an "erev rav." We welcome everyone into these nights of freedom stories, and engage with many symbols to find different ways into diverse liberation stories. At the same time, Torah's insistence that the Pesach offering is for b'nei Yisrael can be a jumping-off point to notice the differences, specific contexts of different freedom struggles, and to name, rather than to gloss over, power differences around the table today. We name where specific rituals and songs come from, and need to think about whether they are ours to lead. This is especially important for white assimilated Jews in the U.S. context. For white Jews, taking ritual practices from Black culture is appropriation, of which there is a long history and active present. This is true even when those practices reference the Exodus story, if they were developed in the context of U.S. chattel slavery.

Larks writes:

> Explore how you can hold space for Jews like the Abayudaya, who have observed Passover in secret in recent memory. Listen to the stories of Ukrainian Jews who currently find themselves in an exodus. Talk about your commitment to fighting for the liberation of Black Jews who have yet to be free. Encourage yourself to consider if Jews are indeed free if we are not yet all free. Use Be'chol Lashon's Haggadah inserts and other resources to make your Passover celebration multicultural and inclusive![12]

There are endless creative and powerful ways for us, whoever is our "us" at any given table, to explore freedom stories. The key is to dive, with specificity, into our own stories, naming our specific relationships to others' stories and why they matter to us in this time. This can take more, and a different kind of, preparation than we are used to for Pesach seders, leading us to research our histories and lineage. This specificity of freedom stories is also possible through curiosity and generous discussion, something for which seders are built.

Christian Seders

Because of Christian telling of the Exodus as part of their Scripture, and the role of Christianity in the conquest and colonization of Africa and the Americas, the Exodus has had a many-centuries-long journey through different traditions. The Exodus came to have a central role in Black Liberation Theology because of the lived experience of enslavement of Black people and the collective memory of the direct descendants of enslaved people. This is materially different than Christians, historically and contemporarily in a position of collective power over Jews, appropriating Jewish rituals. "Christian seders" refer to Christians hosting meals that take the elements of the seder, and making a ritual that, they claim, is within Christian tradition because of Jesus's Jewish context. This is historically inaccurate and culturally inappropriate, and calls up harmful supersessionist theologies.

While Pesach is rooted in biblical tradition, the bulk of the ritual of the seder dates from after the life of Jesus; the text of the Haggadah dates from the periods of the Mishnah and the Gemara, 200–700 CE. Given the history of early Christian disavowal of Jewish ritual, and centuries of Christian anti-Jewish violence, especially prevalent around Easter and Pesach, it is hurtful for Christians today to cherry-pick Jewish rituals to explore. Supersessionist, or replacement, theology is the belief that God's covenant with the Jews has been replaced by a covenant with Christians. This theology is one of the threads underpinning Christian supremacy and current right-wing movements for white Christian dominance.

We have many Christian beloved friends and family, and people from all traditions, who we are grateful to have as seder guests. We want our Christian friends to want to learn about Judaism and Jewish history, for the sake of loving and caring for us, challenging Christian supremacy, and ending and making repair for millennia of Christian antisemitism. An invitation to a Christian seder can be an opportunity to open up these kinds of conversations and strengthen relationships, as part of our ongoing work to create a world without any religious supremacy.

NISAN

During Pesach, we say Hallel as part of the Shacharit service (see Sukkot Liturgy to read more about Hallel). There are special Torah readings for every day of Pesach:

First day (Shemot 12:21–51; maftir Bamidbar 28:16–25): The instruction is given to put blood on the doorposts so the Angel of Death will pass over the homes of the Israelites. The Passover sacrifice is described, and the instruction to retell the story to future generations is given. After the tenth plague, the death of the firstborn, the Israelites flee Egypt, robbing the Egyptian people as they go. There are also instructions for eating the paschal offering. Maftir reading: There are instructions to make the paschal sacrifice on the fourteenth of Nisan, hold a festival on the fifteenth, eat unleavened bread for seven days, observe the first day as a holiday, and bring offerings all week.

Second day (Vayikra 22:26–23:44; maftir Bamidbar 28:16–25): Appointed sacred days are mentioned and, like on Shabbat, no work is to be done. There are instructions to make an offering on the fourteenth of Nisan, and the fifteenth of Nisan is the beginning of the Feast of Unleavened Bread. The text establishes the days when it is permissible to work. Bringing the firstfruits, the Omer period, is described. The text specifies that the corners of the fields and dropped sheaves must be left for the poor and the stranger. Rosh HaShanah, Yom Kippur, and Sukkot are described and instructions are given to give sacrifices, to rest, and to create a lulav. Maftir reading: Details are given for making the Passover sacrifices and observing Passover.

Third day (chol ha'moed) (Shemot 13:1–16): The Torah says to consecrate every firstborn, both human and animal, to God. The people are reminded of their liberation and obligation to observe Passover even when they are settled in the Land. Important obligations are described: to "bind it as a sign" (rabbinically imagined as tefillin) and to redeem firstborn human children and animals. For all of the days of chol ha'moed and for the last days of Pesach, the Maftir reading, Bamidbar 28:19–25, provides details of the offerings that should be brought on Passover.

Fourth day (chol ha'moed) (Shemot 22:24–23:19; Bamidbar 28:19–25): Instructions for just practices when it comes to giving loans, bringing offerings from the harvest, spreading rumors, and giving false witness are provided. The text warns not to bring death on the innocent, accept bribes, or oppress the stranger, "for you know the feelings of the stranger, having yourselves been strangers in the land of Egypt." Shmita, the seven-year cycle of working and resting the land, is discussed. There are, again, instructions to keep the Festival of Unleavened Bread in the springtime, and the Harvest of Shavuot, and the Ingathering of Sukkot, which are named as pilgrimages.

Fifth day (chol ha'moed) (Shemot 34:1–26; Bamidbar 28:19–25; Shabbat reading: Shemot 33:12–34:26; Bamidbar 28:19–25): This portion describes the creation of the second set of Ten Commandments, including Moses' second ascension of Mount Sinai. There is a declaration of the thirteen attributes of God, a renewal of the covenant between God and the people, and instructions for conquest upon entering the Land. There are instructions to observe Shabbat, Passover, Shavuot, and Sukkot, and pilgrimage is commanded three times a year.

Sixth day (chol ha'moed) (Bamidbar 9:1–14; Bamidbar 28:19–25): On the first new moon in the second year after the Exodus, the people observe Passover for the second time. Some people are unclean due to being near dead bodies and cannot offer the Passover sacrifice. God establishes Pesach Sheni (a second Passover) for all those traveling or unclean because of contact with dead bodies on the first Passover. Pesach Sheni is fourteen Iyyar.

Seventh day (chol ha'moed) (Shemot 13:17–15:26; maftir Bamidbar 28:19–25): The people are led to the Sea of Reeds by a pillar of cloud by day and a pillar of fire by night. Moses carries with him the bones of his ancestor Joseph. Pharaoh's heart is hardened once again and the Egyptians pursue the Israelites. The Israelites cry out in fear, but God splits the sea and they cross as if on dry land. When they have all crossed, God drowns the Egyptians in the sea, and the people's faith is restored in God and Moses. Chapter 15 records Moses and Miriam's Song of the Sea, a poetic and musical moment that features the prayer Mi Chamocha.

Eighth day (Devarim 15:19–16:17; maftir Bamidbar 28:19–25): Tithing is established, as is the commandment to make pilgrimage and bring sacrifices and offerings. There is to be an accommodation if the travel is too great to allow people to convert money and then make pilgrimage. Supports and protections for the Levite, the stranger, the orphan, and the widow are described, including the instruction: "There shall be no needy among you." Prohibitions against restricting loans to the poor and instructions for treating Hebrew slaves are also given.

SEDER HOSTING

Hosting a seder or creating a Haggadah is a gorgeous and brave act of love for your tradition, yourself, and your communities. It is also a whole lot of work. Here are some questions to think about to make planning and making your seder more politically meaningful, more communally and self-empowering, and more nourishing than exhausting.

Who Is It for? Who Is It from?

We've been to transformative four-person seders with our closest people, we've been in overflowing rooms with people squished on top of each other on the couch. When starting to plan, first think about what you want out of the holiday this year, and what seder formations would be meaningful. Do you want to be surrounded by a boisterous crowd? Is the goal building new connections with new people, or going deep into hard questions with people with whom you organize day in and day out? Do you want to hold the reins and steer the ship on your own, or do you want to build and offer the seder with people, and have the experience of planning together? Think about personal and communal needs, the team and table that feels most possible, joyful, and meaningful this year. A seder for one, a seder connecting beloved ones over Zoom, and a seder on the third, or eighth, night, or even before or after Passover, are all holy.

Taking It to the Streets

There have been beautiful seders in the streets, where the ritual retelling is brought to the doorsteps of today's oppressive regimes, such as Jews for Racial and Economic Justice's 2017 Seder in the Streets, which ended with four arrests for civil disobedience. There is power in mobilizing people around Pesach and calling on the resonant themes and powerful imagery of the holiday. To plan a seder as part of a public action, start by asking oneself:

* What is the goal of the action? How does telling the Pesach story and making Pesach practice public support the goal of the action?
* What is the ritual experience that participants should have?
* What is the story that needs to be visible to the target?

Taking It Home

Public and in-home seders have different goals and thus require different strategies. The goal of a home seder is *not* to move an outside target. At home, rituals can be created that will affirm and celebrate where our people have come from, where they are now, where people want to go, and ask hard questions about how to get there. A home seder can encourage people to work together to better understand the ways that oppression functions and how it impacts people individually and collectively, and to strategize about how to get free. Public seders are trying to communicate a clear and usually simple message; home seders are more nourishing and interesting when there is disagreement, questioning, and debate.

In 2020 at the beginning of the COVID-19 pandemic, we hustled to figure out virtual sedarim, the first "Zoom ritual" most of us had ever attended. As in so many parts of life, the rush to virtual access made it clear how necessary online accessibility is to get everyone a seat at the table. Disabled activists made clear the hypocrisy early on in the pandemic, pointing to how reluctant our religious communities and workplaces were to provide virtual access for programs and meetings, and how immediate the switchover was when it impacted nondisabled people. When in-person gathering is more possible in the future, we must remember to always provide hybrid and online offerings.

Virtual ritual was for others not possible, for those who do not use technology on Shabbat and Yom Tov. This meant more people either did solo sedarim or benefited from the leniencies many halachic rabbis and denominations offered so that use of technology on Passover for the seder was possible.

We've learned, a few zoom rituals in, how to make these sacred spaces more meaningful. Zoom rituals can be interactive and participatory, not just frontal. Send out a supplies list in advance, and make use of music,

NISAN

video, and visuals. Sometimes we love an active chat, and sometimes we turn the chat off so that speakers can have the floor. Communication Access Realtime Translation (CART) provided in real time by live captioners makes calls accessible for deaf readers and the hard of hearing. Some software provides auto-captions but there are none yet that can accurately capture Hebrew. Sign language interpreters can be pinned so their video is always featured on the screen.

Crafting the Ritual

In Mishna Pesachim 10:4, there are instructions for making a seder, including: "begin with shame and conclude with glory" (מַתְחִיל בִּגְנוּת וּמְסַיֵּם בְּשֶׁבַח) matchil bignut umsayem bshevach. This traditionally refers to beginning by telling about the Hebrews' enslavement, and concluding with recounting God's glory and verses of praise. Jews in many times and places understood this ritual as an opportunity for transformation and healing, and the arc of the seder was crafted to reflect that transformation. The instructions lead to beginning in the muck and the mud of oppression and heartbreak, and moving the participants to enact and experience the liberation that the seder is describing.

There are many ways to do this. The structure of the seder offers an outline, and many generations of Jews and radicals have created material to inspire, challenge, and uplift. As you are crafting a seder, picking and choosing what to include, think about the arc of moving from narrowness to expansiveness, from oppression to liberation, and how you will create that motion.

The craft of the seder is designed so that it is impossible to disengage from our bodies. It is structured around a meal, and participants are instructed to sit and lie around the table in specific ways. Some seders, however, involve looking at the Haggadah and other printed material, reading and listening, with short breaks to snack. Other seders involve participants in acting out sections of the story, such as crossing the Sea of Reeds. The seder ritual is distinct in that it involves bodies, minds and intellects, spirits and hearts. Different people have different comfort levels with embodied practices, reading aloud, chanting, and singing, and a seder is an amazing opportunity to exercise and grow both collective and individual muscles.

Embodied ritual practices to try on at a seder might include:

*   Lighting candles and sending the light to specific people and places.
*   Passing a pitcher of water and a bowl around the table and doing hand washing at the table, collectively. Inviting people to name something they're washing off, something they're committing to, or something they are preparing for.
*   Removing a drop of wine from one's cup when naming the plagues.
*   Carrying out the Red Sea Ritual from the Love and Justice in Times of War Haggadah.[13]
*   Opening the door for the Prophet Elijah and asking who else someone would like to invite in.
*   Singing songs or nigunim (wordless melodies).
*   Reading poetry and thinking about the ways that many voices will amplify and enhance that specific poem or reading. See Fringes Havurah Reading Style guide for reading tips.[14]

NISAN

Picking a Haggadah, Making a Haggadah, Crowdsourcing a Haggadah

We grew up with hand-bound photocopies, new inserts ripped from Jewish newspapers or magazines, and supplemental readings borrowed from books and other Haggadot. Some years, we make a whole new Haggadah, based on a theme or the group itself, and some years we continue to use a favorite, personal creation, updated with a few new readings, poems, songs, and rituals.

With a close and committed enough group, it is possible to make a fully crowdsourced seder experience, and invite people to sign up for and lead a portion of the seder.[15]

Part of the role of the seder facilitator is to craft a ritual that brings the table's attention to specific questions, goes deep on meaningful discussions, and connects people to each other. A leftist seder can explore the intersections of campaigns addressing different issues, and/or can go deep on specific struggles and strategies. What does the seder have to teach us about prison and police abolition? How can the Exodus story bring us to more embodied clarity about justice in Palestine and anti-Zionist Judaism? What does removing chametz teach us about moving into socialist, communist, and postcapitalist economies? What does dedicating four cups of kiddush to Black liberation and ending white supremacy have to teach us?

Preparation for this kind of seder can start weeks or months before, when we turn to our comrades and ask, what's on your heart this season? We can craft our seders to be spaces of learning and deepening, of the real hard questions of our time.

Feeding People

It is difficult to coordinate logistics, craft and lead the ritual, *and* make and serve an involved meal for a room full of people with varying dietary needs. Feeding people is its own body of work, making food that is delicious and nourishing or coordinating other people to do so. Think about having a food captain or lead chef who is a different person from the ritual leader.

CHOL HA'MOED

The first two days of Pesach, the fifteenth and sixteenth of Nissan, are chag, festival time with specific prohibitions. Days three through six are known as chol ha'moed, literally the "weekdays of the festival." In Diaspora, days seven and eight of Pesach are once again chag time.

How do we make the entire eight days of Pesach meaningful, not only a few hours at a seder? Traditionally, the Amidah liturgy switches from praying for rain to praying for dew, morid ha'tal, on the afternoon of the second day of Pesach. In a season when new life and growth are celebrated, knowing that there will be a balance of rain and dew allows people to trust that everything comes at the right time.

Each day of Passover has a specific Torah reading that is selected from mentions of the Exodus in the books of Shemot, Vayikra, and Bamidbar. They refer to both the events of Yetziat Mitzrayim, the Exodus, and the occasions of pilgrimage and sacrifice that commemorate the Exodus. In addition to the Torah reading, Shir haShirim, Song of Songs, is a beautiful addition to a daily observance. What is the Torah, broadly understood, that we want to read for the whole week of Pesach? We envision our communities learning expansive liberation theologies. Each day during the week we can sing songs, read poems, and hear stories of people fighting, sacrificing for, and creating liberation in our time.

Jewish schools are closed for the whole week of Pesach, and many families take chol ha'moed trips. These days are considered special, but the rules and restrictions of chag of not traveling or spending money are not in effect. Even for those who don't get the week off from work and school, it is still possible to break out of our usual routines and make time for outdoor adventures to celebrate the coming of spring.

YOM HASHOAH

Remembrance of the Holocaust is a necessary part of the Jewish yearcycle. We are obligated to remember the names of our dead—Jewish people, queer people, political prisoners, disabled people, Roma people, alongside all victims of Nazi terror. We must remember the results of extremism, fascism, and xenophobia, as they have impacted Jewish people in the Shoah and throughout history, and all peoples who have been targeted by genocide. We must take space to mourn personal and collective loss, and let this grief mobilize us to solidarity with other people mourning genocide. Yom HaShoah, however, is a complex day for those of us who want to grieve the overwhelming violence of the Nazi Holocaust while not being part of perpetuating harm against Palestinians.

Yom HaShoah is the Israeli-originated observance of Holocaust Remembrance Day, now observed in most Jewish communities around the world. Instituted by the Knesset (the Israeli parliament) in 1951, Yom HaShoah was set to be observed on the twenty-seventh of Nisan. Its placement on the calendar was not a foregone conclusion: in 1949 the Chief Rabbinate of Israel observed a day of remembrance of the Holocaust on the tenth of Tevet, which is already a day of mourning on the Jewish calendar, in lieu of creating a new holiday. International Holocaust Remembrance Day was designated by the United Nations in 2005 and is observed on January 27, the date that Auschwitz-Birkenau was liberated.

Yom HaShoah was set on the twenty-seventh of Nisan to be after the anniversary of the Warsaw Ghetto Uprising (15 Nisan 5703) and Passover (beginning 15 Nisan), while staying connected to the Pesach season of liberation on the Jewish calendar. Yom HaShoah was also established at this time because of its proximity to Israeli national holidays. Yom HaShoah is seven days before Yom HaZikaron, literally, the day of remembrance, a memorial day for Israeli soldiers, and eight days before Yom Ha'Atzmaut, Israeli Independence Day. Observance of Yom HaShoah involves memorial services and hearing from Holocaust survivors, and, in Israel, a country-wide siren followed by two minutes of silence. This same siren and two minutes of silence is repeated a week later on Yom HaZikaron, ritually and emotionally tying the two together. We are appalled at the ways in which the devastating tragedy of the Nazi Holocaust has been used to allow the modern State of Israel to behave with impunity against the Palestinian people. Observing Yom HaShoah in Nisan because of its proximity to Yom Ha'Atzmaut attempts a ritual embodiment of this dynamic.

At the same time, because of the ways the memory of the Shoah is misused for right-wing political goals, we have seen some on the Left shying away from engaging with the legacy and memories of the Holocaust. Many on the Jewish Left rarely allow the grief of the Nazi Holocaust to take up explicit communal space, or allow ourselves to publicly mourn, to acknowledge the loss of Jewish life and its impact on the generations that have followed. We encourage our communities to engage with these questions deeply, to not minimize one sadness to make room for another.

There are many ways to mark this date, and no easy or right answers. Perhaps you observe Yom HaShoah, despite how it was established, on the twenty-seventh of Nisan, because that is when the majority of Jews around the world mourn the Nazi Holocaust. Perhaps you create ritual mourning space on the UN's International Holocaust Remembrance Day. Whenever we do it, we must find ways to remember the specific targeting of Jews, alongside the specific targeting of Roma people, queer and trans people, disabled people, communists, socialists, and anarchists, and all who rose up in anti-facist solidarity.

COUNTING THE OMER

Though the seder and telling the story of the Exodus seem like the final acts in the long struggle for liberation from slavery, they are also the first acts in the next journey of the Jewish people. On the second night of Pesach, Sefirat HaOmer counting the days of the Omer, begins. The Torah instructs, in Vayikra 23:15–16:

וּסְפַרְתֶּם לָכֶם מִמׇּחֳרַת הַשַּׁבָּת מִיּוֹם הֲבִיאֲכֶם אֶת־עֹמֶר הַתְּנוּפֶה שֶׁבַע שַׁבָּתוֹת תְּמִימֹת תִּהְיֶינָה: עַד מִמׇּחֳרַת הַשַּׁבָּת הַשְּׁבִיעִת תִּסְפְּרוּ חֲמִשִּׁים יֹום וְהִקְרַבְתֶּם מִנְחָה חֲדָשָׁה לַיהֹוָה:

And from the day on which you bring the sheaf of elevation offering—the day after the sabbath—you shall count off seven weeks. They must be complete: you must count until the day after the seventh week—fifty days; then you shall bring an offering of new grain to HaShem.

Using an agricultural seasonal calendar, the days are counted from the barley harvest on Pesach to the wheat harvest on Shavuot. In our people's story, we are counting from the liberation from Mitzrayim to receiving the Torah at Sinai. Counting the Omer is also a spiritual journey and a practice that acknowledges that the experience of oppression is mental, emotional, and spiritual, as well as physical. The liberation of the Exodus is one step in a many-layered journey of freeing minds and spirits as well as physical bodies.

To count the Omer, the blessing is said, and then the nights are, literally, counted:

בָּרוּךְ אַתָּה יְיָ אֱלֹהֵינוּ מֶלֶךְ הָעוֹלָם, אֲשֶׁר קִדְּשָׁנוּ בְּמִצְוֹתָיו, וְצִוָּנוּ עַל סְפִירַת הָעֹמֶר.

Barukh ata Adonai Eloheinu Melech ha'olam asher kid'shanu b'mitzvotav v'tzivanu al Sefirat HaOmer.

Blessed are you, Adonai our God, Sovereign of the Universe, who has sanctified us with your commandments and commanded us to count the Omer.

הַיּוֹם יוֹם אֶחָד לָעֹמֶר.

Hayom yom echad la'omer

Today is the first day of the Omer.

The Kabbalists assigned a sefira, a different facet of God, to each week of the Omer, and similarly, a different facet of God to each day of the week. The first week of the Omer is chesed, the second week is gevurah, the third is tiferet, and so on. The first day of the week is chesed, the second is gevurah, and the third day tiferet. On the second day of the first week of the Omer, for example, we explore the gevurah of chesed—that is, the boundaries needed in love. This practice offers a way to deepen the practice of counting and expand one's exploration of self and the Divine.

Forty-nine days is a lot to count. Collective counting in minyanim, using digital or tangible Omer counters, and calendars help us keep our places. There are many more layers of tradition of counting the Omer that we will discuss in Iyar, the month to come.

The movement from the intensity of Nisan into the counting of the Omer shows us, again, the wise rhythm of the Jewish year. We are offered practices of ramping up and down, gently drawing our attention toward freedom, in all its forms. In the next month, we will focus on the journey.

FOR TIMES SUCH AS THESE

Illustration © Sol Weiss. Incantation © Dori Midnight.

a spell for wandering:
pay attention to what is bright and blooming before your eyes
find a stone and sing to it until it gives forth water
harvest only the wild greens that grow in abundance
make a flag of no nation from cloth torn in grief

we can't solve exile with more exile
we won't satisfy longing with theft
we remember every land is a holy land

count the days
name them:
beauty within discernment, outpouring of persistence,
splendor within splendor, multiplicity of connection,
compassion at the roots, coursing of divine presence,
generosity of earth

count the losses
count the harm done in our name:
700,000 Palestinian refugees forcibly displaced from their homes in 1948
2,000,000 Palestinians living under blockade in Gaza
3,000,000 Palestinians living under occupation in the West Bank

bear a litany of 418 destroyed villages: Lifta, Lydda, Safad, Ramia,
Al Majdal, Der Yassin, Beisan, Al-Tirabin, Amqa, Iqrit, Yasur, Sunayd,
Dimra, al-Faluja, Hawsha, Ijzim, Zikrin, Saqiya . . .

do not look away
do not offer empty prayers

Indwelling Presence,
let us find home in the wandering and in each other
let our marching be prayer
and our prayers be fire

Shekhinah,
You who know exile and desire return,
carve pathways home for all who are dispossessed
from the rushing rivers to the churning sea
may Palestine be free!

WELCOME TO אייר IYAR

What journey are you on at this moment in your life? Where are you coming from and where are you going? What small thing can you do every day to remind you of how far you have come and where you are going?

What are the texts that bring you back to what's most important to you? What are the books filled with the wisdom of ancestors that guide a return to core commitments and values?

On the "journey" from Pesach to Shavuot, our daily practice and weekly study invite us to reflect on what kind of people we want to be in the world: how we experience and manifest holiness, how we treat each other, how we live into liberation and live into Torah. What daily practice of noticing will you try on this year?

Introduction to Iyar

הֱווּ זְהִירִין בָּרָשׁוּת, שֶׁאֵין מְקָרְבִין לוֹ לָאָדָם אֶלָּא לְצֹרֶךְ עַצְמָן. נִרְאִין כְּאוֹהֲבִין בִּשְׁעַת הֲנָאָתָן, וְאֵין עוֹמְדִין לוֹ לָאָדָם בִּשְׁעַת דָּחְקוֹ:

Be careful with the ruling authorities for they do not befriend a person except for their own needs; they seem like friends when it is to their own interest, but they do not stand by a person in the hour of their distress.

—Pirkei Avot 2:3

Iyar is a month of journeying. In the Northern Hemisphere, it is time to truly cross into spring. In Jewish ritual time, we mark the days between Passover and Shavuot through counting the Omer (one practice during the Omer is reading Pirkei Avot, including the gem cited above). On the one hand, Iyar has no major holidays. On the other hand, Iyar is one of the few months with a special practice, layered with meaning, that we do every day. The word Iyar is from the Akadian word for "blossom." In 1 Kings 6:1, this month is known as Ziv, "brightness." Iyar calls us to pay attention to where we are headed, to be present right where we are, and to notice what is bright and blooming each day.

Iyar begins in most years in late April and early May. May Day (May 1) and Nakba Day (May 15) often take place during Iyar. May Day is rooted in the Celtic spring festival of Beltane, and celebrated in many communities and cultures. In 1889, anarchist and socialist organizers designated May 1 as International Workers' Day, in commemoration of those killed in Haymarket Square in Chicago during the 1886 strike for an eight-hour workday. While there have been many attempts over the years to co-opt and depoliticize May Day, celebrating militant workers' right to organize as part of the cycle of the Jewish year emphasizes the important connection to Jewish and non-Jewish labor movements past, present, and future.

On May 15, Palestinians mark Nakba Day, commemorating the waves of displacement of Palestinians from the State of Israel in 1948 and throughout the following decades. People gather in Palestine, and in cities around the world, for memorials and marches, remembering and making visible the history of Palestinian resistance and continued struggles for justice. Marking Nakba Day as a community focuses attention on the Palestinian demand for the right of refugees from the Nakba, and their descendants, to return to homes and lands from which they were forcibly and violently displaced. In recent years, the Israeli government has criminalized the commemoration of Nakba Day,[1] passing a law that allows the state to fine any institution that marks Israeli Independence Day as a day of mourning. In this context, taking part in public Nakba Day demonstrations, teach-ins, actions, and more makes visible the strong and growing support for Palestinian liberation.

Because of this, we who are living in Jewish time and leftist movements for justice experience the liberatory journey from Pesach to Shavuot, woven through with contemporary action for transformation. In Iyar, as the world greens and blooms around us, we let every day invite us into a different aspect of wonder at creation, at the world in which we live, and at the world of which we dream.

The parashiyot in Iyar are Ta'azria, Metzora, Acharei Mot, Kedoshim,

Emor, Behar, and Bechukotai. This month's parashiyot contain challenging material about bodies—disease, disability, desire. They ask: Who has access to holy places, like temples or community? What makes a body ready to encounter divinity? What boundaries keep us connected to each other and the Divine? Some years we read these portions ready to answer the questions we see the Torah failing to answer, some years we see the wisdom behind the text waiting for us to uncover it. Some years we disengage from the responses Torah offers, trusting our own intuition and revelation.

Iyar in Action

COUNTING THE OMER
See also: Nisan

On the night of the second seder, counting the Omer began. During Iyar, the sixteenth to the forty-fourth days of the Omer are observed. In the earliest agricultural counting from the barley harvest to the wheat harvest, the Omer was associated with a feeling of precariousness, of anxiety about what the harvest would bring. This may be the root of the Omer period being associated with a time of mourning: it is traditional not to have weddings, get haircuts, listen to instrumental music, or purchase or wear new clothes during this time. Eventually, these mourning practices came to be associated with the death of the students of Rabbi Akiva (see: Lag b'Omer).

Kabbalistically, the seven days and weeks of the Omer are each associated with one of the seven lower sefirot:

1. חֶסֶד Chesed: loving-kindness
2. גְּבוּרָה Gevurah: strength, discernment, boundaries
3. תִּפְאֶרֶת Tipheret: beauty, harmony, balance
4. נֶצַח Netzach: endurance, victory
5. הוֹד Hod: presence, acknowledgment
6. יְסוֹד Yesod: foundation, grounding
7. מַלְכוּת Malchut: sovereignty, manifestation

The seven weeks of the Omer are an invitation to layer these different aspects of the world and their spiritual experiences on top of each other, and think about them in forty-nine combinations. We can hold each of these spiritual aspects up to our sense of self, our relationships, our justice work and organizing. Where do we feel chesed present in our organizing? Where is it lacking? How can we focus our attention on chesed in ways that bring about a world with more chesed? Some of the sefirot bring clear and empowering questions; others, some years, can feel more slippery or confusing. All of them we get to explore with curiosity: these are elements that our ancestors saw moving in the world, found meaningful and spiritually enhancing.

Another minhag during the Omer period is to study Pirkei Avot (Ethics of our Fathers)—one of the six chapters every Shabbat afternoon between Pesach and Shavuot. Some congregations and communities continue studying Pirkei Avot through the Omer until Rosh Hashana. The content of Pirkei Avot is focused on ethical behavior. It includes dictums and guidance to live by that our ancestors found particularly meaningful to reengage with every year on the spiritual journey from Mitzrayim to Sinai.

CREATIVE COUNTING IN COMMUNITY

In recent years, there has been an explosion of creative Omer counting opportunities. More are emerging every year, and it's exciting to learn more ways of counting in community.

Beautiful Omer calendars, art, books and counting cards abound. In 2012, Rabbi Yael Levy published *Journey through the Wilderness*, an offering of mindfulness practices for the Omer. Kohenet Nomy Lamm and Rav Kohenet Taya Mâ Shere created the Omer Oracle deck, with forty-nine days of images and sefirot-based invitations. Gold Herring offers a self-care Omer workbook, with teaching and journaling prompts for the seven weeks. Taya Mâ Shere and Bekah Starr offer a deck that explores erotic pleasure and embodiment called *Diving Pleasure: An Oracle for SephErotic Liberation*. Since 2020, Mitsui Collective has been offering embodiment and wellness practices for every day of the Omer.

People are coming together in a variety of ways to practice together during the Omer. In 2016, the Jewish Voice for Peace Havurah Network first came together to count the Omer every night, with different teachers and ritual leaders offering creative practices for each week of the Omer. In 2018, Jews for Racial and Economic Justice invited members to use the period of the Omer to study the full 2016 Movement for Black Lives platform. Each day of the Omer, they shared insights from the platform on social media and brought people together in counting #Omer4BlackLives. In 2021, Hazzan Sabrina Sojourner offered "We are Expected to Love Ourselves: An Omer Journey Towards Healing," weekly gatherings for Jews of African, Latinx, Mizrahi, Mixed, Indigenous, Melungeon, Asian, and Sephardic heritage.

Each year, Sefirat HaOmer provides a chance to journey with greater intention from the liberation of Pesach to the revelation of Shavuot, developing a spiritual practice that connects getting free and getting inspired. Each year, the question to ask ourselves is: What Omer practice will strengthen and deepen our capacity to work collectively for liberation? May we uncover more and more ways of deepening our feelings about and commitment to the rhythm of this season.

LAG B'OMER

Lag l'Omer (Sephardi) or Lag b'Omer (Ashkenazi) is the thirty-third day of the Omer (lamed = 30, gimel = 3), which falls on 18 Iyar. The abbreviated modes of mourning that are observed in the first weeks of the Omer are broken by Lag b'Omer. Ashkenazim have a custom of getting haircuts and having weddings on this day, and Sephardim have weddings on Lad b'Omer (the thirty-fourth day of the Omer).

Lag b'Omer is Rabbi Shimon bar Yochai's yahrtzeit. Rabbi Shimon bar Yochai is the traditional author of the Zohar. As such, bonfires and pilgrimages to his tomb to celebrate him are common. The first weeks of the Omer are observed as a mourning period, due to the plague that annihilated twenty-four thousand of Rabbi Akivah's students. (Rabbi Shimon bar Yochai was one who survived.) The Gemara explains the cause for the plague: because the students did not treat one another with respect.[2] We do not believe that sickness or death is something that can be blamed on a person's behavior or morality. From this story, however, we can reflect on the necessity of kavod across different beliefs and schools of thought. What

IYAR

a life-changing, life-ending power cruelty has between people. When we think of the ways our leftist communities can so often tear one another down instead of building each other up, we think of the loss of Rabbi Akiva's students.

Tradition says the plague finally ended on Lag b'Omer, a cause for celebration. Some Orthodox members of the Jewish world express concern that it is a "new holiday" and should not be observed, and they also express concern at the joyous observation of a yahrtzeit, traditionally a somber observance.

Early Zionists shifted from the rabbinic celebration of the cessation of the plague to a celebration of Shimon bar Kochba and the Bar Kochba revolt in 132–136 BCE. As with the history of the Massada resistance, early Zionists reframed celebrations of Lag b'Omer to focus on the (failed, but lengthy) resistance to the Roman occupation. Bows and arrows are shot in honor of the rebellion, but also have earlier connections to Shimon bar Yochai.

It is said that a rainbow appeared in every generation, except in the generation of Shimon bar Yochai. The rainbow is the symbol of the covenant between God and Noah that the earth would never again be destroyed by a flood. Midrash Rabbah 35:9 explains that, in the absence of the rainbow in Shimon bar Yochai's generation, he was that rainbow.

Lag b'Omer is an example that throughout history Jewish people have created holidays and celebrations to mark current events and major victories. May the legacy of Lag b'Omer embolden us to celebrate on the dates the last weapons manufacturing plant closes, the last prison closes, the Occupation ends, and the last unhoused person moves into their home, and call them holidays.

PESACH SHENI

In Bamidbar chapter 9, we read about Pesach Sheni, Second Passover, in verses 10–14:

דַּבֵּר אֶל־בְּנֵי יִשְׂרָאֵל לֵאמֹר אִישׁ אִישׁ כִּי־יִהְיֶה־טָמֵא ׀ לָנֶפֶשׁ אוֹ בְדֶרֶךְ רְחֹקָה לָכֶם אוֹ לְדֹרֹתֵיכֶם וְעָשָׂה פֶסַח לַיהוָה: בַּחֹדֶשׁ הַשֵּׁנִי בְּאַרְבָּעָה עָשָׂר יוֹם בֵּין הָעַרְבַּיִם יַעֲשׂוּ אֹתוֹ עַל־מַצּוֹת וּמְרֹרִים יֹאכְלֻהוּ: לֹא־יַשְׁאִירוּ מִמֶּנּוּ עַד־בֹּקֶר וְעֶצֶם

לֹא יִשְׁבְּרוּ־בוֹ כְּכָל־חֻקַּת הַפֶּסַח יַעֲשׂוּ אֹתוֹ: וְהָאִישׁ אֲשֶׁר־הוּא טָהוֹר וּבְדֶרֶךְ
לֹא־הָיָה וְחָדַל לַעֲשׂוֹת הַפֶּסַח וְנִכְרְתָה הַנֶּפֶשׁ הַהִוא מֵעַמֶּיהָ כִּי ׀ קָרְבַּן יְהֹוָה לֹא
הִקְרִיב בְּמֹעֲדוֹ חֶטְאוֹ יִשָּׂא הָאִישׁ הַהוּא: וְכִי־יָגוּר אִתְּכֶם גֵּר וְעָשָׂה פֶסַח לַיהֹוָה
כְּחֻקַּת הַפֶּסַח וּכְמִשְׁפָּטוֹ כֵּן יַעֲשֶׂה חֻקָּה אַחַת יִהְיֶה לָכֶם וְלַגֵּר וּלְאֶזְרַח הָאָרֶץ:

Speak to the Israelite people, saying: When any of you or of
your posterity who are defiled by a corpse or are on a long
journey would offer a Passover sacrifice to HaShem, they shall
offer it in the second month, on the fourteenth day of the month,
at twilight. They shall eat it with unleavened bread and bitter
herbs, and they shall not leave any of it over until morning. They
shall not break a bone of it. They shall offer it in strict accord
with the law of the Passover sacrifice. But if a man who is clean
and not on a journey refrains from offering the Passover sacrifice,
that person shall be cut off from his kin, for he did not present
the Divine's offering at its set time; that man shall bear his
guilt. And when a stranger who resides with you would offer a
Passover sacrifice to HaShem, he must offer it in accordance
with the rules and rites of the Passover sacrifice. There shall be one
law for you, whether stranger or citizen of the country.

Mishnah Pesachim 9 explores more details of Pesach Sheni, including
what kind of impurity and how long a journey qualifies one for this second chance at the offering. One way of marking the day is by eating some
matzah, and in some communities Tachanun (תחנון), prayers of supplication following the Amidah, are omitted.

We've never taken part in a do-over seder on the fourteenth of Iyar.
But there is comfort in knowing that, millennia ago, our ancestors understood that life happens, that our holiday calendar must shift and be flexible
to account for life's events, and that second chances are possible. Iyar is a
month when the consistency of daily practice can support us through all
kinds of journeying: times of volatility and grief, and the cycles of struggle
in resistance, in organizing, and in our day-to-day lives. Every day, Iyar
teaches, counts.

IYAR

Illustration © Sol Weiss. Incantation © Dori Midnight.

open the mountain
like a glory hole of revelation
open to me
and bury me in blossoms of text
garland and adorn me,
drape me in your wisdom!
tilt my head back, face to the sky
and pour milk and honey down my throat

when the Holy One turned the mountain upside down
and shook it over our heads
we were there
all of us
trembling in receptivity
all of us, receiving our own torah

torah of worms
torah of black fire written on white fire
torah like the sea, endless currents, alive and always changing
torah of silence
torah of stone fruits
torah of Black Lives Matter
torah of No More Cages
torah of Trans Power, Trans Rage, Trans Beauty
torah of All Bodies are Holy
torah woven in spider silk
torah of tarot, of star poetry, of witchcraft, of spells
torah of dreaming deep
torah wrapped in velvet, crowned in silver bells
torah ora, for she is the tree of life
torah cradled and kissed

You who Opens, You who Reveals,
You who Gives, You who Guides,
humble us
that we might open like soft earth
to everything everything everything

 # WELCOME TO סיון SIVAN

Where do you find inspiration, learning, and wisdom in your life? What people and places offer teaching, stories of where you came from, or skills you want to learn? What do you do to invite new and old knowledge into your life?

Where have you been since Pesach? What's been revealed to you in this season specifically?

What core teachings guide your life? What are you hungry to learn and explore?

Introduction to Sivan

Celebration is also asked of us tonight. Our joy is bound to that of our ancestors, and it is the fuel that feeds our collective future. We bring into this space our ancestors who finally got word of Lincoln's decree, after slaving two and a half years longer than the law allowed. We are here to recreate their resilience and self-love. Our tradition tells us: "B'chol dor vador chayav adam lirot et atzmo k'ilu hu yatza mimitzrayim. In every generation, each person must see themselves as if they had come out of Mitzrayim." As though we ourselves are coming into liberation during this time. It is our duty to act as the Royalty we really are, as a profound act of resistance and radical choice.

May we continue to create liberation every day in every way.

—Jews for Racial and Economic Justice,
"Juneteenth Seder Haggadah," 2018

In Sivan, our collective attention turns to Shavuot, one of the three pilgrimage festivals of the year. Some years, Juneteenth falls within Sivan. The oldest commemoration of the ending of chattel slavery within the United States, Juneteenth marks June 19, 1865, when Black people in Texas received news of the Emancipation Proclamation. In June 2018, Black members of the Jews for Racial and Economic Justice Jews of Color caucus hosted a Juneteenth seder. The seder blended the Pesach seder plate and four ritual cups of wine with the telling of freedom stories and visioning a future without policing and with reparations for slavery. In 2020, amidst the uprisings for Black liberation following the murder of George Floyd z"l, many more Jewish communities observed and celebrated Juneteenth. It is incumbent upon anti-racist Jewish organizers to make Juneteenth as much a part of our calendar as Rosh Hashanah every year, bringing the community's collective attention to the liberatory organizing of Black people on this land across many centuries.

Sivan is the Northern Hemisphere's peak spring month, and it is a time that invites us into reception and revelation in all of its forms: receiving and revealing Torah, receiving and revealing firstfruits, and receiving and revealing spring. After the journey of winter, after the voyage through the Omer, through many weeks of slowly exploring our internal lives, this is a month of trying to crack ourselves wide open, personally and collectively, and to uncover what is inside to harvest.

Occasionally, Sivan reaches all the way to the summer solstice. In Sivan, many more of us can meet out of doors, can picnic and swim, and can mobilize in the streets more easily and for longer. Jewish tradition invites us to receive Torah on Shavuot in the time of elongated days and bright nights, in a time of turning toward each others' summer blossoming. Sivan shines the literal sun on all that we know, and all that is yet to be revealed.

The parashiyot of Sivan are Bamidbar, Naso, Beha'alotcha, and Sh'lach. This month's parashiyot explore who counts—literally, in the form of the census. This month we read about explicit conflict between the people and authority, questions of power and control. Rabbinic tradition offers a reading that upholds divine rule, Moses' authority, elders, and men. When we read closely, we find and celebrate the voices of dissent and disobedience memorialized in these parashiyot.

Sivan in Action

SHAVUOT

Shavuot, as with all of the Jewish calendar, celebrates multiple moments at once, and has multiple names. The wheat harvest, a pilgrimage to the Temple, and the revelation of Torah on Mount Sinai are woven together in the festival of Shavuot.

Shavuot is Zman Mattan Torah (זְמָן מַתַּן תּוֹרָה), the time of receiving Torah, and we are transported to the base of the mountain where Torah is revealed. It is taught that every soul who was, is, or will be Jewish was present at the foot of Mt. Sinai at the time of receiving Torah,[1] and on Shavuot Jews reenact the moment when heaven and earth met at revelation.

וַיּוֹצֵא מֹשֶׁה אֶת־הָעָם לִקְרַאת הָאֱלֹהִים מִן־הַמַּחֲנֶה וַיִּתְיַצְּבוּ בְּתַחְתִּית הָהָר: וְהַר סִינַי עָשַׁן כֻּלּוֹ מִפְּנֵי אֲשֶׁר יָרַד עָלָיו יְהוָה בָּאֵשׁ וַיַּעַל עֲשָׁנוֹ כְּעֶשֶׁן הַכִּבְשָׁן וַיֶּחֱרַד כָּל־הָהָר מְאֹד: וַיְהִי קוֹל הַשּׁוֹפָר הוֹלֵךְ וְחָזֵק מְאֹד מֹשֶׁה יְדַבֵּר וְהָאֱלֹהִים יַעֲנֶנּוּ בְקוֹל: וַיֵּרֶד יְהוָה עַל־הַר סִינַי אֶל־רֹאשׁ הָהָר וַיִּקְרָא יְהוָה לְמֹשֶׁה אֶל־רֹאשׁ הָהָר וַיַּעַל מֹשֶׁה:

Moses led the people out of the camp toward God, and they took their places at the foot of the mountain. Now Mount Sinai was all in smoke, for the Divine had come down upon it in fire; the smoke rose like the smoke of a kiln, and the whole mountain trembled violently. The blare of the horn grew louder and louder. As Moses spoke, God answered him in thunder. The Divine came down upon Mount Sinai, on the top of the mountain, and the Divine called Moses to the top of the mountain and Moses went up.
—Shemot 19:17–20

It is also taught that an erev rav, a mixed multitude, left Mitzrayim with the Israelites,[2] making the Exodus a mass movement for liberation. The classical commentaries imagine that the other nations became proselytes of the Israelite God when they joined the Israelites in leaving,[3] restricting it to a Jewish exodus. But, looking past that homogenizing commentary, it is possible to imagine a movement of other enslaved peoples, non-Jewish partners, midwives, and neighbors, who joined this Jewish freedom movement. Perhaps they traveled with the Israelites through the split sea to the mountain. Then, while imagining every soul who was, is, or would be Jewish present at Sinai, we can visualize every non-Jewish soul who was, is, or would be part of Jewish community and solidarity movements. This midrash also teaches us that our multifaith families are there too.

Shavuot is also Chag HaShavuot (חַג הַשָּׁבֻעוֹת), the Festival of Weeks, marking the end of the counting of the Omer, seven weeks since Passover. As we read in Vayikra 23:15–16:

וּסְפַרְתֶּם לָכֶם מִמָּחֳרַת הַשַּׁבָּת מִיּוֹם הֲבִיאֲכֶם אֶת־עֹמֶר הַתְּנוּפָה שֶׁבַע שַׁבָּתוֹת
תְּמִימֹת תִּהְיֶינָה: עַד מִמָּחֳרַת הַשַּׁבָּת הַשְּׁבִיעִת תִּסְפְּרוּ חֲמִשִּׁים יוֹם וְהִקְרַבְתֶּם
מִנְחָה חֲדָשָׁה לַיהוָה:

And from the day on which you bring the sheaf of elevation offering—the day after the sabbath—you shall count off seven weeks. They must be complete: you must count until the day after the seventh week—fifty days; then you shall bring an offering of new grain to the Divine.

At Shavuot we honor the spiritual harvests of the Omer counting practice. Coming into Shavuot after weeks of counting, we experience revelation as something that does not always fall in our laps. Instead, it is cultivated through daily, ongoing practice. Our active role in counting the Omer, and whatever practices we have taken on during the seven weeks, helps us experience ourselves and our communities as partners in revelation.

Yet another name for Shavuot is Chag HaBikurim (חַג הַבִּכּוּרִים), Festival of the First Fruits, in which farmers bring the produce of their first harvest to the Temple, acknowledging the holiness of the day. The priest takes the basket and sets it before the altar, and the farmer recites a full liturgy as proscribed in Devarim 26:1–11 that recounts the ancestors journeying into Egypt, the enslavement and oppression there, the miracles of the Exodus, the wandering in the desert, and the arrival in the Land.

Shavuot is Atzeret, a holy day of no work, as we read in Bamidbar 28:26:.

וּבְיוֹם הַבִּכּוּרִים בְּהַקְרִיבְכֶם מִנְחָה חֲדָשָׁה לַיהוָה בְּשָׁבֻעֹתֵיכֶם מִקְרָא־קֹדֶשׁ יִהְיֶה לָכֶם כָּל־מְלֶאכֶת עֲבֹדָה לֹא תַעֲשׂוּ׃

On the day of the first fruits, your Feast of Weeks, when you bring an offering of new grain to HaShem, you shall observe a sacred occasion: you shall not work at your occupations.

Shavuot is observed as a two-day festival in Diaspora, one of feasting and study.

הַכֹּל מוֹדִים בַּעֲצֶרֶת דְּבָעֵינַן נָמֵי לָכֶם. מַאי טַעְמָא? יוֹם שֶׁנִּיתְּנָה בּוֹ תּוֹרָה הוּא.

With regard to Atzeret, the holiday of Shavuot, that we require that it be also "for you," meaning that it is a mitzvah to eat, drink, and rejoice on that day. What is the reason? It is the day on which the Torah was given, and one must celebrate the fact that the Torah was given to the Jewish people.

—Pesachim 68b:10

Parallel to Shimini Atzeret's conclusion to Sukkot in the fall, Shavuot is the conclusion of the journey from Pesach to Shavuot and the counting of the Omer. In this cycle, the freedom that began with leaving the narrow places concludes with receiving Torah in joyful celebration.

TIKKUN LEYL SHAVUOT

In honor of receiving Torah at Mount Sinai, many people stay up all night studying sacred wisdom, at an event called Tikkun Leyl Shavuot. This mystical practice, started by Rabbi Isaac Luria in the sixteenth century, has many inspirations. Perhaps it is because the Israelites slept in and missed the revelation,[4] or perhaps it is to repair the catastrophe of the first time Moses came down from the mountain with the tablets and found the Israelites worshiping the egel hazahav (עֵגֶל הַזָּהָב), the Golden Calf. We commit to not making the same mistake this time, and in anticipation of the Revelation, we stay up all night, to not sleep on Torah. Shavuot is imagined as a wedding, with the Torah being the ketubah (marriage contract) between the Jewish people and God, so we stay up all night in anticipation, as for a wedding day.

Confirmation, a contemporary ritual that is celebrated when Jewish young adults are sixteen, is often held on erev Shavuot. Originated in the Reform movement in the early nineteenth century,[5] students continue their religious school studies in preparation for their confirmation, and celebrate with a ceremony during which they teach and receive blessings. The confirmation ritual moved the young adult coming of age ceremony, traditionally a Bar Mitzvah, into a school or home setting, modeling it after a graduation, and was part of the assimilation efforts of the early Reform movement. Before Bat Mitzvah was available for women, confirmation was the major coming-of-age ritual, and remains a very popular life cycle event in many communities. Two hundred years later, young people in our communities get to decide if confirmation is a ritual that is still meaningful to them, and how they want to mark transitions in their Jewish lives and learning. Depending on the denomination of a synagogue community, confirmation will be more or less emphasized.

Yizkor, memorial prayers, are recited on the second day of Shavuot as a part of the liturgy, and provide another touchpoint throughout the year to gather and remember our beloved dead. See the section on the Yizkor of Yom Kippur in Tishrei for more on the foundations of Yizkor. On Shavuot we can take special care to remember and mourn those teachers and wisdom givers who have shaped us, as we intertwine remembrance with our honoring of Torah.

LITURGY AND TORAH READING

Hallel is recited on both days of Shavuot (see Sukkot Liturgy to read more about Hallel).

The Book of Ruth is the megillah associated with and read on Shavuot. The Book of Ruth tells of economic oppression and systems to subvert it, chosen family, queer love, and the harvest season.

Set during the time of the barley and wheat harvests, around Shavuot, the megillah tells the story of Ruth and her mother-in-law Naomi. Following the death of both of Naomi's sons, she decides to return to her birthplace of Bethlehem. Ruth refuses to leave her, saying "Do not urge me to leave you, to turn back and not follow you. For wherever you go, I will go; wherever you lodge, I will lodge; your people shall be my people, and your God my God. Where you die, I will die, and there I will be buried. Thus and more may HaShem do to me if anything but death parts me from you." (Ruth 1:16–17). Rabbinic tradition understands Ruth to be the first convert to Judaism. Dyke tradition understands Ruth and Naomi to be lovers, that Ruth's vow was not (only) to the Jewish people but a love vow to Naomi. As such, these words are often spoken between brides under a chuppah.

Ruth and Naomi's story continues in Bethlehem, detailing the process of gathering pe'ah, the corners and remains left in the field for the most vulnerable. Ruth seduces and partners with Boaz, a land-owning relation of Naomi. They marry, and Ruth gives birth to a child, "born of your daughter-in-law, who loves you and is better to you than seven sons" (4:15). Naomi becomes the child's foster mother, and her neighbors name him Obed. This queerspawn was the grandfather of King David, who is the ancestor of the one who will be the Mashiach.

On both days of Shavuot, two Torah scrolls are removed from ark, and different sections are read from each scroll:

Shemot 19:1–20:23 is the reading for day 1. This is the story of the encounter between the Israelite people at the foot of Mount Sinai, Moses, and God during the giving and receiving of the Ten Commandments. It is customary in many congregations to rise for the reading of the Ten Commandments, which is chanted in a special trope. For the maftir, we read, in Bamidbar 28:26–28:31, instructions for the offerings given on Shavuot.

Devarim 15:19–16:17 is the reading for day 2. This reading begins with laws of animal tithing, and continues with instructions on how to observe the three pilgrimage festivals: the Feast of Unleavened Bread (Pesach), the Feast of Weeks (Shavuot), and the Feast of Booths (Sukkot). For the maftir, Bamidbar 28:26–28:31 is read again.

Ezekiel 1:1–28 and 3:12 is the haftorah reading for the first day of Shavuot. The first chapter details Ezekiel's visions of God, including that of the merkavah (chariot). This text depicts a revelation, which is the reason it is read on Shavuot. Various discussions of this connection in midrashic commentary explain Ezekiel's personal revelation, and the connection between chariots and Sinai.

Habakkuk 2:20–3:19 is the haftorah reading for the second day of

Shavuot. It recounts praying for God's power in military battle and recalls images from the revelation at Sinai.

Additional liturgy, Akdamut, Yatziv Pitgam, and Azharot, are recited before these Torah readings. Akdamut is an Ashkenazi piyyut, a liturgical poem, written in Aramaic, in the early eleventh century, by Rabbi Meir bar Yitzchak in Worms. It is read as part of the Torah service right before the reading of the Ten Commandments. Yatziv Pitgam is another Aramaic piyyut that is read on the second day of Shavuot before the haftorah. Azharot is a liturgical poem about the 613 mitzvot. The first known example appears in the tenth century siddur of the Saadia Gaon.

Hallel, the celebratory service of praise that includes Psalms 113–18, is recited on Shavuot, and Yizkor, the memorial service, is recited on the second day of Shavuot.

FOOD AND DECOR

There are many symbolic foods and rituals that help us connect to the beauty of Shavuot and our gratitude for the harvest. Shavuot is lush, abundant, fertile, and we eat and drink to get cozy in that luxury.

Homes and synagogues are decorated with greenery and flowers for several reasons. Hiddur mitzvah—"beautification of the commandments" or "making the necessary beautiful," honors what we cherish the most through art and beauty. There is a midrash that teaches that in anticipation of the moment of the revelation all the flowers bloomed on Mount Sinai.

Another is a pun: The rose, in Hebrew shoshana, is a popular choice for decoration based on a play of words in the Book of Esther. Esther 8:14 reads: "וְהַדָּת נִתְּנָה בְּשׁוּשָׁן" "And the law was proclaimed in Shushan." Reading "Shushan" (in context a city) instead as "shoshana" (rose), the line can playfully be heard as The Torah [which literally means "law"] was given with a rose.

According to the Mishnah, the judgment for trees takes place on Shavuot.

בְּאַרְבָּעָה פְרָקִים הָעוֹלָם נִדּוֹן, בְּפֶסַח עַל הַתְּבוּאָה, בַּעֲצֶרֶת עַל פֵּרוֹת הָאִילָן,

בְּרֹאשׁ הַשָּׁנָה כָּל בָּאֵי הָעוֹלָם עוֹבְרִין לְפָנָיו כִּבְנֵי מָרוֹן, שֶׁנֶּאֱמַר (תהלים לג)
הַיּוֹצֵר יַחַד לִבָּם, הַמֵּבִין אֶל כָּל מַעֲשֵׂיהֶם. וּבֶחָג נִדּוֹנִין עַל הַמָּיִם:

At four times of the year the world is judged: On Passover
judgment is passed concerning grain; on Shavuot concerning
fruits that grow on a tree; on Rosh HaShana, all creatures pass
before Him like sheep [benei maron], as it is stated: "He Who
fashions their hearts alike, Who considers all their deeds" (Psalms
33:15); and on the festival of Sukkot they are judged concerning
water, i.e., the rainfall of the coming year.
—Mishnah Rosh HaShanah 1:2

Other reasons for the custom include reminders of the basket of reeds
in which baby Moses floated down the Nile, or the lushness of Mount
Sinai because animals did not graze there, or a reminder of the firstfruits
brought to the Temple on Shavuot. The Shulchan Aruch suggests it is to
spread joy and happiness, like the joy that filled the people when they
received the Torah.[6] However, the Vilna Gaon, concerned that decorating
with trees was too similar to Christian celebrations of Christmas, objected
to the tradition of flowers and trees as decorations for the holiday.[7]

Perhaps that is why shavuoslekh (Yiddish, "little Shavuots") papercuts
are a traditional Ashkenazi decoration. They are more cost effective, and
distanced from the flora and fauna decorations the Vilna Gaon was so concerned about. Create papercuts with a floral theme or a Torah theme and
hang them in your windows and around your home. This is a joyful activity
for Christian-Jewish multifaith homes to combine snowflake-cutting skills
with Shavuot celebration skills!

Dairy, such as cheesecake, ice cream, and blintzes, is traditionally
eaten on Shavuot. Why? There are a wide variety of possible explanations.
This custom teaches that Torah is like mother's milk.[8] Or perhaps it is a
reminder of the egel hazahav, the Golden Calf. Maybe, for those staying
up all night, dairy lasts longer in the body. Or perhaps it could be because,
according to Midrash, at the time of the revelation the Israelites learned
that all of the meat in their possession was unkosher and how detailed
kosher slaughter would be, and could eat only dairy.[9]

El pan de siete cielos, Seven Heavens cake, is a Sephardi Shavuot dish
sculpted to show the story of Shavuot with Mount Sinai in the middle.

SIVAN

"Mount Sinai" is then ringed by seven ropes of dough, which denote the clouds surrounding the mountain. The symbolism of seven clouds is unclear. In his book "The Sephardic Kitchen," Rabbi Robert Sternberg provides a spiritual explanation for the seven heavens. According to him, the seven heavens are the "seven holy living spaces through which the soul ascends to heaven," after a Jew's body dies.[10]

Some Jewish communities reenact bringing firstfruits to the Temple. At Isabella Freedman Jewish Retreat Center, those gathered to celebrate bring wheat, fruits, and animals under a chuppah. At Beth Elohim in Saint Albans, New York, the community bakes loaves of bread to bring to the Tikkun Leyl Shavuot, in honor of the breads brought to the Mishkan, or the wheat offering on Shavuot.

HOSTING A TIKKUN

Hosting a tikkun for Shavuot can be as big or as small an effort as the year calls for. It can be as simple as gathering a few friends for a dairy meal on erev Shavuot, and asking everyone to bring a brief lesson to share. Or you might organize an event on, or near, Shavuot for some political education on the topic your organizing collective is currently learning about and working on. Plan a book drive for a local group that sends books to people who are incarcerated. Host an all-night study session for the local Jewish communities, asking people to submit workshop topics in advance. Or freestyle it, spending the first hour brainstorming ideas and building breakout spaces and workshops together, and the night free flowing with learning.[11] A skill-share of Jewish and non-Jewish wisdom and skills can honor multiple generations of wisdom and revelation.

Shavuot is an invitation to understand Torah, conceptually and broadly defined, as any wisdom text that inspires and challenges us. And the Book of Ruth provides many jumping-off points for study. We can dig into questions such as: How is our community providing for all people, inspired by the mitzvah of pe'ah? What are the relationships of care that are unseen and uncelebrated in our communities? Inspired by Ruth and Naomi's love, we reflect, how are we valuing all kinds of loving connections? Many progressive and politically left Jewish communities struggle to accept Jews who come to Jewishness through conversion. Studying Ruth on Shavuot is an opportunity to challenge our individual and collective biases, learn about conversion throughout Jewish history and in our times, share stories about and affirm the validity of diverse pathways to Judaism, and reflect on how we want to welcome all people to our spaces.

Contemporarily local movements have organized teach-ins on campaign issues, dedicating learning to issues of justice, such as Jewish Voice for Peace's Deadly Exchange Campaign Shavuot learning in 2018,[12] or Jews for Racial and Economic Justice's Shavuot for Black Lives in 2018.[13] In 2020, eight synagogues joined together to host a tikkun for six hundred people across the country on Zoom, learning about a range of topics, both about movement work and about Torah. Justice-centered Tikkun Leyl Shavuot celebrations underscore the ongoing work of revelation, in lifting up the wisdom of this generation alongside the wisdom revealed to our ancestors.

What wisdom do you hope to receive at the base of the mountain this year? What would revelation look like for your people? Plan your Shavuot learning from that place of curiosity and desire, humility and wonder. As leftists, we know that political education and collective study are integral parts of revolutionary transformation. Sivan teaches that our ancestors also knew that learning is part of liberation journeying.

Sivan is a month to consider where the journey from Pesach has brought us, to uncover what has already been revealed, to share with each other the harvest bounty of what we know and feel. We know, as Jews and as leftists, that revelation is available to us all, when we open ourselves to it, together.

SIVAN

who to pray to in a godless season?

our ancestors built a calf of gold
and who can blame them?
don't we all want something beautiful,
something to do with our hands when we are
alone and afraid?

the season of high sun is abundant with fruit
and grain
destruction and death and durational grief
cycles of violence that break us
another life shattered by the state
another altar on a street corner

the prophets say injustice is a state of
dryness,
a drought of life loving life

god of our ancestors, the waters have ceased
to flow here

this is the prayer that calls us into our
collective body
our collective thirst
our collective mourning
our collective uprising

Source of Mercy,
lend us rigor and tenacity, strength to not
turn away
be with us, Breath of Life,
as we take a hammer to the hydrants
flood the summer streets with our bodies
our tears our rivers of song
our holy unrest
as we chant:
life is precious where life is precious

Illustration © Sol Weiss. Incantation © Dori Midnight.

WELCOME TO תמוז TAMMUZ

What's growing in your garden right now? What is feeding you? What does the sun have to offer?

Where do you see signs of what's been destroyed in your communities? What destruction needs attending to?

How are the hurts of your communities' histories manifesting in the collective body? What grief is unresolved and impacting your community?

Introduction to Tammuz

It took me years to realize that the forest and the struggle move to the same rhythms. Coffee trees and communities blossom when the conditions are right. Ponds and people get depleted if we're used up faster than we replenish. Some tasks are right for the rainy season, others for the dry season. Trees with the deepest roots withstand the mudslide. And another thing. The life of the forest is hope-based. Hope is the force that sends the rootlets of ferns snaking toward moisture, mice scouring the leaf litter for seeds and tenants striking for building repairs. It guides each living being along the path from what is to what might be. Without it nothing moves but the wind and the waves.

—Ricardo Levins Morales

We enter the Hebrew month of Tammuz in the height of summer, at the peak of heat and dryness. The Hebrew month of Tammuz is named for the Mesopotamian god of shepherds and growing plants, Dumuzid. Tammuz's Assyrian parallel is the month of Araḥ Dumuzu, a time of mourning for the yearly anniversary of the death of Dumuzid. In the Jewish calendar, Tammuz brings us into a season of mourning, the Three Weeks, which stretch from the seventeenth of Tammuz until the ninth of Av.

On Turtle Island, the summer months of long days and high temperatures call us outdoors. This is often a time to reconnect with our bodies and to connect with the earth in a new way. Many of us live in places where this is the time to get in the water, to dig in the dirt, and to eat food we or our friends have grown.

This is also often when we see some of the most sustained protests against state violence: from the protests at the 1968 Democratic National Convention, to the Ferguson uprisings in August 2014 after the police murder of Mike Brown, through the uprisings of the summer of 2020 after the police murder of George Floyd. What can be learned from the Jewish observation of a month of collective mourning in the midst of summer? The teachings of Ricardo Levins Morales remind us to pay attention to seasons and their conditions, of earth and movements. Tammuz calls us to demand a world in which no one's life is ended through state violence, and to bring our bodies into the hot streets to publicly mourn and proclaim, through our grief, that another world is possible.

The parashiyot of Tammuz are Korach, Chukat, Balak, and Pinchas. This month's readings are dramatic, with characters revolting, being swallowed by the earth, dying, mourning, being swayed by talking donkeys, exacting extremist political puritanical ideological violence, demanding women's financial futures and independence . . . the works. As we move through the books of Vayikra, Bamidbar and Devarim the material is less often narrative, and these parashiyot are a boost of story to keep us going. Though the majority of our text focuses on the relationship of Moses and God, and Moses as broker between God and the people, these parashiyot reveal a glimpse into the experiences of the Israelites and those who come into contact with them.

Tammuz in Action

THE SEVENTEENTH OF TAMMUZ AND THE THREE WEEKS

From the middle of Tammuz into the first week of Av, we immerse ourselves in an extended period of collective mourning called the Three Weeks. Known in Hebrew as בין המצרים, bein ha'Metzarim, "between the narrow straits," this period begins with a minor fast day on the seventeenth of Tammuz. The mourning practices of the Three Weeks include refraining from playing musical instruments or listening to music, getting a haircut or shaving, celebrating weddings, and reciting the Shehecheyanu (the effect of which is not eating new fruits or wearing new clothing).

The seventeenth of Tammuz commemorates, first and foremost, the Roman breaching of the walls of Jerusalem, alongside other events that the Tannaim, the rabbis of the Mishnaic period, considered communal disasters. In the Mishnah Taanit 4:6 we read:

חֲמִשָּׁה דְבָרִים אֵרְעוּ אֶת אֲבוֹתֵינוּ בְּשִׁבְעָה עָשָׂר בְּתַמּוּז וַחֲמִשָּׁה בְּתִשְׁעָה בְאָב.

בְּשִׁבְעָה עָשָׂר בְּתַמּוּז נִשְׁתַּבְּרוּ הַלּוּחוֹת, וּבָטַל הַתָּמִיד, וְהָבְקְעָה הָעִיר, וְשָׂרַף אַפּוֹסְטְמוֹס אֶת הַתּוֹרָה, וְהֶעֱמִיד צֶלֶם בַּהֵיכָל.

> Five calamitous matters occurred to our forefathers on the seventeenth of Tammuz, and five other disasters happened on the ninth of Av. On the seventeenth of Tammuz the tablets were broken by Moses when he saw the Golden Calf; the daily offering was nullified; the city walls of Jerusalem were breached; Apostemos burned a Torah scroll; and an idol was placed in the Sanctuary. [To be continued in Av.]

What do these events have in common, and how are they relevant today?

All of the calamities remembered on the seventeenth of Tammuz are collective traumas—that is, harm that happened to the community as a whole. While many other holidays in the Jewish year include experiences of Jewish collective traumas, Hannukah, Purim, and Pesach, for instance, bring us into experiencing our survival and celebrating our power. The seventeenth of Tammuz, the Three Weeks, and Tisha b'Av, create the time of year most focused on hurt, harm, and grief.

Each of these events strikes at what the rabbis considered core and essential to the Judaism they were constructing. Interestingly, these threats come from both inside and outside the community. There is the story of the Golden Calf, made by our biblical ancestors, and an account of the Roman attacks on Jerusalem. The attack against the walls of Jerusalem paralleled with the desecration of the Temple spotlights the ways in which colonizing forces intentionally attack the culture, spiritual practices, and sacred lifeways and traditions of people and places they are trying to dominate.

It is painful to acknowledge our individual struggles with accessing sacredness; on the seventeenth of Tammuz we see how our ancestors attempted to shift and transform these struggles through investigating the ways the collective body is impacted. Our ancestors gathered multiple experiences of collective harm and marked them all together on one day. They then moved into Three Weeks of collective decreased joy: during bein ha'Metzarim, minhag in many places is to have no big celebrations, and some do not shave or get a haircut, swim, or listen to music.

The seventeenth of Tammuz invites us to reflect on our relationships to spiritual and cultural practices that connect us to the sacred, and what constitute threats to those practices. The Tannaitic rabbis put idol worship in the same mishnaic breath as Roman colonization, both heinous to their understanding of Judaism. We are in the ideological lineage of Rabbinic Judaism, where the Golden Calf and idol worship are both seen as total violations of Jewish law. Yet we who claim Torah as inherited tradition are all just as much the descendants of the people who made the Golden Calf as we are of the rabbis who condemn it. We can wonder about the desires that motivated our calf-building ancestors. What animated and sustained practices that were deemed idol worship by the authorities? The story of the Golden Calf can be understood as patriarchal rabbinic authority demeaning worship that they could not control. In this reading, we honor our ancestors' complex theologies and desire for multiple forms of worship.

At the same time, idol worship can be understood as parallel to materialism today, focusing on the gold of the calf instead of the immaterial but deeply real Divine the people have encountered. We can understand the rabbi's rejection of idol worship as parallel to our rejection of the violence of cultural appropriation—reducing a complex, detailed, layered being or civilization into a symbol divorced from its real power. It is then possible to comprehend the rabbis' understanding that spiritual practice can collude with empire, and use the seventeenth of Tammuz to mourn the desecration of the Jewish people's holiest places and practices from inside and outside of the tradition.

Wherever we place ourselves in the tradition, the seventeenth of Tammuz is about the overwhelming impact of our cultural and spiritual traditions being harmed. It is a powerful gateway into the Three Weeks, which culminates with the ninth of Av, marking the complete destruction of the Temple. Some of us have never had access to cultural practices that feel spiritually supportive, and some of us are just beginning the journey of discovering what a relationship with our spiritual selves and the holiness of the world feels like. Some of us have no interest in exploring anything in the realm of spiritual practice. Across a range of relationships to tradition, we can ask: when we allow ourselves to mourn the ruination of our modalities of accessing the holy, how much deeper can we feel the heartbreak of the wreckage of our sacred sites?

MARKING THE SEVENTEENTH OF TAMMUZ

Marking the seventeenth of Tammuz and coming into the Three Weeks in community could become a time for looking back on the last year and years to see what loss has been experienced in the community. What sacred communal spaces, like bookstores, community centers, encampments, bars, parks, and monuments, have been shut down by the state and the forces of gentrification and capitalism? What organizations have collapsed or closed in the past year? What collective events have come to an end? What ritual or acknowledgment does the community need to collectively grieve these losses? Some of these things may have ended abruptly, too soon, and unjustly; others may have closed after a long run and in good time. Often, endings hold both and all. The seventeenth of Tammuz is an invitation to make space for all of these losses.

The traditional practices of marking the seventeenth of Tammuz include a personal fast for those who are able, and additions of Selichot liturgy to the Shacharit and mincha services. Those who don't go to synagogue but are looking for ways to creatively engage in the seventeenth of Tammuz and Three Weeks have the challenge and opportunity of a wide open space in which to experiment. As leftist communities find more ways to take public action on the ninth of Av, the seventeenth of Tammuz, and the Three Weeks, they can become spiritual and political days and weeks of preparation. They can be times to reflect, gather with each other, plan, and build.

Tammuz is a spacious month, with very little on the Jewish calendar. This collective breath is particularly notable for where it falls squarely between two intense holiday arcs: sandwiched between the packed Exodus journey of Nisan, Iyar, and Sivan and the slow and steady ramp-up to the High Holidays that will begin in earnest in Av. With intention, Tammuz can be a month to notice this hinge of the year, and to make space for more subtle changes, within us and around us. In Tammuz, we are encouraged to notice our gardens growing, all around us, all the time.

bless the mugwort in abandoned lots
bless the shattering that scattered sparks
bless the disturbance, the storm and the fire
bless this mess and bless our desire
bless the courage to stay with the trouble
bless our mistakes, our misdeeds, and our
fumbles
bless the uncertainty and bless the collapse
bless the fragments and bless the scraps
bless the longing, the yearning for home
bless these bodies, bless the stones
bless our hearts, cracked open in pain
bless what we have lost and what remains
bless our weeping, bless our grief
bless our fasting, bless our feasts
bless our kisses, bless our bliss
bless our asses, bless our fists
bless our romps in borrowed clothes
bless our pleasure, bless what grows
bless the broken, bless new and old
bless the way we mend with gold
bless the margins, bless the center
bless the way we fall apart, together

bless the breaking, bless the fall
Holy One of Blessing,
bless it all

Illustration © Sol Weiss. Incantation © Dori Midnight.

WELCOME TO אב AV

What losses do you carry with you from your life, families, ancestors, histories? What has happened to Jewish communities that breaks your heart? What communities are you a part of or in relationships with that have been devastated by empire?

What experiences do you have of moving through loss and grief? What pain stays with you? What ways of remembering loss support your living in the present?

Where do you feel love in your life? Where do you offer love? How do you nurture your sexual self?

Introduction to Av

מִשֶּׁנִּכְנַס אָב, מְמַעֲטִין בְּשִׂמְחָה:

When Av begins, one decreases their rejoicing.

—Mishnah Taanit 4:6

Av, in the peak of summer, opens with destruction and consolation. The Three Weeks of counting that began on the seventeenth of Tammuz ends at Tisha b'Av's doorstep. The season grows hotter, the world intensifies. Over the journey of the month, grief melts away or burns up into love, with Tu b'Av. Av is an emotional rollercoaster of a month.

We begin with Tisha b'Av, compressing time and space. Our tradition stitches together moments in history separated by millennia by teaching that they all happened on the same day. Tisha b'Av commemorates the destruction of the First and Second Temples and more, offering a container for all of this sorrow to mingle, where we can allow our hearts to break open. On Tisha b'Av, generations are compressed as well. Ancestors walk through the door and join us on the floor, their pain and suffering mingling with ours. At the same time as we are marking in the holiday cycle violence done to our people, we are reading in the weekly Torah cycle about violence that our people are doing and planning to do to others in conquering Canaan.[1] This is folded into the layers of grief through which we time travel.

Av comes at the height of summer in the Northern Hemisphere, when in our time greater violence has erupted (or been reported), like bombardment and war in Gaza, police brutality and murder in the US. In the summer systems of death dealing often seem to increase their frenetic pace. "If past is prologue, my community can look forward to another summer of intense, relentless, and surely illegal police harassment of young people of color and specifically of young Black men," wrote Mariam Kaba.[2] When we sink down to mourn moments in Jewish history of dissolution, death, and despair, we also sink into the more recent yahrtzeits of primarily Black and brown people murdered by police in the US, and other horrors that have happened in this season.

With layers of intensity, Av demands reflection on how we act under pressure. What family patterns, core beliefs, or traumatic impacts are operating to inform our actions, and how might we implement our higher values even in times of great stress and intensity? When the heat is turned up, how do communities and movements react? How do we respond to devastation, how do we create space to mourn and give despair our full attention? And then, how do we refuse to linger in sorrow?

Tisha b'Av begins a holiday circuit that ends with Simchat Torah, months later in Tishrei. We break our hearts open at Tisha b'Av, in preparation for the New Year and the work of teshuvah. But the grief of Tisha b'Av does not linger long—by the afternoon we welcome in more comfort. Only a week later, we flirt our way into a new world with Tu b'Av, the Jewish love day. Matches are made, love and lust are celebrated, and we mend our broken hearts to dream of a fulfilling, pleasurable future. In the Shabbatot following Tisha b'Av, we head into seven parashiyot of consolation. It will soon be Elul and, after lamenting the year that was, people will be newly ready for the year ahead.

When Av begins, rejoicing decreases, allowing us to truly mourn. We sink into the depths, but not forever. We rise more connected to grief and the people and places we've lost. When Av exits, having been immersed in grief and welcomed in love, we arrive at the doors of accountability and transformation.

The parashiyot of Av are Mattot, Ma'asei, Devarim, Va'etchanan, Eikev, and Re'eh. In this month we read about the plan to enter the land and make home, as well as Moses' learning that he will never be able to enter. This yearning and heartbreak, the threats that are scattered through the instructions for right action once entering the land, evoke the struggles of Av. As the book of Devarim begins this month, Moses illuminates the strongest modality for hope and resilience our people have—storytelling. Moses recounts his life and the covenant between God and the Jewish people, with hopes for a future of peace and abundance. Av can contain the fullness of these emotions.

Av in Action

NINE DAYS

We are now in the midst of another significant arc of Jewish time within the calendar. In each of these journeys there are signposts, moments when we take notice of the spirit of the time, through shifting our attention and intention. The journey from Pesach to Shavuot is characterized by counting the Omer toward deepening insight on the journey from Mitzrayim to Sinai. From Rosh Chodesh Elul through Rosh Hashanah to Sukkot, specific psalms and prayers are said or skipped to explore teshuvah and renewal. The journey of the seventeenth of Tammuz through Rosh Chodesh Av until Tisha b'Av is a time of grief, most distinguished by embodiment practices.

Since the seventeenth of Tammuz, it has been a time of mourning, bein ha'metzarim, between the straits, a time of restricting particularly joyful activities. With Rosh Chodesh Av, the Nine Days begin, and grief and the accompanying practices increase. We refrain from washing clothes and bathing ourselves for pleasure. Many refrain from eating meat or drinking wine during the Nine Days, in commemoration of the ending of the meat and wine offerings with the destruction of the Temple, a practice likely dating from the time of the Rishonim, the rabbinic commentators from the eleventh to the fifteenth centuries.

As we turn our attention to collective harm, death, destruction, and overwhelming violence, Jewish tradition suggests that words are not enough. Fear and grief live in our bodies, and the ritual practices of the Three Weeks and the Nine Days demonstrate centuries of accumulated knowledge about this. In this time, we can experiment with any practices that let us experience mourning without being completely overwhelmed or overcome. Many who refrain from wine during this time, for example, do use it for kiddush on Shabbat and to make havdalah. This allows us to, while immersing in mourning, stay tethered to the present moment.

Shabbat Chazon is the Shabbat immediately preceding Tisha b'Av. It takes its name, "prophesy," from the haftorah parshah in the book of Isaiah. It is known as Black Sabbath, contrasted with the White Shabbat of Shabbat Shuvah, the Shabbat between Rosh HaShanah and Yom Kippur. Shabbat Chazon is the last parshah of the three weeks of punishment.

TISHA B'AV ROOTS AND DEVELOPMENT

The first mention of the ninth of Av as a day of collective mourning is in the Mishnah. In Taanit 4:6 it says:

חֲמִשָּׁה דְבָרִים אֵרְעוּ אֶת אֲבוֹתֵינוּ בְּשִׁבְעָה עָשָׂר בְּתַמּוּז וַחֲמִשָּׁה בְּתִשְׁעָה בְּאָב . . . בְּתִשְׁעָה בְּאָב נִגְזַר עַל אֲבוֹתֵינוּ שֶׁלֹּא יִכָּנְסוּ לָאָרֶץ, וְחָרַב הַבַּיִת בָּרִאשׁוֹנָה וּבַשְּׁנִיָּה, וְנִלְכְּדָה בֵיתָר, וְנֶחְרְשָׁה הָעִיר. מִשֶּׁנִּכְנַס אָב, מְמַעֲטִין בְּשִׂמְחָה:

Five calamitous matters occurred to our forefathers on the seventeenth of Tammuz, and five other disasters happened on the ninth of Av . . . On the ninth of Av it was decreed upon our ancestors that they would all die in the Wilderness and not enter Eretz Yisrael; and the Temple was destroyed the first time, in the days of Nebuchadnezzar, and the second time, by the Romans; and Beitar was captured; and the city of Jerusalem was plowed. From when the month of Av begins, one decreases acts of rejoicing.

How could all of these calamities possibly have happened on the same day, centuries apart? The rabbis in the Gemara on this Mishnah wrestle with divergent accounts of the actual dates of the destruction of the Temples. They do impressive calendrical and historical wrangling, debating what happened when, what to mark, and why, to land them both on the ninth of Av.[3]

Why? In *Seasons of Our Joy*, Rabbi Arthur Waskow posits:

> The very anxiety of the rabbis to justify the date of Tisha b'Av might be taken to support a theory of some modern scholars that the date was partly affected by the religious patterns of Babylon. Among the Babylonians, the ninth of Av was a day of dread and sorrow, a climactic moment in a month-long celebration focused on torches and firewood. (Perhaps this Babylonian holy season also had to do with midsummer and a sense of the raging sun.) Once the Jews had gone into the Babylonian exile, in seeking to commemorate the day of their disaster they may have chosen the fiery day already set aside by the Babylonians around them— the day whose date was so close and whose fiery significance echoed so well with the burning of the Temple.[4]

By now, the rabbis creating and enhancing the holiday calendar by layering stories on top of seasonal and agricultural observances is familiar. On Tisha b'Av, this is maximized, with the rabbis layering their relatively recent political contexts on top of distant biblical stories. This is, perhaps, what laid the groundwork for Jews centuries into the future to even more thickly fold their histories into Tisha b'Av.

The rabbis of the Talmud wrestled with questions of why these catastrophic events happened, and tried on different explanations. In Shabbat 119b, it says that Jerusalem was destroyed because the people desecrated Shabbat.[5] In Yoma 9b, the destruction of the First Temple was said to be caused by forbidden sexual relations, the degradation of consecrated ritual objects, and bloodshed,[6] and the destruction of the Second Temple was said to be due to sinat chinam (שִׂנְאַת חִנָּם), baseless hatred. Perhaps most cinematically of all the reasons given, in Gittin 55b-56a, there is the story of Kamtza and Bar Kamtza. In a layered and dramatic story, public humiliation, power relations, and Jewish infighting lead to the destruction of the Temple.

In this waterfall of explanations for the destruction of the Temples, some are resonant with Jewish experiences today, and some are steeped in and radiate misogyny. What is incredibly noticeable and painful is the length the rabbis go to, to find or invent internal communal reasons for what was, by and large, the caused by the impacts of empires. Exploring Tisha b'Av as a location of and container for experiences of collective and historical trauma and its impacts, part of our work is reckoning with the shame and self-blame that centuries of Jewish ancestors associated with Tisha b'Av. While both Tanakh and Talmud are multivocal and nuanced texts, strands of each of them are shaped by the development of identities based in exile. For centuries, our ancestors told each other that Israelite sinning and Jewish infighting caused God to retract God's self, and that that was what created the space for the Babylonian and Roman conquests. We can see how powerless these ancestors were, how weak their systems of governance, and the overwhelming violence of conquest. They developed reasons for the destruction that gave them collective responsibility, agency, and control.

In the Gemara, alongside the mourning of the destruction, there are diaspora-positive stories, which makes sense given the context of the Babylonian Talmud. In Gittin 56b, Rabbi Yohanan Ben Zakkai negotiates with Roman general Vespasian. Having impressed Vespasian and been invited to make a request of him, Ben Zakkai famously asks, "Give me Yavne and its sages," securing a political future for diaspora rabbinic leadership, but not asking for protection for Jerusalem.

There is much to learn from the rabbinic wrestling with the destruction of the Temples and exile from the land, while at the same time holding a different perspective on this history. There were Jews outside of the land before the Babylonian exile,[7] and many Jews who stayed in Babylonia and did not return with Ezra and Nehemiah in 583 BCE and the years that followed. Susanna Heschel teaches:

> The paradox of Jewish exile is that it never happened. There
> was no edict of exile from the land of Israel after the Romans

destroyed the Second Temple in 70 CE; Jews continued to live in Palestine, even composing the Palestinian Talmud and various Midrashim. Most Jews lived in diaspora, at least since the sixth century BCE, flourishing and transforming Israelite religion into Judaism. Although Jews were never exiled from the land of Israel, the Jewish belief that Jews live in exile shaped Jewish self-understanding as a major theme in religious literature and liturgy.[8]

Holding the historical record next to the traditional story can be confusing. How is it possible to relate to the tradition when the stories that frame them are undermined? We can regain a sense of continuity with ancestors by stepping into the lineage of people who have long been wrestling with place, home, and longing. 70 CE meant the loss of access to a centralized site of worship and governance, fundamentally changing Jewish technology for accessing the Divine and each other. Jewish ancestors, like Jews today, experienced a whole range of feelings about this loss, and it is always important to honor the wrestling.

Over the centuries, other catastrophes of Jewish history came to be marked and mourned on the ninth of Av: the declaration of the first Crusade on August 15, 1096, the expulsion of Jews from England on July 18, 1290, and from Spain on July 30, 1492. In some ways, this is parallel to local Purim celebrations and freedom seders, in that the act of weaving contemporary political events into Jewish ritual, like at Tisha b'Av, is truly not new. In the kinot for Tisha b'Av, elegies and lamentations written to commemorate these events are recited, weaving the Crusades into a narrative arc with the destruction of the Temples. Some contemporary Tisha b'Av observances reach all the way into recent memories and lifetimes, including commemorations of the Holocaust and attempts to shift practices based on the modern state of Israel.

While condensing these varied and nuanced events into one mythologized retelling is part of the core ritual of Tisha b'Av, It also can play into what historian Salo Wittmayer Baron famously characterized, in 1928, as the "lachrymose conception of Jewish history." In lachrymose history, Jewish life is told as tragedy after tragedy and endless persecution. Today, this resonates with claims that antisemitism is cyclical and inevitable.

As students of nuanced and diverse Jewish histories, we know our

AV

lineages contain tragedy *and* great adaptation and thriving. As anti-racist organizers, we are working for an end to all forms of oppression, including antisemitism. And yet, Tisha b'Av instructs us to condense all anti-Jewish violence and persecution into one day, and to sit on the floor weeping. How is it possible to honor the ancestral wisdom of this holiday that time travels through the centuries while remaining clear about our time, places, and commitments?

TISHA B'AV AND TRANSFORMATION

With intention, it is possible to create Tisha b'Av observances that are antidotes to the lachrymose view of Jewish history and containers for processing and moving through historical and intergenerational traumas. For starters, Tisha b'Av can be welcomed as a ritualized commemoration of collective memory, not an objective retelling of history. How we frame rituals matters. During Pesach seders, given our contemporary context of Islamophobia and anti-Arab racism, we open by reminding ourselves and each other that biblical Mitzrayim is not contemporary Egypt. At Tisha b'Av, it is critical to articulate that the Babylonian and Roman empires are not one and the same as the empires of today, even as we then move into experiencing the resonances and similarities.

One of the incredible tools available to create Tisha b'Av as a practice of transforming historical trauma is the ritual of the day itself. While our ancestors marked many instances of violence on one day, they also created a container with strong boundaries on this grief. The arc of time from the seventeenth of Tammuz through Tisha b'Av to Tu b'Av to Rosh Chodesh Elul creates a peak immersion into collective violence, *and then back out of it.* Erev Tisha b'Av is spent in the dark, and in the morning the congregation sits on the floor. But by the afternoon people sit in the seats, and embody the movement of closure that we hope to experience. A week later, at Tu b'Av, we are dancing in the fields. In contrast, many Jews experienced Jewish education that put the Holocaust at the center, showing and telling both subtly and explicitly that to stop mourning is to forget, and to forget is to die. Tisha b'Av offers us the wisdom of movement into and out of grief: of fully immersing ourselves in embodied grief, and, then, getting up. Transformed by, but not stuck, in mourning.

Within the container of the day and the season, the invitation of Tisha b'Av is to feel feelings, not think about grief as an abstract construct. Before there were words for or books about collective, intergenerational, and historical trauma, people knew these concepts intuitively and created the rituals of this day to move through them. Now, there are newer methods and practices for mourning and transforming trauma to integrate with the traditional practices. We tell, sing, and weep over these stories of overwhelming violence. We face the heartbreak and fear together on this day, so that it is possible to rise up and. together, live.

DAY OF MOURNING

וכל המצות הנוהגות באבל נוהגות בתשעה באב

All of the mitzvot of observances for mourning are observances for Tisha b'Av

—Kol Bo 62:15

The embodied practices of Tisha b'Av will be familiar to anyone who has been in a Jewish house of mourning, because on Tisha b'Av the community constructs a collective shiva house. The five prohibitions of Tisha b'Av are refraining from eating, washing, applying makeup or ointment, wearing shoes made with leather, and sex. Torah is not studied on Tisha b'Av because it gladdens the heart, although passages that are appropriately sad are allowed. Work is avoided, though not prohibited, and it is suggested that people start work in the afternoon. Some will read books or watch movies that are related to the tenor of the day, about tragedies in Jewish history or the world. If Shabbat falls on the ninth of Av, the observance of Tisha b'Av begins Saturday night following Shabbat. Some particulars are changed, abbreviated, or omitted when Tisha b'Av is observed on the tenth of Av. In this case, an abbreviated havdalah is made to separate Shabbat from the observance.

יֵשְׁבוּ לָאָרֶץ יִדְּמוּ זִקְנֵי בַת־צִיּוֹן הֶעֱלוּ עָפָר עַל־רֹאשָׁם חָגְרוּ שַׂקִּים

Silent sit on the ground The elders of fair Zion; They have strewn
dust on their heads and girded themselves with sackcloth

—Eicha 2:10

FASTING

Before Tisha b'Av begins, there is a seudah hamafseket, a pre-fast meal.
Traditionally, it is forbidden to eat meat, wine, or more than one cooked
food. Eggs, a mourner's food and symbol of life, as well as bread dipped in
ashes, are permitted. This meal is often eaten while sitting on the ground.[9]
In the case that Tisha b'Av begins Saturday night, the third meal before
the end of Shabbat (seudah shlishit) should be a hearty and festive meal
without the mourning foods of the usual seudah hamafseket.

Tisha b'Av is the second most important fast of the year, next to Yom
Kippur. They are the only sundown to sundown fasts, though Yom Kippur
may fall on Shabbat while Tisha b'Av is deferred to the following day. If a
fast jeopardizes one's physical or mental health in any way, it is forbidden
to fast. For those who are not fasting on Tisha b'Av, the symbolic foods of
the seudah can be incorporated into what is eaten in order to emphasize
the symbolism of the observance. For those eating on Tisha b'Av, Birkat
haMazon (grace after meals) replaces the word rachem, "have compassion,"
with nachem, "comfort."[10]

SPACE, PLACE, AND GREETINGS

The parochet (curtain in front of the Torah ark) is removed, furniture is
overturned, and the lights are dimmed as Tisha b'Av begins with Ma'ariv
(the evening service). Many will sit low to the ground.[11] We re-enact in our
sacred places destruction, and even the resting place of the sacred Torah is
disturbed.

The Torah as we know it today did not exist at the time of the destruction of the Temple. The destruction of the Temple is re-enacted using the
symbols and holy spaces that have developed since the destruction. The
centering of the synagogue following the destruction of the Temple, as
well as and focusing on Torah study, and even the ark that holds the Torah
is based on the kodesh kodashim (Holy of Holies) separated by a paro-

chet. For non-synogogue-based observance, how can one disturb restful or sacred spaces to more deeply connect to the discord of the day?

We do not greet or say goodbye to one another throughout the observance of Tisha b'Av, as it is not a "good morning!" Similarly, in a shiva house we do not greet mourners so as not to require them to in turn say "fine, thanks, how are you?" Not saying hello or goodbye adds to the eerie, unresolved, isolated feelings of the day.

LITURGY

The Tisha b'Av service focuses on the chanting of Eicha, the Book of Lamentations. The prophet Jeremiah is credited by tradition with writing Eicha, and is said to have been born on Tisha b'Av.[12] The text is a heartbreaking account of the destruction of Jerusalem, the destruction of a people, and the feelings of despair, shame, and humiliation felt by the Jewish people at the time. It is chanted in the minor key in a specific Eicha trope (cantillation). This trope also appears in a verse from the Torah reading of Shabbat Chazon (which begins with "eicha"), the haftorah for Shabbat Chazon (right before Tisha b'Av), in much of the haftorah for Tisha b'Av, and in chapters throughout the book of Esther. In Ashkenazi trope melodies, the Esther and Eicha trope are "cousins."

Kinot, elegies, are poetic works written by Jewish people experiencing persecution. Drafted during the time of the Crusades and the Spanish Inquisition, kinot were also written following the Nazi Holocaust. They speak to shame, yearning, fear, and grief, relying on biblical and rabbinic images and themes. Modern kinot express deep mourning and devastation at the violence of death-dealing forces of white supremacy, transphobia, and capitalism.

Traditionally, instrumental music is not played or listened to during the three weeks prior to Tisha b'Av, nor on Tisha b'Av.

WEEPING

עַל־אֵ֣לֶּה ׀ אֲנִ֣י בוֹכִיָּ֗ה עֵינִ֤י ׀ עֵינִי֙ יֹרְדָ֣ה מַּ֔יִם

For these things do I weep, My eyes flow with tears . . .

—Eicha 1:16

Eicha is filled with images of Rachel weeping for her children, of Jeremiah weeping for the destroyed Temple, and in the midrashic literature on Lamentations, God weeping for the people. Tisha b'Av is a day of tears, and the observance, liturgy, and chanting all work to create space for us to pour out our hearts.

For those familiar with synagogue life that is formal, measured, and often "Protestant" in practice, the idea of sitting on the floor, eating ashes, and weeping with synagogue community members might sound uncouth or even absurd. For our cynical leftist organizer brains, tears are not to be shed in public; tears are more comfortable as agitation rather than from personal grief. Tisha b'Av calls for public mourning of two-thousand-year-old events. How do we create spaces that allow for, or even cultivate crying?

Tisha b'Av calls Jews to sink into vulnerability and powerlessness, to pour out our hearts.

ד"א "בלילה" שכל הבוכה בלילה קולו נשמע

ד"א "בלילה" שכל הבוכה בלילה כוכבים ומזלות בוכין עמו

ד"א בלילה שכל הבוכה בלילה השומע קו"ו בוכה כנגדו

Another meaning, "in the night": whoever weeps at night, his voice is heard.

Another meaning, "in the night": whoever weeps at night, the stars and constellations weep with him.

Another meaning, "in the night": whoever weeps at night, the one who hears, weeps with the weeping.

—Sanhedrin 104b:4–6

As with any other practice, Tisha b'Av weeping might take years to grow into, and will look different for different people. We begin by inviting people into rituals where vulnerability is visible and grief is welcomed, where heartbreak is explored out loud. We try not to perform sadness for each other, but to let ourselves touch down into, in public, the devastation we may barely hold at bay each day. This practice allows us to begin to trust that community, ritual, and tradition can hold it with us.

REDEMPTION AND THE END OF TISHA B'AV

The afternoon of Tisha b'Av marks a shift in the tone. The Shir Shel Yom (psalm of the day) that is usually said in the morning, but omitted on Tisha b'Av, is recited in the afternoon.[13] Some verses of comfort are also recited in the afternoon, though Torah is traditionally not learned or included in the evening and morning liturgy. By the afternoon of Tisha b'Av, it is permitted to start cooking for the break-fast meal, sitting in chairs of regular height, and restoring the parochet and other furniture in the synagogue.

It is taught that the Messiah will be born on the afternoon of Tisha b'Av. Therefore, some families have the custom of sweeping the house that afternoon. Hameiri[14] reports that in the community of Narbona, the women would begin to wash their hair in the afternoon to honor the birth of the Messiah, and to welcome feelings of comfort and hope at the pending redemption.[15] We turn our attention from utter despair to the practice of faith and preparation for justice.

As we make clear connections between the history of the observance and the current world, the afternoon of Tisha b'Av can be a potent time to take action for justice. Public mourning, community care, and direct action in opposition to the war machine honors the Jewish history of this day, and hastens the coming of liberation.

The fast is broken with a hand washing with no blessing. After Tisha b'Av ends, Kiddush Levanah (קִדּוּשׁ לְבָנָה), the blessing over the new moon, is recited. Traditionally, it is said on the first Shabbat of the new month, but postponed in Av until after the mourning of Tisha b'Av ends. Due to the timeline of the destruction of the Temple (it still burned through the tenth of Av),[16] the prohibitions against eating meat, swimming, or washing continue through the afternoon of the tenth of Av. If Tisha b'Av ends Thursday night, it is permitted to wash and cook to prepare for Shabbat![7]

TISHA B'AV IN THE TIME OF JEWISH EMPIRE

A day of sitting on the ground, listing horrible things that have happened and weeping in public? This sounds like a queer leftist Jewish dream! And yet, we have complicated feelings about contemporary Tisha b'Av. As the inheritors of Rabbinic Judaism we are part of a tradition completely shaped by the destruction of the Temple and exile from the land. By and large, we are not praying for a literal Third Temple. We also know that the exile didn't happen the way the mainstream of the tradition wants to say that it did; Jews continued to live in the land.

The stakes here are raised exponentially by Zionism and Israeli apartheid. One strand of the weave of stories on Tisha b'Av is about the end of Israelite sovereignty in the land. We now live in a time of Jewish nationalism violently embodied in the Israeli apartheid state. Some Zionists posit that Tisha b'Av need not be as high a day of mourning because, once again, Jews have control of the land. As anti-Zionists who do not long for a return to Temple worship, some of us might consider not mourning the destruction of the Temples at all. The questions loom large: What is the destruction of the Temple to a diaspora Jew? Should an anti-Zionist Jew observe Tisha b'Av while living in a time of Jewish empire?

There are many reasons for the answer to be "yes." Tisha b'Av is about mourning the loss of safety and the loss of sacred sites. It is possible to understand and honor the deep grief of the destruction of a holy site, even when we are not wishing or trying to return to that exact same conception of sacredness and form of worship. Restricted access to and continued violence inside sacred sites, as described in Eicha, is mirrored in violence at the Al-Aqsa Mosque (particularly in spring 2021); the attack at the Tree of Life Synagogue in October 2019; the devastating legacy and continued violence against Black churches, mosques, synagogues, and temples; and the genocidal violence against Indigenous traditions and lifeways. Tisha b'Av is a doorway into the specific rage and grief when sacred sites are destroyed. On Tisha b'Av, we mourn the unchecked conquest and existence of all empires.

The concept of sinat chinam still resonates. It is critical to expand it from solely focusing on relationships with other Jews, to understanding the way cruelty and ego tear apart our movements and undermine our collective striving for a better world. With care not to blame ourselves and our communities for systemic oppression, it is still possible to examine the deep ancestral wisdom about how we hurt each other amidst greater collective violence, and create space on Tisha b'Av to name and shift those patterns.

We mourn on Tisha b'Av because Zionism is not Judaism. If we refuse to mourn the destruction of the First and Second Temples because of the current Israeli nation-state, we are, in effect, supporting Zionist claims that Israel is the rightful and sole inheritor of the biblical tradition. The destruction of the Temples and dissolution of Jewish autonomy in 70 CE can be vivid in our memories without being copy-pasted onto our contemporary time. It is anachronistic to apply a contemporary vision of what Jewish control of the land is onto what it looked like in the time of the Temple. Nothing about the state of Israel does anything to allay the grief at the destruction of the Temples. There is a lineage of anti-Zionist, diaspora Jewishness that continues to mourn and long for home, on this one day of the year and at other select moments in Jewish ritual life, while also creating interdependent homes in all the places Jews live.

There is plenty of theological and cultural wrestling left to do. Tisha b'Av was part of Jewish life for over 1,700 years before the creation of Israel as a settler-colonial state, and we have just barely begun to experiment with the ritual, emotional, and critical tools that help us to make meaning of this day. It is impossible to know what Tisha b'Av will look like in the future, or if the next generation of liberation-seeking Jews will discard it as no longer resonant. However, Jews will always find ways to tell their stories and make new meanings.

TISHA B'AV FOR OUR TIMES

Contemporary, creative, and politically aligned Tisha b'Av observances are, of course, already happening. In 2014/5774, the Jewish Voice for Peace Rabbinical Council created a Tisha b'Av ritual to mourn and respond to the assault on Gaza, drawing many parallels between the tradition and our current time:

The expulsion of the Jewish people from Spain, France, England, the loss of home, community, and safety, [is] also said to have happened on the 9th of Av. Today we bear witness to the loss of home, community, and safety for Palestinians in Gaza at the hands of the IDF.[18]

In the summer of 2019, when the United States' ongoing deportations and violence against immigrants gained national attention, Jews and allies took direct action at ICE headquarters and offices of politicians all over the country on Tisha b'Av. Actions resulted in many planned arrests and wide media coverage, and cities continuing to organize in solidarity with immigrant-led movements. Never Again Action and Jewish Voice for Peace coordinated local and national actions, as did local groups such as Jews United for Justice in Washington, DC, and Baltimore.

In 2020, at the height of Black-led uprisings to defund the police and defend Black lives, Jews for Racial and Economic Justice created 40 Days of Teshuvah:

How does Teshuvah and Tisha B'Av connect to our work of Racial Justice: We know the fight for justice is both in the streets and in the heavens—that it's both physical and spiritual. On Tisha B'Av, we repent and mourn baseless hatred and destruction. We mourn the ways in which we, as a collective, have participated in and perpetuated racism and anti-Blackness. We grieve the fact that we have abandoned *Hashem*—that we have abandoned our values and the true meaning of love and justice—and have practiced the idolatry of white supremacy. As we do *teshuvah* and mourn, we commit to our collective return.[19]

Through these ritual actions, we now have an incredible collection of contemporary Lamentations, taking inspiration from and echoing the rhythms of Eicha. Rabbis Tamara Cohen and Arthur Waskow created "Eicha for the Earth," drawing deep parallels between the Temple *as* the Earth, and the whole Earth as the in-dwelling of Shechina, the destruction of which must be mourned.[20] In 5777/2016, Rabbi Brant Rosen offered Lamentation for a New Diaspora, a heartbreaking and poetic exploration of mourning for all that Zionism has created:

all that we once considered sacred
was sheer profanity
we created holidays and festivals
to celebrate our cruelty
we venerated leaders
who should have been tried
for their crimes[21]

During the COVID-19 pandemic, Tisha b'Av has been an opportunity to mourn overwhelming loss of life and community devastation. In 2022, Svara's Disability Justice Torah Circle organized a Tisha b'Av ritual that seamlessly weaved together destruction of the Temples with destruction in our time. Organizer and Talmud teacher Jessica Belasco wrote:

> We are gathering on Tisha b'Av to hold space for personal and communal grief, with specific attention to the ways in which the COVID-19 pandemic, and our society's disastrously ableist response to the pandemic, has created enormous grief for disabled people. This space will actively center the experiences of disabled people, as we mourn the losses the pandemic has wrought in our lives and the toxic individualism that it has highlighted in our society—and the existential blows inherent in it all.[22]

What can Tisha b'Av look like for you and your community? We can weep and fight against empire with direct action or days of education, tell ancestral stories of grief, and open our hearts to deeply hear the stories of others.

Leftist communities already know how to mourn in the heat of the summer, how to make public containers for grief, and how to move from grief into action. What might be more challenging is creating containers where you and your people can truly weep, and not just perform weeping. Hopefully, we can create public rituals where participants are so in it, so much doing it, that tears are possible, but for others that will not be accessible. For those of us facilitating and leading public action rituals, we are differently present then when we are at homes or in synagogues: having to mind the choreography, cop watching, and livestreaming of an action can

AV

make it challenging to experience the vulnerability needed to be open and express one's own grief. If you're planning a large public action on Tisha b'Av, be sure to make time to take care of yourself and allow the tears to fall.

Many of us on the Left have conflicted relationships with weeping, all of them impacted by race, class, gender, sexuality, and layers of identities and socializations. For some of us, public shows of emotion are particularly fraught; white tears have been weaponized against Black and brown people and communities. Men and masculine people have been trained not to cry. In a cultural and economic system that values some people's feelings over other people's lives, how is it possible, publicly, to grieve?

There is not one answer, but Tisha b'Av is an invitation to explore. Overwhelming harm and violence are devastating life on the planet, and it is not possible merely to think and talk our way to a new world. As people living into more wakefulness than capitalism and white supremacy want for us, it is possible and necessary to assert our full range of human emotions as part of our full humanities. We grieve so that we may live.

Shabbat Nachamu is the Shabbat immediately following Tisha b'Av, the Shabbat of Consolation. It takes its name from the haftorah parshah for the week, from the Book of Isaiah, where it is written: "Nachamu ami" ("Be comforted, my people"). This begins the seven weeks of consolation leading up to Rosh HaShanah.

TU B'AV

אָמַר רַבָּן שִׁמְעוֹן בֶּן גַּמְלִיאֵל, לֹא הָיוּ יָמִים טוֹבִים לְיִשְׂרָאֵל כַּחֲמִשָּׁה עָשָׂר בְּאָב וּכְיוֹם הַכִּפּוּרִים

Rabbi Shimon ben Gamaliel said: There were no days of joy in Israel greater than the fifteenth of Av and Yom Kippur.

—Mishnah Taanit 4:8

Dating back to the Temple period, Tu b'Av is described in the Mishnah and Gemara as a socialist Jewish love festival where all Jews go cruising in vineyards! Like the naming conventions of Tu b'Shvat and Tisha b'Av, Tu b'Av literally means "the fifteenth of Av." Unsurprisingly, the Gemara[23] offers many reasons why this minor holiday is such a joyous day, and in exploring them there is found texture and variance for the ways that intimate love exists between human beings, and with the Divine.

Tu b'Av honors the day, in biblical times, that intermarriage between tribes was first permitted, leading, today, to a time ripe for honoring multi-faith families. It celebrates the autonomy of Mahlah, Noa, Hoglah, Milcah, and Tirzah, the daughters of Zelophehad, who were able to marry whomever they wished without fear of losing their inheritance,[24] and, therefore, encourages honoring bodily, sexual, and romantic autonomy. It celebrates the day on which the deaths of the last generation that fled Mitzrayim ceased, and God resumed communication with the people, illustrating that communication is as integral to intimacy as it is to survival and resilience.[25] On this day, a Jewish king removed the guards that kept people from ascending to the Temple whenever they wanted, encouraging a celebration of police abolition and removing guards and cops out of our sacred places. And on Tu b'Av, when harvesting trees for wood to burn on the altar ended and the hot days began to get shorter and cooler, it was "a day of celebration for the trees."[26] Today we are encouraged to celebrate living in mutual relationships, especially with the earth.

On Tu b'Av, women would borrow white clothing from one another, "in order not to shame anyone who had none,"[27] and go out and dance in the vineyards.[28] Anyone looking to find a partner would go to the vineyards on this day.

Celebration of Tu b'Av fell out of practice between the destruction of the Second Temple and the establishment of modern Israel, where it is marked both secularly and religiously today. There are many ways to reach for the jubilation of Tu b'Av, like organizing a speed dating event, drinking wine with beloveds, redistributing resources, or wearing white outfits and flower crowns all day! In 5783 Baltimore hosted the first ever Tuba Av celebration, with a tuba concert, speed dating, and a clothing swap!

Tu b'Av helps move one from grief to love, and creates a bridge into the month of Elul, when "the King is in the field." We can find ourselves in the field while still in Av, nursing our heartbreak while reaching for earthly and cosmic pleasure.

blow me open, Divine Transformer!
meet me in the field, Queen!
ready us for the work of repair, Holy Mender!
unravel us, Artisan of Being!
gentle me as I take a long hard look at myself, Rock of Refuge!
remind me I am love itself, Beloved!
let me dwell in your house, Becoming, all the days of my life.

oh my god, I hardly know how to pray but

if I am my Beloved's and my Beloved is mine
and there is no time but now
and God is Change
and wounds are portals
and just to live is a blessing
and the only way is through
        and together
and prayer is subversive
        then

            show me how to love this broken self
                this broken world

Illustration © Sol Weiss. Incantation © Dori Midnight.

WELCOME TO אלול ELUL

What has grown in the last year of your life? What have you cultivated in the past year? What has fallen away? What have you thrown away?

In the past year, when have you felt most alert, oriented, grounded, awake, powerful? What was happening in those times? What people, practices, stories, and understanding can you bring forward from those times?

What do you want to bring your energy to in the new year? What do you want to pay attention to every day?

Introduction to Elul

אֲנִי לְדוֹדִי וְדוֹדִי לִי

I am my beloved and my beloved is mine.

—Shir haShirim 6:3

In the heat and height of summer, Rosh Chodesh Elul often comes on surprisingly suddenly. Av has been a time of extreme experiences: grief, rage, sadness, desire, longing, and joy. With Rosh Chodesh Elul, the high highs and low lows of the summer land in the brass tacks of spiritually and interpersonally preparing for a new year. There is much to be done.

Though there are no holidays in Elul, it is the month with the most day-to-day spiritual and mystical potential, and the most month-specific practices, liturgy, and ritual invitations. Elul is a paradox; it is about looking back over the year that was, being fully present in every moment of each day, and being immersed in preparations for the future, for the coming new year. Elul is what we make of it. Our ancestors understood that

ELUL

in order to be renewed in a new year, we must prepare. They could not light holiday candles on the evening of the first of Tishrei and be reborn. Instead, they gave themselves—and us—a month of introspection, values alignment, relationship reckoning, and tools to support this work.

The classic Chassidic metaphor for the month of Elul is of a time when, as the story goes, "the king is in the field."[1] Eleven months of the year, we have to go toward Divinity, seeking out God in the places where God dwells. One month of the year, "the king" comes out "to the field" to literally meet people where they are. How can those of us who don't experience God as a King, and don't think of going to a palace when in prayer and ritual, understand this wisdom of our ancestors about the potency of Elul? Some of us might resonate with the dramatic flair, the pomp of picturing God as bejeweled and all powerful, visiting us in our daily grinds. Some of us might reinterpret Melech, usually translated as King, as Sovereign, and experiment with what it means for divine sovereignty to come to the fields of our lives. And if God as Melech, the King in the field, doesn't resonate, there are, as always, endless other Jewish offerings.

Because through the emotionally rigorous month of Elul, it is also a time of divine love, abounding forgiveness, and generosity for ourselves and others, where and whenever possible. The name of the month, אלול Elul, it is taught,[2] corresponds to verse 6:3 in Shir Ha'Shirim:

$$\text{אֲנִי לְדוֹדִי וְדוֹדִי לִי}$$

I am my beloved and my beloved is mine.

Elul is a time of experiencing God as Beloved and Lover. Centuries of Jewish tradition have built up infinite understandings of, metaphors for, and expressions of the Divine. It is notable that in the month when instructed to do the most self-reflection, to sit with harm we've committed and ways we've missed the mark, all of the significant God-talk is about love and care. And for those who don't experience God as King, Sovereign, or Beloved, it is still possible to distill and apply the wisdom that there can be no transformation, individual or communal, without love and care. It is necessary to envision the forces of love and care as present, active, and acting in the world and our lives.

In Elul, we who spend our days thinking about and working on transforming the world are invited to bring that attention inward. This is the month where we begin, again, to engage with the work of teshuvah: return for the sake of repair, personal transformation in the context of collective transformation. Our ancestors understood and created practices for how we survive and thrive as interdependent beings, interwoven in community, that many of us are, today, remembering and relearning.

Today, we explore Jewish practices of teshuvah in the context of the incredible flowering of transformative justice. Mia Mingus writes:

> Transformative Justice (TJ) is a political framework and approach for responding to violence, harm and abuse. At its most basic, it seeks to respond to violence without creating more violence and/or engaging in harm reduction to lessen the violence. TJ can be thought of as a way of "making things right," getting in "right relation," or creating justice together. Transformative justice responses and interventions 1) do not rely on the state (e.g. police, prisons, the criminal legal system, I.C.E., foster care system (though some TJ responses do rely on or incorporate social services like counseling); 2) do not reinforce or perpetuate violence such as oppressive norms or vigilantism; and most importantly, 3) actively cultivate the things we know prevent violence such as healing, accountability, resilience, and safety for all involved.[3]

Teshuvah is a Jewish practice with millennia of wisdom that we get to bring to transformative justice. Teshuvah requires an understanding of each person's imperfections, each person's capacity to commit harm *and* each person's holiness and reflection of the Divine, and each person's ability to choose accountability, make repair and reparations, and transform. Elul, in theology and practice, reminds us, daily, of our goodness and inherent lovability, at the same time it brings us face-to-face with all we want to change. Elul is a time to remind ourselves of and grow our visions for our lives, communities, and the world, and to do it all with love.

The parashiyot in Elul are Shoftim, Ki Teitzei, Ki Tavo, Nitzavim, and Vayelech. Just action, Temple worship, and promises of the covenant are themes of the Torah readings for this month, giving our Elul preparations rich soil in which to grow. There are many verses of empowerment in this

ELUL

month, including the oft quoted "justice, justice you shall pursue" (Devarim 16:20) and "It is not in the heavens, that you should say, 'Who among us can go up to the heavens and get it for us and impart it to us, that we may observe it? . . . No, the thing is very close to you, in your mouth and in your heart, to observe it" (Devarim 30:11–14). This month brings reminders of our personal and collective responsibility as we prepare for the new year.

Elul in Action

SHOFAR

In Elul, daily practices and liturgy change. The shofar is blown every day to prepare for the new year, to announce its arrival and its process of becoming. While daily shofar in Elul is a minhag (custom), not a mitzvah, as it is on Rosh Hashanah, it is a powerful practice. The blasts of the shofar open our hearts and act as an alarm clock to wake us up. For those used to only hearing it on Rosh Hashanah and Yom Kippur, daily shofar might, at first, seem to detract from the shock of the first blast. But a daily shofar sounding is a beautiful example that nothing is sudden. Making a full repair requires time to reflect, recommit, repair, and make a different choice the next time.[4] The process of teshuvah is not flipping a switch. Similarly, a new year in the Jewish imagination is not just the act of the sun setting, but the preparation and the anticipation for the coming month of Tishrei that pulls us through five holidays to the other side, in a new year. Hearing the shofar daily helps peel back layers that have built up over the past twelve months, and gently eases one into the month ahead.

Daily shofar, as well as other Elul practices, urge us to dedicate the necessary time to take stock of what has become rote and mechanical. The shofar is blown after morning davening in Ashkenazi communities, and after Selichot prayers in Sephardi communities, beginning on the second day of Elul.

We conjure the story of the Akedah, the binding of Isaac, when the ram's horn shofar is blown.[5] Isaac is bound on an altar atop a mountain, about to be killed by his father, Abraham, when a messenger of God intervenes. In lieu of sacrificing Isaac, Abraham sacrifices a ram caught in the nearby thicket. Perhaps the ram can be understood as a symbol of selfless sacrifice, if that is the invitation needed this Elul. Perhaps the ram is a symbol of the bystander, who watches as harm plays out before him. Though it was not a self-sacrifice, the ram may also be seen as an invitation to be an active participant in the new year and to stop harm when possible.

The shofar is most commonly made of a ram's horn (although the kudu's horns make beautiful shofarot; technically the horn from any kosher animal can be made into a shofar except a cow).[6] Vegan shofarot options include inheriting or being gifted a shofar, or sourcing a horn from a ram that has lost its horn, usually due to an injury. (Contact farms and ask, and plan for a long lead time.) Conch shells, spiritual and ritual musical objects in many cultures around the world, can also be blown and create a shofar sound.

The shofar has been used throughout Jewish history to announce the new moon from mountaintop to mountaintop, as a call to war, and in the Temple, and there was a loud shofar blast when the people received the Ten Commandments on Mount Sinai.

There are different customs about how many blasts are played in Elul daily, including:

Tkiyah
Shevarim
Teruah
Tkiyah g'dolah
Tkiyah Shevarim Teruah Tkiyah
Tkiyah Shevarim Tkiyah
Tkiyah Teruah Tkiyah g'dolah
T'kiyah g'dolah

Because hearing the shofar in Elul is minhag, not mitzvah, no blessing is said. Some may wish to say a Shehecheyanu blessing, though, the first time they hear it.

PSALM 27

Psalm 27 is added to the daily liturgy from Rosh Chodesh Elul through, depending on one's custom, Yom Kippur, Shemini Atzeret, or Hoshanah

ELUL

Rabbah. The first documentation of this liturgical addition is in eighteenth-century siddurim. Psalm 27 is full of imagery of divine protection, safety, and care. We ask "to dwell in the House of the Divine." What did our ancestors imagine when they chanted this line? What do we envision as a house of holiness and protection?

Chanting Psalm 27 during Elul is an invitation to ask for protection, care, and support, and to pray for spaces, physical or imagined, that strengthen and embolden us. If the text of Psalm 27 doesn't achieve this for you, are there other poems and songs that do?[7] What can be discovered by returning to the same chant every day for a season, a month, or even a week? Psalm 27 asks, "that I may dwell in the House of the Divine forever." In Elul, some people have the custom of getting the klaf (parchment) in mezzuzot checked to ensure that neither weather nor time have degraded the lettering.

SELICHOT PRAYERS

Selichot prayers are said both in the month of Elul and during the High Holy Day services. The Elul Selichot service happens in Sephardi communities daily, beginning on the second day of Elul, and in Ashkenazi communities on the Saturday night right before Rosh HaShanah. Literally meaning "penitence," the prayers associated with the Selichot service are an invitation into the deep work of teshuvah. The melodies associated with them are the first moments the congregation hears the nusach (נוסח), melodic mode of the Yamim Noraim, (יָמִים נוֹרָאִים) Days of Awe, as well as many of the High Holiday greatest hits: the Thirteen Attributes of God, Ki Anu Amecha, Vidui, and Avinu Malkeinu. We chant these prayers in Elul to musically, spiritually, jumpstart our new year kavvanah. In communities where musical instruments are not played on Shabbat or Yom Tov, Selichot services often involve musical instruments in particular because they are permitted to be used. Some Selichot services are contemplative and meditative, others musical and expressive, and others a combination of the two.

Selichot offers us a space for embodied practice. In this season, we don't only think and reflect about what we've done wrong. Selichot prayers are an invitation to experience in our bodies what teshuvah feels like. Many of us as leftists have refined our skills in analysis and critique. Selichot gives us a place to sing into what hurts—instead of just thinking about what we *should* say, we have the opportunity to strengthen the muscles of letting our hearts break open and being curious about how we feel. The songs and prayers of Selichot are one practice of breaking open, and can encourage us to find our own ways of feeling into the emotions of this time.

BLESSINGS AND FAREWELLS

At the end of the month, attention shifts most fully toward the New Year. People begin wishing one another a sweet year, and to be inscribed in the Book of Life for good. These words of blessing are incredibly tender when we pause and think about what they mean, casually at the end of emails wishing one another long lives, healthy years.

Some of the most common greetings[8]:

Shanah tovah u'metukah (שנה טובה ומתוקה): Hebrew, "a good
   and sweet year."
Gmar chatimah tovah (גְּמַר חֲתִימָה טוֹבָה): Hebrew, "a good final
   sealing" referring to the Book of Life.
A zees, gebentsht yor (אַ זיס, געבענטש יאָר): Yiddish, "A sweet,
   blessed year," used as farewell
Gut yontif (גוט-יום-טוב): Yiddish, "Happy holiday."
   Respond with a gut yontif, a gut yor, "happy holiday and a
   happy year."
A ksiveh vakhsimeh toyve (אַ כתיבה וחתימה טובה): Yiddish, Roughly,
   "May you be written and sealed into the Book of Life," used
   as farewell.
Tizku Leshanim Rabot (תזכו לשנים טובות): Hebrew, Sephardi cus-
   tom. "May you merit many years," used as greeting.
   Respond with Tizkeh vetihyeh ve-ta'arich yamim (תזכה ותחיה
   ותאריך ימים), "May you merit and live and increase your days."
Anyada Buena, Dulse i Alegre (אנייאדה בואינה, דולסי אי אליגרי):
   Ladino, "May you have a good, sweet, and happy New Year."
Moadim shalom: Jewish Persian, "Times of peace."
   Respond with sad sāl be sālhāye khoob, "100 years of good
   years."

Pitka tava (פתקא טבא): Aramaic; A gut kvitl (אַ גוט קוויטל) Yiddish: "a good note," used as farewell after Yom Kippur. Wishing at good judgment and a last ditch note in the Book of Life before the verdicts are delivered.

CHESHBON HA'NEFESH AND TESHUVAH: REPARATIONS AND ACCOUNTABILITY

Why is there all of this praying and singing and horn tooting? It all is for the sake of cheshbon ha'nefesh and teshuvah: the accounting of one's soul and making repair. This is the heart of Elul and the High Holiday season: to excavate our lives, to examine how we are treating each other, to reflect on how we are living our values, to try to know and understand the harm we have caused and experienced in the past year, and to make amends.

Cheshbon ha'nefesh (חֶשְׁבּוֹן הַנֶּפֶשׁ), soul searching, can happen through the traditional practices of Elul, through a musar practice of looking at particular aspects and values, through journaling, meditation, somatic practices, in therapy, and through discussion with friends. Anything you do to take a serious and heartfelt account of how you're doing is cheshbon ha'nefesh. The question then is what do we do with what we've found?

First and foremost, we are called to "make teshuvah." Teshuvah comes from the root of the word "to return." But to what do we return? We return to events of the past year and years, with the gift of time and perspective, to better understand what happened and why, our behaviors and roles in the event. We return, through the practice of making amends, to ourselves. One of rabbinic Judaism's core theological foundations is an understanding that people are made b'tzelem Elohim, in the image of the Divine. When we commit harm, we are moving away from our core selves. When we make teshuvah, we return to our essential goodness.

For those of us with inherited wealth, or experiences of privilege in white supremacy, patriarchy, and more, teshuvah offers a framework of reckoning with the harm we cause that honors our wholeness and holiness. We cause extreme harm for which we must be accountable. And, we are, in our core selves, good and holy. As we work to build models of accountability for harm outside of policing and incarceration, teshuvah offers a framework within which survivors' experiences and needs are centered and healing is possible for all. This is a framework within which we know that all people cause harm and all people experience harm, and that it is necessary to fundamentally restructure our communities to make more room for transforming harm.

How do we make teshuvah? One of the gifts of taking a whole season for teshuvah and not trying to fit it all into twenty-five hours on Yom Kippur is to give ourselves time to luxuriate in studying the centuries of wisdom the Jewish community has inherited. There are centuries of legal and spiritual wisdom from our ancestors on the nature of teshuvah and how to *do* it. In Elul, we can examine Rambam's Hilchot Teshuvah, Rabbeinu Yonah of Gerona's Shaarei Teshuvah, and Rabbi Ira Stone's Mesillat Yesharim. We are also blessed to live and organize in a time of incredible outpouring of Torah on transformative justice. Elul is an incredible time to dive into *Beyond Survival: Strategies and Stories from the Transformative Justice Movement*, edited by Leah Lakshmi Piepzna-Samarasinha and Ejeris Dixon, the *Creative Interventions Toolkit: A Practical Guide to Stop Interpersonal Harm*, by Mimi Kim; and *Fumbling Towards Repair: A Workbook for Community Accountability Facilitators*, by Mariame Kaba and Shira Hassan. There are so many tools for personal reflection during Elul. Check out Return: 30 Days of Reflection by Rabbi Jill Zimmerman, and https://doyou10q.com/, which asks ten questions and locks them for a year!

In Hilchot Teshuvah 2:9, Rambam teaches that there are different processes for rectifying harm bein adam l'Makom (between a person and the Divine) and bein adam l'chavero (between a person and another person. Literally: his other, his friend). Bein adam l'Makom refers to mitzvot that we have transgressed in a way that does not impact other people. In these instances, it is possible to make repair privately, through prayer and reflection, through our "direct line" to the Divine. But in order to make teshuvah for harm that we have committed that impacts other people, we must go to the person, apologize, and do our best to receive their forgiveness. We must take accountability and make literal repair for the harm we have caused. That can include paying damages and fixing what is broken. Teshuvah is not complete until there is an opportunity to commit the same action again, until we are in the exact same situation and faced with the same choice, and choose to do something different.

As Jews living in a settler-colonial state, where all wealth has been built through stolen Indigenous land, and the stolen labor and extreme violence of chattel slavery, teshuvah includes the lifelong process of land back and reparations. Elul is a time to renew commitments to individual and collective reparations. This is a time to learn about and deepen our relationships with campaigns for city and national reparations and to learn about, uncover, and take action to make repair for the legacies of our personal, familial, and communal harm. We do this through moving money and organizing for systemic change in our communities. We do this knowing we are in a long lineage and wide community of people for whom material accountability for harm is essential spiritual work.

We will spend our whole lives learning and practicing how to be in better relationships with ourselves and each other and the world. Jewish tradition offers us seasons and wisdom and practices, and community in which to do this work.

COLLECTIVE TESHUVAH

Alongside personal reflection and teshuvah processes, Elul can be a time for collective reflection and teshuvah. This can take place in organizations, congregations, institutions, movements, classrooms, and collective houses: anywhere we gather, collaborate, and are trying to learn ways of living together that are generative, collaborative, loving, and supportive. Living in capitalism and white supremacist systems and culture, we are rarely taught how to cooperate and tend to the health and wellness of a group. In many movement spaces that are under-resourced and where people are often exhausted, we can carry personal and organizational beef for years. People are hurting themselves and each other, slowing down and hindering our revolutionary work. Without tools for dealing with conflict or containers for what happens when things explode, groups and organizations can collapse. We are blessed to be in a moment where many people are naming this struggle and offering theory and practice for creating healthy collectives.[9] Elul is a time that the Jewish calendar offers much-needed collective care to our groups.

Think about local collectives and organizations you're a part of: Are there already processes in place for collective reflection? If not, is there someone in the group to partner with to create space for reflection? Is there time in regularly scheduled meetings that can be designated for reflection and real talk?

If the group has never done collective reflection before, it might take time to create the structures and build the muscles of group evaluation and reflection. Collective teshuvah can be as contained as setting aside time in a monthly meeting for a brief reflection on relationships and the year, or as expansive as a full organizational evaluation process. There is no one-size-fits-all process for organizational teshuvah, but, as always, we can apply the wisdom of our ancestors to our groups and see what emerges that serves the work for transformation and justice.

One way to begin is with an organizational cheshbon ha'nefesh. Tradition teaches us to look at the differences between harm committed bein adam l'Makom (between people and God), and bein adam l'chavero (between two people). Applying this to collectives, we can look at the conflict and dynamics in our relationships:

* Among and within a group working together on shared goals.
* Between individuals across different organizations.
* Between two allied organizations working together in coalition.
* Among multiple organizations working in coalition.
* Between organizations working on different strategies on the same issues.

In these relationships, some questions to begin reflecting on are:

* What's happened in the past year? What has been won? What has been lost?
* When have we disagreed? When have we struggled and why?
* When have we worked together well? What have I learned or gained from you?
* What power dynamics are influencing our relationship and ability to work together? Are the people with more power in our relationship aware of and in any way accounting for that power differential?
* Looking at our visions and goals, where are they aligned, and where are they different? Have they changed over the year?

ELUL

Once you've taken time to reflect on your own, create a spacious time to share, listen, and be heard. Know that these conversations will very likely bring up hurt feelings; that doesn't mean you're doing it wrong. Ask people from different organizations to facilitate and hold space, setting aside sufficient and spacious time for these conversations, and for the personal preparation and after-care that will be required. Long term, our movements are only as effective as the health and strength of our relationships.

The teshuvah between people in the same organization, coworkers and colleagues and comrades, which might seem like individual and personal teshuvah, can often be deeply influenced by the collectives we organize in, and can have implications for the rest of the community.

We take inspiration from the many stories of intercommunity movement beef between our ancestors. Rabbi Yonah ben Avraham Gerondi (died 1264) was one of the leaders of the opponents of Maimonides, and the instigator of the public burning of Rambam's *Guide for the Perplexed*. Yonah of Gerona involved Christian authorities in his anti-Maimonidean organizing, which eventually led to the public burning of wagonloads of copies of the Talmud. He then recanted his critiques and dedicated his life to publicly making teshuvah. For Yonah, this included teaching in Rambam's honor and always quoting him, as well as writing three works on teshuvah: Iggeret ha-Teshuvah (Letter on Repentance), Sha'arei Teshuvah (Gates of Repentance), and Sefer ha-Yir'ah. Teshuvah has the power not only to transform individuals but to transform communities and the world. Rabbeinu Yonah didn't only stop the harm but worked to rectify and change his actions. What from our communal and collective teshuvah shows the ways to places of growth, different actions, and transformation of harm to materially different ways of being in the world?

While often translated as repair, teshuvah literally means return. Jewish time, as we frequently rediscover, is a spiral. In Elul, we end the year with the beginning. We return, again and again, to ourselves, and to each other.

PART 3

TORAH

TORAH PORTIONS

The Torah portions are read in the same season each year, though there is some variance each year on which month some parashiyot fall within. The Jewish calendar is on a nineteen-year cycle, with a leap month added seven times in that cycle (on the years 3, 6, 8, 11, 14, 17, and 19.) This intervention ensures that the holidays happen in the appropriate seasons—Sukkot following the harvest, Pesach at the time of planting and new blooms. Major holidays have their own Torah readings, which pause the Torah reading cycle and insert the special selection for the holiday. Depending on what day of the week on which a holiday falls, a week's parshah may be shifted to the next week. There are fifty-four Torah portions. In non–leap years, some of the Torah portions are read as double portions, up to fourteen parashiyot that get combined.

To honor the variance from year to year, as well as the spirit of the month and the role Torah plays in it, we have based the parshah summaries off the first year of the nineteen-year cycle as a model year, in the style of Scott-Martin Kosofksy's *The Book of Customs*, published in 2004 and based on the Yiddish *Minhogimbukh* from Venice 1593. Please consult a radical Jewish calendar to confirm what the Torah portions are for any particular year.

Tishrei

The parashiyot in Tishrei are Ha'azinu, V'zot haBracha, and Beresheet. We finish reading Devarim, then we begin again with Beresheet! This month calls us to notice endings and beginnings. We read Torah without end— each year V'zot haBracha blends into Beresheet, the ending of the Torah and beginning blending together. Moses' death, on the cusp of making it into the land but not being allowed to enter, gives us space in this season to name disappointment, loss, betrayal. Beresheet gives us opportunity to begin again, call in hope, or even start a new practice of study. Destruction and creation are inherently interconnected.

Ha'azinu הַאֲזִינוּ (Devarim 32:1–52): Moshe delivers his closing words poem. In the scroll, the text is written in two columns, and it contains mostly rebukes and threats for turning away from God, exhortations of God's power, and a description of what returning to the Divine will be like. God then tells Moshe to ascend Mt. N'vo. From there, he will be able to see the land but will not enter it, and will then die on the mountain.

While all of Torah is, in a sense, poetic, at certain key moments the authors of Torah give us a poem as a sign that something transformative and very impactful is happening. This teaches us that our ancestors knew that something can happen in poetry that cannot happen in prose. Reading Moses' poem of Ha'azinu can be an opportunity to revisit Miriam's song in Shemot 13, to look forward to the Song of Devorah in the book of Judges, and to turn to the poetry of our leftist teachers at key moments in their lives. It can be an opportunity to write and share our own stories as poems. What must be said singing that cannot be said any other way?

V'zot haBracha וְזֹאת הַבְּרָכָה (Devarim 33:1–34:12): The final parshah of the Torah, this is often read during the weekday Torah reading but not on Shabbat due to the date of Simchat Torah. This parshah concludes the cycle of reading, culminating in Moshe's death. Moshe, "the man of God," says goodbye to the people, offering a blessing to each of the tribes. God tells Moses that "this is the land I swore to your ancestors . . . I let you see it with your own eyes, but you shall not cross there." Moshe dies at the age of 120 and is buried (by whom, the Sages debate for centuries!). The Israelites mourn for thirty days, and Joshua takes up the mantle of leadership.

With its title words, Torah ends with a blessing, This is the blessing. We learn that our lives are just one in an unending chain: even Moses, the prophet most intimate with God, does not make it into the promised land. The work of our lives, of building a new world, will inevitably always be incomplete, and we begin again, and again, in every generation. We see that Torah ends in the Wilderness: a diaspora story through and through. Joshua will pick up with the people entering and conquering, and Nevi'im (prophets) and Ketuvim (writings) are, indeed, essential, canonical texts of

Jewish tradition. And yet, it is notable that the story arc that our ancestors chose to make central in our ritual lives, the Torah cycle, ends balanced on the precipice, giving us the choice: What's next? Where do we want to go, and how?

Beresheet בְּרֵאשִׁית (Beresheet 1:1–6:8): We begin at the very beginning. Beresheet 1–2 tells the story of each day of creation, separated into categories, with humans being created on the sixth and final day. The last day is followed by Shabbat, when God rested from this work. Then follows the second telling of the creation myth, in which the world has already been created, and the focus is on the creation of the first two humans. The humans eat from the Tree of Knowledge and are expelled from the Garden. Cain and Abel, the first brothers, are born and Cain kills Abel in a fit of jealousy and anger. Divine beings have children with human women, but God stops them saying, "No, wait, humans have to be mortal." God becomes filled with regret about the creation of the world, and pledges to blot out all living things . . . but Noach finds favor in the eyes of God. He and his family, and the pairs of animals he saved in the ark, live to repopulate the world.

Reading this origin story, we wrestle with the ways it has been used to justify the subjugation of women and femmes, and a theology of human superiority over and domination of all other life on earth. Upon close read, we see that the first human was created "male and female," long understood in traditional rabbinic commentary to mean that the first person was both male and female in one body, then split.[1] From centuries of midrashic wrestling, we receive the story of Lilith, Adam's rebellious first partner.[2]

Cheshvan

The parashiyot of Cheshvan are Noach, Lech Lecha, Vayera, Chayyei Sarah, and Toldot. Cheshvan comes like a release in so many ways, with space to process all that Tishrei brought. The narratives at the beginning of Beresheet that we read this month are easier to follow, but bring deep ethical challenges: the destruction of the world and its recreation with Noah's ark, the dissolution of connection at the Tower of Babel, the creation of the Jewish people with Abraham and Sarah and the violence against Hagar and Ishmael, the covenant and the near-sacrifice of Isaac, visiting angels and Sodom and Ammorah. Newly reinvigorated to reflect on our behaviors and relationships, we dig in to the parashiyot of Cheshvan to consider just action and right relationship in practice.

Noach נח (Beresheet 6:9–11:32): God announces a plan to end life on earth to Noach, and gives instructions for building a boat and saving the world's animals. The classical midrash tells of Noah's wife, Naamah, who is described by Rabbi Sandy Eisenberg Sasso as the original seed keeper.[3] Noach does as he's told, and in the six hundredth year of his life, the rains begin, falling for forty days and nights. After the waters recede, Noach sends a raven, then a dove, to find signs of dry earth. When the land is dry, Noach and his family are told to come out of the ark. He makes a burnt offering and God promises never to destroy humankind again. God then blesses Noach and his sons, and hands over stewardship of the animals to them. God once again promises not to destroy humans, this time sealing the deal with a rainbow.

Sometime later, Noach plants a vineyard and, while drunk, gets naked. One of his sons, Ham, sees his father's nakedness and tells his brothers. The brothers, Shem and Japheth, cover Noach without looking at him, thus preserving his dignity. When Noach recovers and hears what happened, he curses Ham and his descendants, those of Canaan. Noach lives another 350 years and dies at age 950. The story then continues, telling about the descendants of Shem, Ham, and Japeth. Over centuries a story developed that Ham was Black, and the "Curse of Ham" was used by white slave owners as a justification for slavery.[4] There is nothing about race or skin color mentioned in the Torah text, and reading Noach is an opportunity to expose and counter the centuries of racist violence justified through a projection onto this text.

The parshah closes with the story of the Tower of Babel. All people on earth at that time spoke the same language. They learn to make bricks and build a city with a tower reaching to the heavens. God sees this and causes the people to speak different languages, causing everyone to spread out across the earth. The parshah ends with another section of lineages, closing with the family of Terah, including his son Abram, who takes a wife named Sarai.

The stories in Noach, the first family drama in Torah, spark questions about family and harm, community and interdependence. How do we want to live with each other? For many of us, divine interventionism with direct reward and punishment is not among our theologies. And, yet, this story of the earthly impacts of human behavior is incredibly relevant in our time of human-caused climate chaos. What can we learn from our ancestors' experience and retelling of their vulnerability on the changing earth? How do we want to treat each other and care for each other as the waters rise?

Lech Lecha לֶךְ-לְךָ (Beresheet 12:1–17:27): In Beresheet, everything is very rapidly unfolding. Week three, and God makes a covenant with Abram, saying, "Lech lecha," "go forth" (or "go into yourself"), and "I will make of you a great nation, and I will bless you." Abram, Sarai, and his nephew, Lot, move from Haran to Canaan, and God promises the land to Abram and his descendants, despite the fact that Canaanites are already living in the land. When there is a famine, Abram and Sarai go to Egypt to buy food, and Abram tells Sarai to pose as his sister so the governing forces will not kill him in order to capture her. Indeed, the Pharoah does capture (and, we are led to imagine, assault) Sarai. Because of this, "Abram acquired sheep, oxen, asses, male and female slaves, she-asses, and camels." (12:17). As punishment for Sarai's capture, God sends plagues on Pharoah's house. Pharoah confronts Abram, and Abram is sent away with Sarai but allowed to keep all the wealth they have acquired. They return to reside in Canaan, where Lot then leaves them to go to Sodom.

During a protracted battle of the local kings, Lot is captured, and Abram gathers his troops to free him. Abram refuses any reward for also liberating other prisoners and their possessions, saying, "I will not take so much as a thread or a sandal strap of what is yours; you shall not say 'It is I who made Abram rich.'" (14:23)

In a prophetic dream, Abram says his servant Eliezer will be the one to inherit his household, since he has no child. But God promises that he will have a child of his own, saying, "Look toward heaven and count the stars, if you are able to count them. So shall your offspring be." (15:5). Abram makes a covenant with God, a sign of his faith that he will possess the land. God then tells him that there will come a time when Abram's descendants will be strangers in a strange land, that they will be enslaved, but eventually will be free.

Sarai cannot have a child, and tells Abram to have a child with their slave Hagar. Jealous, Sarai then punishes Hagar for getting pregnant, and Hagar runs away. However, an angel appears telling her to return, with the words, "I will greatly increase your offspring, and they shall be too many to count" (16:10). Hagar calls God "El Roi," becoming the first person in the Torah to name God. She returns and gives birth to a son, Ishamel, when Abram is eighty-six years old.

Thirteen years later, God renews the covenant with Abram, giving him and Sarai new names, Abraham and Sarah. God commands Abraham to circumcise himself and every male in his household as a sign of the covenant and tells them that he and Sarah will have a son, Isaac. Abraham obeys God, circumcising himself, his son Ishmael, and all of the enslaved people in his household.

Lech Lecha offers us a chance to reflect on callings and journeys, on destiny and holy work. The spiritual wisdom is, as always in Torah, side by side and interwoven with interpersonal harm: Sarai's violence against Hagar, and systemic violence:-, with God promising already populated land to Abram to conquer. In our time of the ongoing occupation of Palestine, while ancient texts like Lech Lecha are misused as contemporary land deeds and permission to expel Palestinian people from home and land, this parshah can be a jumping-off point to explore what we are spiritually called to do in this lifetime. Given the experiences not only of Abraham and Sarah but also of Hagar, Ishmael, and the Canaanites, what is the holy work that we are called forth to do?

Vayera וַיֵּרָא (Beresheet 18:1–22:24): God appears to Abraham, along with three men, and Abraham offers them food and water. One of them declares that Sarah will have a child within the next year. Sarah, who has stopped menstruating, laughs at this. God asks why Sarah would doubt God's power, and Sarah lies in fear.

God declares that the cities of Sodom and Gomorrah will be destroyed, and Abraham negotiates with God to save the cities on behalf of the righteous who live there. God promises to save the cities if even ten righteous people are found. Two angels arrive in Sodom, and Lot welcomes them to stay with him for their safety. People of the town come to threaten the men, and Lot offers his daughters instead. The angels protect Lot and his family, sending them away in the morning. As they flee, Lot's wife looks back and is turned into a pillar of salt.

Abraham continues on his journey, and Sarah gets pregnant and gives birth to Isaac. Sometime later, Sarah sees Ishmael, the son of Hagar, play-ing with Isaac and demands that Abraham send them away so that Isaac and Ishmael won't have to share an inheritance. Abraham sends Hagar into the desert, but God hears Ishamael's cries and sends an angel to help them, promising to make a great nation of Ishmael.

In the final dramatic scene of this packed parshah, God commands Abraham to take Isaac to the land of Moriah and sacrifice him as a burnt offering. Abraham begins to fulfill this command, but at the last minute God makes a ram appear and Isaac is saved. Because of this show of loyalty, God promises Abraham that he and his descendants will be blessed. This story, known as the Akedah, is traditionally read on Rosh Hashanah, and raises questions about literal and metaphorical sacrifice, what God and the world ask of us.

This parshah contains layered and devastating acts of violence, whose impacts ripple through generations of Jewish lives, and in our time. Throughout this parshah, God is incredibly active in individual lives, punishing and saving, testing and promising. In reading this parshah, we confront the homophobic legacy of the Sodom and Gomorroah story. Homophobic interpretation claims the reason Sodom and Gomorrah were destroyed was because of homosexuality, but an actual reading of the text understands violence and inhospitality to strangers and the vulnerable to be the transgression. This parshah also contains the story of Ishmael and Isaac, Abraham's sons, who go on to be patriarchs of Islam and Judaism. The conflict of their birthright is used to justify conflict between Jews and Muslims, a family rift that continues on in violent occupation and bloodshed between Jews and Muslims today. We reject this kind of biblical determinism, as our Judaism sees no theological inevitability of conflict between any communities. There are a myriad of other ways to approach Vayera, for the stories it has to offer us about families in struggle across millennia, and the legacies of harm that are ours to heal.

Chayei Sarah חַיֵּי שָׂרָה (Beresheet 23:1–25:18): Sarah dies at the age of 127, and Abraham seeks a burial place for her in Hebron. He negotiates with Ephron, the Hittite, for use of a burial cave, and Ephron tries to give it to him for free. Abraham insists on buying the field and the cave, and buries Sarah. Abraham sends a servant to find a wife for Isaac. The servant encounters Rebekah at a well, and she proves her generosity by offering water to the servant's camels. Rebekah agrees to go with the servant to meet Isaac. Finally, Abraham takes another wife, Keturah, and we read of another line of Abraham's descendants.

This parshah has taken on extremely painful significance, as it is now used as justification for Israeli occupation and extreme military control of current Hebron. From 2011 to 2019, Project Hayei-Sara has gathered and shared divrei Torah and created text study and learning spaces on Hebron, working to "reclaim parshat Hayei-Sara" from the violence that settlers in Hebron perpetrate in the name of this parshah. When we read this parshah, we will continue to find ways, ritually and in our organizing, to unsettle this text and demand an end to the occupation of Hebron and Palestine.

Toldot תּוֹלְדֹת (Beresheet 25:19–28:9): We pick up with the life of Isaac, one of Abraham's sons. He and his wife, Rebecca, struggle to conceive, and she eventually becomes pregnant with twins. The Torah documents a painful pregnancy, with Rebecca saying, "if so, why do I exist?" God responds that two nations are in her womb, one mightier than the other, and the older son shall serve the younger. Esau, the elder by mere minutes, grows into an outdoorsy hunter favored by their father Isaac, while Jacob "dwells in tents," and is favored by their mother Rebecca.

The rift continues when Esau returns from hunting, starving. Jacob convinces Esau to sell his birthright to him in return for a bowl of red lentil soup. There is yet another famine, eerily similar to the previous one, and Isaac both builds his wealth and makes a pact with the king of the Philistines, also named Abimelech. Toward the end of his life, Isaac tells Esau to prepare a meal for him, after which he will give Esau his blessing (which is separate from the birthright and more intimate in nature). Rebecca overhears this and has Jacob dress like Esau, putting pelts on his arms to be hairy, cook his favorite meal, and take advantage of Isaac's blindness to trick his father into thinking he is Esau. The trick works, and only after Jacob receives the blessing meant for his brother does Esau find out. Esau vows to kill Jacob after their father dies. Hearing this, Rebecca sends Jacob to the family in Paddan Aram to marry and escape Esau's wrath. Esau realizes he can never make his parents happy with the Canaanite women he has married, and goes to his Uncle Ishmael, forming a chosen family of rejected brothers.

While Jacob is understood as one of the patriarchs of the Israelites, Esau, his literal twin, we're told is the patriarch of the Edomites, a rival biblical tribe. Traditional rabbinic commentary generally explains away and justifies Jacob's and Rebecca's actions. We can write new commentaries and new midrash that work to repair the interfamily harm within our ancestral narratives, and derive new meanings and different lessons.

Kislev

The parashiyot of Kislev are Vayetzei, Vayishlach, Vayeshev, and Miketz. We follow the continued growth of the Jewish family, the second generation of covenanted relationship with HaShem. This month we see family dysfunction continue, yearning for connection in so many forms—parental approval, romantic partnership, peace between siblings, conception, affirmation from family, healing in family after violence. Amidst all this tumult is the presence of dreaming, the force that connects humans to the Divine and gives them insights to navigate earthly relationships. As winter looms larger in the Northern Hemisphere, Kislev invites us to reach toward the gifts of dreaming—to have imagination and inspiration to break out of hopelessness, cycles of cruelty, and generational harm.

Vayetzei וַיֵּצֵא (Beresheet 28:10–32:3): Jacob sets out as instructed, but suddenly night falls and he must settle down for the evening. He takes a stone to use as a pillow, falls asleep, and dreams. He sees a ladder reaching from the earth to the sky, with angels ascending and descending. God speaks to Jacob in the dream, saying, "the ground on which you are lying I will assign to you and your offspring" (28:13), and God renews the covenant with Jacob. Upon waking, Jacob says, "God is in this place and I did not know it." ("מַה־נּוֹרָא הַמָּקוֹם הַזֶּה" "mah norah hamakom hazeh, how awesome is this place.") He builds a monument there from the stone he used as a pillow and names it Bethel, though it had already been named Luz. He then makes a traveler's prayer vow to God that if he is protected on the journey and arrives safely he will accept God and donate a tenth of his possessions to God. Finally, Jacob continues on his way.

When Jacob arrives at Haran, he sees Rachel for the first time. Overcome with desire, he single-handedly pushes the rock off the well. They kiss, and Jacob weeps. Jacob asks to marry Rachel and agrees to work for seven years for the right to marry her. On the wedding night, Laban tricks Jacob into marrying Rachel's older sister Leah, and also transfers the enslaved Zilpah to Leah. Jacob then agrees to work for another seven years in order to actually marry Rachel, and acquire the enslaved Bilhah. This is a painful story in which women are considered property, and we also see the literary parallel of Jacob, who tricked his father into giving him his brother's birthright, getting himself tricked.

Rachel cannot conceive, but Leah is incredibly fertile. Thus begins a breeding war, with Leah giving birth multiple times, Bilhah bearing children on behalf of Rachel, and Zilpah bearing children on behalf of Leah. Rachel begs Leah to give her mandrakes to help her conceive, and offers a night with Jacob in return, after which Leah has another son. Leah also gives birth to Dinah, the one named daughter in the family. Rachel finally conceives, and gives birth to Joseph.

Jacob holds a family meeting with Rachel and Leah, and they decide to leave for Canaan. Jacob takes only the huge herd of speckled sheep, Rachel steals Laban's household idols, and they flee in the middle of the night. God comes to Laban in a dream, and warns him against trying Jacob. Laban then confronts Jacob in the desert of Gilead in the middle of the night, but after conflict they make a pact. Jacob continues on, having ended it poorly with another family member. On the way, he meets an angel of God. This parshah contains mystical angels and inspiring dreams, and also the messy struggles of women competing in a misogynist family system and community. Many of us include Bilhah and Zilpah when we say the opening blessing of the ancestors of the Amidah, to honor their legacies as our foremothers and to rewrite our understanding of labor and ancestry.

Vayishlach וַיִּשְׁלַח (Beresheet 32:4–36:43): Vayishlach is a difficult parshah that contains sexual violence, revenge, and mass killings. Among many other parashiyot, this week might bring up questions about why, and how, to read such troubling texts. We will have different answers from each other. From year to year, we will change our own answers. Sometimes the answer to the question "how do I read this text?" will be, right now, I can't. We are blessed, when we choose to read them, to never have to do it alone, but to have community in our time and across time to read next to.[5]

We begin with the continuation of Jacob's journey, as he sends word that he is coming to Esau. The messengers return, telling Jacob that Esau is coming to meet him with four hundred men. Jacob panics, sure Esau is going to exact revenge for his trickery, and divides his camp into two, such that if one is attacked, the other half might survive. He also sends a huge gift of livestock to buy Esau's favor.

Jacob sends his family across the Yabbok River and spends the night alone until a man appears and "wrestled with him until the break of dawn" (34:25). A messenger of God? A midnight hookup? Jacob's leg is wrenched from the socket, but he receives a new name from the angel, "Yisrael," meaning "God-wrestler" because, as the angel told him, "You have wrestled with beings divine and human and have prevailed."

The next day, Jacob and Esau meet and Esau falls on Jacob's neck, kisses him, and they weep. Here the word וַיִּשָּׁקֵהוּ is written with dots above the letters, a scribal oddity. Some classical commentary claims that it means the kisses were actually bites. Or perhaps, it represents the fractured nature of making peace with someone who caused him harm. Despite Jacob's fears, Esau is only happy to see him, and desires no revenge. They introduce their families to each other, and Esau offers to travel with Jacob for a while, but Jacob resists and they part ways.

Jacob arrives at the Canaanite town of Shechem, home of a man named Shechem, the son of the town's chief, Hamor. Dinah goes out to visit with the young women of the town, but is captured and assaulted by Shechem. He then decides he wants to marry her, but Jacob's sons say that they cannot give their sister to an uncircumcised man. Moreover, they insist that every man in the city must be circumcised. Shechem accepts and convinces all of the other men to agree. While the men are recovering from the surgery, two of Jacob's sons, Simeon and Levi, massacre all of them and take Dinah home. The other brothers then raid and plunder the town.

Jacob and God talk again, and Jacob brings everyone to Bethel. The Torah takes a verse to name Deborah, Rebecca's nurse, who died and was buried under an oak tree. Rachel dies while giving birth to Benjamin, and is buried on the side of the road. She is the only one of the Matriarchs or Patriarchs not buried in the Cave of Machpelah. Reuben, Jacob's firstborn son with Leah, has sex with Bilhah. Jacob finally arrives at Kiryat Arba (Hebron), and Isaac dies. Esau and Jacob come together again to bury him.

Parshat Vayishlach can provoke conversations about how our ancestors understood consent, the relationship between conflict, harm, and accountability, and transformation. We can read the parshah through asking questions about what we imagine each person involved was experiencing, making new and necessary midrash that value listening to survivors of harm and centering healing and transformation. With careful facilitation, this parshah can be a jumping off point to asking how we respond to harm in our communities, and what systems we need to build to create communities of care and transformation in relationships.

Vayeshev וַיֵּשֶׁב (Beresheet 37:1–40:23): The narrative now focuses on Joseph, second youngest son of Jacob, firstborn of his favorite wife, the late Rachel. Jacob gives Joseph a כְּתֹנֶת פַּסִּים, ktonet pasim, which, perhaps, is a beautiful dress. The only other time this word is used is in II Samuel referring to a princess's garments. Joseph's brothers are extremely jealous, and the situation only worsens when Joseph tells them of his dreams of celestial bodies and sheaves of wheat bowing down to him. The tension boils over one day when Joseph is sent by Jacob to check on his brothers, who are out in the fields, and they throw Joseph into a pit. The eldest, Reuben, tries to prevent them from killing him, and then leaves for a short time. While he is gone, the rest of the brothers sell Joseph into slavery to a passing group of Midianites. Upon returning home, the brothers present Jacob with Joseph's bloody coat, and he begins a life of mourning his beloved son. Joseph is taken to Egypt, where he ends up in the palace of Potifar, a high official in Pharaoh's court.

At this point, there is a story about Tamar, daughter-in-law of Jacob's fourth son, Judah. Tamar is widowed when God causes her husband, Judah's firstborn, Er, to die. Judah's second son, Onan, is duty-bound to enter into a levirate marriage with Tamar, so that their potential child would be considered his elder brother Er's. He refuses to impregnate her and spills his seed on the ground, for which he is killed by God. This is the origin of the term "onanism," and the biblical source cited by the rabbis for the prohibition against masturbation. Blaming Tamar, rather than God, for his sons' deaths, Judah refuses to allow his third son to marry her.

Judah's wife dies and, sometime later, he goes to Timnah for the sheepshearing. Hearing that her father-in-law is going there, Tamar dresses up like a sex worker and waits at the gate of the town. Not recognizing his daughter-in-law, Judah propositions her and gives her his seal, cord, and staff as collateral. Only months later when she is pregnant and Judah threatens to kill her, does she reveal to him that it is he who is the owner of those items and the one who got her pregnant. Tamar gives birth to twins, and the midwife is careful to monitor which child is born first, having learned from the family drama of twins and birthright in Jacob and Esau.

Meanwhile, back in Potifar's palace, Joseph has become a favored servant of Potifar's, but is assaulted by Potifar's wife. Joseph is sent to a prison for political prisoners, where he is given power over the other prisoners, again favored as a power broker by those above him. In prison, he meets the chief cupbearer and chief baker. He interprets their dreams, saying that the baker will be sentenced to death and the cupbearer will be restored to his position, and asks the cupbearer to remember him. Joseph's predictions come to pass, but the cupbearer forgets about Joseph once he is restored.

Joseph's life offers so much for us to unpack. In our time, trans Torah scholars have come to recognize and celebrate Joseph as a vibrant trancestor. Vayeshev can be a jumping-off parshah to explore the complex gender experiences within Torah, brilliantly compiled by scholar and organizer Binya Kóatz in "Toldot Trans: Tracing a Trans Lineage through the Torah."[6] How do Joseph's gender expressions and Joseph's interactions in family and community resonate with our lived experiences? What does it do for our reading and relationship with Joseph to name Joseph as part of trans lineage? Joseph's experience in prison brings our collective attention to incarceration in our time, and compels us to lift up Torah from incarcerated Jews and listen to the voices of all incarcerated people. How does prison function in this text, how does it relate to and differ from prisons as they function today? What are our responsibilities, as the spiritual descendants of an ancestor for whom the experience of incarceration had an impact?

Miketz מִקֵּץ (Beresheet 41:1—44:17): The Joseph cycle continues. Two years pass, and Pharaoh is tortured by dreams that none of his advisors can interpret. He dreams of seven healthy cows, at the edge of the Nile, swallowed by gaunt cows, and of seven ears of grain on a single stalk swallowed up by seven thin ears of grain. Finally the cupbearer remembers Joseph and tells Pharaoh about him. Joseph is brought to the palace and interprets the dreams in a way that makes sense to Pharaoh, suggesting a plan to save grain in the abundant years ahead of the lean ones. Pharaoh puts Joseph in power as second-in-command, in charge of the grain-saving efforts.

Joseph, now thirty-five, is recast as an Egyptian with clothing, a new name, and an Egyptian wife. The plan to save grain during the seven rich years works. His wife, Asenat, gives birth to Menashe and Efraim. The seven years of famine begin, and many people, including Joseph's brothers, go to Egypt to find food. Jacob keeps Benjamin at home, to protect him from the danger the rest of his sons may encounter.

The brothers come before Joseph, and do not recognize him, although he recognizes them. He accuses them of being spies, imprisons them for three days, and demands they bring Benjamin to Egypt to prove they are not lying. The brothers journey back to Egypt to try to convince Jacob to let them bring Benjamin with them. He resists until the famine becomes unbearable. The brothers are afraid of Joseph, especially when he greets them with hospitality and generosity. Joseph asks about their father, and, when he meets Benjamin, he breaks down. When it is time to leave, Joseph has a silver goblet put in Benjamin's bag. On the way home, one of Joseph's servants catches up to them and accuses them of theft, saying that only the one who has the cup shall stay and be Joseph's slave. They tear their clothing and return to the city to grovel at Joseph's feet. The parshah shows us one family narrative of revenge and repair. Joseph's assimilation to Egyptian elite society gifts us yet another interfaith marriage in our ancestral lineage.

Parshat Miketz calls us to plan for the future, and asks how we plan to share our resources. Joseph colludes with power and takes part in creating an economic system of centralized control that leads to the people's enslavement. We can use this parshah as a time to study socialist, communist, and other anti-capitalist economic texts, such as on just transition and solidarity economics.[7] How would we have advised Pharoah? How are we working toward a world where all have enough?

Tevet

The parashiyot of Tevet are Vayigash, Vayechi, Shemot, and Vaera, which complete the story cycle of Joseph and his brothers and bring the people from Canaan into Mitzrayim. We begin the book of Shemot this month, the enslavement of the Jewish people, and the beginning of the Exodus story, starting with some of the plagues. In one month of parashiyot our ancestors become climate refugees, then are enslaved, and then are redeemed from slavery. How powerful that this descent and ascent happens in only one month, that the most embittered moments of the Torah are contained and do not bleed over into another month. Another prophetic text written to help humans survive environmental disaster and human cruelty is the medicine written by Octavia Butler in Lauren Olamina's The Book of the Living. She reminds us that "the only lasting truth is Change. God Is Change."[8] Tevet contains within it descent and ascent to remind us of this fact.

Vayigash וַיִּגַּשׁ (Beresheet 44:18–47:27): Joseph, whose brothers still do not recognize him, demands that Benjamin, the youngest brother, be brought to Egypt. The brothers resist, but ultimately return home with food and attempt to convince Jacob to send Benjamin to Egypt with them in Judah's care. Jacob eventually relents and the brothers return to a warm welcome by Joseph.

When they attempt to leave a second time, Joseph has his silver chalice hidden in Benjamin's bag; a second test. Judah, in an attempt to save Benjamin, recounts to Joseph his own favored status, assumed death, and Jacob's mourning. Joseph sends everyone away but his brothers and, weeping, reveals his true identity to them. He sends them to collect Jacob and bring the family to Egypt where they can settle in Goshen and thrive. Joseph and Benjamin meet and weep with each other. Pharoah welcomes Joseph's brothers and promises them safety in Egypt. The brothers reveal to Jacob that Joseph is alive. The midrash credits Serach bat Asher, Jacob's granddaughter, with telling him the news in a way he could accept. Jacob travels to Mitzrayim to be reunited. On the way God comes to Jacob in a dream and promises them safety. "Fear not to go down to Mitzrayim for I will make you there into a great nation" (46:3). Pharoah welcomes Joseph's brothers and promises them safety in Mitzrayim. All the souls who descended into Mitzrayim are listed. The famine continues and Joseph amasses the wealth of the land for the Egyptian palace, first by accepting money, then livestock, then the very freedom of the people seeking food to live.

This parshah contains the more detailed backstory of how the Israelites came to be enslaved in Mitzrayim, a story many of us don't talk much about around the seder table. Reading this parshah in Tevet, we are confronted with Joseph's instrumental role in Israelite serfdom and wrestle with Joseph's relationship to the empire. How have our ancestors navigated and made brutal compromises with those in power? How are we doing the same? Vayigash gives us a case study heavy with these questions to unpack.

Vayechi וַיְחִי (Beresheet 47:28–50:26): Jacob lives in Egypt for 17 years. At the age of 147, as he prepares to die, he makes Joseph vow that he will not be buried in Egypt, but will be brought to the family burial plot.

Jacob blesses Joseph's sons, Ephraim and Menasheh, as his own, but he bestows the blessing for the firstborn on Ephraim, the younger son. He also blesses his own sons, some blessings more generous than others, and dies. Joseph has Jacob embalmed, and all of Egypt mourns for him. Joseph gets Pharaoh's permission to bury Jacob, and is sent with a full entourage. Once in the land, he mourns for seven days and buries Jacob in Ma'arat HaMachpela, where Abraham, Sarah, Isaac, Rebecca, and Leah are buried. The brothers fear that now that Jacob is dead, Joseph will take revenge on them, but there is peace. The next generation is born, Joseph lives to 110. He makes his brothers vow to carry his bones out of Egypt when they leave. When Joseph dies, he is embalmed and put in a coffin in Egypt.

Vayechi is the last parshah of Beresheet, a parshah of endings, reconciliation, and blessings written in a language of prophetic finality. It can be an opportunity to reflect on all we've just journeyed through in this action-packed first book of Torah. When we zoom out and look over the stories of our collective first families, we see competition for presumably scarce resources, in a patriarchal system where conquering and land struggles are the norm. We also can experience our ancestors' deep intimacy with God, protective care for those they considered family, and visions of a world transformed. And we're just getting started.

Shemot שְׁמוֹת (Shemot 1:1–6:1): A new king gains power in Mitzrayim (Egypt), who does not know Joseph. He fears the Israelite people who have increased in number, enslaves them, and commands that the Israelite boys be killed at birth. In an act of resistance, midwives defy the decree, and Moses is born, his mother hides him in a basket in the river, and he is found and adopted by the Pharaoh's daughter. When he is grown, he kills an Egyptian taskmaster whom he sees beating an Israelite, and, when word of this deed spreads, flees to Midian. There, he marries Zipporah, one of seven daughters of Yitro, a local priest, and works as a shepherd. God remembers the Israelites, and appears to Moses in a burning bush, instructing him to go to Pharaoh, along with his brother Aaron, and demand that Pharaoh free the Israelite people. Pharoah refuses, and instead makes the work harder for the Israelites. Moses returns to God, who promises to overpower Pharaoh and free the people.

For many of us, this and the following parashiyot contain the stories in Torah that we're most familiar with. When we read Shemot in the weekly Torah cycle, in Tevet, far from seder preparations, we get the chance to slow down, dwell in the details, and take our time with the myriad hard questions of this parshah, which are as thick as the inspiration. Why does it take God so long to hear the Israelites and remember the covenant? What is happening in the burning bush? What do we do with God's hardening of Pharaoh's heart, in essence elongating the suffering of Israelites and Egyptians? How do we read this as a liberation story, when God's promise of freedom is directly linked in the text to bringing the people to the already populated land, saying: "I will take you out of the misery of Mitzrayim to the land of the Canaanites, the Hittites, the Amorites, the Perizzites, the Hivites, and the Jebusites, to a land flowing with milk and honey." (Shemot 3:17). Shemot, as with every story of resistance and rebellion, in our ancestors' times as in ours, comes replete with contradictions and struggle.

Vaera וָאֵרָא (Shemot 6:2–9:35): God continues to tell Moses how God will free the Israelites, and Moses throws up roadblocks and objections throughout. God sends Aaron, Moses' brother, to help him, and says, "I will harden Pharaoh's heart, that I may multiply My signs and marvels in the land of Egypt" (7:3). God lays out the plan to send plagues to the Egyptians. Before Pharaoh, at God's instruction, Aaron turns his rod into a snake. Pharaoh's magicians do the same, but Aaron's snake swallows the Egyptian snakes. This does not sway Pharoah, so God turns the Nile, and all the water in Egypt, into blood. God next sends a plague of frogs (or, according to 8:2, one big frog), followed by a plague of lice, then insects. Pharaoh relents for a brief period, allowing Moses and Aaron to return to Canaan to make sacrifices to God, but his heart hardens again and he refuses to let them leave. God sends the next plague that kills all the Egyptian livestock, followed by a plague of boils, then of hail. Still, Pharaoh does not relent.

In our time of forest fires, floods, pandemics, and more, it can be painful to read about God's direct action in causing the plagues to prove a point. At the same time, this parshah contains deep collective theological intimacy, with God promising "And I will take you to be My people, and I will be your God" (Shemot 6:7), tied directly to the promise of freedom. Where do we feel divine intimacy and how do we cultivate collective theologies of liberation in our time of plagues?

Shvat

The parashiyot in Shvat are Bo, Beshalach, Yitro, and Mishpatim. This month the Israelites cross the sea and on the other side begin to learn how to become a free people. We learn that that entails celebrating victories with song, distributing responsibility and asking for help, feeling awe, making collective commitments for the future, and agreeing upon norms and behaviors. How can receiving rules make us free? We learn in Shvat that entering into agreements, choosing how we want to be treated and treat others, is a mark of liberated people. This glimmer of freedom starts moving in Shvat, preparing to blossom in the spring.

Bo בֹּא (Shemot 10:1–13:16) tells of the final three plagues (locusts, darkness, and the death of the firstborn) with increasing intensity. God gives the Israelites instructions for Yetziat Mitzrayim (the Exodus). This parshah contains the first commandment, to set up a calendar and that this month, Nisan in the text, will be the first month of the year, followed by the commandments to observe Passover.

In Bo, we continue to wrestle with the way the Israelites' liberation and the biblical roots of our sacred calendar are directly tied to the suffering of the Egyptians with the killing of the firstborn. As the people leave, however, we're told that it is an erev rav, a mixed multitude, that goes up. Rashi says it is a mingling of nations, and Ibn Ezra specifies it is Egyptians who mix with the Israelites and go out in the Exodus. We know that in resisting empire, poor and working-class people have always created mutual solidarity, and that mass movements for liberation require coalition. Despite what we're told about Jewish isolation and chosenness, we, and our ancestors, have experiences of solidarity and reciprocity with our neighbors woven into our earliest origin stories.

Beshalach בְּשַׁלַּח (Shemot 13:17–17:16) is read on this special Shabbat, Shabbat Shirah, because the Song of the Sea is included in this parshah. See below for more discussion of Shabbat Shirah. B'nei Yisrael, (The Children of Israel), are led out of Egypt through the splitting of the sea, and Moshe brings the bones of Joseph to bury in the land of Yisrael. The people are protected by God in the form of a "pillar of cloud" by day and a "pillar of fire" by night. In November 2012, the Israeli military launched what they called "Operation Amud Anan," co-opting the name for military action against Palestinians in Gaza from Exodus. And yet, when we read the text, we understand the cloud and fire create guidance and light and are not a source of violence. When we read this parshah, we recommit to opposing Israeli military violence done in the name of our sacred texts.

On the other side, Moses and Miriam lead the people in a joyful song of liberation as the Egyptians and their chariots drown in the Sea of Reeds. The people complain about the lack of water and food and safety, and are comforted. The enemy nation of Amalek attacks the weak and the old and is defeated by the Israelite army, actions that later, in Devarim 25, we are commanded to remember, and not to forget.

In Torah, when the people are crushed between the sea and the oncoming Egyptian army, the sea is split through the power of Moses' raised staff. In multiple rabbinic sources we read the classic midrash of Nachshon, jumping into the sea before it split, his human action creating the conditions for miracles. In our time, Kohenet Shoshana Jedwab and Dori Midnight tell the midrash of Miriam and the tachash, "a magical creature, a kosher sea unicorn, [that] dwelled in the Sea of Reeds and assisted the Jews in their passage out of Egypt."[9] Reading about miracles that our ancestors experienced can inspire us to look for the daily miracles around us, and to create organizing cultures that believe in the potential of seemingly unlikely transformations.

Yitro יִתְרוֹ (Shemot 18:1–20:23) finds Moshe working from dawn to dusk as the sole judge, ruling for the people on legal matters. Yitro, Midianite chief/judge/magician/healer and Moshe's father-in-law, arrives with his family, sees Moshe suffering, and helps institute a system of rule involving multiple heads of tribes to share the labor. The people the arrive at Mount Sinai, and the Ten Commandments are revealed to Moses, who transmits them to the gathered people. This moment of revelation requires preparation from all the people, who are warned that touching the mountain will lead to death. There is a dynamic interplay between Moshe's individual leadership, as the only person who can speak directly with God, and all of the people, who are present at Sinai and all of whom receive the direct transmission of God's original instructions.

Yitro, coming directly after Yetziat Mitzrayim, is a parshah of collective formation. Who are the Israelites now that they've left slavery, how will they organize themselves, and what is holy to them? In Yitro we read the seemingly mundane, how to organize judicial decisions, next to the wildly mystical and holy, God revealing Godself and proclaiming the Ten Commandments. This is familiar to us, how we need to figure out our organizing structures, roles, and responsibilities in order to make transformation possible. In Yitro we are encouraged to learn from every person, and from the earth's holiness, to create consistent and transparent methods of communication, *and* to be open to spontaneous bursts of receiving wisdom from all kinds of places.

Mishpatim מִשְׁפָּטִים (Shemot 21:1–24:18) expands upon the first ten commandments and enjoins a series of ethical and ritual laws on the people. These include laws about marriage and sex, a system of ethical payment of workers and slaves, and the commandment to "not oppress the stranger, for you were once strangers in Egypt" (22:20). The people respond by saying na'aseh v'nishma (נַעֲשֶׂה וְנִשְׁמָע), "We will do and we will listen" (24:7). Moses finally ascends to the top of Mount Sinai with Joshua to receive the tablets, and remains there for forty days.

In this parshah, we begin to get the instructions that so much of the rest of Torah is filled with, and it is a mixed bag. It is painful, following so soon after the Israelites' liberation story, to read instructions for enslaving and owning people, including other Hebrew people. We read this right up next to methods for accountability for harm. The injunction to "Not tolerate a sorceress" (Shemot 22:17) is a breath away from "You shall not wrong or oppress a stranger, for you were strangers in the land of Egypt" (Shemot 22:20). Luckily for us, we are inheritors and in the lineage of the rabbinic tradition, and halacha, Jewish law, has always involved interpreting and revaluing Torah instructions. When we read Parshat Mishpatim, we begin this process in earnest again, year after year.

Adar

The parashiyot in Adar are Terumah, Tetzaveh, Ki Tisa, Vayakhel, and Pekudei. This month the Israelites build the Mishkan and adorn the priests in the most lush and beautiful creations the Holy One of Blessing can dream up. Aaron and his lineage are named as the high priests, and the craftspeople Bezalel and Oholiab are lifted up to lead the greatest theater build our people have known to that point. The people create the Golden Calf and are punished. The desire for a Golden Calf comes at the time the Israelites are waiting alone at the base of the mountain. Creating a place for God to dwell in the Mishkan gives the Israelites a place to direct their attention and passions. This month's travel through the Torah focuses on the world of aesthetics, and the pride and comfort it can bring.

· **Terumah** תְּרוּמָה (Shemot 25:1–27:19) begins the instructions for the creation of the Mishkan, the traveling tabernacle in which the Ten Commandments would be carried, and God's presence would dwell when wandering in the desert. The parshah is an extended holy building guide, with lots of construction instructions and interior decorating details, including size, materials, and ornamentation.

It is fitting to begin Adar, the month in which we focus more on aesthetics, glamour, and art than in other months, with this parshah. Meaningfully, this parshah begins and is named after the instruction to build this holy place with terumah, gift offerings from all of the people. The Mishkan, the first holy dwelling that our ancestors collectively build, requires everyone's contributions to become holy. It is constructed in the Wilderness, on the journey; our holy place in diaspora from the very beginning.

Tetzaveh תְּצַוֶּה (Shemot 27:20–30:10) continues the instructions for the Mishkan, including the design of the sacred clothing worn by Aaron and the priests. They dress in blue, purple, and crimson, and bells adorn the hem of Aaron's clothing so the Israelites can hear him coming. The breastplate with symbols for the twelve tribes is created, as well as the urim and turim (אוּרִים וְתֻמִּים), mysterious stones used for divination by the priests, "for dignity and adornment" (Shemot 28:40). Moshe is given instructions on ordaining Aaron as high priest. The ornateness of the priestly garb showcases our ancestors' appreciation of art and beauty as integral to ritual, and the details of placement of specific pieces over Aaron's heart demonstrate an ancient understanding of what today we often refer to as embodiment.

The ordination of Aaron as the high priest begins a lineage of inherited ritual leadership. The rabbis, postdestruction of the Second Temple, opened up spiritual authority to more men and developed a culture in which allegedly all nondisabled men had access to learning (while still by and large rejecting ritual power of women, trans, and disabled people). The hierarchy of the priestly lineage can still be felt in top-down forms of charismatic leader–centered Jewish communities, something that leftist communities are not immune from creating. Tetzaveh thus can be an invitation to intentionally interrogate how spiritual leadership is held in our communities, and to talk about how we can practice distributed, collective, rotating, and diverse forms of leadership in Jewish ritual and community.

Ki Tisa כִּי תִשָּׂא (Shemot 30:11–34:35) recounts the first census of all adult men. Craftsmen, Bezalal and Ohiolab, are singled out by name, identified as skilled, and blessed, in a sacred moment of God and Torah valuing physical labor. The reminder to observe Shabbat is repeated. God gives Moshe the Ten Commandments. Meanwhile, the Israelites begin to fear that Moshe is never returning and convince Aaron to create a Golden Calf. God tries to destroy all the people but is stopped by Moshe. However, when Moshe descends the mountain and hears the celebration, he smashes the tablets and has three thousand Israelites killed. Moses ascends the mountain again to receive the commandments a second time, sees God's back, and descends with a face so radiant he wears a veil the rest of his life (Shemot 34:33).

Much can be said about what the Golden Calf represents. Impactful drashot parallel the Golden Calf with idolatry of materialism, capitalism, and white supremacy. We can read with compassion for the Israelite people needing to construct something they can see in this time of massive uncertainty. They were led into the Wilderness by a God they didn't know and couldn't see, and they reached for physical comfort. Though Moshe reacts in rage, in this parshah we can build the muscle of empathy with the people who we are working to move, and with the parts of ourselves that crave comfort and certainty in a chaotic world.

Vayakhel וַיַּקְהֵל (Shemot 35:1–38:20): In Vayakhel, the commandment to observe Shabbat is repeated, and the people gather their fine goods for the Mishkan and offer all their skills to its creation. They give so abundantly that Moshe calls for them to stop.

While Bezalel and Oholiab lead the artisans in constructing the Mishkan, the people are overflowing with abundant offerings, and a spirit of generosity flows from the community toward this collective project. "Their efforts had been more than enough for all the tasks to be done" (Shemot

36:7). This is a parsha where we can explore collective dayenu, enoughness, when we come together and focus on all of our gifts. This can also be a parshah to explore what it means to feel abundance and enoughness in ourselves and our communities, embodied today in the politics and practice of wealth redistribution.

Pekudei פָּקוּדֵי (Shemot 38:21–40:38): All the materials used in the creation of the Mishkan are calculated, the garments for the priests are made, and all is consecrated. God's presence appears in a cloud to dwell in the Mishkan.

In the final parshah of Shemot, the construction of the Mishkan is complete. It can feel impossible sometimes to know when a project or organization has run its course. When the Mishkan is finished, God declares it done and fit for the Divine Presence to dwell. May we find such clarity in knowing when to lovingly end projects.

Nisan

The parashiyot in Nisan are Vayikra, Tzav, and Shmini. We read of the offerings, the reasonings for them, and the logistics of temple sacrifice. Aaron and his sons are ordained, and then Nadav and Avihu, his eldest, die after bringing an unrequested offering. In the month of Nisan we are called to think about our location in the collective Jewish story of Exodus and to find ourselves in this story of freedom. One of the ways we do this is through the minutiae—the cleaning and preparing and obsessing over getting our homes ready for Passover. It is the tension between minute detail and cosmic questions that electrifies the month of Nisan and creates such holiness in bringing sacrifices. It is the swing between mundane and Divine where Judaism lives, in this month in particular.

Vayikra וַיִּקְרָא (Vayikra 1:1–5:26): This parshah has the most letters and words of all the parashiyot in Vayikra, and comprises instructions on korbanot, animal and meal offerings. These include: olah, an offering burnt fully that lifts the smoke up; mincha, meal offerings of flour, oil, and frankincense; shelamim, a peace offering, that is meat that can be eaten by the offerers and the priests; chatat, a sin offering, and asham, a guilt offering, for sins regarding the use of consecrated goods or for those wondering if they've made a mistake, or for those who are lying when making vows.

What does all of this meat, smoke, fire, and oil have to do with us today, after the destruction of the Temple, when offerings have been replaced in Rabbinic Judaism by prayer? While often translated as "sacrifice," the root of korban, קרב, means closeness. Korbanot are meant to bring human beings and the Divine closer together, and to fix ruptures between people. Our ancestors had hands-on ways of coming close, for the sake of building intimacy, toward collective connection and healing. We can ask how our rituals are serving to bring us closer together and closer to holiness. What are offerings that we want to make for the sake of intimacy?

Tzav צַו (Vayikra 6:1–8:36): Included in this portion are instructions for the priests on temple logistics for processing offerings, including how to dress, how to tend ashes, who can eat the edible offerings, and how to tend the fire on the altar. There is a description of the process for anointing the high priest. The prohibition from eating ox, sheep, or goat fat, fat from animals that died of natural causes or are killed by other animals, and blood appears here.

Finally, Moses is instructed to ordain Aaron and his sons as priests. As this happens, in Vayikra 8:23, is one of only four appearances of the trope sign shalshelet, the rarest musical notation in Torah, a long drawn out sound that many commentators have suggested indicates hesitation or jealousy. In this instance, it is often interpreted as communicating Moses' ambivalence at ordaining his brother. The trope tradition transmits one layer of complex feelings about hierarchical leadership. Reading this parshah, we can explore the concept of the high priesthood, and our own feelings about Torah's inherited leadership. What are our questions, hesitations, and ambivalence? How do the leadership models in Torah impact our community formations today?

Shmini שְׁמִינִי (Vayikra 9:1–11:47): On the eighth day after their ordination, God commands Aaron and his sons, as well as the people, to bring offerings. Nadav and Avihu, Aaron's sons, bring an offering not requested by God, and an eish zarah (אֵשׁ זָרָה), a strange fire, consumes them instantaneously. Moses commands Aaron and his remaining sons not to mourn for the two, and gives them renewed instructions for their safety and honoring the Temple. This instruction is fraught within the family system. The parshah closes with a description of kosher and unkosher animals, and instructions for what to do with an oven or cistern that interacts with an unkosher substance.

The deaths of Nadav and Avihu are another painfully dramatic moment in Torah. What was so wrong with their offerings? Centuries of commentators have asked and answered in different ways. From where we sit, we see how the punishment of Nadav and Avihu shows youth power as threatening to established hierarchies. While Aaron was commanded not to mourn, we are able to have the full range of feelings about these deaths, and how their story is shared. We are able to celebrate the lives and mourn the deaths of Nadav and Avihu, and declare their memories to be a blessing.

Iyar

The parashiyot in Iyar are Ta'azria, Metzora, Acharei Mot, Kedoshim, Emor, Behar, and Bechukotai. This month's parashiyot contain challenging material about bodies—disease, disability, desire. They ask: Who has access to holy places, like temples or community? What makes a body ready to encounter Divinity? What boundaries keep us connected to each other and the Divine? Some years we read these portions ready to answer the questions we see the Torah failing to answer, and some years we see the wisdom behind the text waiting for us to uncover it. Some years we disengage from the responses Torah offers, trusting our own intuition and revelation.

Ta'azria תַזְרִיעַ (Vayikra 12:1–13:59): Ta'azria, the b'nei mitzvah student's worst nightmare. Instructions are given for the amount of time a person is in a state of tumah, ritual impurity, following childbirth (spoiler: the lengths of time are different depending on the sex of the child). The parshah describes in detail the skin condition of tzara'at, often mistranslated as leprosy. The priest becomes the medical provider, quarantining the sick person and administering the course of action. A person with tzara'at is taken outside the camp while infected. In non–leap years, Ta'azria is combined into a joint reading with the following parshah.

On the literal and physical level, this parshah makes us confront the treatment of sick and disabled people in our communities. COVID-19 has taught us the risk and cost of isolation, of pushing vulnerable people out of our circle of care, and this parshah can catalyze conversations about how we want to build community practices of gemilut chasidim, acts of loving-kindness that leave no one outside the camp.

Adding to our discomfort, from the earliest commentaries on this parshah, tzara'at is understood as not physical but an outward expression of internal spiritual struggle. This is explored in Vayikra Rabbah, midrash on Vayikra compiled in the fifth to seventh centuries CE. Tzaar'at is understood as a punishment for l'shon ha'ra, evil speech, gossip, and incitement of harm. The phenomena of tzara'at infecting a house is seen as a consequence of hoarding: if your neighbors ask to borrow things and you say no despite having them, your house may be afflicted with tzara'at, forcing you to bring all of your things out into the open for the community to see. These rabbinic interpretations feed the culture of ableism in our traditional texts, in attributing the root cause of physical ailments to a person's harmful behavior.

Reading the text today, we wrestle with our ancestors' imperfect attempts to understand the relationship between body, mind, spirit, action, and community. While people afflicted with tzara'at were isolated from the rest of the community, the separation was never permanent; built into the Torah of tzara'at is the ritual of purification and reentering the community. By wrestling with this text, not trying to solve the contradictions or smooth over the edges, but instead taking different lessons from the text than our ancestors did, we create our own ritual of transformation and purification.

Metzora מְצֹרָע (Vayikra 14:1–15:33): The discussion of tzara'at continues, with increasingly challenging applications. The parshah discusses the offerings that are brought after recovering from the condition, as well as the cases of buildings that contract the disease. There are rules and rituals for a person who has had a genital infection or regular discharge or emissions, with separate laws for men and women experiencing genital discharge.

Finally, we read the first instructions for niddah, the state of separation when someone is menstruating. Even in Torah, this does not read as a celebration of the holiness of a menstruating body, grouping menstruation with tza'arat, proclaiming that everything the menstruant's body touches is tamari (ritually impure) and enforcing separation between the menstruant and everyone else. Rabbinic law expanded on Torah, the time and conditions of ritual separation. The laws of niddah both influenced and were influenced by the patriarchal culture of Rabbinic Judaism, and leave a long legacy, still active in many Jews' lives today, of menstruating bodies being seen as perpetually untouchable and inherently dangerous. While there is gender diversity in Torah and Rabbinic text, in this parshah there are only men and women, with menstruating seen as solely and the sole distinguishing feature of women's bodies.

Yet we know that women, femmes, and queers have always resisted patriarchy, in our bodies, spirits, and actions. We know and resonate with those who cherished a time of being untouchable to husbands and separate from men. We know that not all women menstruate, and that many who menstruate are not women.

While this text has a specific impact on bodies that menstruate, we read it today in a culture of all-around silencing, fear, and shame toward bodies experiencing sexually transmitted infections. Our ancestors clearly observed real things about the nature of disease transmission, but their knowledge, as ours so often is today, was blended with a culture of patriarchy and misogyny. When we read Metzora, we are invited to directly confront these legacies and the understanding of what is a "healthy body" within Torah and Rabbinic Judaism, and to work to actively create Jewish cultures that celebrate all bodies.

Acharei Mot אַחֲרֵי מוֹת (Vayikra 16:1–18:30) is named "after death," referring to the death of Nadav and Avihu, Aaron's oldest sons. Priests, like their father, they were killed by fire that came from God when they offered God a sacrifice of "alien fire" that God had not commanded. The parshah dictates the centralization of sacrifices to the Temple and strictures around the consumption of blood and flesh. Specific instructions are given for the sacrifices on Yom Kippur, the tenth day of the seventh month. The people are warned, "You shall not copy the practices of the land of Egypt where you dwelt, or of the land of Canaan to which I am taking you, nor shall you follow their laws."

Finally, there is a list of prohibited sexual relationships. This parshah is, famously and disturbingly, the source of "man shall not lie with a man." (18:22). There are as many ways to respond to this harmful text as there are Jews in the beit midrash. Some of us reject it outright, saying, there is no Torah, no wisdom, in this particular piece of Torah text. Some wrestle with the translation and reevaluate the meaning, and others let this text be a gateway to celebrating how long queer people and gay sex have been present and visible in our tradition (if the text prohibits it, people were doing it). Because it comes in the same parshah with the instructions for Yom Kippur, we are confronted with all of the teshuvah, all of the repair and transformation, that our tradition needs and calls for.

In non–leap years, Acharei Mot is combined into a joint reading with the following parshah.

Kedoshim קְדֹשִׁים (Vayikra 19:1–20:27) opens with the powerful affirmation from HaShem: "You shall be holy, for I the Divine your God am holy." Instructions are given for observing Shabbat, bringing offerings, and maintaining the corners of the field and the vineyard for the poor and the stranger to harvest. Prohibitions continue, this time against bearing false witness. The focus is on ethical behavior between people, injunctions against child sacrifice, and additional laws about sexual ethics.

In Kedoshim, we continue to wrestle with the Torah as a lawbook. This can feel like a dry, storyless parshah, a list of do's and don'ts. Why should we care? Some of us find Torah meaningful and fascinating for its own sake, some of us experience it as holy. When we are struggling with the text, we can also remember that this is our ancestors' original instructions, the boundaries with which the people in charge were attempting to shape the culture, and there's so much we can learn in this text about what was important to them. This parshah is full of instructions we can get behind: giving family members honest feedback, and not hating them or bearing a grudge (Vayikra 19:17); mysterious instructions: to not cut the side hairs on your head or beard (Vayikra 19:27); and instructions we reject: once again putting men's sexual relations with each other in the category of sexual prohibitions (Vayikra 20:30). Our challenge can be to not cherry-pick the instructions that resonate with us and throw away the rest but to actively engage with all of it: working to understand, contextualize, rage at, and grieve with some instructions while celebrating and lifting up others. We reflect on how these instructions, and millennia of engagement and interpretation of them, have shaped our communities and lives today.

All of this is built on two concepts: That the people are holy, because God is holy and declares "I have set you apart from other peoples to be Mine" (Vayikra 20:26); and that when the people go into the land, "You shall not follow the practices of the nation that I am driving out before you. For it is because they did all these things that I abhorred them" (Vayikra

20:23). This parshah can be a time to wrestle with chosenness and the spiritual roots of Jewish supremacy's role in apartheid in Palestine today. Can we retain God's declaration of our holiness, being set apart, while moving away from a theology of chosenness, being set above?

Many of our ancestors and elders already have. We can study this text alongside a century of Jewish reinterpretation and outright rejection of chosenness theology, most prominently from Rabbi Mordechai Kaplan's rejection of chosenness as a foundational principle of Reconstructionist Judaism that has, in turn, influenced other denominations. Unfortunately, rejection of chosenness theology has not, in many sources, flowed into a rejection of Jewish supremacy and nationalism. There is still much work to be done, not only to debate chosenness in the abstract but to connect the dots for our communities and to mobilize all Jews who reject chosen people ideology in text to also reject its embodiment in Zionism. This is work we are called to, year after year, by our sacred text. For many of us, it is this dynamic process, of studying text in the world and the world in our texts, that make it holy.

Emor אֱמֹר (Vayikra 21:1–24:23): The parshah focuses on the behavior of and laws controlling the priests. A priest may encounter a dead body of only a member of his immediate family; otherwise, they are not permitted to mourn. The high priest is forbidden to encounter any dead body, even a close family member, in order to maintain his tahara, ritual purity, which is necessary for him to perform the work of the Temple. The parshah states that a person with a disability is disqualified from priestly duties in the Temple, inviting us to confront ableism in both the text and our contemporary communities: Who is, today, directly or inadvertently disqualified from ritual leadership? What harm is happening, and what do we all lose? The sacredness of the sacrifices is again described, as are which members of the priestly family can be sustained by the sacrifices. The people are warned that their offerings must not have defects or blemishes.

The calendar and events of Shabbat, Passover, Shavuot, Rosh HaShanah, Yom Kippur, and Sukkot are described. God instructs the people about the oil for the lamps of the Mishkan, as well as bread and frankincense for Shabbat. A conflict between an Israelite with a Jewish mother and Egyptian father and an Israelite with two Israelite parents breaks out, and the former blasphemes God and is taken out of the encampment and stoned. The people learn that God has an ineffable name, and that there are certain prohibitions that will incur the death penalty. While proclaiming one law for everyone in the community, stranger or citizen, this story insinuates that there is a connection between the blasphemy and having a non-Jewish parent. In this parshah we unpack concepts of community belonging and leadership: What did our ancestors think was important? What do we?

Behar בְּהַר (Vayikra 25:1–26:2): After weeks and weeks of wrestling with sexual prohibitions and stoning people for witchcraft, we get to parshat Behar, which focuses on the laws of shmita, a Shabbat for the land. Every seven shmita cycles is a jubilee year. Torah says, "In this year of jubilee, each of you shall return to his holding," and goes on to describe how this will happen, saying, "My blessing for you in the sixth year, so that it shall yield a crop sufficient for three years" (Lev. 25:21). The parshah continues to instruct on financial ethics and another reminder not to make false idols.

In parshat Behar, we get to dive into shmita as one of the core practices that illuminates Torah as a precapitalist text, with different economic values and logics. We should by no means idealize the economic system presented, which includes permission for slavery. And in this time of capitalism's prolonged death throes and climate catastrophe, we can explore the laws of shmita and jubilee, uncovering and lifting up a profoundly different relationship to land, resources, and community care, and engage in the large-scale collective processes of reparations and landback needed in our time.

Shmita has been an invaluable part of Jewish wisdom and movements for environmental justice for many decades, brought to the forefront by teachers like Rabbi Arthur Waskow and more. In 5782 (2021–2022), many in our communities experienced their first shmita year, learned shmita Torah and halacha, asked questions about how to practice shmita todah, and lived into the answers, creating new ways of practicing shmita in our time. We don't have to wait until 5789 for our next deep dive into shmita; the release of the seventh year requires us to live sustainably in years one through six. This parshah, as well as Re'eh, read in Av, calls us every year to return to the laws of shmita and ask: how are we tending to the land, our home?

In non–leap years, Behar is combined into a joint reading with the following parshah.

Bechukotai בְּחֻקֹּתַי (Vayikra 26:3–27:34): We've reached the final parshah in Vayikra, which opens with the ultimate stakes for all of the laws that have come before: "If you follow My laws and faithfully observe My commandments, I will grant your rains in their season, so that the earth shall yield its produce and the trees of the field their fruit" (Vayikra 26:3). Promises of goodness, safety, and closeness to God are ensured if the commandments are kept. However, if the people do not follow all of the commandments, God promises, "I will wreak misery upon you, your land shall become a desolation and your cities a ruin" (Vayikra 26:16). Finally, however, the people will repent, and God will remember the covenant. At the end of the parshah, instructions are given for computing the values of land and animals that are given as vows to God, prorating offerings based on the jubilee, and tithing and redeeming of animals.

Capping off Vayikra as a text of difficult instructions, Bechukotai is a parshah of difficult consequences to those instructions. The arc described here, of the people going astray, God punishing them physically, collectively, emotionally, and spiritually, the people repenting, and God remembering the covenant and returning, is not a theology that many of us adhere to. And yet some of this text feels descriptive rather than prescriptive: we've just received instructions on how to care for the land, and this parshah proclaims that if those instructions are ignored, the land will take its rest on its own terms. God affirms that at no time will God reject the people completely, and God will not annul the covenant (Vayikra 26:44). For some of us, some of the time, this feels like an unhealthy bond, not a model for relationships. For others of us, or at other times, this is sacred, one-of-a-kind, God love that is ever present even in the hardest of times. We close the parshah and Vayikra with the prayer and the promise that, as with all Torah, we will encounter it, learn from it, and struggle with it, year after year.

Sivan

The parashiyot of Sivan are Bamidbar, Naso, Beha'alotcha and Sh'lach. This month's parashiyot explore who counts—literally, in the form of the census. This month we read about explicit conflict between the people and authority, questions of power and control. Rabbinic tradition offers a reading that upholds divine rule, Moses' authority, elders, and men. When we read closely, we find and celebrate the voices of dissent and disobedience memorialized in these parashiyot.

Bamidbar בְּמִדְבַּר (Bamidbar 1:1–4:20): The opening parshah of the book of Bamidbar is primarily concerned with the census: tribe by tribe, clan by clan, counting adult males who can bear arms. Each tribe is given a place around the Tabernacle. The Levites are not counted in the military census, but instead are instructed on the care of the Tabernacle. They are given specific roles, clan by clan. Finally, there is a separate census of the Kohathites, and a description of their assigned roles and responsibilities.

Bamidbar means "wilderness," the location of this entire book of Torah. The Israelites have left Mitzrayim and not yet arrived at their promised destination. It is painful, as always, that the census counts only men, and that it is so focused on military abilities; it is very clear in this parshah what's important to Torah. While the military census and the assignment of altar service roles can feel far away from our Jewish life today, the process outlined in Bamidbar is at its core about knowing who's in the community, who's doing what, and how the community will be kept safe, spiritually focused, and aligned. In our times of wilderness and wandering, uncertainty and upheaval, this parshah can invite us make sure we count and account for *everyone* in our communities. Bamidbar invites us into consideration about our roles and responsibilities, and our collective strength when we each find our unique offerings.

Naso נָשֹׂא (Bamidbar 4:21–7:89): Parshat Naso opens with a continuation of the census process; there is a description of the duties and a count of the Merarite and Gershonite clans of the Levites. The details of the laws of sotah, the ritual of accusation when a man suspects his wife of adultery, are described. This is followed by the laws of Nazirite vows. These laws come into play when someone decides to nazir, separate themselves and dedicate themselves to God, taking on a priestly status for a period of time. This means that they abstain from wine, do not have their hair cut, and have no contact with a dead person. In Bamidbar 6:24–27, Aaron and his sons are instructed on the proper way to bless the people; this has become what is known as, and continues to be integrated into contemporary liturgy as, the "priestly blessing." Naso closes with the heads of each of the twelve tribes bringing offerings to the newly consecrated altar of the Mishkan.

For all of us concerned with misogyny within Jewish text and Judaism, this parshah requires us to wrestle with the treatment of the accused adulterer, and the rabbinic tradition of the laws of sotah that follow from it in the Mishnah and Gemara. In the text, women accused of adultery are forced to drink bitter waters with a priestly spell infused in them, while the accused man undergoes no such public humiliation. This public ritualized shaming is one of the countless ways that women's bodies and sexualities are denigrated in Jewish tradition, and it describes an enactment of women's bodies being property of their husband. While the ritual might seem irrelevant in today's context, it is a harmful text that needs to be named as such in our continued work to heal from and create a world without misogyny. In more than half of a tractate of Talmud, the laws of sotah were predicated on, and furthered a culture of, distrusting women and considering women's bodies property.

At the same time, we wonder, did the waters ever work as they are described? Or were they just a bad drink that would have created a path for the woman to be inevitably absolved? The laws of sotah come, as so much of the harm transmitted in Torah does, a few verses from the spiritual gift of the priestly blessing, in Numbers 6:24–27. While sotah is no longer practiced, if it ever was, the priestly blessing is a protective spell that is still present in our liturgy millennia later. We can invoke this blessing as a source of empowerment when choosing to do the at times overwhelming work of confronting oppressive texts, in this parshah and beyond.

Beha'alotcha בְּהַעֲלֹתְךָ (Bamidbar 8:1–12:16): After the consecration of the altar in the previous parshah, Beha'alotcha begins with lighting the lamps in the Mishkan and the initiation of the Levites into priestly service. Moses reviews the instructions for Pesach and receives the instructions for Pesach Sheni, a second chance at the Pesach offering for those who were absent or impure on Pesach (Second Pesach, see *Iyar: Holidays*). On the day that the Mishkan is erected, a cloud covers it, at night appearing as fire. The Israelites stay in camp when the cloud is present, continuing on their journey when the cloud disperses. There are other instructions for encampment and journeying. During the journey, the Israelites complain, to Moses and to God, in general and specifically, about the food. Moses gathers seventy elders, and God puts God's spirit on them.

This parshah is full of stories of people who feel the call to prophecy and are rebuked, as the community wrestles with collective leadership.

Beha'alotcha closes with the story of Miriam and Aaron speaking against Moses because he married a Cushite woman. They point out that they are both capable of receiving prophecy from God, implicitly questioning Moses' elevation in leadership. God calls all three siblings together, defends Moses as the one able to receive the most direct prophecy, and punishes only Miriam, and not Aaron, with tzara'at, the spiritual skin infection. Moses prays for Miriam's healing, with the lines "אֵל נָא רְפָא נָא לָהּ" "el na refa na la," "Oh God, heal her" now used in our liturgy. However, God decrees that she remain stricken with the skin infection and stay out of the camp for seven days. When we sing this prayer for healing, we are calling back to complex family and communal leadership dynamics, and wrapping the words themselves in new, transformative meanings.

Sh'lach שְׁלַח (Bamidbar 13:1–15:41): On God's instructions, Moses sends twelve men to scout the land of Canaan and learn about the land, the people, the cities, the soil, and the fruit. The scouts come back with giant fruits and reports of the abundance of the land. Ten of the scouts believe the people of the land are too powerful and that the Israelites should not try to conquer them. Only Joshua and Caleb report that the land and people are conquerable. The people believe the ten scouts and, once again, say they wish they could go back to Mitzrayim. Moses and Aaron plead with the people to trust God's power and protection, but the people threaten to pelt Moses and Aaron with stones. God appears and threatens to destroy everyone; Moses says this will make God look bad, and pleads for forgiveness for the people. God condemns the scouts to death and punishes the people with wandering in the Wilderness for forty years, one year for each day of the scouts' expedition. The next day, a group says they have learned their lesson and are ready to go into the land. They do, but are defeated by the Amalekites and Canaanites. The parshah closes with the laws of offerings when the people come into the land, the story of the stoning of a man found gathering sticks on Shabbat, and instructions for putting tzitzit (fringes) on the corners of garments.

In Rabbinic tradition, we are generally assumed to identify with and root for Joshua and Caleb and the project of conquering Canaan. Today, as Israel continues its decades-long occupation of Palestine, we are confronted with the militaristic and conquering urges within Torah. Even while we question the historicity of this origin story, it is painful to read the command to go into a populated land and conquer it. We who do not take Torah as historical fact or modern land deed can, as many of our ancestors have done, read this story as a metaphor for our spiritual lives and personal journeys of transformation. At the same time, while the occupation of Palestine continues, we are obligated to create decolonial Torah study. One way to do this is to read the story and create midrash from the perspective of those who did not want to go into the land. Did they have more objections than what is communicated through the text? As we listen deeply to the words and between the lines, we can hear new old voices speaking their wisdom.

Tammuz

The parashiyot of Tammuz are Korach, Chukat, Balak, and Pinchas. This month's readings are dramatic, with characters revolting, being swallowed by the earth, dying, mourning, being swayed by talking donkeys, exacting extremist political puritanical ideological violence, demanding women's financial futures and independence . . . the works. As we move through the books of Vayikra, Bamidbar, and Devarim, the material is less often narrative, and these parashiyot are a boost of story to keep us going. Though the majority of our text focuses on the relationship of Moses and God, and Moses as broker between God and the people, these parashiyot reveal a glimpse into the experiences of the Israelites and those who come into contact with them.

Korach קֹרַח (Bamidbar 16:1–18:32): Korach, a Levite, along with 250 leaders of the community, rises up against Moses' authority. Proclaiming that all of the community is holy and that God is with them all, they question why Moses is putting himself above others. They bring firepans of incense, and the ground opens up and swallows them. When people protest what happened to Korach and his followers, a plague comes. When it ends, God commands the heads of each tribe to come with a staff, and selects Aaron's staff to bloom with blossoms and almonds, to demonstrate who God has chosen for leadership. God then instructs Aaron how to make priestly offerings.

The story of Korach is an opportunity to discuss sacred leadership, humility, and collective power. Some years, we might read Korach and feel firmly aligned with his challenge to Moses' authority. Other years, Korach seems like an egotistical charismatic leader subverting the collective good. We read Korach and ask, how do we organize in ways where all of us get to bring our unique and varied skills and power?

Chukat חֻקַּת (Bamidbar 19:1–22:1): Chukat opens with the laws for the offering of the Red Heifer, and continues with additional laws regarding purity and impurity upon contact with a dead body. The Israelites arrive at Kadesh, where Miriam dies and is buried. Immediately, the community is without water and complains to Moses, who hits a rock in rage. The water flows, but God tells Moses that because he didn't trust God, he will not be able to enter the Promised Land.

The Israelites try to cross through Edom and are turned away. There, Aaron dies, and the people mourn for thirty days. The people again complain about the lack of food, and God sends serpents to bite the people. Some die, the rest repent, and God instructs Moses to put a serpent on a staff; anyone bitten by a serpent can look at the copper serpent and be healed. The Israelites try to pass through the land of the Amorites but are refused. However, they march on and settle the land, and continue into the land of Bashan. Most years, Chukat is read as a double parshah with the following parshah.

Chukat is a parshah full of sickness, death, dying, mourning, and the magic of healing. We note the discrepancy between the community's thirty days of mourning for Aaron, and no such collective time allowed for grieving Miriam. The lack of water and the uprisings against Moses, Moses' rage and subsequent punishment, this all seems to flow directly from having no time for grief and mourning. When we read parshat Chukat, we can create healing in our tradition by setting aside time in our ritual spaces to honor and mourn Miriam, great prophetess, bringer of water, song, and healing.

Balak בָּלָק (Bamidbar 22:2–25:9): While much of Torah is concerned with God's power, Parshat Balak communicates this in a particularly weird way. Balak, king of the Moabites, fears the Israelites will come to conquer their land. He calls Balaam to come and put a curse on the Israelites. After initially resisting, Balaam goes, but the Angel of God blocks his way. At first, only Balaam's donkey can see the Angel, and resists going forward. God speaks through the donkey, and tells Balaam to continue, but that he will only be able to speak God's words. Three times, Balak and Balaam build altars and offer bulls and rams. Each time, Balaam speaks blessings instead of curses, saying that this is what God has spoken through him. We learn that, according to Torah, God's power extends through all creatures.

Finally, the story continues with the Israelites, who have been staying at Shittim. Some of them are now in relationships with Moabites and offering sacrifices to Baal-peor. God is enraged and commands Moses and the officials to publicly impale those in Moabite-Israelite relationships, which Pinchas immediately does. This story is in sharp contrast with Balaam, in which God's protection from those outside the community comes through empowering donkeys and blocking curses. In Pinchas, we see the early tendrils of a culture of fear of others, manifest through the rejection of intermarriage, and linking intermarriage with idol worship. This parallels fears in our time that intermarriage leads to assimilation and erasure of Jewishness. We can understand these fears while rejecting their imprint in Jewish culture today and working to build communities where all of our families, friends, beloveds, and neighbors are welcomed.

Pinchas פִּינְחָס (Bamidbar 25:10–30:1): Picking up moments after the last parshah ended, Pinchas's violent zealotry of slaying the Israelite and Moabite couple is rewarded, and God commands Moses to attack the Midianites. God also demands a census be taken; the Israelite people total 601,730. The names of the clans are listed, and the system for land allotments is laid out. Five sisters, Mahlah, Noah, Hoglah, Milcah, and Tirzah, come to Moses and Eleazar the priest and demand a land allotment in their father's name, saying, "Let our father's name not be lost to his clan just because he had no son" (Numbers 27:4). God tells Moses to grant their request, and makes daughters second in line after sons for inheriting property. God then tells Moses to appoint Joshua as the leader who will succeed him. In this parshah we have more stories of action and leadership in Torah. We reject the misogynist violent leadership of Pinchas, and celebrate the power of the five sisters' collective organizing for their own dignity and resourcing.

The parshah closes with the instructions for ritual offerings on Shabbat, New Moons, and the festivals and holidays we know as Pesach, Shavuot, Rosh Hashanah, Yom Kippur, Sukkot, and Shemini Atzeret.

Av

The parashiyot of Av are Mattot, Ma'asei, Devarim, Vaetchanan, Eikev, and Re'eh. In this month we read about the plan to enter the land and make home, as well as Moses' learning that he will never be able to enter. This yearning and heartbreak, the threats that are scattered through the instructions for right action once entering the land, evoke the struggles of Av. As the book of Devarim begins this month, Moses illuminates the strongest modality for hope and resilience our people have—storytelling. Moses recounts his life and the covenant between God and the Jewish people, with hopes for a future of peace and abundance. Av can contain the fullness of these emotions.

Mattot מַטּוֹת (Bamidbar 30:2–32:42): Moses describes the laws of oaths, including different rules for men and women, and the power of fathers and husbands to annul their daughters' and wives' oaths. It is disappointing, though not surprising, to read this so soon after the inheritance ruling in favor of the five sisters in the last parshah. The Israelites go to war with the Midianites, and Moses commands them to kill all of the Midianite survivors. Moses gets angry when the troops initially spare the Midianite women, whom he blames for seducing Israelite men and leading them to worship Baal Peor (in Parshat Balak). He instructs them to "slay every woman who has known a man carnally," demonstrating violent misogyny traditionally not associated with Moshe. God instructs Moses and Elezar on how to divide the resources captured from the Midianites, which, as described in the parshah, include the "females who had not had carnal relations."

The leaders of the tribes of Reuben and Gad ask Moses for permission to stay east of the Jordan River, as it is better for cattle grazing. Moses becomes angry at this request, but the tribal leaders promise that they will send men to be the first troops to enter the land. The leaders of the Gadites, Reubenites, and Manasseh then go and conquer various cities and territories. As we begin to reach the end of the book of Bamidbar, and with it the close of the journeys of the Wilderness, we get more and more details of the conquest of Canaan. It is painful to read this in the time of Israeli military occupation of Palestine. We long to study Torah in a free Palestine, with this text relegated to literal ancient history.

Mattot is read as a double parshah with Ma'asei.

Ma'asei מַסְעֵי (Bamidbar 33:1–36:13): The parshah reviews the journey of the Israelites from Mitzrayim to their current encampment. God instructs Moses on the division of the land among the tribes when they conquer Canaan. God gives instructions on the laws concerning murder, including where and how to set up cities of refuge for people who have killed someone unintentionally. The sisters Mahlah, Noah, Hoglah, Milcah, and Tirzah marry men in their father's clan and receive their inheritances.

The Torah of the cities of refuge is a thought-provoking text to study as abolitionists, in the context of the U.S.' current system of mass incarceration. The cities of refuge are designed to keep people safe who have killed someone accidentally, at the same time ascribing the death penalty to those who strike someone with a tool that could cause death. Without taking this text as prescriptive for us today, we can study this portion to understand the principles that our ancestors considered important, which included fair trials, safety for those who are accused of doing harm, and considering both intent and impact. This can be a jumping-off point for our discussion of harm, teshuvah, and justice today.

Devarim דְּבָרִים (Devarim 1:1–3:22): The Book of Devarim is Moses' final words to the Israelites בְּעֵבֶר הַיַּרְדֵּן, on the other side of the Jordan, a book-length recounting of the journey from the Exodus to this moment, balanced on the precipice of the land. Devarim, the opening parshah of the book, is the retelling of the Israelites' journey from Horeb through the Wilderness. Moses recounts stories of the previous books, such as appointing judges, the episode of the twelve spies, and the criss-crossing of the land encountering and making war with other peoples. Moses' recounting of the forty years of wandering is as harsh as the first telling was, not glossing over the challenges but instead retelling of the people's fears, anxieties, and infighting. Parshat Devarim invites us to think about movement history in our collectives: How do we retell the story of how we got here? Who gets to narrate our histories? What stories are important to retell, in our lifetimes, to each other?

Va'etchanan וָאֶתְחַנַּן (Devarim 3:23–7:11): This parshah is always read on Shabbat Nachamu, the Shabbat of Consolation following Tisha b'Av, and takes its name from the first word, "and I pleaded." It begins with

Moses recounting how he pleaded with God to allow him to enter into the Land but was denied, and Joshua was established as the next leader in line. Moses reminds the people of the immutability of the Torah, the revelation at Sinai, and the close encounter with God. He also blames the people for not being able to enter the Land, and threatens that if they follow false idols they will be scattered and driven out of the Land. Moses establishes three cities of refuge, as described in Ma'asei, where a person who has accidentally killed someone can escape from their vengeful family. This is a powerful passage to study in the context of abolitionist work to dismantle the police and prison systems. What principles guided our ancestors in confronting violence and its impacts in their communities?

In a moment of revelation for the generation that was not physically present at Sinai, Moses affirms that "it was not with our fathers that HaShem made this covenant, but with us, the living, every one of us who is here today" (Devarim 5:3). This assertion is often cited as proof that the covenant is inherited by and renewed with us, the living, in every generation, and that Torah is ours to interpret and reinterpret in our lifetimes.

The people then receive a repetition of the Ten Commandments, and the first two paragraphs of what becomes the Shema (Devarim 6:4) and V'ahavta (Devarim 6:6–9). Distressingly, this is immediately followed by instructions to destroy the nations residing in the land when the Israelites arrive. We note and take solace that our rabbinic ancestors chose the specific verses that they pulled from this passage to include in the daily liturgy, focused on love and dedication, mindfulness and teaching the generations. They left the instructions for occupation in Torah, not elevating them by including them in the siddur. We who proclaim the Shema and V'ahavta, as so many generations before us have, take on the commandments to listen and to love holiness in our world. For many of us, this includes hearing the call to work to end the occupation of Palestine, and to love ourselves, all our people, our movements, and our neighbors as we do this.

Eikev עֵקֶב (Devarim 7:12–11:25): In Eikev, the Israelites learn the blessings that flow from following God's instructions: living in a rich land, raising healthy animals, and protection from sickness. Moses reminds the people of their salvation from enslavement and how God provided for them in the desert, and reminds them not to forget this when they become comfortable. Moses then instructs the people to conquer and dispossess the people already living in the land, and reminds them of the egel hazahav (the Golden Calf) and God's compassion in not destroying them. He recounts receiving the Ten Commandments, the egel hazahav, and placing the new set in the Mishkan (traveling ark). He reminds them of their travels in the desert and Aaron's death. Finally, Moses instructs the people to befriend the stranger and protect the widow. The continuation of the Shema appears in Devarim 11:13–21.

In our times of climate catastrophe, parshat Eikev reads as relevant and prophetic. We are taught that our actions impact the earth, that our behavior can lead to overwhelming catastrophes of rain, fire, and famine. With the reminder of the egel hazahav, we can transpose the instructions against worshiping other gods as a warning against materialism and capitalism, that put accumulation above care for each other and the earth. In this text, we are invited to reflect on how we can walk in the divine paths in our lifetimes, in love, toward the protection and care of the whole earth.

Re'eh רְאֵה (Devarim 11:26–16:17): In Re'eh's opening words, "See, I set before you blessing and curse," God gives the people both the choice to follow the mitzvot, and a framework of consequences for disobeying. The Israelites are instructed to destroy all of the sacred sites of the residing people, demolishing their altars, pillars, and images of their gods. They are reminded that they must bring sacrifices to a central place that God selected, and do so in the exact manner instructed. There are warnings against following dream-diviners or others who would draw one to idol worship. In this parshah, we must confront the legacy of destruction of sacred sites, on Turtle Island and in Palestine, brought by colonization. The Torah was shaped by people who experienced the destruction of their sacred sites, and then enshrined in sacred text the instruction to perpetrate that harm on others. How can we make learning this parshah a pathway to creating more blessing, and not further these curses?

There are also laws enumerating the foods that may and may not be eaten (yes antelope, no hare). Instructions are given to put aside a tenth of the field's yield and the firstfruits of flock and land for God. While kashrut is a unique body of food law in its own right, this can be a parshah to think about food justice in our time: from seeds and soil health, farm workers' rights and food apartheid, there are ample issues to unpack how we make fruit and land holy for God in our times.[10] The laws of shmita, a remission of debts every seventh year, are explained (see parshat Behar, read in Iyar). Instructions are given to make the Passover sacrifice, and to remember the

Exodus, and its rituals, as well as to observe the Omer, Shavuot, and later Sukkot. The people are instructed to make pilgrimages, three times a year, to the sacred place God will choose.

Elul

The parashiyot in Elul are Shoftim, Ki Teitzei, Ki Tavo, Nitzavim, and Vayeilech. Just action, Temple worship, and promises of the covenant are themes of the Torah readings for this month, giving our Elul preparations rich soil in which to grow. There are many verses of empowerment in this month, including the oft quoted "Justice, justice you shall pursue" (Devarim 16:20) and "It is not in the heavens, that you should say, 'Who among us can go up to the heavens and get it for us and impart it to us, that we may observe it? . . . No, the thing is very close to you, in your mouth and in your heart, to observe it" (Devarim 30:11–14). This month brings reminders of our personal and collective responsibility as we prepare for the new year.

Shoftim שֹׁפְטִים (Devarim 16:18–21:9): Shoftim is concerned with human justice and divine justice. It is fitting that we study this parshah of how to justly govern in Elul, as we collectively turn toward reflection and repair. In 16:20 we read the much beloved, and oft quoted, verse, "Justice, justice you shall pursue," an invitation to not to simply be curious about justice but to commit one's life to pursuing it with fervor. Encountering this line in the context of Torah, we are forced to wrestle with the second part of the verse: "so you may thrive and occupy the land that the Lord your God is giving you (16:21)." For a nuancing of this verse, we can turn toward the rest of the parshah, which includes instructions to establish courts, and not to worship gods or goddesses besides God. God gives half-hearted consent for the establishment of kings; instructions to support the landless Levites; warnings against assimilation; warnings against magic, divination, spell casting, or ghost or ancestral work; as well as instructions on conducting a just war, and the communal accountability/absolution ritual of the Egla Arufa, the broken heifer. Our ancestors understood the unbreakable link between justice, governance, and collective living and thriving. They had very different assessments of what was just and right, based on hierarchy and chosenness. We can reject many of their conclusions while still embracing the same questions of Shoftim, of judges.

Ki Teitzei כִּי-תֵצֵא (Devarim 21:10–25:19): This parshah contains the violent narrative of the "beautiful captive," and instructions on a wide variety of subjects. These include: family dysfunction, including favored children and defiant sons, and returning lost property. There are also warnings against many things, such as men wearing women's attire and women wearing men's attire, and shatnez (using certain fabrics mixed with other fabrics). There are bans on who can engage in Temple worship. We have the instruction to chase away the mother bird before collecting eggs. There is a reminder to "remember to forget Amalek" instructions on how to poop, and instructions to leave the corners of one's field for the hungry to collect.

In Kiddushin 39b we read that witnessing a young child die after completing the mitzvot named in this parshah of shooing a mother bird from a nest before collecting eggs is what caused Elisha ben Abuyah, famed heretic of Talmud, to lose his faith and turn away from Torah. We can expand on this rabbinic tradition, honoring that our lineage includes skeptics. There is so much in this parshah that we know is violent, and as with many other parashiyot, there are parts that are irredeemable to us, such as justifying patriarchal abduction of women. Especially as we continue to live in patriarchal and misogynist cultures, there is power in naming out loud what we are rejecting, interwoven with living a life engaged in Torah and mitzvot.

We can also, following in the rabbinic tradition, interpret and understand certain verses and mitzvot. The rabbis of the Talmud are deeply troubled by the ben sorer u'moreh, the rebellious son whom Torah commands be put to death. They affirm that a case, as specified in this parshah, has never happened, and suggest it will never happen. Why is it there? "Study and receive reward," we are told. That is to say, wrestling with and reinterpreting this text is its own benefit. In this lineage, as part of their work of TransTorah and TransText, Rabbis Elliot Kukla and Reuben Zellman compiled many centuries of rabbinic interpretation of Devarim 22:5's prohibition against women and men wearing each other's garments. They offer the teaching that this is prohibited only in cases of intentionally disguising one's identity for the purpose of committing harm, and is permitted for the sake of spiritual joy.[11] There are many more mitzvot, in this parshah and beyond, for us to study, challenge, and receive reward.

Ki Tavo כִּי-תָבוֹא (Devarim 26:1–29:8): The people are told that firstfruits must be given to the Temple. A ritual is described for remembering that the land belongs to God, including the line אֲרַמִּי אֹבֵד אָבִי "Arami oved avi," which is often translated as "my father was a wandering Aramean." There are instructions about how to set up altars in the land when the people get there, and there are curses and blessings for following or refusing to follow God's instructions. Finally, the parshah recalls the journey from Mitzrayim to the Land, including miracles and military conquest.

This parshah gives us an opportunity to talk about migration and movement of people across time and place. Our tradition ties ancestral wandering to honoring land, the sacredness of land, and the practice of spiritual and material gratitude and giving back to the land.

Nitzavim נִצָּבִים (Devarim 29:9–30:20): In years that are not a leap year, this parshah stands alone. In leap years, it is a joint parshah with Parshat Vayeilech. God affirms that the covenant being made with the generation about to enter the land is also with the generations that will follow. God expounds on the responsibilities and consequences of the covenant, that all those who turn away will be punished, and those who observe the mitzvot will be granted prosperity. This parshah includes the notable psukim affirming Torah's accessibility: Devarim 30:11–14, "It is not in the heavens, that you should say, 'Who among us can go up to the heavens and get it for us and impart it to us, that we may observe it? Neither is it beyond the sea, that you should say, 'Who among us can cross to the other side of the sea and get it for us and impart it to us, that we may observe it?' No, the thing is very close to you, in your mouth and in your heart, to observe it."

These verses form a bedrock upon which so much of our engagement with Torah grows. Here, approaching the pinnacle moments of Torah's culmination, as Moses and HaShem sum up the most important instructions, we read that these mitzvot come from inside of us, are in our mouths and our hearts. It is with this enjoinment that we hear what we know in our bodies to be spiritually true: the holy work of mitzvot, of living a life of sacredness, must come from, and resonate with, our embodied experiences of justice and wholeness.

Vayeilech וַיֵּלֶךְ (Devarim 31:1–31:30): Moses reveals to Joshua he will not go to enter the land, but that Joshua will lead the people; he instructs: have faith and trust in the Divine. The holiday of Sukkot is established, and Moses tells the story of the journey to all who are there so that they can share the legacy and ancestral wisdom. God tells Moses he is about to lie with his ancestors, and that there will be a time when the people rebel against all Moses told them, and that there will be punishment from God. God instructs Moses to write down all of the lessons of Torah as a poem, and to teach it to the people.

As Moses looks back on his legacy and forward into the future beyond his lifetime, it is an opportunity for us to reconnect with ancestors and envision descendants. Who are the Moseses in our lives, who remember the previous generations' politicization, actions, and development and can share their lessons with us? Who are the Joshuas in our lives, younger generations with more courage and vision, who will carry the work on to places we can't yet imagine? As Torah begins to end (only to begin again), Vayeilech is an opportunity to strengthen the links between the generations in our communities and organizations.

CLOSING

At the close of this book, we call in the wisdom of the Jewish year: cycles of time endlessly flowing one into the next, while affirming the newness of each year, season, month, and day.

When we come together to work for justice, it is called a "movement," because people are individually and collectively transformed as we organize for our conditions to change. Life-denying forces that try to crush movements for justice want us to stay still or go backward in time.

It is this motion to which we are called: we can't stay still, and we won't go back. All that is alive grows, dies, and makes way for new life. We will bring our ancestors and their wisdom with us, live in the present, and dream of the future. Our hope is that this book offers the traditions that we can root in and be held by as we transform.

Tradition doesn't require us to make ourselves smaller; instead, it encourages us to expand, to bring it along with us as we grow. Our calendar shows that we can bring the past with us without being frozen or constrained, through living in cyclical time while telling about the past and visioning the future. Every year we meet the same holidays, same Torah portions, and same prayers. There is always something different, from year to year—what's changed is always us.

Over the last many pages, we have explored the Jewish year, in this moment in time. We began by exploring some of the core concepts and values that undergird our work. Within the framing concepts of behaving, belonging, and believing, we explored big questions in leftist Jewish life today: What does leftist Jewish organizing and ritual space look like? How are we organized? What do we believe? We then dove into the months of the Jewish year: the nature of each of the months and the ways we connect to the rhythms of the season, and how the cycles of our life and organizing, the earth, and our prayers nourish one another. We unpacked a small part of each Torah portion as the foundational text of the Jewish year. We know that for every holiday we explored, for every Torah portion we dipped our toes into, there is infinitely more we could have included. We offer our profound gratitude for everyone who is uncovering old magic and creating new rituals, even as we write these words.

Where are we headed? More of everything: more Torah, more community, more solidarity! We will come into more confidence: at the power of the orchard of wisdom we are harvesting and planting, and at the beauty and rightness of our embodying it. In the coming years, radical Jewish communities will gain deeper knowledge in our many ways of being Jewish. Our newness, for those of us approaching Jewishness after generations of assimilation, will become a point of pride: students approaching with fresh experiences have so much to offer. We will build new structures and find new ways of organizing ourselves that meet the changing conditions of our time. We will experiment, leave behind what is not serving, and grow our imaginations and creativity. We will plant seeds, not knowing when they will mature or if we will ever see the day, but knowing that the next generations will be there to eat the fruit and plant more seeds.

May we know and feel our interwovenness with all life.
May we experience being held by the power of our ancestors.
May the gifts we carry from our tradition make us braver.
May the work of our hands transform the mundane into sacred,
    and in turn, may sacred time transform us.

ACKNOWLEDGMENTS

We are thankful to the Source of Life and Creativity for bringing us to this moment. Thank you for sustaining us through five years of writing, rewriting, retreating, praying, crying, and teaching on this book. Thank you for inspiration, motivation, and life. We give thanks to our ancestors, whose blessings we feel flowing through us as we write. To the revolutionaries and ritualists who have come before, names known and unknown: we praise you, we thank you! We wrote this book on Lenapehoking, the homelands of the Lenni-Lenape people, on Mni Sóta Makoce, the homeland of Dakota people, long home to the Anishinaabe people, and on Piscataway and Susquehannock land. We are uninvited settlers in these places, and we offer our deep gratitude to original and forever stewards of these lands. We give thanks to the earth, and these specific lands, their rivers and trees and lakes. We pray that this book is in service of movements for land back and indigenous sovereignty.

We give thanks to you, dear readers, whom we called in every time we sat down to write. Thank you for engaging with it, exploring your political and spiritual practice with it, disagreeing with it, chevruta learning over it. We offer our abundant gratitude to all our beloved teachers, comrades, loves, and publishers for helping us arrive at this moment. This book comes from, and is an offering to, our communities. Thank you.

A raucous and throaty thank you to Sandra Korn, our editor at Wayne State University Press. Thank you for believing in this project from its very beginning and championing it at every turn. Thank you for your patience, co-scheming, and teaching. It is a joy to create this book with you as a gift to the radical Jewish communities that have cared for all of us.

Thank you to the team at Wayne State University Press. Thank you to Sandra Judd, our copy editor, and to designers Emily Gauronskas, Lindsey Cleworth, Carrie Teefey for making our book beauty dreams come true. Thank you to Traci Cothran and Kelsey Giffin for your work getting the book out into the world. Thank you to Stephanie Williams for your leadership at WSUP.

Thank you, Dori Midnight, for blessing this book with spells. Thank you for all the ways you have schemed, scrapped, studied, and nourished us individually and as a team. Thank you for weaving such healing for our people. Thank you, Sol Weiss, for illuminating the months with your art, and for the ways you bless our movement with such beauty. Thank you, Dori and Sol, for being game at the last minute to bring te'amim, the cantillation and flavor of art and magic, to color this book.

Thank you to Rabbi Rebecca Alpert for paving the way and for generously sharp feedback on this manuscript. Thank you to Rabbi Julia Watts Belser for all your friendship, support, and guidance on this book. Thank you to Claudia Horwitz and Nadav David for your insightful reading and skilled feedback. Thank you to the inimitable Shelley K. Rosenberg for being our first reader and biggest cheerleader.

Thank you to our teachers: Bobbi Brietman, Rabbi Elisa Goldberg, Rabbi Lynn Gottlieb, Rabbi Margaret Holub, Rabbi Linda Holtzman, Dr. Tamar Kamionkowski, Rabbi Sarra Lev, Rabbi Mordechai Liebling, Rabbi Nathan Martin, Aurora Levins Morales, Rabbi Vivie Mayer, Rabbi Dev Noily, Rabbi Brant Rosen, Rabbi Jacob Staub, Dr. Elsie Stern, Elliott bat-Tzedek, Rabbi Laurie Zimmerman, and so many more. We are honored to be your students.

Thank you to our shared beloved friends and comrades, Rabbis Leora Abelson, Max Reynolds, Nora Woods, Alissa Wise, Eli DeWitt, and Ari Lev Fornari, and to Annie Sommer Kaufman, Stefanie Fox, Stefan Lynch, Kate Poole, and Irit Reinheimer. Thank you to Elissa Martell for many years of scheming and creating, and the Radical Jewish Calendar Team for inspiration and collaboration. Thank you to the Jewish Voice for Peace Rabbinical Council for years of building the rabbinic community we want to be a part of.

Thank you to the seasons for holding us, to the earth for loving us, and to Jewish time for teaching us about long arcs and steady yet ever-changing cycles.

Though we are a two-headed, four-limbed, back-to-back being[1] in most ways, we do have some individual thank yous!

---

[1]   Beresheet Rabbah 8:1.

Ariana

Thank you to my parents, Alex and Linda Katz, for teaching me that Judaism nourishes our politics, and our politics nourish our Judaism and covering it all in joy.

In order of appearance (in my life), thank you to Abigail Katz z"l, Ernest Katz z"l, Claire Singer z"l, William Singer z"l, Joe Miele, Andy Helaine and Danielle Schattner, Mendel Katz-Dean, Lisa Scheeler z"l, Matthew and Lia Schattner, Shahrzad Noorbaloochi, Michelle Weiser, Sarah McAndrews, Duncan Hewitt, Tyler Cullis, Liza Behrendt, Asher Bruskin, the YJVP Boston Crew, Leslie Wright, Mildred Wright z"l, Patrick McAndrews, Marvin and Terry Marsh, Shannon Katz-Dean, the Robins Fam, Lura Groen, Jesse Hammons, Missy Smith, Emily Parker, Willow Hewitt, Misha, and Khashayar. I am deeply blessed and forever shaped by your love.

Thank you to Marjorie Berman, Lawrie Hartt, and Em House. Thank you to my Hinenu community for shaping me, teaching me Torah, and being my landing. Thank you to all of the organizers and teachers who have shown me patience and delight as I grow and learn from you.

Thank you to Jess, my dear comrade and work wife, the Reish Lakish to my Rabbi Yochanan. Thank you for sharpening my strategy and softening my self-criticism. Thank you for bringing joy and heart and honesty to everything you weave, every ritual you make, every word you write. I am forever transformed by marking the changing of each month and year alongside you.

And thank you to my beloved Ever for being my chevrusa, co-schemer, patient world builder, and delight. Thank you to my sweet baby and book delayer Meir Gamzu, who brings joy to each season. I am so grateful to move through this life with you two.

Jessica

To the people and communities that have taught, nurtured, challenged, pushed, and loved me for so many years, thank you for making me possible, thank you for making this book and everything I do possible.

To the Jewish communities in which I am gratefully entangled, thank you to all of the people whose Shabbat and seder tables, organizing meetings, and actions fed and stretched me. There are blessedly more of you than I can name. In particular, I am profoundly grateful to: Josina Manu Matlzman, Kohenet Sharon Jaffe, Ezra Nepon, Nava EtShalom, Irit Reinheimer, Rabbi Leora Abelson, Wendy Elishva Somerson, MJ Kaufman, Margot Seigle, Laynie Soloman, Zahara Zahav, Graie Hagans, Nadav David, Beth Blum, Mai Schwartz, Rabbi Alissa Wise, Noa Grayevsky, Kate Poole, Michal David, Kayla Glick, Alana Krivo-Kaufman, Sarit Cantor, and Enzi Tanner. Thank you to Matir Asruim comrades and the South Minneapolis radical Jewish community: I'm so grateful to be learning new ways of being together and I'm deeply honored to be growing together.

Thank you to the people and places who help me believe I can write: Roan Boucher for reading everything, Josina Manu Maltzman for telling me I'm a writer, Sara Yukimoto-Saltman for structure, Sarina Partridge for song, Mary Lynn Ellis for decades of teaching in every conversation, Claudia Horwitz and Susan Raffo for writing and organizing and deep care in both, and the Fields at Rootsprings, stewarded by Signe V. Harriday, Alice Butts, Zoe Hollomon, and Erin Sharkey, for sacred space to write.

Thank you to my friends who are family. Katie, thank you for making house and being home. Cindy, for decades of friendship, learning each other and the world together. Becky, Lex, Devika, Moe, Roan, Cindy, Katie: thank you for loving me, rooting for me, and allowing me the blessing of loving you.

Ariana, thank you for every mikvah, every blessing, every word of love and support, every moon. I love learning each other's hearts and speech patterns, walking each other's dogs, holding hands in the hardest things. Being partners in our many schemes and dreams makes everything I do infinitely more possible and more joyful.

To my parents: Thank you for truly everything. Thank you for instilling in me the profound embodied knowing that I am held in fiercely loving community stretching back and forward beyond what I can comprehend. Mom, thank you for making me a writer. Dad, thank you for believing in me, even, especially, when you didn't agree with me. This is for you both.

GLOSSARY &
TEXT LIBRARY

Glossary

Ableism: The system of oppression that marginalizes disabled people, creates the concept of a normal and able body, and celebrates and privileges those bodies and minds.

Abolition: The act of ending and dismantling violent systems and institutions. Growing out of the movement to abolish slavery in the nineteenth century, today current movements work to abolish prisons and police. Scholar Ruth Wilson Gilmore teaches, "Abolition is not absence, it is presence. What the world will become already exists in fragments and pieces, experiments and possibilities. So those who feel in their gut deep anxiety that abolition means knock it all down, scorch the earth and start something new, let that go. Abolition is building the future from the present, in all of the ways we can."[1]

Anti-Black racism: The specific ways that race-based hatred particularly targets Black people and Blackness. Naming anti-Black racism illuminates the ways in which the U.S. was constructed on anti-Blackness stemming from the transatlantic slave trade.

Anti-racism: Commitment to fighting against racist ideology and the material consequences of racism. Racism creates a hierarchy of racial identities and allocates resources and freedoms accordingly. Anti-racism is the ongoing practice of challenging racism in ourselves, dismantling racist systems, and working to repair the harms caused by centuries of structural racism.

Antisemitism: Hatred of and violence against Judaism and Jewish people.

Anti-Zionism: Philosophy, practice, and movements that counter Zionism as a Jewish supremacist form of nationalism. At the advent of modern political Zionism in the late nineteenth/early twentieth centuries, most Jews opposed Zionism as unrealistic, counter to Jewish messianic theologies, and at odds with contemporary Jewish life. Opponents of Palestinian freedom often claim anti-Zionist positions are inherently antisemitic, in efforts to discredit legitimate critiques of Israel's foundational inequalities. Contemporary anti-Zionist positions range across a spectrum of beliefs and organizing strategies.

Ashkenazi אַשְׁכְּנַז: Jews of European descent. Originally the designation was specific to Jews of the Rhineland in what is now Germany, beginning around 800–900CE; over time the term expanded to include Central, Eastern, and Western European Jews.

Beit din בֵּית דִּין, plural batei din: A Jewish governing body, made up of three learned Jews, versed in halacha and/or the particular Jewish communal guidelines and values of that community, that rules on status and makes decisions.

Beit midrash בֵּית מִדְרָשׁ, plural batei midrash: Literally, house of study. Place where Jewish learning happens.

Beta Yisrael ቤተ እስራኤል: Ethiopian Jewish community. Traces roots to exiles from the destruction of the First Temple, 586 BCE.

BIJOCSM: Acronym for Black, Indigenous, Jew of Color, Sephardi, and Mizrahi.

Bikur cholim בִּקּוּר חוֹלִים: The mitzvah of visiting the sick.

BIPOC: Acronym for Black, Indigenous, People of Color.

Boycott, Divestment and Sanctions (BDS) Movement: Inspired by the South African anti-apartheid movement, BDS is a Palestinian-led movement launched in 2005 to pressure Israel to comply with international law and to end its discriminatory apartheid policies through mounting boycott, divestment, and sanction campaigns targeting corporations, governments, and other institutions that are invested in or otherwise enabling Israel's practices that violate Palestinians' human rights. Its three baseline demands are (1) the end of the occupation and colonization of Palestinian lands; (2) full and equal rights for Palestinians inside Israel; and (3) the right of Palestinian refugees to return home.

Capitalism: Unsustainable economic system and violent set of social relations; capitalism is based on production and profit, and requires the exploitation of land, resources, and people's labor.

Chag חַג, plural chaggim חַגִּים: Holiday. *See also:* Moed

Challah חלה: Bread that has had challah "taken" from it. If the dough is made with at least four cups of flour, an ounce of the dough is separated from it and burned, in remembrance of the sacrifices in the Temple. For dough over fourteen cups, the blessing on separating challah is said.

Cheit חֵט: Literally "missing the mark." Sin.

Chevra kadisha חֶבְרָה קַדִּישָׁא: Jewish burial society, a group that ritually washes and prepares the bodies of our beloved dead for burial.

Chiyyuv חִיּוּב: Obligation. In halacha, chiyyuv refers to the obligation to perform certain mitzvot. Expanding on this concept, we may feel chiyyuv to ethical and moral practices or actions (i.e., chiyyuv to practice solidarity).

Chol ha'moed חוֹל הַמּוֹעֵד: Intermediate days of the weeklong festivals of Passover and Sukkot. Chol ha'moed days are different from the first and last days of a festival, in that work is not prohibited, but these days are still part of sacred time and include the particular practices of the festival (i.e., refraining from eating unleavened bread, living in the sukkah).

Christian hegemony: The concept that describes Christianity's power and dominance and the assumption of Christian norms in culture and thought.

Chumash חוּמָשׁ: A compiled version of the five books of Torah, organized by the weekly Torah portions, including the haftorah readings. From the root word חמש, five.

Chuppah חֻפָּה: Wedding canopy. Originally the marriage bed.

Colonization: Invasion, land theft, and genocide of Indigenous people. Colonization is ongoing, and includes the destruction of cultures and lifeways, the intentional separation of families and communities, the outlawing of spiritual practices and traditions, and the ongoing erasure of Indigenous peoples. Both the U.S. and Israel are settler-colonial states, founded on colonization perpetrated by Europeans. Indigenous people continue to exist and resist, in the face of five hundred years of colonization of Turtle Island.

Conservative Movement: In nineteenth-century Germany, the Conservative Movement emerged from the Positive-Historical School of Judaism as a middle way between the Reform and Orthodox strains of Judaism. The movement advocates for adherence to tradition and halacha, while allowing for certain modernist changes, decided by a central collective rabbinic authority.

Diaspora גָּלוּת, galut: The Greek word for dispersion, first used in the Septuagint, the Greek translation of the Hebrew Bible. Commonly understood also as exile.

Diasporism: A set of ethical, political philosophies and creative expressions that embrace, rather than shun, Jewish dispersion around the globe, outside of the land of Yisrael.

Disability justice: A movement and an ideology working to dismantle ableism, the systemic and interpersonal oppression of people with disabilities. The term was developed in 2005 by the Disability Justice Collective, a group including Patty Berne, Mia Mingus, Stacey Milbern, Leroy F. Moore Jr., and Eli Clare.

Drash דְּרַשׁ: An interpretation of a text. "To drash," to expound upon. A "drasha" is a teaching on the text.

Eretz Yisrael אֶרֶץ יִשְׂרָאֵל: Biblical name for the land now known as Palestine/Israel.

Erev עֶרֶב: lit: the evening, eve. Jewish days begin at sundown, and so holidays begin at sundown, usually with a post-sunset service (i.e., erev Rosh Hashanah).

Feminism: Political ideology that works to dismantle systemic and interpersonal oppression of women and gender minorities, and sees the liberation of people of all genders as central to the liberation of all people. From its origins in the Suffragist movement of the 1900s, through the Women's Liberation movement in the 1960s, and still to this day, so-called feminists have too often centered white, straight, middle- and upper-class women. The "Trans Exclusionary Radical Feminist" moniker refers to transphobic self-identified feminists who have co-opted the language of feminism to further transphobia. Bell hooks wrote in her 2000 *Feminism Is for Everybody: Passionate Politics*, "As long as women are using class or race power to dominate other women, feminist sisterhood cannot be fully realized."

Haftorah הַפְטָרָה: Supplemental weekly readings from Nevi'im (Prophets) read in some communities on Shabbat and on holidays following the Torah reading.

Halacha הֲלָכָה: Literally "the way to walk." Rabbinic Judaism's legal framework. Halacha is pluralist and multivocal, which is to say there is no one definitive halachic answer to any question: different Jewish communities have always created specific halacha.

Havurah חֲבוּרָה: A self-organizing Jewish community with a horizontal organizational structure, typically without a rabbi as leader. The havurah movement began in the 1960s.

Igbo Jews: Jewish communities among the Igbo people in Nigeria. Some Igbo Jews trace their lineage back to the tribes of Gad, Zevulun, and

Menasseh, Jacob's sons and grandson. They likely made their way to Nigeria in waves of migration and diaspora from the Babylonian and Roman exiles, and perhaps grew with the entry of Jewish traders.

Indigenous: People with collective belonging to a specific place. Kim Tallbear writes in the 2013 "Genomic articulations of indigeneity," "Indigenous peoples . . . have evolved a more multifaceted definition of 'indigenous' that entangles political self-determination and mutual networking for survival in a global world."[2]

Intersectionality: Coined by Black feminist scholar Kimberlé Crenshaw in 1989 to describe the ways that systems of oppression are overlaid onto each other, and how they affect, magnify, and change each other to become more than the sum of their parts. Gender, sexuality, class status, disability, and more influence the ways we experience oppression and privilege regarding our racialization.

Islamophobia: Hatred and bias against Muslim people, expressed interpersonally and weaponized by the U.S. and other colonial powers.

JOCISM: Acronym for Jews of Color, Indigenous, Sephardi, and Mizrahi Jews.

Kabbalah: Influential Jewish mystical tradition that blossomed in thirteenth-century Spain, centering around study of the Zohar.

Kahal קָהֵל: Assembly, community.

Karaite Judaism יהדות קראית: A stream of Judaism that holds Torah law to be supreme authority, does not participate in halacha or consider the Talmud to be oral Torah or divinely inspired. Traces early roots, emerges as a distinct, named movement in 9th century Baghdad.

Kavannah כַּוָּנָה: Spiritual intention.

Keva קֶבַע: Fixed parameters.

Kittel קיטל: Yiddish. A white linen or cotton robe. Ashkenazi in origin. Worn under the chuppah, at the Passover seder, on Yom Kippur, and when buried. The kittel is first worn at the wedding. It is a powerful link between sacred moments of life and death. Traditionally worn only by men; in many communities people of all genders wear a kittel.

Leftist: A person who holds politically left, progressive politics that center social, cultural, economic justice, and human rights. Originated at the 1789 National Assembly in France when supporters of the king rallied to his right and supporters of the revolution rallied to his left. Refers to a wide spectrum of political tendencies and movements.

LGBTQIA2S+: Acronym for Lesbian, Gay, Bisexual, Transgender, Queer, Intersex, Asexual, Two-Spirit.

Maariv מַעֲרִיב: The evening prayer service. Traditionally connected to the patriarch Jacob.

Machzor מַחְזוֹר: literally "cycle." Refers to the special prayerbook used on the High Holy Days.

Megillah מְגִילָּה: Scroll. Each megillah is associated with a different holiday. The megillot and their holidays are: Ruth (Shavuot), Esther (Purim), Lamentations (Tisha b'Av), Song of Songs (Pesach), and Ecclesiastes (Sukkot).

Melacha מְלָאכָה: Work that is forbidden on Shabbat and Yom Tov. Torah gives a few examples of work that is forbidden on Shabbat (like labor in a field, kindling fire). In the Mishnah, the rabbis list thirty-nine categories of work that are prohibited on Shabbat, all related to the labor required to build the Mishkan in the Wilderness.

Midrash מִדְרָשׁ: Exegesis on Torah. Creative process of storytelling or using grammar to account for inconsistencies in theology or content of Torah. AKA "fan fiction."

Mincha מִנְחָה: The afternoon prayer service. Traditionally connected to the patriarch Isaac.

Minhag מִנְהָג, plural minhagim מנהגים: lit. custom. In some cases of a conflict between a custom or the letter of the law, the rabbis rule with minhag because of the meaning it has in people's lives.

Minyan מִנְיָן, plural minyanim מִנְיָנִים: Literally count, number. A gathering of ten Jewish people needed to recite certain prayers.

Mitzvah מִצְוָה, plural mitzvot מִצְוֹת: Commandment.

Mizrahi מִזְרָחִי: Jewish cultures of the SWANA region, the oldest locations of Jewish cultures. Term primarily came into use as a political identity to counter Ashkenazi dominance and anti-Arab racism in Israel.

Moed מוֹעֵד: Festival, referring specifically to Sukkot, Pesach, and Shavuot.

Musaf מוּסָף: Meaning "additional sacrifice," it refers to the additional service that is added to the liturgy on Shabbat, holidays, and Rosh Chodesh that takes the place of sacrifices that were offered in the time of Temple. Some denominations may omit Musaf.

Mussar מוּסָר: Jewish ethical movement that began in nineteenth-century Lithuania focusing on spiritual and ethical discipline and values-aligned ways of fulfilling mitzvot.

Mutual Aid: collective organizing to meet each other's needs, integrated with an analysis of systemic and root causes, and aligned with actions to change the current systems in which we're living. Dean Spade writes: "We see examples of mutual aid in every single social movement, whether it's people raising money for workers on strike, setting up a car pooling system during the Montgomery Bus Boycott, putting drinking water in the desert for migrants crossing the border, training each other in emergency medicine because ambulance response time in poor neighborhoods is too slow, raising money to pay for abortions for those who can't afford them, or coordinating letter-writing to prisoners."[3]

al-Nakba النكبة: Literally "the Catastrophe" in Arabic, referring to the mass displacement and forced exile of Palestinians leading up to the establishment of the State of Israel in 1948 continuing to this day.

Neiilah נְעִילָה: Literally "closing," the final service on Yom Kippur. The name references the closing gates of repentance evoked in the service.

Nusach נֻסַּח, plural nusachot נוסחאות: Can refer to the text or the musical mode of a service. Nusach differs across geographic region and community, and for specific services. For example, Shabbat nusach is different from weekday nusach.

Organizing: Bringing people together to build power for the sake of changing material political conditions.

Orientalism: Term coined by Edward W. Said in his 1978 book *Orientalism*, to refer to how the West engages with SWANA people and places, presuming superiority, in ways that empower and fuel Western imperialism and colonialism.

Orthodox: Originally Orthodoxy grew in nineteenth-century Germany as a response to the Reform movement, advocating for adherence to traditional, halachic Jewish observance. Not a denomination with a single, articulated leadership body, Orthodoxy can be seen as an umbrella term for a range of movements and affiliations, including Modern Orthodoxy, Haredi, Hasidism, and Open Orthodoxy.

Parshah ha'Shavua פָּרָשַׁת הַשָּׁבוּעַ, plural parashiyot: Literally portion of the week, referring to the part of the Torah read each week. There are fifty-four portions, meaning that at least two weeks of every year are a "double portion," two parashiyot read together. The vast majority of Jewish communities read the same parshah every week. Many communities read in a triennial cycle, which now refers to sectioning the parshah into thirds, and reading the first third of the parshah in year one, the second third in year two, and the third third in year three. Divisions between parashiyot were made by the Masoretes (lit, 'Masters of the Tradition'), groups of scribe-scholars active from the fifth to the tenth centuries CE, in the cities of Tiberias, Jerusalem, and Babylonia.

Piyyut פִּיּוּט, plural piyutim פִּיּוּטִם: liturgical poems from various generations of Jewish history and geographies that are read, chanted or sung during the liturgy, often of specific holidays.

Prekante, plural Prekantes: Ladino, Personal women's prayers written in the vernacular. From *Ritual Medical Lore of Sephardic Women: Sweetening the Spirits, Healing the Sick* by Isaac Jack Lévy and Rosemary Lévy Zumwalt, "Often in published works, the term prekante has not been translated at all. When translated, it has been rendered as 'incantation,' more often than not, giving the Latin or Portuguese meaning of 'enchantment' and 'bewitchment.'"

Queer: Umbrella term for gender and sexuality that is outside cisgender and heterosexual. Reclaimed slur.

Rabbinic Judaism: All the streams and cultures of Judaism that trace lineage through the rabbis who created the Talmud and halacha. Most contemporary denominations are rabbinic (i.e., Conservative, Reform, Reconstructionist, Orthodox, etc.).

Radical: Latin for "root." Radical politics refers to investigating root causes of problems, and working for transformative change to systems of oppression.

Reconstructionism, Reconstructionist Judaism: Jewish movement founded by Rabbi Mordechai Kaplan in the 1920s to the 1940s. Reconstructionism understands Jewishness as evolving over time, based in historical context, and not only being composed of religious practice and theological belief but also encompassing a sense of belonging in community and taking part in Jewish life, practices, customs, and ritual.

Reform: Tracing its origins to nineteenth-century German Jewish organizing for modernizing Judaism to be more compatible with European Christian life, the Reform Movement is now the largest denomination of affiliated Jews. Historically, the Reform Movement has emphasized personal choice over halachic or rabbinic authority.

Renewal: Growing out of the havurah movement and counterculture of the U.S. 1960s, led for many years by founding rabbi Zalman Schachter-Shlomi, the Renewal Movement is known for bringing together Kabbalistic and Chassidic Jewish mystical traditions with socially progressive, egalitarian Jewish communities.

Reparations: Financial compensation for wide-scale harm caused, most notably the campaign for reparations to Black Americans whose African ancestors were kidnapped and enslaved, as well as from the German government to Jews whose ancestors were killed during the Nazi holocaust, and from the South African government to Black South Africans following Apartheid.

Rosh Chodesh רֹאשׁ חֹדֶשׁ: The beginning of the new month. Each month begins at Rosh Chodesh, literally the head of the month, on the new moon. Rosh Chodesh is celebrated by praying Hallel, the service of Psalms sung in praise for new months and holidays. Rosh Chodesh traditionally was a day of rest for women, and the tradition of Rosh Chodesh circles has been continued by feminists. Rosh Chodesh circles sometimes connect the moon to menstruation, which for some is deeply meaningful, but is also exclusionary and reductive. We are grateful to be part of communities and Rosh Chodesh circles that do not essentialize biology to experiences of womanhood or femmeness.

Salting: The process by which union organizers obtain jobs in nonunionized workplaces to agitate and organize their coworkers to create a union.

Selichot סְלִיחוֹת: Penitential prayers, primarily recited in the Jewish month of Elul and during Rosh Hashanah and Yom Kippur

Sephardi: Jewish cultures of the Iberian Peninsula, now called Spain and Portugal.

Shacharit שַׁחֲרִת: The morning prayer service. Traditionally connected to the patriarch Abraham. Torah is read during this service on Mondays, Thursdays, Shabbat, and Rosh Chodesh (the new month).

Shalosh Regalim שָׁלֹשׁ רְגָלִים: Literally, the three pilgrimage festivals. Refers to Pesach, Shavuot, and Sukkot.

Shlilat ha'golah שְׁלִילָת הַגָּלוּת: Literally, "negation of the diaspora." Zionist philosophy developed in the early twentieth century that believes life in diaspora made Jews weak and inferior.

SWANA: South West Asia and North Africa: decolonial term for what is often referred to from a Eurocentric perspective as the "middle east."

Ta'anit תַּעֲנִית: A ritual fast.

Tachanun תחנון: Literally, "supplication," aka נפילת אפיים nefilat apayim, falling on the face. Recited from a seated and hunched over posture. Penitential prayer following the recitation of the Amidah during Shacharit and mincha during the week, but not on Shabbat.

Tallit טַלִּית: Four-cornered garment that has tzitzit, sacred fringes, dangling off the four corners of the garment. Tallit is worn during the Shacharit service and once a year in the evening for the Kol Nidre service on Yom Kippur.

Te'amim טְעָמִים: Hebrew. טראָפּ Trope in Yiddish. Diacritics in English. Musical system of chanting from Tanakh, with marks indicating musical notes. There are different systems of te'amim for different holidays. The trope marks are consistent in Jewish communities around the world, while the melodies vary in different communities by region and culture. Te'am means flavor in Hebrew, and the music is understood to be another layer of commentary and flavor on the text.

Teshuvah תְּשׁוּבָה: Repentance. From the root שׁוב, meaning return.

Tfillah תְּפִלָּה: prayer. Plural, tefilot, תְּפִלּוֹת. Can refer to prayer in general. Is also a name for the Amidah, central prayer of the whole service, said three times a day (morning, afternoon, and evening).

Tikkun Olam תִּיקּוּן עוֹלָם: Repairing the world. First appearance in the Mishnah refers to actions that keep society functioning—making decisions מפני תיקון עולם, mipnei tikkun olam, for the sake of Tikkun Olam. Later, in Lurianic Kabbalah, Rabbi Isaac Luria describes the creation of the world and the myth of the shattering vessels that could not contain God's goodness. Following the shattering, these sparks of the Divine landed on earth, contained in klipot, husks. Mitzvot (in its most religious understanding, not "good deeds") reveal these sparks. In the 1960s Jews began using Tikkun Olam as a term to refer to acts of social justice.

Tkhine תְּחִנָּה, plural tkhines תְּחִנּוֹת: Yiddish, "supplications." Personal women's prayers written in the vernacular.

Trans, transgender: Gender identity of someone who identifies with a different gender than the one assigned to them at birth.

Transformative Justice: Mia Mingus writes: "(TJ) is a political framework and approach for responding to violence, harm and abuse. At its most basic, it seeks to respond to violence without creating more violence and/or engaging in harm reduction to lessen the violence." (See Elu, page 277.)

Turtle Island: In some Indigenous creation stories the land is supported on the back of a turtle; Turtle Island is a name for the North American continent used by many Indigenous people and allies.

Tzedakah צְדָקָה: Just giving of money or other resources.

Tzedek צֶדֶק: Justice.

White supremacy: Belief that white people are superior to other racialized people, manifesting in interpersonal prejudice, systemic violence and oppression, institutionalized policies and practices, and international warfare and domination.

Yahrtzeit יאָרצײַט: German for "year's time." The date of death as observed on the Jewish calendar. On this day the Mourner's Kaddish is recited. There is a minhag of lighting a yahrtzeit candle that burns for the twenty-four hours of the day, as well as visiting the graves of the dead.

Yamim Noraim יָמִים נוֹרָאִים: Literally, days of awe. Refers to Rosh Hashanah and Yom Kippur, and the ten days in between. Sometimes used to refer to the entire holiday season beginning with Elul.

Yom Tov יוֹם טוֹב: Holiday. Melacha, productive labor, is prohibited on Shabbat and Yom Tov. Reminder—the Jewish day begins at sundown, and Jewish holidays begin at sundown!

Zichrono l'vracha זִכְרוֹנוֹ לִבְרָכָה: "May his memory be a blessing," phrase that is said after saying the name of someone who has died. Abbreviated in writing as *z"l* or ז״ל. Feminine singular is זיכרונה לברכה (zikhrona liv'rakha), the masculine plural is זיכרונם לברכה (zikhronam liv'rakha), and the feminine plural is זיכרונן לברכה (zikhronan liv'rakha). While there are other similar phrases to say after saying the name of a deceased person, zichrono/a livracha is most common.

Zionism: Jewish nationalist movement to create a Jewish nation-state. As a political movement, Zionism originated in late nineteenth-century Europe.

˙ Text Library

Tanakh תָּנָ"ךְ: abbreviation that comprises Torah, Nevi'im (Prophets), and Ketuvim (Writings)

> **Torah** תּוֹרָה: Five books of Moses. Beresheet (Genesis) Shemot (Exodus) Vayikra (Leviticus) Bamidbar (Numbers) Devarim (Deuteronomy).
>
> **Nevi'im** נְבִיאִם: Prophets. Joshua, Judges, I Samuel, II Samuel, I Kings, II Kings, Isaiah, Jeremiah, Ezekiel, Hosea, Joel, Amos, Obadiah, Jonah, Micah, Nahum, Habakkuk, Zephaniah, Haggai, Zechariah, Malachi
>
> **Ketuvim** כְּתוּבִים: Writings. Psalms, Proverbs, Job, Song of Songs, Ruth, Lamentations, Ecclesiastes, Esther, Daniel, Ezra, Nehemiah, I Chronicles, II Chronicles.

Talmud תַּלְמוּד: a vast compendium of Jewish practice, law, stories, and debate. There are two versions of the Talmud, the *Talmud Bavli* (originating in Babylonia) and *Talmud Yerushalmi* (from Palestine). The Babylonian Talmud is the dominant of the two. The Talmud is made up of two parts:

> **Mishnah** מִשְׁנָה: compiled around 200CE, covering hundreds of years of ritual practice and legal development, the Mishnah is the first major work of Rabbinic literature. Organized into six orders, known as sedarim, singular seder סֵדֶר, subdivided into chapters, known as masechet מַסֶּכֶת, and subdivided into numbered lines.
>
> **Gemara** גְּמָרָה: structured as commentary on the Mishnah, but covering content way beyond the material in the Mishnah. The Gemara was compiled from the third to the eighth centuries CE.

Responsa: Answers to questions on Jewish practice that arise from new situations otherwise not imagined or discussed by halacha established in previous generations. Responsa establish new law that can then become precedent for future questions.

Shulchan Aruch שֻׁלְחָן עָרוּךְ: Literally "the set table," the Shukchan Arukh is the foremost code of halacha. Sixteenth century, compiled by Rabbi Yosef Karo.

Kol Bo כֹּל בּוֹ: Halachic guide compiled in c.1250–c.1450 CE.

Vayikra Rabbah וַיִּקְרָא רַבָּה: a midrash on the book of Vayikra (Leviticus), compiled between the fifth and seventh centuries.

Zohar זֹהַר: literally, splendor, radiance. Central text of Jewish mystical tradition, first appeared in thirteenth century Spain, written primarily in Aramaic.

NOTES

Introduction

1   When we call on our ancestors, we are calling on genetic connections, biblical forebears, chosen family, and friends who have become ancestors too soon. We use this word widely, with great hope for how it might nourish us to rely on the wisdom of those who came before us, who link us to other more possible worlds. Whether you are genetically or culturally linked to Jews or not, your Jewish and non-Jewish ancestors have wisdom and help waiting for you.

2.   Z"l is an abbreviation of zichrono livracha (זִכְרוֹנוֹ לִבְרָכָה), may her memory be for a blessing. It is a minhag, a Jewish custom, to say or write when naming a person who has died. There are a range of other honorifics to say, but this is the most common.

3.   A lifetime organizer and writer, Melanie Kaye/Kantrowitz was the founding director of Jews for Racial and Economic Justice in 1990. Her 2007 book *The Colors of Jews: Racial Politics and Radical Diasporism* has shaped understanding of the Jewish Left for decades. She deeply impacted Jewish lesbian culture through her organizing and writing, including editing *Sinister Wisdom* from 1983 to 1987. Learn more about her and read tributes to her at: melaniekayekantrowitz.com/.

4.   We differentiate between Jewish relationships to Eretz Yisrael over the millennia of Jewish life, and modern political Zionism. For further discussion, read "Judaism Beyond Zionism" on page 32.

5.   Grace Lee Boggs and James Boggs, *Revolution and Evolution in the Twentieth Century* (New York: NYU Press, 2008), www.jstor.org/stable/j.ctv12pnr39.

6.   Elisheva Carlebach, *Palaces of Time: Jewish Calendar and Culture in Early Modern Europe* (Cambridge, MA: Belknap Press of Harvard University Press, 2011).

7.   Some Rosh Chodesh circles connect the moon to menstruation, which for some is deeply meaningful, but is also exclusionary and reductive. We are grateful to be part of communities and Rosh Chodesh circles that do not essentialize biology to experiences of womanhood or femmeness.

8.   1 Tishrei: Rosh HaShanah, new year for the world and human beings; 15 Shvat: Tu B'Shvat, new year for the trees; 1 Nisan, spring and new year for kings/change in reign; 1 Elul: new year for animals.

9.   Maimonides, Rabbi Moses ben Maimon, known as the Rambam, calculated the year in his *Mishneh Torah*, compiled in 4930–4940 (1170–1180 CE).

10. The thirty-nine melachot, kinds of work, are drawn from the thirty-nine kinds of labor done to create the Mishkan, the traveling sanctuary, in the Torah.

11. A havurah, חבורה, is an intentional Jewish community that gathers for Shabbat, holidays, and community events. Horizontal leadership is a central facet of havurot, which gained popularity in the 1960s in the US and continue strongly today with organizations like the National Havurah Movement.

12. Aurora Levins Morale. *Medicine Stories: Essays for Radicals* (Durham, NC: Duke University Press: 2019).

13. Arabic for "catastrophe," referring to the displacement of over seven hundred thousand Palestinian people at the founding of Israel in 1948.

14. Coming from the word "explanation" in Hebrew, Hasbara refers to targeted media campaigns to create positive thought about the State of Israel worldwide, relying on misinformation and bias.

15. Students at the Hillel were barred from cosponsoring an event on Pinkwashing with a Palestinian student group, and had to host if off-site. Open Hillel became a movement of student organizers pushing for Jewish life on campus to have space for dissent on Israel. See Laurie Goodstein, "Members of Jewish Student Group Test Permissible Discussion on Israel," *New York Times*, December 28, 2013, sec. U.S., www.nytimes.com/2013/12/29/us/members-of-jewish-student-group-test-permissible-discussion-on-israel.html.

16. As longtime supporters of the movement for Boycott, Divestment and Sanctions of Israel, we support the Palestinian Campaign for the Academic Boycott of Israel, which calls attention to the complicity and actions of Israeli academic institutions in the ongoing occupation of Palestine and discrimination against Palestinians. As of this writing, the college requires students to spend time in Israel for academic credit. We, along with many other students before, during, and after our time at RRC, took part in organizing to challenge this requirement.

17. Jewish relationships to astrology have been, over the millenia, as diverse as they are today. There are debates about astrology in the Talmud: some rabbis state as obvious truth how the month, day of the week, and hour in which we are born impact our personalities, traits, and lives; others proclaim it soothsaying and thus forbidden. Post-Talmudic rabbinic scholars Saadiah Gaon (also known as Rasag, Cairo, 882–942) and Abraham ben Meir ibn Ezra (also known as ibn Ezra, Spain, 1089–1164) embraced astrology; Rabbi Moshe ben Maimon (Rambam, also known as Maimonides, who lived in Spain, Morocco and Egypt, 1137–1204) rejected it. Astrological signs, meanwhile, are all over centuries of Jewish art and decor, including siddurim and synagogues.

18. The incredible Dreaming the World to Come planner by Rebekah Erev and Nomy Lamm explores many more of these connections. Check out: www.dreamingtheworldtocome.com/mystical-associations for more.

Frameworks

1. HaShem, literally means "the Name" and is one of the many ways to refer to the unknowable proper name of God within Jewish tradition.

2. "Judaism is whatever Jews are doing at a given time," is an insight we learned from our teacher of Biblical history, Dr. Elsie Stern.

3. From the same root as the word "to go" or "to walk," halacha can be translated as "the way" and refers to Jewish law, derived from the Oral Torah. The Oral

Torah refers to the Talmud, a compendium of stories and law compiled from approximately 200 to 500CE. This is in contrast with the Written Torah (Beresheet, Shemot, Bamidbar, Vayikra, and Devarim).

4.   Leora Batnizky, *How Judaism Became a Religion* (New Jersey: Princeton University Press, 2013).

5.   Judith Plaskow, *Standing Again at Sinai: Judaism from a Feminist Perspective* (New York: Harper Collins, 1991), xi–xii.

6.   Arielle Isack, "What Comes Next for Jews of Color Activism?" *Jewish Currents*, March 23, 2023, jewishcurrents.org/what-comes-next-for-jews-of-color-activism.

7.   Kenneth Kahn, "The Jewish Chicken Farmers of Petaluma: Why Remember?" *Jewish Currents*, February 19, 2018.

8.   Isaiah 42:6.

9.   In 1917, the UK's foreign secretary Arthur Balfour made the first public statement offering support to the Zionist project of a "national home for the Jewish people" in Palestine.

10. Susannah Heschel, "Ending Exile with the Prophetic Voice of the Diasporic Jew," Contending Modernities, September 25, 2020, contendingmodernities.nd.edu/theorizing-modernities/ending-exile/. Daniel Boyarin, *A Traveling Homeland: The Babylonian Talmud as Diaspora* (Philadelphia: University of Pennsylvania Press, 2015).

11. Inspired by the South African anti-apartheid movement, BDS is a Palestinian-led movement launched in 2005 to pressure Israel to comply with international law and to end its discriminatory apartheid policies through mounting boycott, divestment and sanction campaigns targeting corporations, governments, and other institutions that are invested in or otherwise enabling Israel's practices that violate Palestinians' human rights. Its three baseline demands are (1) end the occupation and colonization of Palestinian lands; (2) full and equal rights for Palestinians inside Israel; and (3) the right of refugees to return home. Learn more at: bdsmovement. net/call.

12. For more, see Ella Shohat, "Sephardim in Israel: Zionism from the Standpoint of Its Jewish Victims," *Social Text* no. 19/20 (1988): 1–35, doi.org/10.2307/466176.

13. The Israeli military referred to its 2012 bombing of Gaza as Amud Anan, Operation "Pillar of Cloud," a reference to the Exodus story and a "pillar of cloud" leading the way and protecting the Israelite people traveling through the Wilderness.

14. Heschel, "Ending Exile."

15. Rabbi Obadiah ben Yaakov Sforno, known as Sforno, lived 1470–1550, in Italy.

16. Thank you to Rabbi Alissa Wise for teaching us this and many other impactful texts.

17. Melanie Kaye/Kantrowitz, *The Colors of Jews: Racial Politics and Radical Diasporism* (Bloomington, IN: Indiana University Press, 2007), 199.

18. In creative projects like *Jewish Currents* (Jacob Plitman, "On an Emerging Diasporism," *Jewish Currents*, Spring 2018, jewishcurrents.org/on-an-emerging-diasporism) and the Diaspora podcast by Jewish Voice for Peace (Tallie Ben-Daniel and Nava EtShalom, Diaspora Podcast, December 5, 2019, diasporapodcast. simplecast.com/), through countless scholars and writers, and through organizing by groups like Jews on Ohlone Land, Miknaf Ha'aretz, and Linke Fligl. Through seven years of leading discussions and workshops on diasporism, Linke Fligl

articulated the need for "diasporism that invites us into more accountable land relationship" with "the lands you call home, the lands your people came from, the land of Israel/Palestine." ("Linke Fligl Land Stories," linkefligl.com/infographics).

19. Kaye/Kantrowitz, *The Colors of Jews*, 199.

20. Ursula K. Le Guin, "Every Land," www.ursulakleguin.com/every-land.

21. Mishnah Pirkei Avot 1:1.

22. See Anna Elena Torres's "The Anarchist Sage/*Der Goen Anarkhist*: Rabbi Yankev-Meir Zalkind and Religious Genealogies of Anarchism," *In geveb*, February 2019.

23. Trans Halakha Project, Svara, svara.org/trans-halakha-project/.

24. Jacob Staub, "Reconstructionist Judaism & Halacha," accessed September 10, 2023, www.myjewishlearning.com/article/reconstructionist-judaism-halakhah/.

25. Plaskow, *Standing Again at Sinai: Judaism from a Feminist Perspective*, xi–xii.

26. See Cara Page and Erica Woodland, *Healing Justice Lineages: Dreaming at the Crossroads of Liberation, Collective Care, and Safety* (Berkeley: North Atlantic Books, 2023).

27. For explorations of emotional, communal, and social needs in movement spaces, see Susan Raffo, "At Least Two Layers of Support: An Anatomy of Collective Care," in *Liberated to the Bone: Histories. Bodies. Futures* (Chico, CA: AK Press, 2022), 116–25, and Maurice Mitchell, "Building Resilient Organizations," the Forge, November 29, 2022, forgeorganizing.org/article/building-resilient-organizations.

28. A version of this section was originally published by Reconstructing Judaism as part of *An Introduction to Trauma, Healing & Resilience for Rabbis, Jewish Educators and Organizers*, by Rabbi Jessica Rosenberg, March 2020, www.reconstructingjudaism.org/introduction-trauma-healing-resilience-rabbi-jessica-rosenberg/.

29. Maria Yellow Horse Brave Heart, "The Return to the Sacred Path: Healing the historical trauma response among the Lakota," *Smith College Studies in Social Work* 68, no. 3 (1998): 287–305.

30. Robert Liberles, *Salo Wittmayer Baron: Architect of Jewish History* (NY: New York University Press, 1995), 117–18.

31. This concept is explored in more depth in Jessica Rosenberg's "Reunderstanding Jewish Historical Trauma: Moving From the River to the Watershed," *Evolve*, December 27, 2021, evolve.reconstructingjudaism.org/reunderstanding-jewish-historical-trauma-moving-from-the-river-to-the-watershed/.

32. Sousan Abadian, "Cultural Healing: When Cultural Renewal is Reparative and When it is Toxic," *Journal of Indigenous Wellbeing* 4, no. 2 (Fall 2006), journalindigenouswellbeing.co.nz/media/2018/10/2_Abadian.pdf.

33. Tisha b'Av is a holiday focused on destruction and grief, and offers us ample ritual technology to mourn Black lives ended by police and state violence. Sukkot traditionally includes a water libation ritual, and brings our attention to the sacredness of the earth and the harvest.

In 2016, Indigenous and settler Jews were among the thousands who traveled to Oceti Sakowin camp at Standing Rock to protest the Dakota Access Pipeline and answer the call from Indigenous leaders to join the water protectors. During Sukkot, Jewish water protectors sought permission from camp elders to build a sukkah, and detailed their experience of connecting the festival to the camp's core statement "mni wiconi" (mini we-choh-nee), Lakota for "water is life." Annie

Kaufman and Liat Melnick, "Called to Standing Rock," *Lilith Magazine*, November 15, 2016, lilith.org/2016/11/called-to-standing-rock/.

34. Julia Watts Belser, "God on Wheels: Disability and Jewish Feminist Theology," *Tikkun Magazine*, Fall 2014.

35. Jess Belasco, "The Needy for a Pair of Sandals: Jacob's Unsettling, and Our Own," Svara Blog, December 2, 2022, svara.org/needy-for-a-pair-of-sandals/.

36. Sins Invalid, "About Us," accessed February 12, 2023, www.sinsinvalid.org/about-us.

37. "10 Principles of Disability Justice," Sins Invalid, September 17, 2015, www.sinsinvalid.org/blog/10-principles-of-disability-justice.

38. Leah Lakshmi Piepzna-Samarasinha, *Care Work: Dreaming Disability Justice* (Vancouver: Arsenal Pulp Press, 2018), 41.

39. Beresheet 18:1–2.

40. Leah Lakshmi Piepzna-Samarasinha, *The Future Is Disabled: Prophecies, Love Notes and Mourning Songs* (Vancouver: Arsenal Pulp Press, 2022), 13.

41. The Combahee River Collective, "The Combahee River Collective Statement," April 1977.

42. "How Tokenism Affects Jews of Color and 5 Ways Allies Can Interrupt It," Jews of Color Initiative Newsletter, January 2022, jewsofcolorinitiative.org/newsletter/how-tokenism-affects-jews-of-color-and-5-ways-allies-can-interrupt-it/.

43. For detailed research and analysis about Jews of Color, see "Beyond the Count: Perspectives and Lived Experiences of Jews of Color," commissioned by the Jews of Color Initiative, August 12, 2021, jewsofcolorinitiative.org/wp-content/uploads/2021/08/BEYONDTHECOUNT.FINAL_.8.12.21.pdf.

44. Gordon Kaufman, "Theology as Imaginative Construction," *Journal of American Academy of Religion* 50, no. 1 (March 1982): 78.

45. B. Talmud Chagigah 14b.

46. Rabbi Dr. Erin Leib Smoker teaches on second naivete: "A term borrowed from Catholic theologian Peter Wust by philosophers Paul Ricoeur and later Emmanuel Levinas, Akiva Ernst Simon, a student of Martin Buber's, wrote extensively on 'ha'temimut ha'shniya' (second naiveté) and brought it to the attention of modern Jewish thinkers. Second naiveté is faith reconstituted in the aftermath of criticism. It is the willingness to re-embrace religious language and religious modalities after a rupture—intellectual or experiential—has robbed one of innocence. In the words of Ricoeur, 'Beyond the desert of criticism, we wish to be called again' (The Symbolism of Evil, p. 249)." www.sefaria.org/sheets/287180.116?lang=bi&with=all&lang2=en.

47. Octavia E. Butler, *Parable of the Sower* (New York: Four Walls Eight Windows, 1993).

48. See the story of Moses in Rabbi Akiva's Beit Midrash in B. Menachot 29b:3–5.

49. Devarim 31:6.

Tishrei

1. Rosh HaShanah, Tu b'Shvat, Rosh Chodesh Nisan, and Rosh Chodesh Elul.

2. Dating back as early as the Mishnah, codified in 200CE, Jewish prayer has centered around three daily prayer times: Shacharit (שַׁחֲרִת), morning, mincha (מִנְחָה), afternoon, and ma'ariv (מַעֲרִב), evening. Each prayer service has a set structure and order. On Shabbat and holidays, we have the same services, following the same basic

N
O
T
E
S

365

structure, with additional prayers, songs, readings, and melodic differences for the holiday. There is Musaf, literally the additional service, on Shabbat, Rosh Chodesh, and holidays.

3. We begin at the end. See Chapter 12 on Elul for an exploration of the king dwelling in the field.

4. Rabbi Moshe ben Maimon, known as the Rambam, influential rabbi and philosopher who lived in Spain, Morocco, and Egypt, 1137–1204.

5. B. Rosh HaShanah 10b–11a.

6. Beresheet 41:14.

7. In some Indigenous creation stories, the land is supported on the back of a turtle; Turtle Island is a name for the North American continent used by many Indigenous people and allies. See: Robin Wall Kimmerer, *Braiding Sweetgrass: Indigenous Wisdom, Scientific Knowledge, and the Teachings of Plants* (Milkweed Editions, 2013), 3–5.

8. Wendy Elisheva Somerson, "The Intersection of Anti-Occupation and Queer Jewish Organizing." *Tikkun Magazine* 25, no. 4 (July/August 2010): 58–73.

9. Ronald L. Eisenberg, *Jewish Traditions: A JPS Guide* (Philadelphia: Jewish Publication Society, 2004), 189.

10. Donna Maher, "The Joys of a Mizrahi Rosh Hashanah Seder," Hey Alma, September 2, 2020, www.heyalma.com/the-joys-of-a-mizrahi-rosh-hashanah-seder/.

11. Ashkenazi Jews may wear a kittel (קיטל), a white robe. This tradition dates to the twelfth or thirteenth centuries. In recent decades Sephardi Jews have taken up the custom, but wearing it only on Yom Kippur, whereas Ashkenazi Jews will wear a kittel at their wedding, at Pesach, and at Yom Kippur.

12. Rabbi Linda Holtzman, text message to author, December 9, 2022.

13. So much so, it lives in a huge range of poetry and song, including Leonard Cohen's "Who by Fire."

14. For further exploration of the book of Jonah, see Rabbi Shmuly Yanklowtiz, *The Book of Jonah: A Social Justice Commentary* (New York: CCAR Press, 2020).

15. Annie Cohen, "Feldmestn & Keyvermestn Ritual," High Holidays at Home, highholidaysathome.com/clip/feldmestn.

16. Eddy Portnoy, "The Festive Meal," *Tablet Magazine*, September 24, 2009, www.tabletmag.com/sections/belief/articles/the-festive-meal.

17. Hannah Gold, "Happy Yom Kippur!" Vashti Media, September 24, 2020, vashtimedia.com/2020/09/24/yom-kippur-ball-yiddish-zionism-jeremy-corbyn/.

18. To learn more about chol ha'moed turn to page 222.

19. Rambam, *Mishneh Torah*, Sanctification of the New Month, 3:11.

20. Mishnah Rosh Hashanah 2:2.

21. Bereishit 33:17.

22. A contemporary adaptation of a Temple-time water libation ritual, often honored through dancing and music.

23. Arukh HaShulchan, Orach Chaim 625:3.

24. Vayikra Rabbah 14.

25. "A kosher sukkah must have at least 3 walls, and each wall must have a minimum length of 28 inches (7 tefachim x 7 tefachim). The walls of the sukkah must extend at least 40 inches high, and the walls may not be suspended more than 9 inches above the ground5 (this is a common problem with fabric sukkahs)." oukosher.org/

faqs/minimum-dimensions-sukkah/, citing The Shulchan Aruch, sixteenth-century law code by Rabbi Yosef Karo. See Shulchan Aruch (O.C. 634:1, 633:8, 630:9).

26. B. Sukkah 11b:15.
27. B. Bava Batra 75a:6.
28. Zohar 3:103b.
29. Great Small Works, Portable Shows, greatsmallworks.org/portable.html.
30. Tina Wasserman, "A Savory Sukkot," Reform Judaism, reformjudaism.org/savory-sukkot.
31. See "Indigenous Solidarity on Turtle Island" in the chapter on Shvat.
32. Vayikra 23:40 and discussion in Bereishit Rabbah 15:7.
33. Sefer ha-Hinukh, #285.
34. Richard Siegel, Michael Strassfeld, and Susan Strassfeld, The Jewish Catalog: A Do-It Yourself-Kit (Philadelphia: Jewish Publication Society, 1973).
35. Shulchan Aruch, Orach Chayim 658:3.
36. B. Sukkah 45b:2.
37. Note how lulav refers just to the palm, as well as to the palm-myrtle-willow bundle, as well as to the etrog-palm-myrtle-willow bundle, depending on the application. "Taking lulav" to say the blessing of shaking lulav includes the etrog, in this instance.
38. Mishnah Sukkah 3:1–15. Further, in Sukka 30a:4, "It was also said: Rabbi Ami said, 'A dry [Lulav] is invalid because it is not beautiful, [and] a stolen [Lulav] is invalid because it is for him (the user) a commandment fulfilled through a transgression.'"
39. Rakia Sky Brown, Gabi Kirk, Noah Rubin-Blose, and Miriam Spaerstein, "The Local Lulav," Jewish Currents, September 28, 2018, jewishcurrents.org/decolonize-sukkot.
40. "Why and When Do We Read the Book of Kohelet (Ecclesiastes) in Public?," Responsa by Rabbi Prof. David Golinkin, November 10, 2006, schechter.edu/why-and-when-do-we-read-the-book-of-kohelet-ecclesiastes-in-public-responsa-in-a-moment-volume-1-issue-no-2-october-2006-orah-hayyim-6632-1/.
41. Songs of Songs Rabbah 1:9.
42. Mishnah Sukkah 4:5.
43. Mishnah Rosh Hashanah 1:2.
44. Rabbi Shlomo ben Yitzchak, known as Rashi, 1040–1105 CE, France.
45. B. Megillah 31a.

Cheshvan

1. Further discussion of shmita, the biblically commanded practice of letting the land rest every seventh year, in parsha Behar.
2. Tricia Hersey, "Our work has a framework: REST IS RESISTANCE!" January 11, 2021, thenapministry.wordpress.com/2021/01/11/our-work-is-has-a-framework/.
3. Mishnah Taanit 1:3–4.
4. Jill Hammer, The Jewish Book of Days: A Companion for All Seasons (Philadelphia: Jewish Publication Society, 2006), 59.
5. Midrash Tanhuma Beresheet 11:6.
6. Machzor Vitry supplement 14, cited in Louis Ginzberg, Legends of the Jews, JPS 1938. 6: 204, n. 109.

7. Hammer. *The Jewish Book of Days: A Companion for All Seasons*, 62.

7. Hammer. *The Jewish Book of Days: A Companion for All Seasons*, 62.
8. Beresheet 22:19.
9. Midrash Rabbah 56:11.
10. Rambam, *Mishneh Torah*, Hilchot Teshuva, 2:1.

Kislev

1. "We eat fried foods on Channukah in remembrance of the fat that allowed our traditions, and by extension our people, to survive. Channukah is, in fact, a holiday that celebrates fat as that which sustains and renews us." *A Miracle of Fat* by Rabbi Minna Bromberg, accessed June 27, 2003, www.fattorah.org/blog/a-miracle-of-fat.
2. Arthur O. Waskow, *Seasons of Our Joy: A Modern Guide to the Jewish Holidays* (Boston: Beacon Press, 1982), 91.
3. Gematria, גימטריה, is the practice of counting up the numbers assigned to Hebrew letters in words and phrases to make meaning and find hidden relationships and teaching.
4. B. Shabbat 21b.
5. Zechariah 4:1–6.
6. B. Shabbat 21b.
7. Ibid.
8. Ibid.
9. www.yadvashem.org/artifacts/museum/hanukkah-1932.html
10. A seven-branched candleholder used in Kwanzaa observance.
11. Kohenet Shoshona Akua Brown, "A Kwanzakkah Story," *Unruly*, December 26, 2019, jocsm.org/a-kwanzakkah-story/.
12. Edmund Case, "A New Theory of Intermarriage," Evolve, March 12, 2020, evolve.reconstructingjudaism.org/new-theory-of-intermarriage/#_ftn1.
13. Dar Williams, "The Christians and the Pagans," track 1 on The Christians and the Pagans (EP), Razor & Tie, 1996.
14. "8 Nights, 8 Actions," Ritualwell, accessed June 27, 2023, ritualwell.org/ritual/8-nights-8-actions.
15. Jewish Voice for Peace, "5776 Chanukah Ritual: Companion: May the Light of Justice Shine," December, 2015, https://www.jewishvoiceforpeace.org/wp-content/uploads/2015/12/5776-Chanukah-Ritual-Companion.pdf.
16. Jewish Voice for Peace, "JVP Chapters Host Channukah Actions Against Islamophobia and Racism in 25 Cities," December 21, 2016, jewishvoiceforpeace.org/2016/12/jvp-chapters-host-chanukah-actions-islamophobia-racism-25-cities/.

Tevet

1. Like so many (most) women in Torah, Noah's wife is unnamed. She is given a name in Bereishit Rabbah 23:3, "Rabbi Abba bar Kahana said: Na'amah was Noah's wife. Why was she called Na'amah? Because all of her deeds were pleasant (ne'imim). The Rabbis said this is a different Na'amah. Why was she called Na'amah? Because she beat on a drum to draw people to idol worship." Sandy Eisenberg Sasso understands Na'amah as the mother of all growing things. You be the judge!
2. Jubilees 6:23–28 in Hammer, *The Jewish Book of Days*, 3 Tevet p129.

FOR TIMES SUCH AS THESE

3. Esther 2:16.

4. B. Yoma 35b:7–8.

5. *Apocrypha* is a Greek word meaning "hidden books," and refers to texts of the Second Temple period (approximately 516 BCE–70 CE) that were not included in the Tanakh when it was canonized, but are included in Roman Catholic and Greek Orthodox versions of the "Old Testament." Sefer Yehudit, while not in Tanakh, is included in midrashic retellings of the Channukah story in rabbinic Judaism.

6. Sapir Shans, "Eid Al-Banat," Sefaria, November 18, 2019, www.sefaria.org/sheets/202481.

7. Esther 2:16.

8. Rabbi Jill Hammer, "Chag HaBanot: the Festival of the Daughters," Ritualwell, accessed July 26, 2021, ritualwell.org/ritual/chag-habanot-festival-daughters.

9. Megillat Taanit, Adar 20.

Shvat

1. Shavuot is also called Z'man Matan Torah, the time of our receiving of Torah, marking revelation at Sinai. Revelation is not a one-time, static event. Rather, each time people are open to learning or innovation, they are part of an ongoing revelation of Torah.

2. Yitzchak Meir Rothenberg Alter, aka the Chiddushei HaRim, the first Rebbe of the Ger Hasidic dynasty, b. 1799.

3. Sefer HaZechus LeTu b'Shvat: "Since the wellsprings of Torah begin to flow on Rosh Hodesh Shvat [when Moshe began teaching *Mishneh Torah*] the ability to reach for great depths of understanding Torah Shebe'al Peh [the Oral Torah] is aroused. [One who has great powers of perception] can tell the difference between Chiddushei Torah [novel explanations of Torah subjects] developed before the first of Shvat and those developed afterward." From *The Wisdom in the Hebrew Months* by Zvi Ryzman (Rahway, NJ: ArtScroll Mesorah Publications, 2009).

4. B. Rosh Hashanah 14a.

5. See the Parshat Behar for further exploration of shmita.

6. Lesli Koppleman Ross, *Celebrate! The Complete Jewish Holidays Handbook* (New Jersey: Jason Aronson Inc., 1994), 279.

7. Eisenberg, *Guide to Jewish Practice*, 701.

8. Ross, "Eating Fruit on Tu Bishvat" in *Celebrate! The Complete Jewish Holidays Handbook* (New Jersey: Jason Aronson Inc., 1994), 239.

9. International Jewish Anti-Zionist Network, "Enduring Roots: Over a Century of Resistance to the Jewish National Fund," March 18, 2014, www.ijan.org/projects-campaigns/stopthejnf/enduringroots/.

10. Al-Haq, "Israel's Punitive House Demolition Policy: Collective Punishment in Violation of International Law," July 19, 2011, www.alhaq.org/publications/8101.html.

11. Chelsea Vowel, "Beyond territorial acknowledgments," âpihtawikosisân, September 23, 2016, apihtawikosisan.com/2016/09/beyond-territorial-acknowledgments.

12. More resources on land acknowledgments from the Native Governance Center at nativegov.org/news/a-guide-to-indigenous-land-acknowledgment/.

13. Jews on Ohlone Land, "About Us," www.jewsonohloneland.org/about.

14. Vayikra 19:23–25.
15. So many Haggadot to choose from! A few we like are:

    "Trees of Reconciliation: A Tu b'Shvat Haggadah," by Elliot batTzedek and Hannah Schwartzchild, 2013, jewishvoiceforpeace.org/wp-content/uploads/2016/01/Tu-Bishvat-Haggadah-2013r.pdf.

    "Tu b'Shvat Haggadah," Hazon, January 14, 2020, issuu.com/hazon/docs/2020_tu_b_shvat_haggadah_final.

    "Seder Tu b'Shvat," by Rabbi Rachel Barenblat, Velveteen Rabbi, accessed June 27, 2023, velveteenrabbi.blogs.com/files/tubhaggadah-adults.pdf.

    "Pray as If the Earth Matters: A Tu Bi'Shevat Seder," by Sarah Barasch-Hagans, Sarah Brammer-Shlay, Miriam Geronimus, Lonnie Kleinman, Chayva Lerman, Michael Perice, Rabbi Arthur Waskow, May Ye, Ritualwell, accessed June 27, 2023, ritualwell.org/ritual/pray-if-earth-matters-tu-bishevat-seder/.
16. Rabbi Yehuda Loew ben Bezalel, known as the Maharal, lived 1520–1609 in Bohemia.
17. Jill Hammer, *The Jewish Book of Days: A Companion for All Seasons* (Philadelphia: Jewish Publication Society, 2006), 177.
18. Rebecca Mark, "D'var for Shabbat Shira," Hinenu Baltimore, February 11, 2020, www.hinenubaltimore.org/blog/2020/2/11/dvar-for-shabbat-shira.

Adar

1. Satirical retelling of the Purim story in a play.
2. Literally "star" but also "good luck."
3. From 1951 until his death in 1994, Menachem Mendel Schneerson, known as the Lubavitcher Rebbe, served as the leader of the Chabad-Lubavicher movement.
4. B. Ta'anit 29a:18.
5. Yiddish, talk and connect.
6. Personal communication with author, July 21, 2020.
7. See also Shir haShirim on Pesach; Ruth on Shavuot; Eikha on Tisha b'Av; and Kohelet on Sukkot.
8. Arthur Waskow, *Seasons of Our Joy: A Modern Guide to the Jewish Holidays* (Boston: Beacon Press, 1982), 116.
9. B. Berachot 28a.
10. Elliot Horowitz, *Reckless Rites: Purim and the Legacy of Jewish Violence* (New Jersey: Princeton University Press, 2006).
11. Susan Schnur, "From Prehistoric Cave Art to Your Cookie Pan: Tracing the Hamentasch Herstory" *Lilith Magazine*, Spring 1998.
12. Reisa Aviva Mukamal, "Revised Blessing after Reading Megillat Esther," Ritualwell, August 17, 2022, ritualwell.org/ritual/revised-blessing-after-reading-megillat-esther.
13. Babylonian Talmud Megillah 7b.
14. Kate Poole and Jessica Rosenberg, "The Newish Jewish Economy," *Jewish Currents*, Spring 2017.
15. Ezra Berkley Nepon, *Dazzle Camouflage: Spectacular Theatrical Strategies for Resistance and Resilience* (Philadelphia, 2016), 53.

16. Rabbi Emily Aviva Kapor, "Cross-dressing and Transmisogyny on Purim," *Planting Rainbows* (blog), February 22, 2013, plantingrainbows.wordpress.com/2013/02/22/cross-dressing-and-transmisogyny-on-purim/.

17. Esther 9:18–9.

18. Deutsch Gotthard, M. Franco, and Henry Malter, "Special Purims," *Encyclopedia Judaica*, jewishencyclopedia.com/articles/12450-purims-special.

Nisan

1. For example, "They set out from Rameses in the first month, on the fifteenth day of the first month. It was on the morrow of the passover offering that the Israelites started out defiantly, in plain view of all the Egyptians" (Bamidbar 33:3).

2. Mishnah Pesachim 10:4.

3. Deborah Glanzberg-Krainin, "Redemption Seemed as Close as the Kitchen Sink," *The Velveteen Rabbi's Haggadah for Pesach*, by Rabbi Rachel Barenblat, March 2020, https://velveteenrabbi.com/2015/02/03/velveteen-rabbis-haggadah-for-pesach.

4. Tosefta Pesachim 2.

5. Yosef Karo, *Shulchan Orech, Orech Chayyim* 470.

6. "Major rise in demand for Shmurah Matzah amid Passover—survey," *Jerusalem Post*, March 19, 2021, www.jpost.com/judaism/major-rise-in-demand-for-shmurah-matzah-amid-passover-survey-662570.

7. Claire Suddath, "So You Think You Know Matzo," April 9, 2009,. *Time Magazine*, content.time.com/time/nation/article/0,8599,1890268,00.html.

8. Rebecca Alpert, *Like Bread on the Seder Plate: Jewish Lesbians and the Transformation of Tradition* (New York: Columbia University Press, 1997), 1–2.

9. Alpert, *Like Bread on the Seder Plate*, 2.

10. "The Abundant Joy of Mimouna," Jews for Racial and Economic Justice, May 14, 2019, www.jfrej.org/news/2019/05/the-abundant-joy-of-mimouna.

11. Shekhiynah Larks, "Rethinking 'Go Down Moses' at the Passover Seder" Be'chol Lashon, April 5, 2022, globaljews.org/jewishand/its-time-to-retire-go-down-moses-at-passover-seder/.

12. Ibid.

13. Micah Bazant and Dara Silverman, "Red Sea Ritual," *Love and Justice in Times of War Haggadah*, 76, April 16, 2003, saltyfemme.files.wordpress.com/2010/03/haggadah.pdf.

14. Fringes: A Feminist, Non-Zionist Havurah, "Fringes-Style Reading," June 27, 2023, fringeshavurah.com/original-liturgy/fringes-style-reading/.

15. There are more accessible tools for creating a Haggadah every year. Check out Haggadot.com for a deep library. Some of the Haggadot that have served as inspirations for us and so many are:

    Rabbi Arthur Waskow, "1969 Freedom Seder," June 24, 2005, https://legacy4now.theshalomcenter.org/content/original-1969-freedom-seder.

    Reuven Abergel, "The Israeli Black Panthers Haggadah," 1971, www.panthershaggadah.com.

    "A New Haggadah: A Jewish Lesbian Seder"—Judith Stein, 1984, ROS_IE2128919, American Jewish Historical Society, accessed February 7, 2023, archives.cjh.org/repositories/3/digital_objects/433586.

Micah Bazant and Dara Silverman, "Love and Justice in Times of War Haggadah," April 16, 2003, saltyfemme.files.wordpress.com/2010/03/haggadah.pdf.

Jews for Racial and Economic Justice, "Black Lives Matter Haggadah," April 12, 2019, www.haggadot.com/haggadah/blacklivesmatter.

Jewish Voice for Peace, "Liberatory Passover Haggadah," March 21, 2018, www.jewishvoiceforpeace.org/2018/03/passover-haggadah/.

International Jewish Anti-Zionist Network, "Legacies of Resistance: An Anti-Zionist Haggadah for a Liberation Seder," April 15, 2014, www.ijan.org/resources/legacies-of-resistance-an-anti-zionist-haggadah-for-a-liberation-seder/.

Iyar

1. "'Nakba Law'—Amendment No. 40 to the Budgets Foundations Law," Adalah: The Legal Center for Arab Minority Rights in Israel, January 2012, www.adalah.org/en/law/view/496.
2. B. Talmud Yevamot 62b.

Sivan

1. B. Shabbat 146a.
2. Shemot 12:38.
3. Rashi on Shemot 12:38, for example.
4. Ibn Ezra on Shemot 19:11.
5. "What is Confirmation?," Union of Reform Judaism, accessed January 9, 2023, reformjudaism.org/beliefs-practices/lifecycle-rituals/what-confirmation/.
6. Shulchan Aruch 494:3.
7. Chayei Adam 131:13.
8. Song of Songs 4:11.
9. Mishna Berurah 494:12.
10. Ronit Treatman, "From Spain to Salonika, a disappearing Shavuot tradition revisited," *Times of Israel*, June 12, 2016, www.timesofisrael.com/from-spain-to-salonika-a-disappearing-shavuot-tradition-revisited/.
11. For resources and skilling up on facilitating cocreated spaces, check out adrienne maree brown, *Holding Change: The Way of Emergent Strategy Facilitation and Mediation* (Chico, CA: AK Press, 2021) and online resources on Open Space Technology.
12. Jewish Voice for Peace Rabbinical Council, "Reclaiming Safety Shavuot Study Guide," May 2018, jewishvoiceforpeace.org/wp-content/uploads/2018/05/Shavuot-Deadly-Exchange-Study-Guide-.pdf.
13. Graie Hagans, Koach Baruch Frasier, and Rabbi Max Reynolds, "Shavuot for Black Lives," Jews for Racial and Economic Justice, May 2018, www.jfrej.org/assets/uploads/Shavuot-WHOLE_Final.pdf.

Av

1. In Av, there are two special Shabbatot, Shabbat Chazon and Shabbat Nachamu. We read parashiyot Mattot and Ma'asei as a double parsha to finish Bamidbar, then begin a new book with parashiyot Devarim, Va'etchanan, and Eikev.

2. Mariam Kaba, "Summer Heat," *New Inquiry*, June 8, 2015, thenewinquiry.com/summer-heat/.

3. B. Taanit 29a.

4. Arthur Waskow, *Seasons of Our Joy: A Modern Guide to the Jewish Holidays* (Boston: Beacon Press, 1982), 208.

5. B. Talmud Shabbat 119b.

6. B. Talmud Yoma 9a.

7. For example, the synagogue in Dura Europa dates from 244 CE. Yale University Art Gallery, "Dura-Europos: Excavating Antiquity," accessed June 27, 2023, media.artgallery.yale.edu/duraeuropos/dura.html.

8. Susannah Heschel, "Ending Exile with the Prophetic Voice of the Diasporic Jew," Contending Modernities, September 25, 2020, contendingmodernities.nd.edu/theorizing-modernities/ending-exile.

9. Rama, Oraĥ Ĥayim 552:1–7.

10. Rama, Oraĥ Ĥayim. 557:1; N.H. p. 198.

11. Rama, Oraĥ Ĥayim., 559:1–3.

12. Midrash Iyov.

13. Kitzur Shulĥan Arukh 124:19.

14. Rabbi Menachem ben Solomon Meiri, also known as Hameiri, who lived in Catalan, 1249–1315.

15. Meiri on Taanit 30a.

16. B. Taanit 29a.

17. Mishna Berura 558:3.

18. Jewish Voice for Peace, "Tisha b'Av Gaza Mourning Ritual," 2014, jewishvoiceforpeace.org/wp-content/uploads/2015/07/JVP-Tisha-B%E2%80%99Av-Gaza-Mourning-Ritual.pdf.

19. Yehudah Webster, "40 Days of Teshuvah Report Back," Jews for Racial and Economic Justice, September 15, 2020, www.jfrej.org/news/2020/09/40-days-of-teshuvah-report-back.

20. Tamara Cohen and Arthur Waskow, "Eicha for the Earth," Ritualwell, www.ritualwell.org/ritual/eicha-earth.

21. Brant Rosen, "Lamentation for a New Diaspora," Jewish Voice for Peace, July 2017, jewishvoiceforpeace.org/wp-content/uploads/2017/07/lamentation-for-a-new-diaspora.pdf.

22. Personal correspondence.

23. B. Ta'anit 30b-31.

24. Ibid.

25. Ibid.

26. Ibid.

27. Mishnah Taanit 4:8.

28. B. Ta'anit 31.

Elul

1. Shneur Zalman of Liadi, known as the Alter (Elder) Rebbe, or Ba'al HaTanya, who lived 1745–1812 in Lithuania and Russia, taught, "There once was a king who before

he entered into his city, all of the people of the city would come to meet him face to face in the field."

2. Mishnah Berurah 581:1, "There is a hint in the verse 'I am for my Beloved and my Beloved is for me' ('*Ani L'Dodi v'Dodi Li*': Shir haShirim) that the first letters spell Elul and the last letters have a numerical value of 40. This alludes to the forty days from the beginning of Elul until Yom Kippur for during these forty days repentance is [more readily] accepted so a person should bring their heart near to their Beloved [God] with repentance, and then the Beloved will be close to them to accept the repentance with love."

3. Mia Mingus, "Transformative Justice: A Brief Description," *Transforming Harm: A Resource Hub for Ending Violence*, January 11, 2019, transformharm.org/transformative-justice-a-brief-description.

4. Rambam, *Mishneh Torah*, Hilchot Teshuva.

5. Beresheet 22:1–19.

6. See: Golden Calf, Shemot 32:4, not a great look for cows and Jewish people or cows and sacred spaces.

7. Alicia Ostriker and Jacob Staub have written two beautiful responses to Psalm 27.

8. Compiled from Yoyneh Boyarin, and "What are Sephardic Rosh Hashana customs?" Stroum Center for Jewish Studies, September 24, 2014, jewishstudies.washington.edu/sephardic-studies/what-are-sephardic-rosh-hashana-customs, and "High Holidays," Jewish Languages, accessed June 27, 2023, www.jewishlanguages.org/high-holidays.

9. We've been influenced by Susan Raffo's book, *Liberated to the Bone: Histories. Bodies. Futures* (Chico, CA: AK Press, 2022); Bryan Mercer and Hannah Sassaman, "Embracing Conflict Didn't Tear Our Organization Apart, It Transformed Us (Part 1)," July 2022, convergencemag.com/articles/embracing-conflict-didnt-tear-our-organization-apart-it-transformed-us-part-1/; and Maurice Mitchell, "Building Resilient Organizations," November 29, 2022, forgeorganizing.org/article/building-resilient-organizations.

Torah Portions

1. Rabbi Elliot Kukla, "Aggada (The way we tell our stories): Text Study on Beresheet Rabbah 8:1," TransTorah, 2006, www.transtorah.org/PDFs/Text_Study_Bereshit_Rabbah.pdf.

2. See Judith Plaskow's influential feminist midrash in *The Coming of Lilith: Essays on Feminism, Judaism, and Sexual Ethics, 1972–2003* (Boston: Beacon Press, 1995).

3. Sandy Eisenberg Sasso, *A Prayer for the Earth: The Story of Naamah, Noah's Wife* (Woodstock, VT: Jewish Lights Publishing: 1997).

4. For an in-depth exploration tracing scholarly attempts to trace this history, see Rebecca Alpert's "Translating Rabbinic Texts on the Curse of Ham: What We Learn from Charles Copher and His Critics," *Re-Presenting Texts: Jewish and Black Biblical Interpretation* (Piscataway, NJ: Gorgias Press, 2013), 39–52.

5. In particular, check out Amy Kalmanofsky, ed., *Sexual Violence and Sacred Text* (Eugene, OR: Wipf & Stock Publishers, 2020).

6. Binya Koatz, "Toldot Trans: Tracing a Trans Lineage through the Torah," August 2, 2018, www.sefaria.org/sheets/125838.

7. There are endless places to learn about capitalism, socialism, and communism, and build our understanding and comfort with economics. Check out David Smith, *Marx's Capital Illustrated* (Chicago: Haymarket Books, 2014); Hadas Their, *A People's Guide to Capitalism: An Introduction to Marxist Economics* (Chicago: Haymarket Press, 2020); and Hada Thier's Marxism in a Minute series available on Haymarket Press's Youtube channel.

   Movement Generation explains: "Just Transition is a vision-led, unifying and place-based set of principles, processes, and practices that build economic and political power to shift from an extractive economy to a regenerative economy." Learn more at: movementgeneration.org/just-transition/.

   "Solidarity economy (SE) is an organizing framework for those who wish to create a systemic commitment to and practice of interdependence and collective liberation in the economic activities that meet our material needs. Solidarity economy rests on our shared values: cooperation, democracy, social and racial justice, environmental sustainability, and mutualism. Interdependence and respect are central." Learn more at solidarityeconomyprinciples.org/what-do-we-mean-by-solidarity-economy/.

8. Octavia Butler, *Parable of the Sower* (New York: Four Walls Eight Windows, 1993), 3.

9. Dori Midnight, "Miriam and the Tachash," accessed September 10, 2023, dorimidnight.com/writing/miriam-and-the-tachash/.

10. Food apartheid is a term coined by farmer and organizer Karen Washington. She teaches: "What I would rather say instead of 'food desert' is 'food apartheid,' because 'food apartheid' looks at the whole food system, along with race, geography, faith, and economics. You say 'food apartheid' and you get to the root cause of some of the problems around the food system. It brings in hunger and poverty. It brings us to the more important question: What are some of the social inequalities that you see, and what are you doing to erase some of the injustices?" (Interview with Anna Brones in *Guernica Magazine*, May 7, 2018, www.guernicamag.com/karen-washington-its-not-a-food-desert-its-food-apartheid.)

11. Rabbi Elliot Kukla and Rabbi Reuben Zellman, "TransTexts: Cross-Dressing and Drag," Keshet, June 3, 2008, www.keshetonline.org/resources/transtexts-cross-dressing-and-drag/.

Glossary and Text Library

1. Ruth Wilson Gilmore, "Making abolition geography in California's Central Valley," *unambulist*, December 20, 2018.

2. Kim Tallbear, "Genomic articulations of indigeneity," *Social Studies of Science* 43, no. 4 (May 2013): 509–33.

3. Dean Spade, "Mutual Aid Is Essential to Our Survival Regardless of Who Is in the White House," *Truthout*, October 27, 2020, https://truthout.org/articles/mutual-aid-is-essential-to-our-survival-regardless-of-who-is-in-the-white-house/.

BIBLIOGRAPHY

Abadian, Sousan. "Cultural Healing: When Cultural Renewal Is Reparative and When It Is Toxic." *Journal of Indigenous Wellbeing* 4, no. 2 (Fall 2006): 5–27. journalindigenouswellbeing.co.nz/media/2018/10/2_Abadian.pdf.

Al-Haq. "Israel's Punitive House Demolition Policy: Collective Punishment in Violation of International Law." July 19, 2011. www.alhaq.org/publications/8101.html.

Alpert, Rebecca. *Like Bread on the Seder Plate: Jewish Lesbians and the Transformation of Tradition.* New York: Columbia University Press, 1997.

———. "Translating Rabbinic Texts on the Curse of Ham: What We Learn from Charles Copher and His Critics." In *Re-Presenting Texts: Jewish and Black Biblical Interpretation,* edited by W. David Nelson and Rivka Ulmer, 39–52. Piscataway, NJ: Gorgias Press, 2013.

Barenblat, Rabbi Rachel. "Redemption Seemed as Close as the Kitchen Sink." "Velveteen Rabbi's Haggadah for Pesach." March 2020. velveteenrabbi.com/2015/02/03/velveteen-rabbis-haggadah-for-pesach/.

Batnizky, Leora. *How Judaism Became a Religion.* Princeton, NJ: Princeton University Press, 2013.

Bazant, Micah, and Dara Silverman. "Red Sea Ritual." *Love and Justice in Times of War Haggadah.* Accessed April 16, 2003. saltyfemme.files.wordpress.com/2010/03/haggadah.pdf.

Belasco, Jess. "The Needy for a Pair of Sandals: Jacob's Unsettling, and Our Own." Svara Blog, December 2, 2022. svara.org/needy-for-a-pair-of-sandals/.

Belser, Julia Watts. "God on Wheels: Disability and Jewish Feminist Theology." *Tikkun Magazine,* Fall 2014.

Belzer, Tobin, Tory Brundage, Vincent Calvetti, Gage Gorsky, Ari Y. Kelman, and Dalya Perez. "Beyond the Count: Perspectives and Lived Experiences of Jews of Color," commissioned by the Jews of Color Initiative. August 12, 2021. jewsofcolorinitiative. org/wp-content/uploads/2021/08/BEYONDTHECOUNT. FINAL_.8.12.21.pdf.

Boggs, Grace Lee, and James Boggs. *Revolution and Evolution in the Twentieth Century*. New York: NYU Press, 2008. http://www.jstor.org/stable/j.ctv12pnr39.

Boyarin, Daniel. *A Traveling Homeland: The Babylonian Talmud as Diaspora*. Philadelphia: University of Pennsylvania Press, 2015.

Bromberg, Minna. "A Miracle of Fat." Accessed June 27, 2023. www.fattorah.org/blog/a-miracle-of-fat.

brown, adrienne maree. *Holding Change: The Way of Emergent Strategy Facilitation and Mediation*. Chico, CA: AK Press, 2021.

Brown, Kohenet Shoshona Akua. "A Kwanzakkah Story." *Unruly* (blog), December 26, 2019. jocsm.org/a-kwanzakkah-story/.

Brown, Rakia Sky, Gabi Kirk, Noah Rubin-Blose, and Miriam Spaerstein. "The Local Lulav." *Jewish Currents*, September 28, 2018. jewishcurrents. org/decolonize-sukkot.

Butler, Octavia E. *Parable of the Sower*. New York: Four Walls Eight Windows, 1993.

Carlebach, Elisheva. *Palaces of Time: Jewish Calendar and Culture in Early Modern Europe*. Cambridge, MA: Belknap Press of Harvard University Press, 2011.

Case, Edmund. "A New Theory of Intermarriage." Evolve, March 12, 2020. evolve.reconstructingjudaism.org/new-theory-of-intermarriage/#_ftn1.

Cohen, Annie. "Feldmestn & Keyvermestn Ritual." High Holidays at Home. Accessed on June 28, 2023. highholidaysathome.com/clip/feldmestn.

Cohen, Tamara, and Arthur Waskow. "Eicha for the Earth." Ritualwell. Accessed June 28, 2023. www.ritualwell.org/ritual/eicha-earth.

The Combahee River Collective. "The Combahee River Collective Statement," April 1977.

Eisenberg, Ronald L. *Jewish Traditions: A JPS Guide*. Philadelphia: Jewish Publication Society, 2004.

Feur, Michael. "What is the 17th of Tammuz about?" Accessed July 16, 2019. www.sefaria.org/sheets/183168.

Fringes: A Feminist, Non-Zionist Havurah. "Fringes-Style Reading." Accessed June 27, 2023. fringeshavurah.com/original-liturgy/fringes-style-reading/.

Gay, Ross. *Inciting Joy*. Chapel Hill, NC: Algonquin Books, 2022.

Gold, Hannah. "Happy Yom Kippur!" Vashti Media, September 24, 2020. https://vashtimedia.com/2020/09/24/issues/the-jewish-left/yom-kippur-ball-yiddish-zionism-jeremy-corbyn/.

Golinkin, David. "Why and When Do We Read the Book of Kohelet (Ecclesiastes) in Public?" November 10, 2006. schechter.edu/why-and-when-do-we-read-the-book-of-kohelet-ecclesiastes-in-public-responsa-in-a-moment-volume-1-issue-no-2-october-2006-orah-hayyim-6632-1/.

Goodstein, Laurie. "Members of Jewish Student Group Test Permissible Discussion on Israel." *New York Times*, December 28, 2013. www.nytimes.com/2013/12/29/us/members-of-jewish-student-group-test-permissible-discussion-on-israel.html.

Gotthard, Deutsch, M. Franco, and Henry Malter. "Purims, Special." *Encyclopedia Judaica*. Accessed June 28, 2023. jewishencyclopedia.com/articles/12450-purims-special.

Hagans, Graie, Koach Baruch Frasier, and Rabbi Max Reynolds. "shavuot4blacklives." Jews for Racial and Economic Justice, May 2018. www.jfrej.org/assets/uploads/Shavuot-WHOLE_Final.pdf.

Hammer, Jill. "Chag HaBanot: the Festival of the Daughters," Ritualwell. Accessed July 26, 2021. ritualwell.org/ritual/chag-habanot-festival-daughters.

———. *The Jewish Book of Days: A Companion for All Seasons*. Philadelphia: Jewish Publication Society, 2006.

Hersey, Tricia. "Our work has a framework: REST IS RESISTANCE!" The Nap Ministry, January 11, 2021. thenapministry.wordpress.com/2021/01/11/our-work-is-has-a-framework/.

———. *Rest Is Resistance: A Manifesto*. New York: Little Brown Spark, 2022.

Heschel, Susannah. "Ending Exile with the Prophetic Voice of the Diasporic Jew." Contending Modernities, September 25, 2020. contendingmodernities.nd.edu/theorizing-modernities/ending-exile/.

Horowitz, Elliot. *Reckless Rites: Purim and the Legacy of Jewish Violence*. Princeton, NJ: Princeton University Press, 2006.

International Jewish Anti-Zionist Network. "Enduring Roots: Over a Century of Resistance to the Jewish National Fund." March 18, 2014. www.ijan.org/projects-campaigns/stopthejnf/enduringroots/.

Isack, Arielle. "What Comes Next for Jews of Color Activism?" *Jewish Currents*, March 23, 2023. jewishcurrents.org/what-comes-next-for-jews-of-color-activism.

Jewish Voice for Peace. "5776 Chanukah Ritual: Companion: May the Light of Justice Shine." December 2015. https://www.jewishvoiceforpeace.org/wp-content/uploads/2015/12/5776-Chanukah-Ritual-Companion.pdf.

Jewish Voice for Peace. "JVP Chapters Host Chanukah Actions Against Islamophobia and Racism in 25 Cities." December 21, 2016. jewishvoiceforpeace.org/2016/12/jvp-chapters-host-chanukah-actions-islamophobia-racism-25-cities/.

Jewish Voice for Peace. "Tisha b'Av Gaza Mourning Ritual." 2014. jewishvoiceforpeace.org/wp-content/uploads/2015/07/JVP-Tisha-B%E2%80%99Av-Gaza-Mourning-Ritual.pdf.

Jewish Voice for Peace Rabbinical Council. "Reclaiming Safety Shavuot Study Guide." May 2018. jewishvoiceforpeace.org/wp-content/uploads/2018/05/Shavuot-Deadly-Exchange-Study-Guide-.pdf.

Jews for Racial and Economic Justice. "Juneteenth Seder Haggadah." 2018. www.jfrej.org/assets/uploads/JFREJ-Juneteenth-Haggadah_Color_HiRes_v6.pdf.

Jews for Racial and Economic Justice. "The Abundant Joy of Mimouna." May 14, 2019. www.jfrej.org/news/2019/05/the-abundant-joy-of-mimouna.

Jews of Color Initiative. "How Tokenism Affects Jews of Color and 5 Ways Allies Can Interrupt It." Jews of Color Initiative Newsletter, January 2022. jewsofcolorinitiative.org/newsletter/how-tokenism-affects-jews-of-color-and-5-ways-allies-can-interrupt-it/.

Kaba, Mariam. "Summer Heat." *The New Inquiry*, June 8, 2015. thenewinquiry.com/summer-heat/.

Kahn, Kenneth. "The Jewish Chicken Farmers of Petaluma: Why Remember?" *Jewish Currents*, February 19, 2018. https://jewishcurrents.org/the-jewish-chicken-farmers-of-petaluma-why-remember.

Kalmanofsky, Amy, ed. *Sexual Violence and Sacred Text*. Eugene, OR: Wipf & Stock Publishers, 2020.

Kapor, Rabbi Emily Aviva. "Cross-dressing and Transmisogyny on Purim." *Planting Rainbows* (blog), February 22, 2013. plantingrainbows.wordpress.com/2013/02/22/ cross-dressing-and-transmisogyny-on-purim/.

Karo, Yosef. *Shulchan Orech, Orech Chayyim.*

Kaufman, Annie, and Liat Melnick. "Called to Standing Rock." *Lilith Magazine*, November 15, 2016. lilith.org/2016/11/ called-to-standing-rock/.

Kaufman, Gordon. "Theology as Imaginative Construction." *Journal of American Academy of Religion* 50, no. 1 (March 1982): 78.

Kaye/Kantrowitz, Melanie. *The Colors of Jews: Racial Politics and Radical Diasporism.* Bloomington: Indiana University Press, 2007.

Kimmerer, Robin Wall. *Braiding Sweetgrass: Indigenous Wisdom, Scientific Knowledge, and the Teachings of Plants.* Minneapolis: Milkweed Editions, 2013.

Koatz, Binya. "Toldot Trans: Tracing a Trans Lineage through the Torah." Sefaria, August 2, 2018. www.sefaria.org/sheets/125838.

Kosofksy, Scott-Martin. *The Book of Customs: A Complete Handbook for the Jewish Year.* New York: Harper Collins, 2004.

Kukla, Elliot. "Aggada (The way we tell our stories): Text Study on Bereshit Rabbah 8:1." TransTorah, 2006. www.transtorah.org/PDFs/ Text_Study_Bereshit_Rabbah.pdf.

Kukla, Rabbi Elliot, and Rabbi Reuben Zellman. "TransTexts: Cross-Dressing and Drag." Keshet, June 3, 2008. www.keshetonline.org/ resources/transtexts-cross-dressing-and-drag/.

Kutler, Dane. *The Social Justice Warrior's Guide to the High Holy Days.* September 2015. www.danepoetry.com/.

Larks, Shekhiynah. "Rethinking 'Go Down Moses' at the Passover Seder." Be'chol Lashon, April 5, 2022. globaljews.org/jewishand/ its-time-to-retire-go-down-moses-at-passover-seder/.

Levins Morales, Aurora. *Medicine Stories: Essays for Radicals.* Durham, NC: Duke University Press: 2019.

Lévy, Isaac Jack, and Rosemary Lévy Zumwalt. *Ritual Medical Lore of Sephardic Women: Sweetening the Spirits, Healing the Sick.* Urbana: University of Illinois Press, 2002.

Liberles, Robert. *Salo Wittmayer Baron: Architect of Jewish History.* New York: New York University Press, 1995.

Maher, Donna. "The Joys of a Mizrahi Rosh Hashanah Seder." Hey Alma, September 2, 2020. www.heyalma.com/the-joys-of-a-mizrahi-rosh-hashanah-seder/.

Mark, Rebecca. "D'var for Shabbat Shira." Hinenu Baltimore, February 11, 2020. www.hinenubaltimore.org/blog/.

Mercer, Bryan, and Hannah Sassaman. "Embracing Conflict Didn't Tear Our Organization Apart, It Transformed Us (Part 1)." July 2022. convergencemag.com/articles/embracing-conflict-didnt-tear-our-organization-apart-it-transformed-us-part-1/.

Mingus, Mia. "Transformative Justice: A Brief Description." Transforming Harm: A Resource Hub for Ending Violence, January 11, 2019. https://transformharm.org/tj_resource/transformative-justice-a-brief-description/.

Mitchell, Maurice. "Building Resilient Organizations." The Forge, November 29, 2022. forgeorganizing.org/article/building-resilient-organizations.

ben Maimon, Moses. *Mishneh Torah*. Hilchot Teshuva.

Mukamal, Reisa Aviva. "Revised Blessing after Reading Megillat Esther." Ritualwell, August 17, 2022. ritualwell.org/ritual/revised-blessing-after-reading-megillat-esther.

Nepon, Ezra Berkley. *Dazzle Camouflage: Spectacular Theatrical Strategies for Resistance and Resilience*. Philadelphia: 2016.

Page, Cara, and Erica Woodland. *Healing Justice Lineages: Dreaming at the Crossroads of Liberation, Collective Care, and Safety*. Berkeley: North Atlantic Books, 2023.

Penniman, Naima. "Concentric Memory: Re-membering Our Way into the Future." In *A Darker Wilderness: Black Nature Writing from Soil to Stars*, edited by Erin Sharkey, 176–77. Minneapolis: Milkweed Editions, 2023.

Piepzna-Samarasinha, Leah Lakshmi. *Care Work: Dreaming Disability Justice*. Vancouver: Arsenal Pulp Press, 2018.

———, *The Future Is Disabled: Prophecies, Love Notes and Mourning Songs*. Vancouver: Arsenal Pulp Press, 2022.

Plitman, Jacob. "On an Emerging Diasporism." Jewish Currents, Spring 2018. jewishcurrents.org/on-an-emerging-diasporism.

Plaskow, Judith. *The Coming of Lilith: Essays on Feminism, Judaism, and Sexual Ethics, 1972–2003*. Boston: Beacon Press, 1995.

———. *Standing Again at Sinai: Judaism from a Feminist Perspective.* New York: Harper Collins, 1991.

Poole, Kate, and Jessica Rosenberg. "The Newish Jewish Economy." *Jewish Currents*, Spring 2017.

Portnoy, Eddy. "The Festive Meal." *Tablet Magazine*, September 24, 2009. www.tabletmag.com/sections/belief/articles/the-festive-meal.

Raffo, Susan. *Liberated to the Bone: Histories. Bodies. Futures.* Chico, CA: AK Press, 2022.

Rosen, Brant. "Lamentation for a New Diaspora." Jewish Voice for Peace, July 2017. jewishvoiceforpeace.org/wp-content/uploads/2017/07/lamentation-for-a-new-diaspora.pdf.

Rosenberg, Jessica. "Reunderstanding Jewish Historical Trauma: Moving From the River to the Watershed." *Evolve*, December 27, 2021. evolve.reconstructingjudaism.org/reunderstanding-jewish-historical-trauma-moving-from-the-river-to-the-watershed/.

Ross, Lesli Koppleman. *Celebrate! The Complete Jewish Holidays Handbook.* New Jersey: Jason Aronson Inc., 1994.

Said, Edward. *Orientalism.* New York: Vintage Books, 1978.

Sasso, Sandy Eisenberg. *A Prayer for the Earth: The Story of Naamah, Noah's Wife.* Woodstock, VT: Jewish Lights Publishing: 1997.

Schnur, Susan. "From Prehistoric Cave Art to Your Cookie Pan: Tracing the Hamentasch Herstory." *Lilith Magazine*, Spring 1998.

Shans, Sapir. "Eid Al-Banat." Sefaria, November 18, 2019. www.sefaria.org/sheets/202481.

Shohat, Ella. "Sephardim in Israel: Zionism from the Standpoint of Its Jewish Victims." *Social Text* 19/20 (1988): 1–35. doi.org/10.2307/466176.

Shohat, Ella. *On the Arab-Jew, Palestine, and Other Displacements.* London, Pluto Press: 2017.

Siegel, Richard, Michael Strassfeld, and Susan Strassfeld, eds. *The Jewish Catalog: A Do-It Yourself-Kit.* Philadelphia: Jewish Publication Society, 1973.

Sins Invalid. "10 Principles of Disability Justice." September 17, 2015. www.sinsinvalid.org/blog/10-principles-of-disability-justice.

Smith, David. *Marx's Capital Illustrated.* Chicago: Haymarket Books, 2014.

Somerson, Wendy. "The Intersection of Anti-Occupation and Queer Jewish Organizing." *Tikkun Magazine*, July/August 2010. https://wendysomerson.net/wp-content/uploads/2022/07/intersection-tikkun-article.pdf.

Spade, Dean. "Mutual Aid Is Essential to Our Survival Regardless of Who Is in the White House." *Truthout*, October 27, 2020. https://truthout. org/articles/mutual-aid-is-essential-to-our-survival-regardless-of-who-is-in-the-white-house/.

Suddath, Claire. "So You Think You Know Matzo." *Time Magazine*, April 9, 2009. content.time.com/time/nation/article/0,8599,1890268,00. html.

TallBear, Kim. "Genomic articulations of indigeneity." *Social Studies of Science* 43, no. 4 (May 2013): 509–33. https://doi. org/10.1177/0306312713483893.

Teutsch, David A. *A Guide to Jewish Practice, Vols. 1–3.* Wyncote, PA: Reconstructionist Rabbinical College Press: 2011.

Thier, Hadas. *A People's Guide to Capitalism: An Introduction to Marxist Economics.* Chicago: Haymarket Press, 2020.

Torres, Anna Elena. "The Anarchist Sage/*Der Goen Anarkhist*: Rabbi Yankev-Meir Zalkind and Religious Genealogies of Anarchism." *In geveb*, February 2019.

Treatman, Ronit. "From Spain to Salonika, a disappearing Shavuot tradition revisited." *Times of Israel*, June 12, 2016. www.timesofisrael.com/ from-spain-to-salonika-a-disappearing-shavuot-tradition-revisited/.

Vowel, Chelsea. "Beyond territorial acknowledgments." âpihtawikosisân, September 23, 2016. apihtawikosisan.com/2016/09/ beyond-territorial-acknowledgments.

Washington, Karen, interviewed by Anna Brones. "It's Not a Food Desert, It's Food Apartheid." *Guernica Magazine*, May 7, 2018. www.guernicamag.com/ karen-washington-its-not-a-food-desert-its-food-apartheid.

Waskow, Arthur. *Seasons of Our Joy: A Modern Guide to the Jewish Holidays.* Boston: Beacon Press, 1982.

Wasserman, Tina. "A Savory Sukkot." Reform Judaism. reformjudaism. org/savory-sukkot.

Webster, Yehudah. "40 Days of Teshuvah Report Back." Jews for Racial and Economic Justice, September 15, 2020. www.jfrej.org/ news/2020/09/40-days-of-teshuvah-report-back.

"8 Nights, 8 Actions." Ritualwell, accessed June 27, 2023. ritualwell.org/ ritual/8-nights-8-actions.

Union of Reform Judaism. "What is Confirmation?" Accessed January
9, 2023. reformjudaism.org/beliefs-practices/lifecycle-rituals/
what-confirmation/.

Yanklowtiz, Shmuly. *The Book of Jonah: A Social Justice Commentary*. New
York: CCAR Press, 2020.

Yellow Horse Brave Heart, Maria. "The Return to the Sacred Path:
Healing the Historical Trauma Response among the Lakota." *Smith
College Studies in Social Work* 68, no. 3 (1998): 287–305.

ABOUT THE AUTHORS

Rabbi Ariana Katz is the founding rabbi of Hinenu: The Baltimore Justice Shtiebl, a warm and joyful congregation in Baltimore, Maryland. She is a graduate of the Reconstructionist Rabbinical College.

Rabbi Jessica Rosenberg is an organizer, educator, and writer based in South Minneapolis. She is a graduate of the Reconstructionist Rabbinical College and a core organizer of the Radical Jewish Calendar project.

Rabbi Ariana Katz (left) and Rabbi Jessica Rosenberg (right).

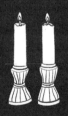